Arkansas Ferns and Fern Allies

Arkansas Ferns and Fern Allies

by W. Carl Taylor

illustrated by Paul W. Nelson

Arkansas Ferns and Fern Allies

This book was designed by Greg Raab.
It was produced by the Publications Section of the Milwaukee Public Museum.
The manuscript was transmitted to Parnau Graphics via telecommunications and typeset in Garamond. Cover photograph by the author.
Printing by Inland Press.

Published by the Milwaukee Public Museum
800 W. Wells St., Milwaukee, WI 53233
© 1984 by the Milwaukee Public Museum
All rights reserved.
ISBN 0-89326-097-5

Library of Congress Cataloging in Publication Data

Taylor, W. Carl, 1946-
  Arkansas ferns and fern allies.
  Bibliography: p.
  Includes index.
  1. Ferns — Arkansas — Identification. 2. Pteridophyta — Arkansas — Identification. I. Title
QD525.5.A8T39   1984   587'.09767   84-60494
ISBN 0-89326-097-5

This book is dedicated to
Dr. Delzie Demaree
and
Dr. Dwight M. Moore
for their enduring contributions
to Arkansas botany

Acknowledgments

I wish to express my gratitude to the many persons who have offered assistance during the course of this study. Without their help this work would not have been possible. Thanks are due to Edward Browne, Jr., George Clark, Beverly Gerdeman, Richard Hauke, James Key, David Lellinger, William Mahler, Daniel Marsh, Sidney McDaniel, Aileen McWilliam, Robert Mohlenbrock, Dwight Moore, Jewel Moore, Ronald Pearman, Paul Redfearn, Leon Richards, William Shepherd, Clarence Sinclair, Edwin Smith, Paul Somers, Robert Stolze, Jerry Taylor, Dale Thomas, Ralph Thompson, Gary Tucker, Warren Wagner, Jr., and Wallace Webber.

Special thanks are due David Johnson, Douglas Ladd, Robbin Moran, Paul Nelson, James Peck, and Jovanka Ristic for reading and improving the manuscript by offering numerous comments and suggestions. Many thanks also go to my typist Roberta Blanks.

Delzie Demaree deserves special acknowledgment for his kind hospitality and invaluable assistance. During our extensive travels throughout the state Doc shared his unique, almost uncanny knowledge of plants which he has acquired through many years of field experience. To have been blessed with the help and encouragement of Dr. Demaree and so many others, I am indeed fortunate.

Preface

Arkansas is a state blessed with naturalness. The topography is varied and is covered with a diversity of vegetation. The flora is rich in species, particularly in ferns and their allies. Dr. Taylor has provided us with an excellent manual to aid us in identifying the ferns of our state. The dramatic illustrations, the simply written keys, and easily understood descriptions provide us with a straightforward means of identifying Arkansas' ferns. Dr. Taylor's research has produced an accurate, up-to-date account of the distribution of each species within Arkansas. Mr. Nelson has carefully prepared illustrations that capture the form and detail of each species. As a result, we now definitely know more about the ferns than any other plant group in Arkansas. Dr. Taylor's book sets a new level of excellence for treatments on Arkansas' plants. Hopefully, we shall see similar treatments of other plant groups to aide us in appreciating and enjoying our natural state.

Dr. James H. Peck
Assist. Prof. Biology
University of Arkansas at Little Rock

Contents

Recognizing Ferns and Fern Allies — 2

Parts of a Fern — 4

Life History of Pteridophytes — 8

Pteridophyte Names — 10

Historic Account of Arkansas Pteridophytes — 11

Natural Divisions of Arkansas and Pteridophyte Distribution — 12

For Further Reading — 16

How to Identify a Pteridophyte Using Keys and Descriptions — 17

Illustrated Key to the Genera of the Arkansas Pteridophytes — 18

County Map of Arkansas — 24

Description of the Arkansas Pteridophytes — 25

List of Herbaria from which specimens are cited — 246

Glossary — 247

Literature Cited — 254

Checklist of Arkansas Pteridophytes — 260

Index to Common and Scientific Names — 261

Recognizing Ferns and Fern Allies

Ferns

Ferns are often imagined as relatively small plants with delicate, dissected leaves growing in shaded forests. While numerous ferns fit this image, a check through this book will reveal that ferns possess a great diversity of size and form and exist in many different habitats. Ferns range in size from less than a centimeter to over several meters in height. The leaves of most ferns are dissected but some have undivided leaves which, at a glance, look like the leaves of flowering plants. A few ferns are aquatic, while others may be found on rocks, exposed to heating and drying by the sun. Some grow as epiphytes on the trunks and branches of trees. Despite a large degree of variation in size, form, and habitat, all ferns possess common characteristics.

A fern is a non-flowering plant consisting of vascular roots, stems, and leaves and reproducing by spores. The roots, stems, and leaves of a fern are called vascular because they contain conducting cells for moving water and nutrients throughout the plant. Spores are tiny, one-celled, reproductive bodies. Ferns are distinguished from other spore-producing plants, such as fungi and mosses, because these plants do not have vascular roots, stems, or leaves. Flowering plants are vascular but unlike ferns they disperse by seeds. In contrast to spores, seeds are multicellular reproductive bodies that contain embryos.

Ferns produce spores in tiny cases usually located on the lower surface of fertile leaves. These spore cases are typically clustered into brownish spots or lines called sori. A sorus may be partly covered by a thin sheet of tissue called an indusium. The shape and location of the sori are often important in identifying a fern. For instance, Polypody Ferns (pp. 191-195) have round sori, Spleenworts (pp. 31-53) elongate ones, and Cliff Brakes (pp. 177-181) linear sori along the edges of fertile leaflets. Royal Ferns (pp. 169-175) have certain leaves partially or entirely modified just to bear spores. In such cases the leaves or parts of them are considered to be dimorphic, meaning they are of two kinds or forms, i.e., they bear sterile, vegetative leaves and different looking, fertile, spore-bearing leaves. Dimorphic leaves are also characteristic of the Net-veined Chain Fern (pp. 129-131) and the Sensitive Fern (pp. 153-155). Grape Ferns (pp. 67-77) and Adder's-tongue Ferns (pp. 157-167) bear spore cases on an erect, fertile segment of the leaf which rises above a leafy segment. When identifying ferns, care should be taken to find and examine spore-bearing or fertile leaves whenever possible as they possess important diagnostic information.

In addition to spore production, ferns can be recognized by the way their leaves develop. As fern leaves mature they unroll from base to tip in such a manner that the developing leaf fancifully resembles the head of a fiddle. These fiddleheads are characteristic of most ferns.

Three significant features which will serve to distinguish a fern from other kinds of plants are:
1. Plants often with dissected leaves
2. Sori borne on the underside of fertile leaves
3. Fiddleheads formed by developing leaves

Fern Allies

Another group of plants reproducing by spores and having vascular roots, stems, and leaves are the fern allies. In contrast to the large, dissected leaves of most ferns, the leaves of fern allies are small or narrow and undivided. The fern allies of Arkansas are represented in the following groups.

1. Horsetails and Scouring Rushes (pp. 113-121) have tubular, jointed stems which bear whorls of very small, scale-like leaves. The tips of the leaves are free but further down, along their edges, they are attached to each other forming a cylindrical sheath surrounding the stem.
2. Clubmosses (pp. 133-137) have their stems clothed with small leaves and superficially appear similar to large moss plants. Their spores are borne in terminal club-like cones or in fertile zones along the stems.
3. Spikemosses (pp. 211-219) also look like mosses but they bear their spores, which are of two different sizes, in four-sided cones at the tips of stems.
4. Quillworts (pp. 123-127) look like tufts of grass with their narrow leaves arising from buried two-lobed corms. Spores of two different sizes are produced in spore cases at the bases of leaves.

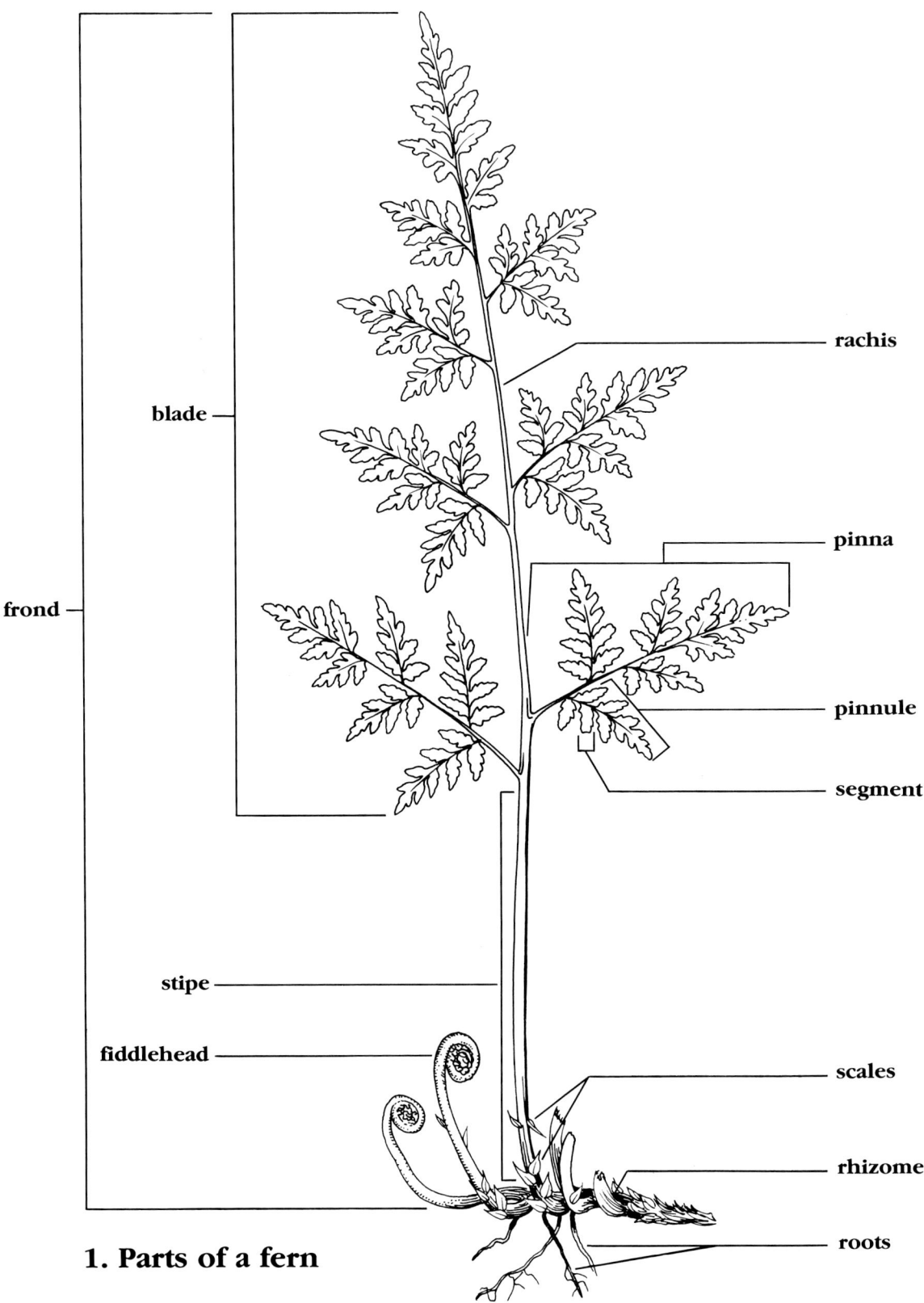

1. Parts of a fern

Parts of a Fern

In a sense, a fern may be visualized as an erect plant which has fallen over on its side. Instead of growing leaves at one end and roots at the other, a fern produces leaves along the upperside of its stem and roots toward the lower side. The horizontal stem growing on or just below the soil surface and producing leaves and roots is called a rhizome.

Other parts of a fern can be described using terminology that has been applied to higher plants, i.e., leaves, petioles, leaflets, etc. However, because of the uniqueness of ferns among the higher plants, different terms are used. (Fig. 1). For instance, the leaf of a fern is called a frond and the stalk which attaches the blade, the flattened, green part of the frond, to the rhizome is called a stipe instead of a petiole. The midrib of a divided blade is termed a rachis and each division of the blade is referred to as a pinna (pl. pinnae). Each division of a pinna is a pinnule and divisions of a pinnule are called segments.

The degree of dissection of a frond is often important in identifying ferns (Fig. 2). A simple, or undivided, frond is characteristic of some ferns. A pinnatifid frond is divided nearly, but not quite all the way, to its midrib or midvein. A pinnate frond has its blade divided all the way to the rachis with the divided parts called pinnae. Fronds with more dissection are described as bipinnatifid, bipinnate, or tripinnate. Terms may be combined to describe fronds with intermediate degrees of dissection, e.g., a pinnate-pinnatifid frond is a pinnate frond whose pinnae are pinnatifid, and a bipinnate-pinnatifid frond is a bipinnate, or twice pinnate, frond whose pinnules are pinnatifid.

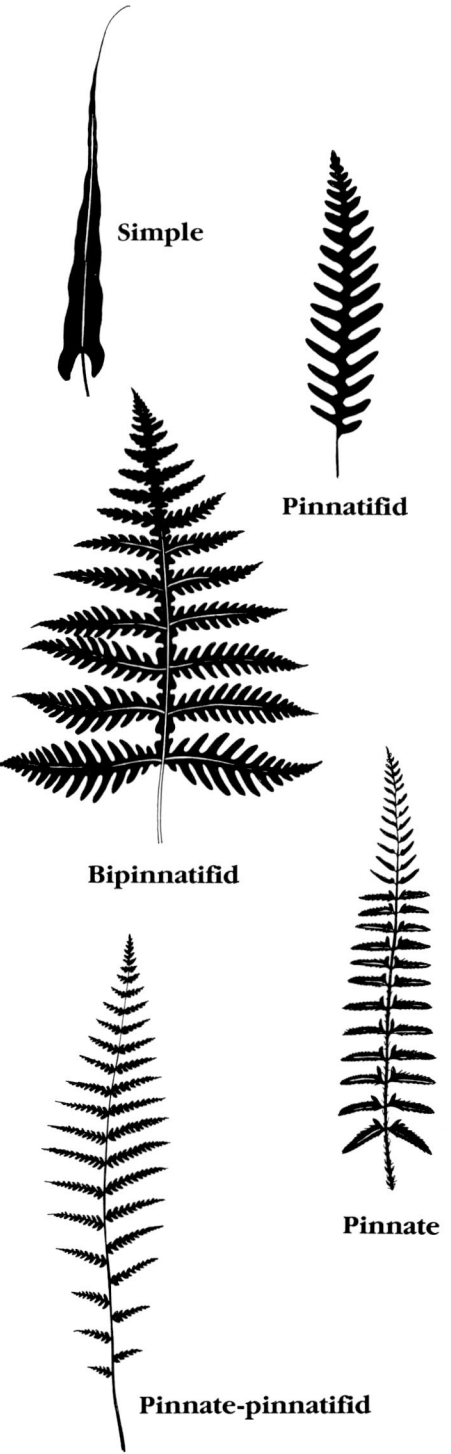

2. Frond dissection

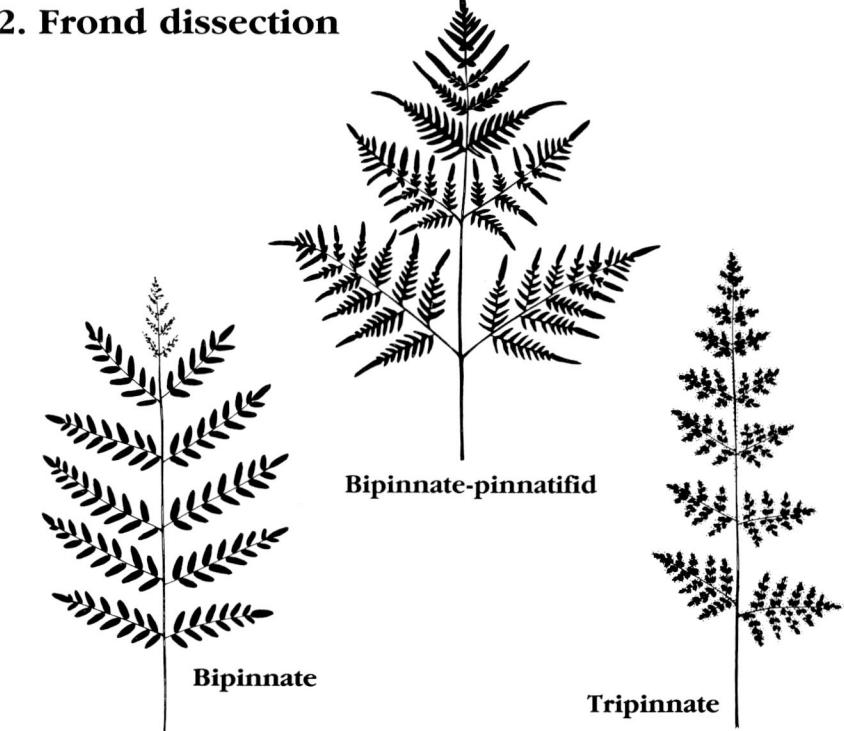

3. Shapes

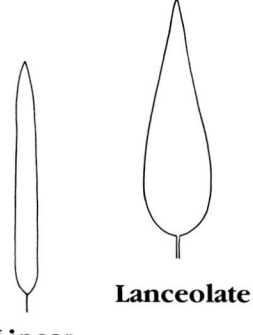

In addition to the location of sori, the shapes of fronds, pinnae, pinnules, segments, or other parts of ferns are often helpful in identification. For example, many ferns have fronds that are lanceolate or lance-shaped in outline while other ferns have fronds that are deltoid, linear, oblong, ovate, or a variety of other shapes (Fig. 3).

Fronds possess a number of additional features that are useful in identification (Fig. 4). For instance, many ferns have veins that are forked and free, that is, they branch as they run from the midvein toward the blade edge, but they do not reunite with each other (Fig. 4a). A few ferns have veins that join with each other to form a network (Fig. 4b). Veins that form a network are called reticulate and each part of the blade enclosed by a reticulum is called an areola (pl. areolae). Unlike ferns, fern allies bear small or narrow leaves that contain only a single, unbranched midvein (Fig. 4c).

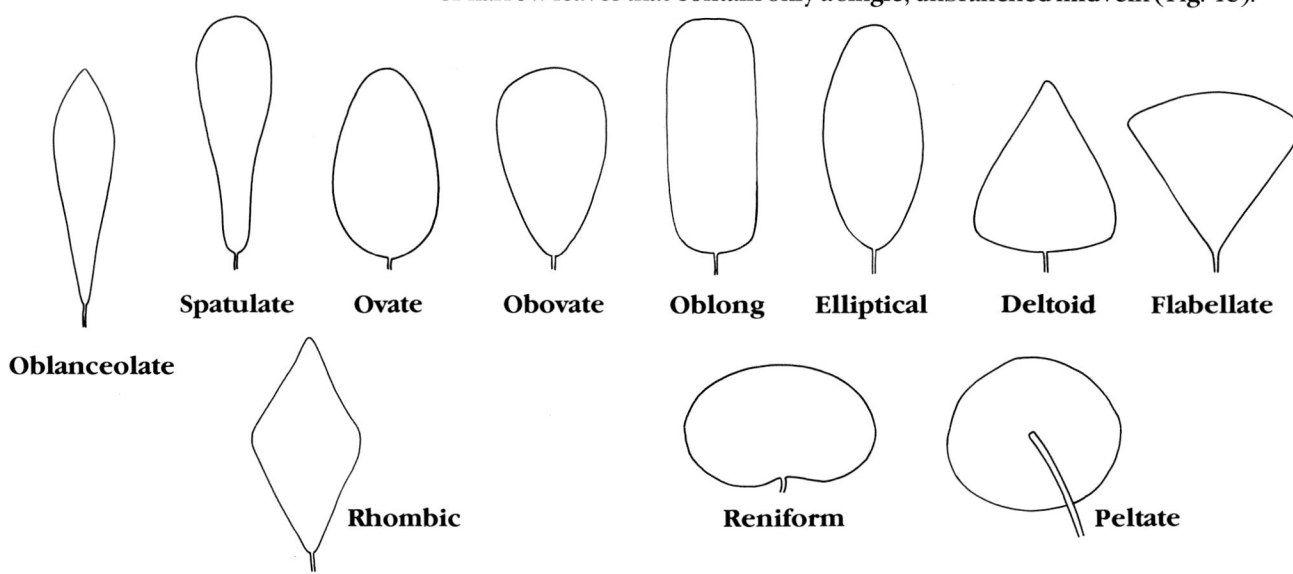

4. Veins, margins, apices, and bases

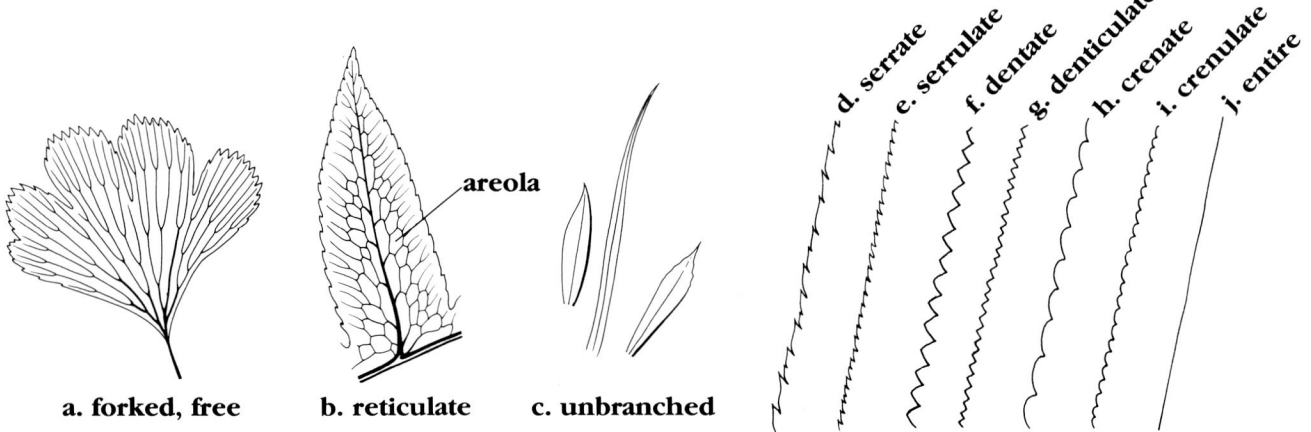

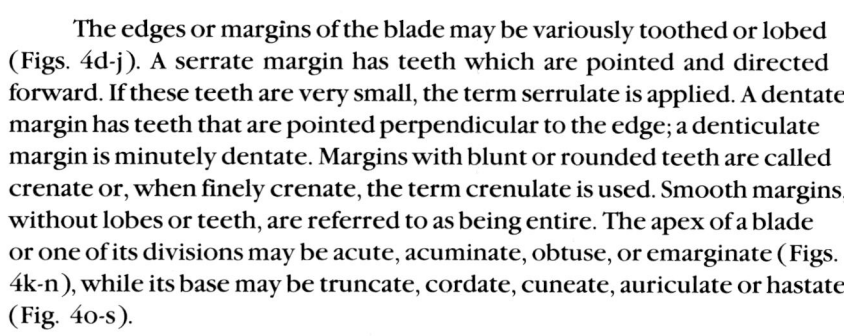

The edges or margins of the blade may be variously toothed or lobed (Figs. 4d-j). A serrate margin has teeth which are pointed and directed forward. If these teeth are very small, the term serrulate is applied. A dentate margin has teeth that are pointed perpendicular to the edge; a denticulate margin is minutely dentate. Margins with blunt or rounded teeth are called crenate or, when finely crenate, the term crenulate is used. Smooth margins, without lobes or teeth, are referred to as being entire. The apex of a blade or one of its divisions may be acute, acuminate, obtuse, or emarginate (Figs. 4k-n), while its base may be truncate, cordate, cuneate, auriculate or hastate (Fig. 4o-s).

Hairs and scales, most often found on stipes and rhizomes but also on other parts, can provide distinguishing characters (Fig. 5). Hairs consist of one or more cells but they are only one cell wide (Figs. 5a-c). Generally, hairs taper toward the apex but they may be secretory and have a bulbous, glandular tip. A hairless surface is termed glabrous. Scales are more than one cell wide and may be of various colors and shapes (Figs. 5d-f). Spleenworts are distinguished from other ferns because they bear latticed or clathrate scales consisting of translucent cells that have thick, dark colored, side walls (Figs. 5g). When viewed with a hand lens the cells of these scales look like miniature leaded glass window panes.

Some of the more commonly used terms in the keys and descriptions have been explained and illustrated in this section. These, and additional terms used in the keys and descriptions, are defined in the glossary at the back of this book.

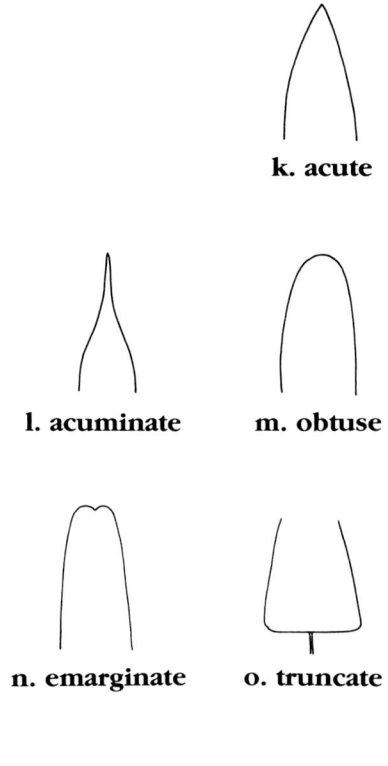

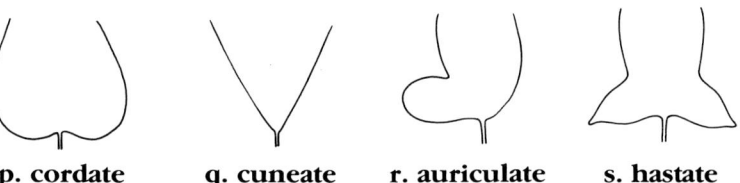

5. Hairs and scales

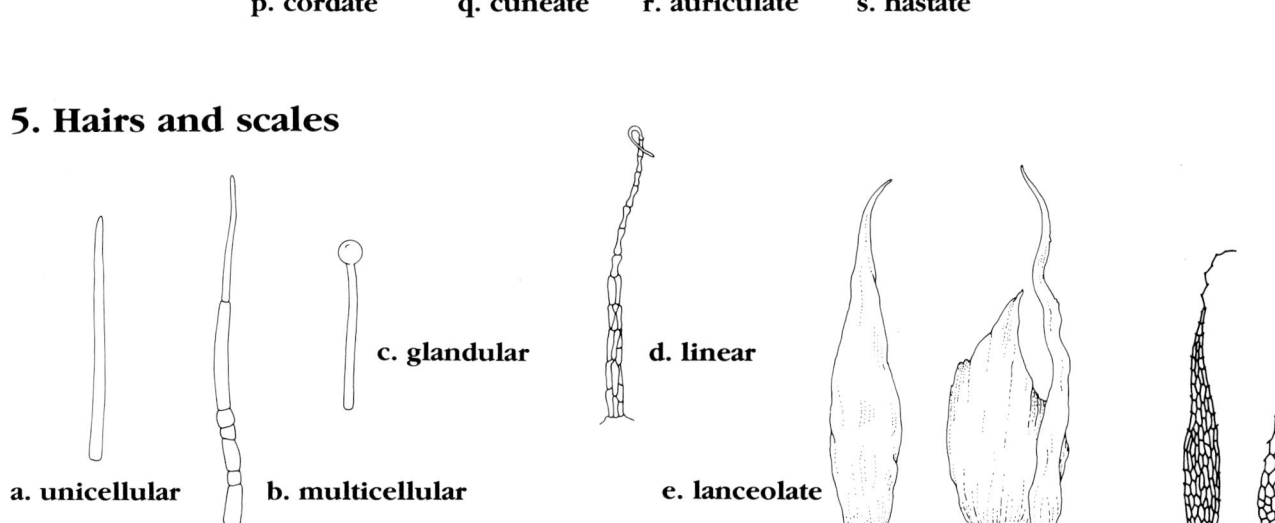

6. Life cycle of a fern

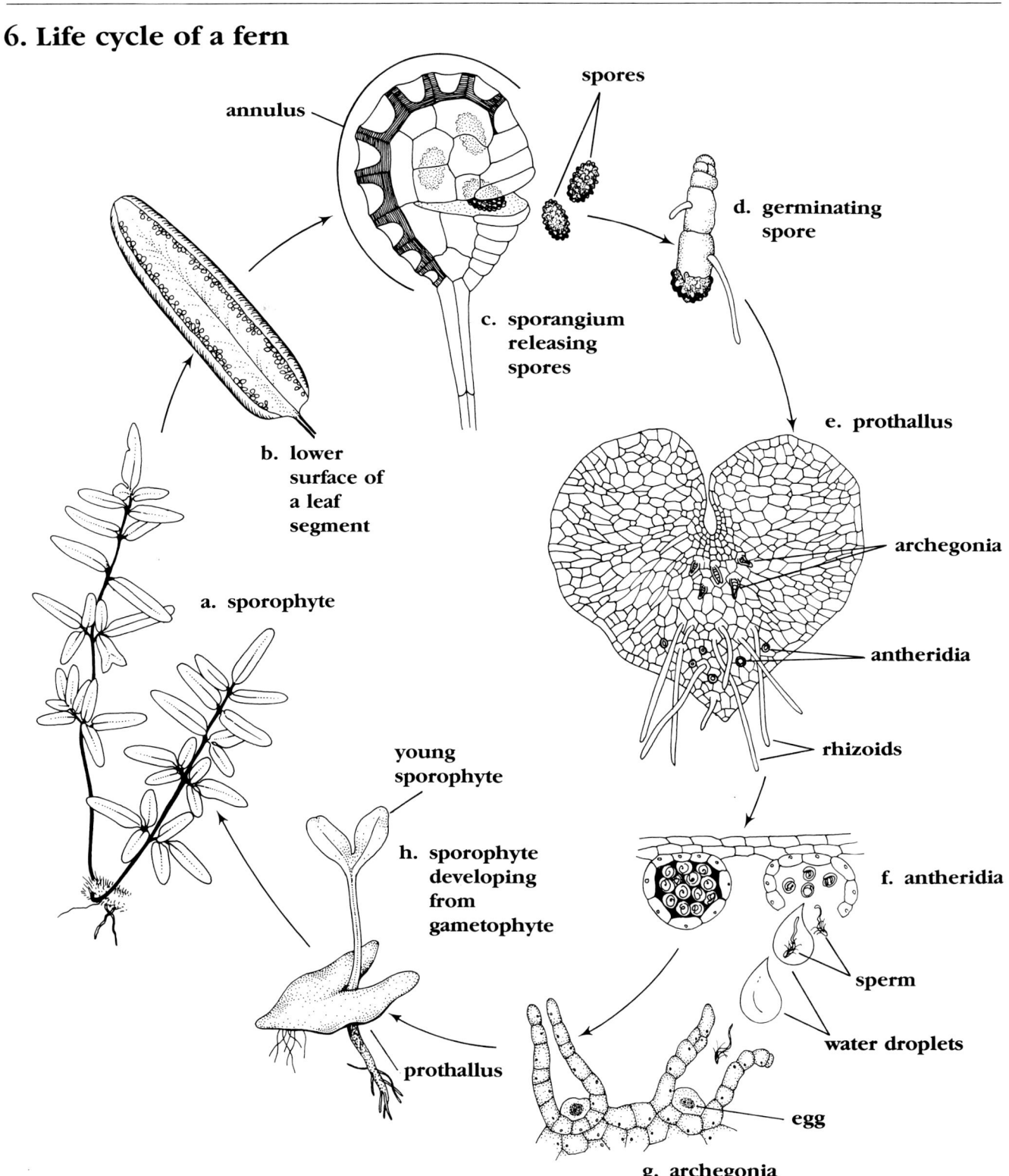

Life History of Pteridophytes

A fern possessing vascular roots, stems, and leaves may be referred to as a sporophyte or spore plant because it is capable of producing spores (Figs. 6a). As mentioned previously, these spores are produced in spore cases called sporangia that are typically clustered into sori which form brownish spots or lines on the lower surface of fertile fronds (Fig. 6b).

Spores develop within each sporangium through a process of successive cell divisions including meiosis or reduction division during which each cell's chromosome number is reduced from two sets (diploid) to one set (haploid). Usually sixty-four or more spores are contained in each sporangium when this process is complete. Upon maturing, spores are catapulted away from the plant by opening and rapid closing of the sporangium made possible by a group of specialized cells called an annulus (Fig. 6c). If a spore lands in a suitable place it will usually begin to germinate in a short time. At first, the spore yields a short filament of cells (Fig. 6d) but later, the plant assumes a flattened, often heart-shaped form which is called a prothallus (Fig. 6e). A prothallus, generally less than one centimeter across, may be referred to as a gametophyte or gamete plant because it is capable of producing gametes, i.e., sperm and eggs. On its lower surface, toward one side, the prothallus bears root-like filaments called rhizoids. Among these rhizoids are borne globose antheridia which, when mature, release swimming sperm (Fig. 6f). Around the notch of the heart, flask-shaped archegonia are formed (Fig. 6g). Inside each archegonium is an egg. In a droplet of water, sperm can swim to an archegonium, go down its neck, and fertilize the egg inside. Union of a sperm and an egg creates a zygote and combines the chromosome sets of both gametes to restore the diploid condition. The zygote develops into an embryo which grows and differentiates to form a sporophyte (Fig. 6h). As the sporophyte matures the prothallus withers.

When prothalli of two different, but closely related, kinds of ferns grow near each other it is possible for a sperm from one prothallus to unite with an egg from the other prothallus. The offspring of such a cross is called a hybrid and combines the features of both parents. Hybrids are usually sterile and produce shrivelled, aborted spores (Fig. 7). On rare occasions, irregularities in the spore development process result in chromosome doubling and the production of a few viable diploid spores in otherwise sterile hybrids. These diploid spores are capable of producing fertile sporophytes in the normal way. The ability of ferns to hybridize makes it possible for new and diverse kinds of ferns to be formed. Research has provided strong evidence that hybridization has played an important role in the evolution of new species of ferns.

The life history of fern allies is similar to that of the ferns and is the main reason for uniting these plants with the term pteridophyte. Besides the simple form of the leaves, major differences between ferns and fern allies include the location and size of sporangia and the production of two kinds of spores by some fern allies. Fern allies have relatively large, solitary sporangia on the upper surface of their sporophylls or spore bearing leaves. These sporophylls may be aggregated into a strobilus or cone, as for example is the case with the Spikemosses and some Clubmosses. Horsetails also have strobili but sporangia are borne on the inner surface of angular segments

7. Spores (greatly enlarged)

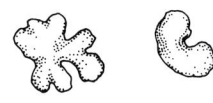

Shrivelled, abortive spores typical of sterile, hybrid ferns. Sterile hybrids usually produce spores of irregular size and shape.

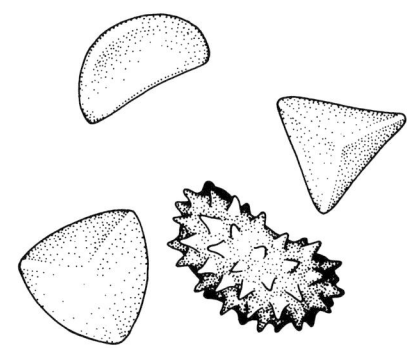

Viable spores from several different kinds of ferns. Normal ferns produce spores of uniform size and shape.

called sporangiophores.

Clubmosses and Horsetails are termed homosporous since they produce only one kind of spore which, as in the ferns, yields a gametophyte bearing both archegonia and antheridia. On the other hand, Spikemosses and Quillworts are called heterosporous because they produce two types of spores. Megaspores, contained in megasporangia, develop into gametophytes which bear only archegonia, while microsporangia hold great numbers of much smaller microspores which develop into antheridia.

The life history of pteridophytes is relevant to their distribution. The need for a droplet of water at the proper time and place to allow the sperm to swim to the egg is crucial for completion of the life cycle. Obviously the lack of this kind of moisture in a habitat would limit the occurrence of a sporophyte. This is the reason why ferns and fern allies are most often found in moist, shady places where water droplets are likely to be present.

A modification in the life cycle of certain pteridophytes removes the requirement for water droplets in completing the life cycle and therefore allows sporophytes to be formed in drier places. The spores of some ferns produce prothalli that lack functional antheridia and archegonia. After a period of time, a bud develops on the prothallus which grows into a sporophyte. Production of a sporophyte from a bud on the prothallus without need for a sperm and an egg is called apogamy. Apogamous ferns usually contain only thirty-two diploid spores in each sporangium.

Pteridophyte Names

Some ferns, like Bracken, are widely known by their common names. Such names are usually simple and easy to remember. However, common names are meaningful in only one language and no international rules govern their usage. Confusion may arise because one plant may have several common names or different plants may share a single common name. The use of scientific names avoids these problems. The system of naming plants using scientific nomenclature is governed by a set of rules followed worldwide. According to these rules a plant can have only one valid name. Any additional names which have been applied to the plant but are no longer thought to be correct are called synonyms.

The scientific name of a plant consists of Latinized words which are italicized or underscored when written. The first name is a capitalized noun and is called the generic name. It identifies the genus to which the plant belongs. A genus is a group of closely related plants. For example, all Maidenhair ferns belong to the genus *Adiantum,* all Spleenworts to the genus *Asplenium,* etc. The second name is the specific epithet. It is a modifier in the lower case (although proper names may be capitalized) that tells something about the plant (e.g., *Onoclea sensibilis,* Sensitive Fern), where it is found (e.g., *Woodwardia virginica,* Virginia Chainfern), or commemorates some person (e.g., *Asplenium bradleyi,* Bradley's Spleenwort). The generic name and the specific epithet together form the species name. A species (sing. and pl.) may be defined as the plants that we recognize as being of one kind.

Below the rank of species are the subspecies (subsp.), variety (var.), and forma (f.). These categories are used to account for variation not sufficiently distinctive to be recognized at the species level. Infraspecific epithets with an abbreviated indication of their rank follow the specific epithet, e.g., *Athyrium filix-femina* subsp. *asplenioides*.

Following the epithet is the author citation. Generally written in abbreviated fashion, the author citation indicates who is responsible for the scientific name. Often there will be one author's name in parentheses followed by another author's name. The name in parentheses is the author who first described the plant but in another genus or at a different rank, e.g., as a variety or forma. The author named outside the parentheses is responsible for the present combination of generic and epithet names.

A hybrid is named by placing an "X" between the generic name and the specific epithet to indicate its hybrid origin, e.g., *Dryopteris* X *leedsii*. A hybrid may also be expressed by its generic name followed by the specific epithets of the parental species in alphabetical order separated by an "X", e.g., *Dryopteris celsa* X *marginalis*.

Historic Account of Arkansas Pteridophytes

Records of ferns and fern allies in Arkansas date back to the travels and collections of Nuttall (1821, 1835), who reported 23 species of pteridophytes from the Arkansas Territory in 1835. Lesquereux (1860) recorded 35 species for the state as part of a geological survey. Harvey (1881) compiled an annotated list of Arkansas ferns with notes on the ranges and habitats of 40 ferns. In a list of Arkansas plants, Branner and Coville (1891) included 45 species of ferns and fern allies.

Buchholz (1924) revised the lists of Harvey and Branner and Coville to arrive at 46 species and 3 varieties of pteridophytes in Arkansas. Buchholz's study was immediately followed by Palmer's (1924) report of two new species for the state. These additions were incorporated in a supplement to the Arkansas plants by Buchholz and Palmer (1926) which lists 15 pteridophytes. Scully (1937, 1939) produced two papers describing the ferns and fern allies found in and around Hot Springs National Park.

The most recent account of Arkansas pteridophytes was written by Moore (1940b). It includes an annotated list of 67 ferns and fern allies. Moore (1941) also published a paper entitled "Some Noteworthy Fern Communities of Arkansas" which contains lists of species found in five different localities within the Interior Highlands. Demaree (1943b) listed 70 pteridophytes in his "Catalogue of Vascular Plants of Arkansas."

Since the early 1940's, thousands of voucher specimens have been added to herbaria and taxonomic research has resulted in a number of nomenclatural changes and revised species concepts. Over a dozen additional pteridophytes have been discovered in the state including those reported by Chandler (1941), Demaree (1943a), Moore (1947, 1950, 1951), Wagner (1962), Bowers and Redfearn (1967), Farrar and Redfearn (1968), Tucker (1971), Buck (1977), Thomas (1978), Taylor and Johnson (1979), and Werth and Taylor (1980).

The latest comprehensive study of Arkansas vascular plants is by Smith (1978). Smith's work includes distribution maps for 70 ferns and fern allies based mainly on studies by Taylor (1976, 1979). The work of Key (1975) on the pteridophytes of the Interior Highlands should also be mentioned as it describes most of the pteridophytes occurring in the state.

Currently there are 72 species of ferns and fern allies, representing 31 genera, known from Arkansas. In addition, five sterile hybrids have been collected in the state and four species are represented by more than one variety. Nearly 20% of the native or naturalized species of pteridophytes found in North America north of Mexico occur in Arkansas.

Natural Divisions of Arkansas and Pteridophyte Distribution

Arkansas constitutes 53,104 square miles in the south-central United States and possesses a diverse terrain, providing a wide range of habitats in which many species of ferns and fern allies can grow. Generally, Arkansas may be divided into two broad geographic areas: the Interior Highlands, occupying the western and northern portions of the state, and the Gulf Coastal Plain Lowlands, comprising the eastern and southern portions.

The Interior Highlands area of Arkansas is a rugged, mountainous region with maximum local relief exceeding 600 meters (Plate 1). In contrast, the Gulf Coastal Plain is a belt of flat to rolling land with elevations varying from about 20 to 120 meters (Plate 2). At least sixty species of pteridophytes can be found in the Interior Highlands, while the Gulf Coastal Plain has about 40 species.

Although these two geographic areas are the most obvious and distinctive, additional information concerning the distribution of pteridophytes is revealed by subdividing each area. Based mainly on differences in topography, surface geology, and vegetation, Arkansas may be characterized as consisting of five natural divisions (Foti, 1974). The Gulf Coastal Plain is divided into the West Gulf Coastal Plain, the Mississippi Alluvial Plain, and Crowley's Ridge. The Interior Highlands area is divided into the Ozark Mountains and the Ouachita Mountains. These natural divisions (Fig. 8) are useful in characterizing the distributions of pteridophytes in the state.

The West Gulf Coastal Plain consists of level to rolling bottomlands, terraces, and hills. Soils of this region are largely sandy loams and the forests are primarily composed of Loblolly Pine and bottomland hardwoods.

The eastern part of Arkansas consists of flat to slightly rolling bottomlands and terraces of the Mississippi Alluvial Plain. The soils of this region are generally deep and impermeable. The forested areas which remain are composed of bottomland hardwoods adapted to the wet, poorly drained soils.

Crowley's Ridge is an eroded, loess-mantled prominence rising steeply over 60 meters above the surrounding Mississippi Alluvial Plain. Its forests are dominated by upland hardwoods that are related to the mixed mesophytic forests of the loess hills east of the Mississippi River.

The Ozark Mountains are remnants of eroded, uplifted plateaus and consist mostly of broad uplands or narrow upland ridges (Plate 3). This region is generally covered by oak-hickory forests, but mixed mesophytic forests may occur on slopes of deep drainage ravines. Surface rocks in the northern half are chiefly limestones and dolomites while sandstones and shales predominate in the southern half.

The Ouachita Mountains are a series of more or less parallel ridges running east and west which were formed by folding (Plate 4). Surface rocks are largely sandstones and shales. The forests of this region are composed primarily of Shortleaf Pine and upland hardwoods.

Many pteridophytes have widespread distributions within the state. *Polypodium polypodioides* seems to be the most ubiquitous species, occurring in all natural divisions, on rocks or as an epiphyte on a number of trees. *Polystichum acrostichoides* is also found in all natural divisions. Although usually occurring on well drained sites, it also grows in the relatively impermeable soils of the Mississippi Alluvial Plain where few other ferns have been collected. Other species showing widespread distributions in Arkansas include *Asplenium platyneuron, Athyrium filix-femina, Botrychium virginianum, Equisetum hyemale, Onoclea sensibilis, Pteridium aquilinum, Selaginella apoda, Thelypteris hexagonoptera,*

Plate 1

Plate 2

Plate 3

Plate 4

8. Natural Divisions of Arkansas

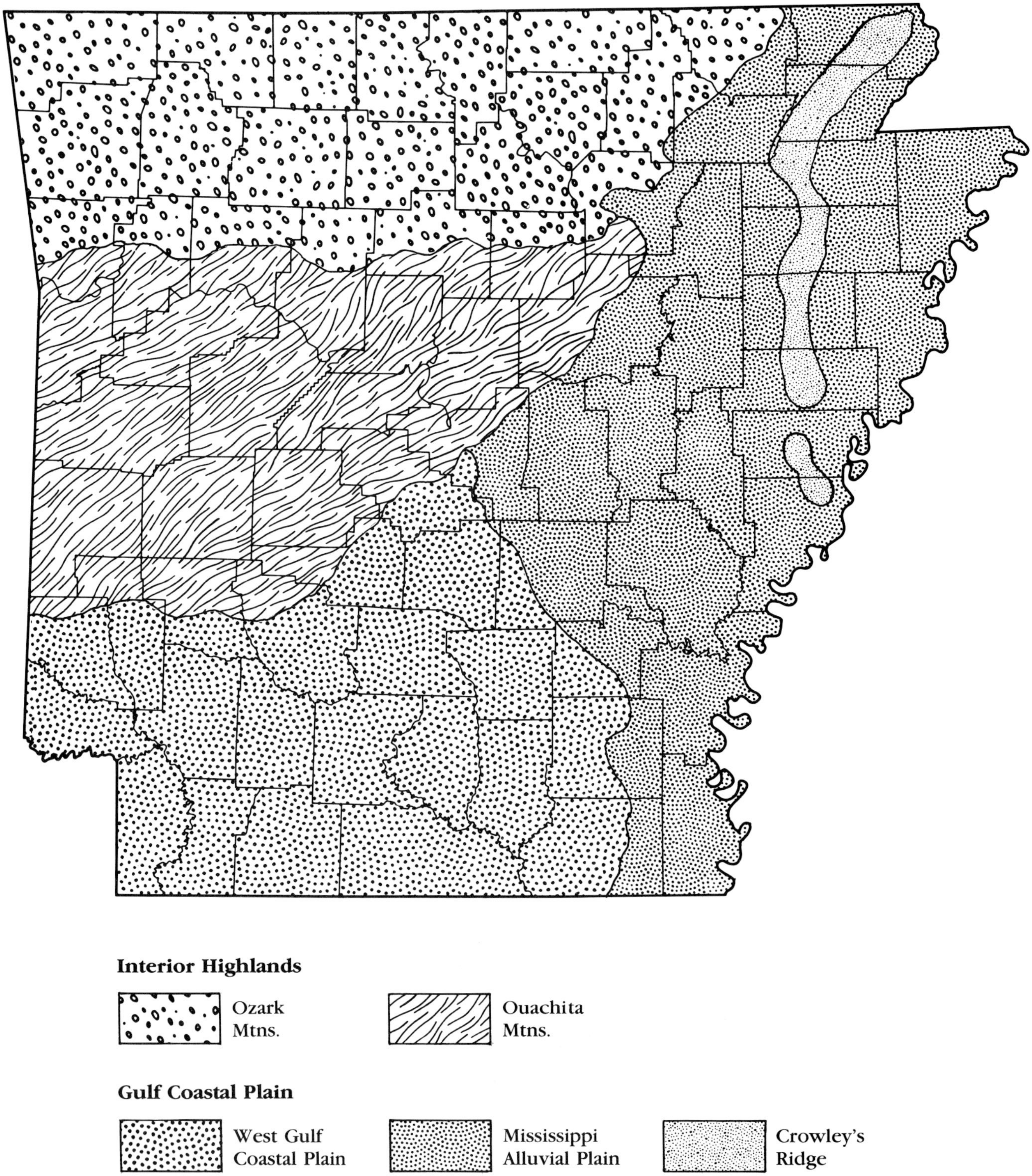

Interior Highlands

Gulf Coastal Plain

Thelypteris palustris, and *Woodsia obtusa.*

Osmunda cinnamomea and *O. regalis,* while also of widespread occurrence in Arkansas, are much more common in the southern portion of the state. These two species appear to be most abundant in the West Gulf Coastal Plain where they are often found together along stream banks and around seepage areas.

Botrychium biternatum and *Lorinseria areolata* are found chiefly in the southern part of the state where they are often collected in the Ouachita Mountains and West Gulf Coastal Plain Regions

Several species appear to be restricted to the West Gulf Coastal Plain, such as *Botrychium lunarioides, Lycopodium appressum, Ophioglossum nudicaule* and *Woodwardia virginica.* As a rule, these species occur in moist, somewhat open, sandy soils.

Thelypteris noveboracensis, which reaches the southwestern limit of its range in Arkansas, is found mostly in the Ouachita Mountains. Here it occurs in moist, shaded, rocky woods along streams.

A number of pteridophytes are distributed throughout the Interior Highlands. Those species which occur mostly within the Interior Highlands and to some extent on Crowley's Ridge include *Adiantum pedatum, Asplenium bradleyi,* and *Cheilanthes lanosa. Adiantum pedatum* occurs in moist, shaded, humus-rich soils, while *Asplenium bradleyi* and *Cheilanthes lanosa* are saxicolous plants, usually associated with sandstone outcrops.

Species which appear to be restricted to the Interior Highlands of Arkansas include *Asplenium trichomanes, Dryopteris marginalis,* and *Cheilanthes tomentosa.* These plants are all inhabitants of a variety of rock outcrops or rocky, wooded slopes. *Asplenium trichomanes* and *Dryopteris marginalis* are usually found in moist, shaded habitats, while *Cheilanthes tomentosa* occurs on dry, exposed sites.

Ferns mostly restricted to the Ozark Mountains include *Asplenium rhizophyllum, Cystopteris tennesseensis,* and *Athyrium pycnocarpon. Asplenium rhizophyllum* and *Cystopteris tennesseensis* occur on limestone, dolomite, and sandstone outcrops. *Athyrium pycnocarpon* inhabits rich woods, stream banks, and moist, shaded, rocky slopes in this region.

Ferns occurring on calcareous rocks mainly in the northern half of the Ozark Mountains include *Asplenium resiliens, Cheilanthes alabamensis, C. feei, Notholaena dealbata, Pellaea atropurpurea,* and *P. glabella.*

Eighteen species and hybrids of pteridophytes are known from three or fewer counties in Arkansas. Some of these sporadically occurring taxa may be recent adventives while others may represent relicts. Coastal Plain species which occur at or near the northwestern limits of their ranges in Arkansas are *Lygodium japonicum, Pteris multifida, Selaginella arenicola, Thelypteris normalis,* and *T. torresiana.*

Dennstaedtia punctilobula, Dryopteris carthusiana, Lycopodium lucidulum, and *Osmunda claytoniana,* all frequently encountered in the northeastern United States, occur sporadically in Arkansas where they reach the southwestern extent of their ranges. These Arkansas stations may represent relicts surviving from a once wider distribution or from past southern migrations during Pleistocene glaciation.

For Further Reading

Listed below are several excellent guides to the ferns of states adjacent to Arkansas and to regions which include Arkansas.

Correll, D. S. 1956. **Ferns and Fern Allies of Texas.** Texas Research Foundation, Renner, Texas.

Cranfill, R. 1980. **Ferns and Fern Allies of Kentucky**. Kentucky Nature Preserves Commission Scientific and Technical Series Number 1, Frankfort, Kentucky.

Key, J.S. 1982. **Field Guide to Missouri Ferns.** Missouri Department of Conservation, Jefferson City, Missouri.

Mickel, J. T. 1979. **How to Know the Ferns and Fern Allies.** Wm. C. Brown Co., Dubuque, Iowa.

Mohlenbrock, R. H. 1967. **The Illustrated Flora of Illinois — Ferns.** Southern Illinois University Press, Carbondale, Illinois.

Shaver, J. M. 1954. **Ferns of Tennessee.** George Peabody College for Teachers, Nashville, Tennessee.

Thieret, J. W. 1980. **Louisiana Ferns and Fern Allies.** Lafayette Natural History Museum, Lafayette, Louisiana.

Wherry, E. T. 1961. **The Fern Guide.** Doubleday & Co., New York; reprinted 1975, Morris Aboretum, Philadelphia.

Wherry, E. T. 1964. **The Southern Fern Guide.** Doubleday & Co., New York; reprinted 1977, New York Chapter American Fern Society, New York Botanical Garden, Bronx.

There are a number of general botany and plant morphology textbooks from which you can learn much more about ferns and fern allies. Visit your library to find out what books are available.

How To Identify a Pteridophyte Using the Following Keys and Descriptions

The following keys consist of a series of indented couplets composed of two contrasting statements. Only one of the two statements in each couplet will correctly describe the fern in question, and following the correct alternative statements through the key will ultimately lead to the fern's identify.

To identify a fern using this key, begin with the first couplet, numbered with ones. The first statement asks if the fern is aquatic or semiaquatic, or, in the contrasting statement, if the fern is terrestrial or epiphytic. If the fern is aquatic or semiaquatic, proceed to the next pair of equally indented statements under the first alternative numbered two. If the fern is terrestrial or epiphytic, choose the other statement of the first couplet and, under that, the most fitting of the two statements numbered four. This process is continued until the fern is identified to genus. The key is supplemented with illustrations to assist you in decision making.

In the initial key, the fern is identified as belonging to a particular genus. The generic name is followed by its page number in the text. Turn to this page and you will find a generic description which should match your plant. This description is followed by a key to the species and hybrids. Using the same procedure as you did with the key to the genera, the fern can be identified to the species level. Turn to the page number following the specific epithet for a description and additional information about that species.

Under the scientific name for each species, variety, or hybrid described you will find: first, a listing of synonyms which have been applied to the fern in Arkansas; second, a suggested common name; third, a technical description of the plant; fourth, the plant's main habitats and distribution in Arkansas; fifth, its range outside of Arkansas; and finally, any additional interesting or useful information about the plant.

Habitat descriptions have been condensed from data on herbarium sheets and from personal field notes. The distribution maps for each species or hybrid have been compiled from specimens contained in the herbaria listed on page 246. A representative specimen is cited for each county in which the species or hybrid taxon has been collected. Each cited specimen is indicated by its collector, his or her collection number, and in parentheses, the acronym of the herbarium in which the specimen is stored. A county map of Arkansas is on page 24.

Illustrated Key to the Genera of Arkansas Pteridophytes

1. Plants aquatic or semiaquatic
   2. Plants free-floating .... *Azolla* (p. 63)
   2. Plants anchored by roots
      3. Pinnae four, borne at tip of stipe; fronds appearing like a four-leaf clover .... *Marsilea* (p. 143)
      3. Pinnae absent, frond merely a naked stipe resembling a small grass .... *Pilularia* (p. 187)
1. Plants terrestrial or epiphytic
   4. Stems tubular, jointed; leaves tiny, scale-like, whorled, laterally attached below their tips to form a cylindrical leaf sheath . *Equisetum* (p. 113)
   4. Stems not tubular, unjointed; leaves or fronds essentially free
      5. Plants grass-like or moss-like; leaves scale-like or linear, less than 3 mm wide, with a single, unbranched vein
         6. Plants grass-like; leaves or sporophylls linear, clustered, spirally arranged on a buried two-lobed corm .... *Isoetes* (p. 123)
         6. Plants moss-like; leaves small, scale-like, clothing stems; sporophylls aggregated in terminal cones or grouped in subterminal cauline zones
            7. Leafy stems more than 5 mm thick; strobili cylindrical or sporophylls aggregated in subterminal cauline zones; homosporous .... *Lycopodium* (p. 133)

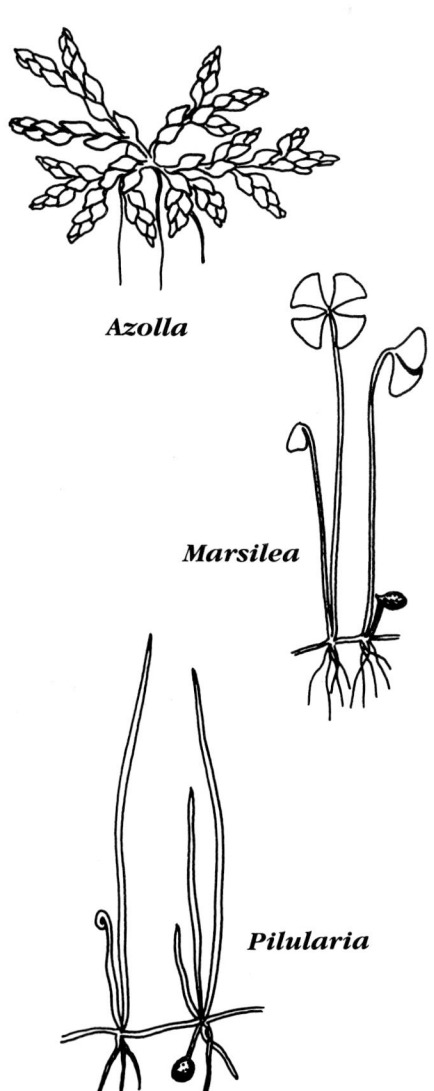

Azolla

Marsilea

Pilularia

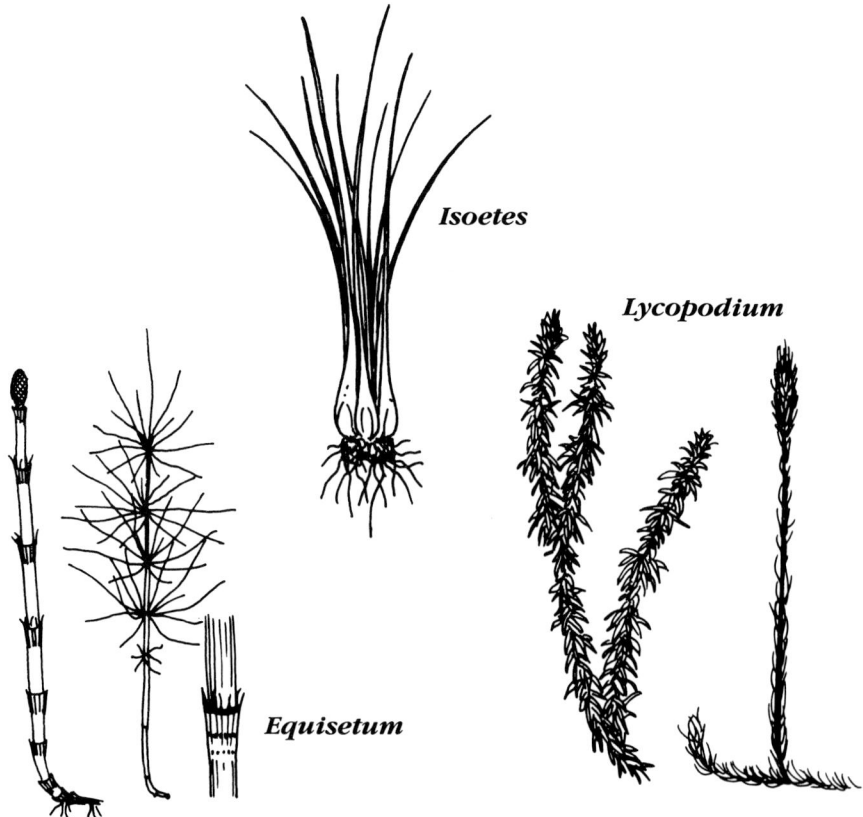

Isoetes

Lycopodium

Equisetum

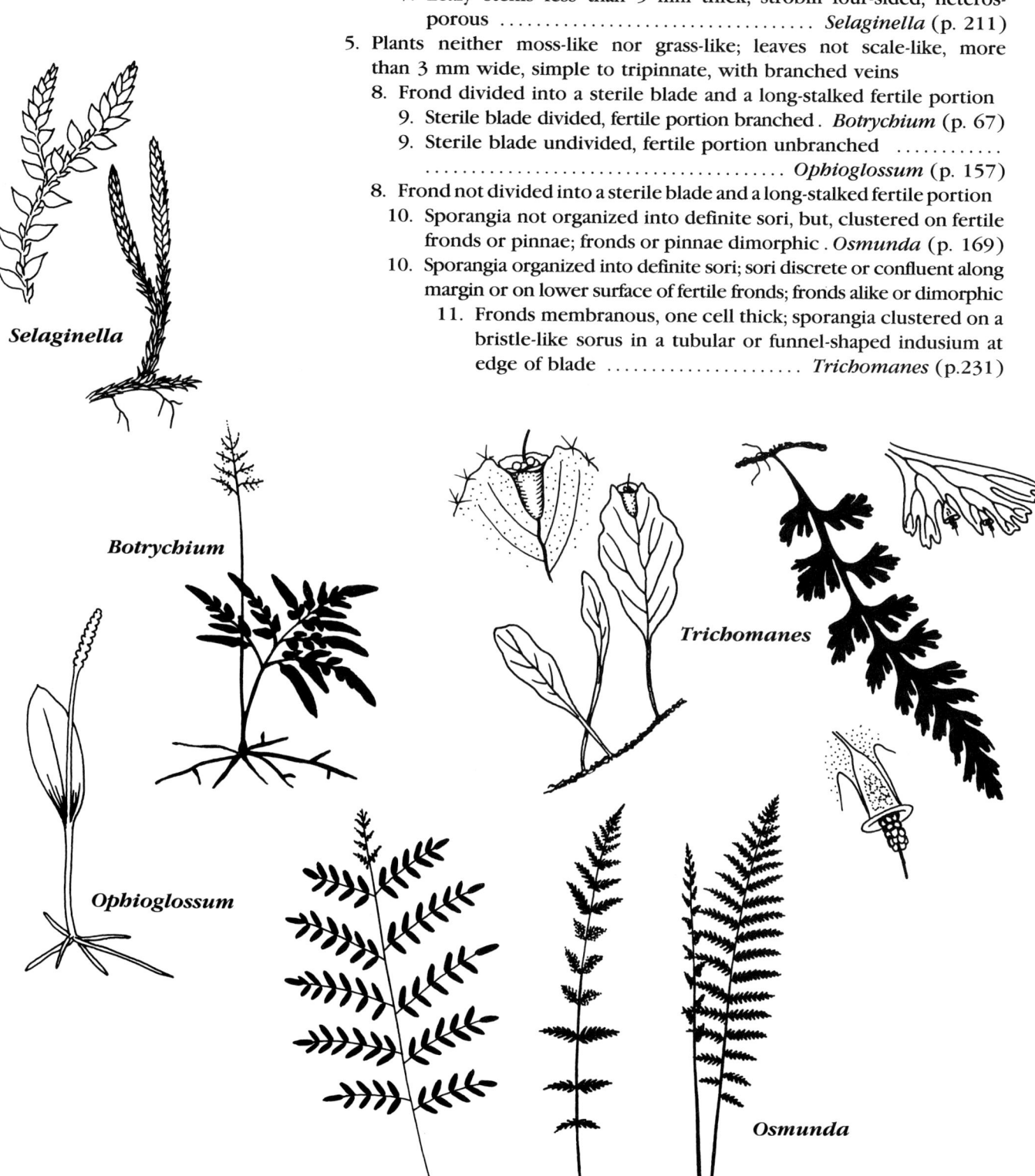

7. Leafy stems less than 5 mm thick; strobili four-sided; heterosporous .... *Selaginella* (p. 211)
5. Plants neither moss-like nor grass-like; leaves not scale-like, more than 3 mm wide, simple to tripinnate, with branched veins
   8. Frond divided into a sterile blade and a long-stalked fertile portion
      9. Sterile blade divided, fertile portion branched . *Botrychium* (p. 67)
      9. Sterile blade undivided, fertile portion unbranched ....
         .... *Ophioglossum* (p. 157)
   8. Frond not divided into a sterile blade and a long-stalked fertile portion
      10. Sporangia not organized into definite sori, but, clustered on fertile fronds or pinnae; fronds or pinnae dimorphic . *Osmunda* (p. 169)
      10. Sporangia organized into definite sori; sori discrete or confluent along margin or on lower surface of fertile fronds; fronds alike or dimorphic
         11. Fronds membranous, one cell thick; sporangia clustered on a bristle-like sorus in a tubular or funnel-shaped indusium at edge of blade .... *Trichomanes* (p.231)

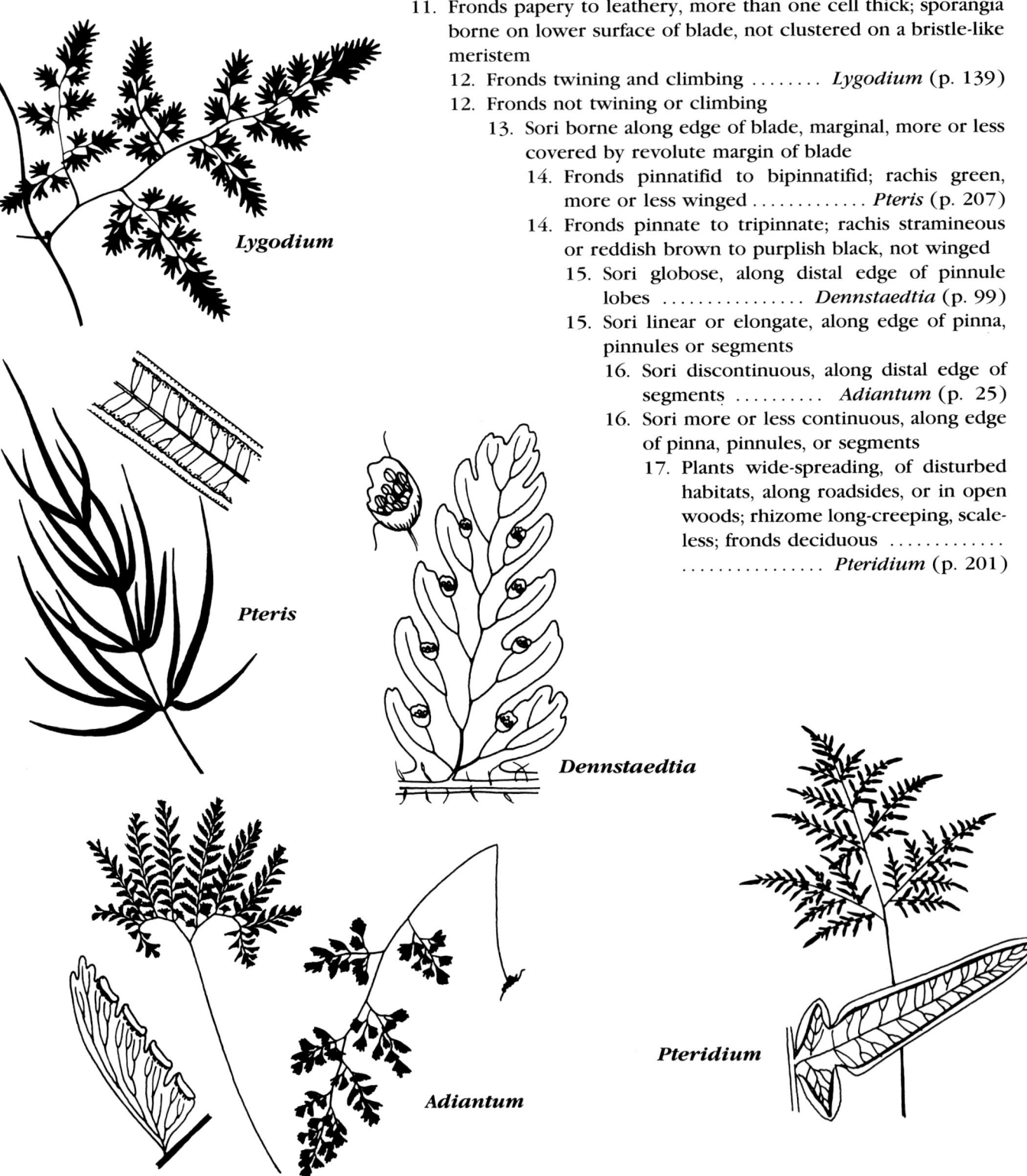

11. Fronds papery to leathery, more than one cell thick; sporangia borne on lower surface of blade, not clustered on a bristle-like meristem
    12. Fronds twining and climbing .... *Lygodium* (p. 139)
    12. Fronds not twining or climbing
        13. Sori borne along edge of blade, marginal, more or less covered by revolute margin of blade
            14. Fronds pinnatifid to bipinnatifid; rachis green, more or less winged .... *Pteris* (p. 207)
            14. Fronds pinnate to tripinnate; rachis stramineous or reddish brown to purplish black, not winged
                15. Sori globose, along distal edge of pinnule lobes .... *Dennstaedtia* (p. 99)
                15. Sori linear or elongate, along edge of pinna, pinnules or segments
                    16. Sori discontinuous, along distal edge of segments .... *Adiantum* (p. 25)
                    16. Sori more or less continuous, along edge of pinna, pinnules, or segments
                        17. Plants wide-spreading, of disturbed habitats, along roadsides, or in open woods; rhizome long-creeping, scaleless; fronds deciduous ....
                        .... *Pteridium* (p. 201)

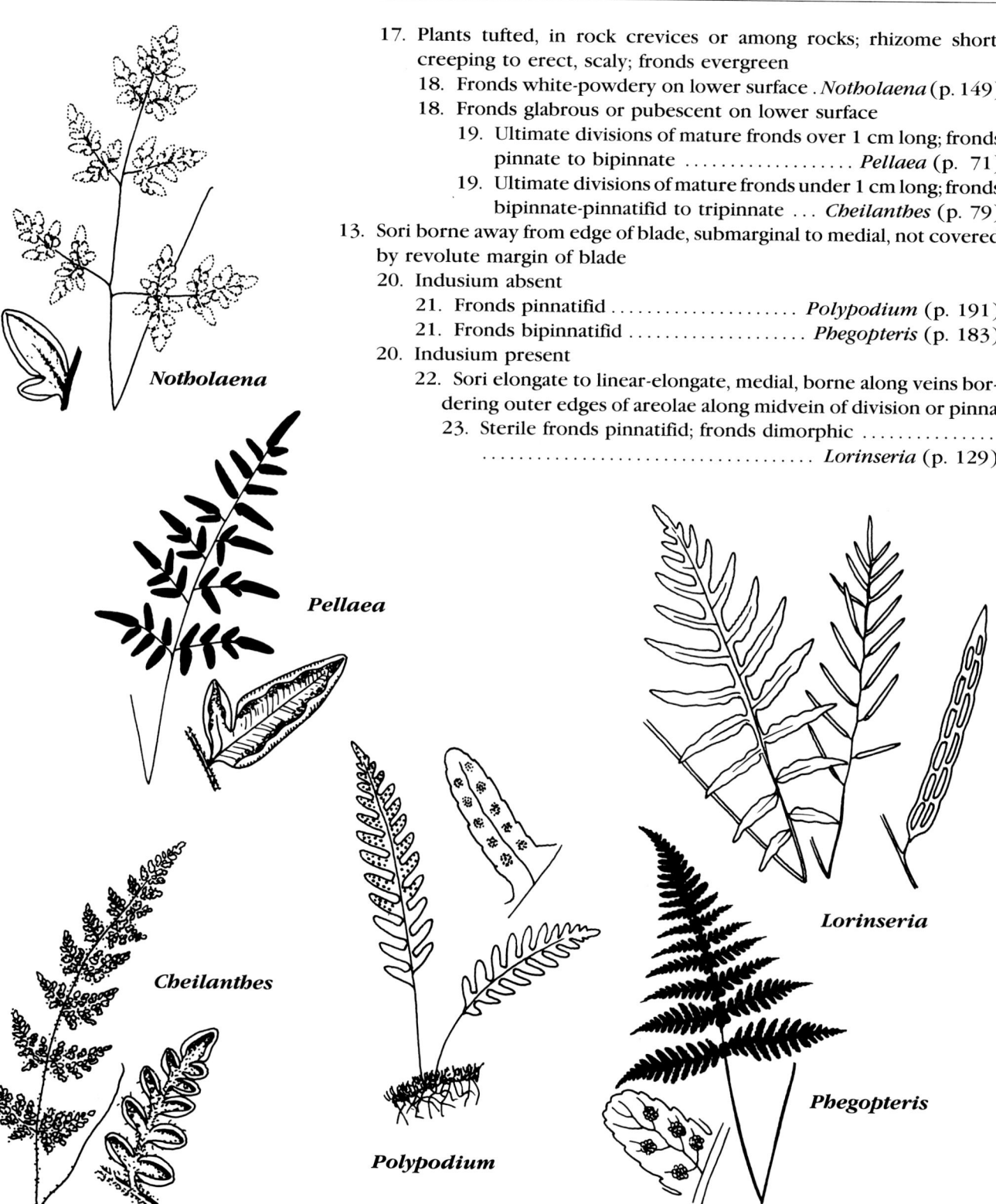

17. Plants tufted, in rock crevices or among rocks; rhizome short-creeping to erect, scaly; fronds evergreen
   18. Fronds white-powdery on lower surface . *Notholaena* (p. 149)
   18. Fronds glabrous or pubescent on lower surface
      19. Ultimate divisions of mature fronds over 1 cm long; fronds pinnate to bipinnate .... *Pellaea* (p. 71)
      19. Ultimate divisions of mature fronds under 1 cm long; fronds bipinnate-pinnatifid to tripinnate ... *Cheilanthes* (p. 79)
13. Sori borne away from edge of blade, submarginal to medial, not covered by revolute margin of blade
   20. Indusium absent
      21. Fronds pinnatifid .... *Polypodium* (p. 191)
      21. Fronds bipinnatifid .... *Phegopteris* (p. 183)
   20. Indusium present
      22. Sori elongate to linear-elongate, medial, borne along veins bordering outer edges of areolae along midvein of division or pinna
         23. Sterile fronds pinnatifid; fronds dimorphic ....
         .... *Lorinseria* (p. 129)

23. Sterile fonds pinnate-pinnatifid; fronds alike .... *Woodwardia* (p. 241)
22. Sori round to linear-elongate, marginal to medial, borne on, along, or across veins on lower surface of frond
   24. Fronds dimorphic; veins of sterile fronds reticulate, forming a series of linear to oblong areolae along pinna midvein; fertile fronds rigidly erect, much contracted .... *Onoclea* (p. 153)
   24. Fronds alike or only slightly dimorphic; veins free, simple or forked
      25. Sori elliptic to linear-elongate, straight to slightly curved along anterior side of vein or recurved or reflexed across and along both sides of vein; indusium attached along one side of sorus
         26. Rhizome scales clathrate ... *Asplenium* (p. 31)
         26. Rhizome scales not clathrate . *Athyrium* (p. 55)
      25. Sori round to reniform, borne on veins; indusium attached under or near center of sorus
         27. Indusium attached under sorus, pocket-like or cup-like
            28. Indusium pocket-like, opening along edge toward pinna margin; stipe glabrous, virtually scaleless .... *Cystopteris* (p. 91)

Woodwardia

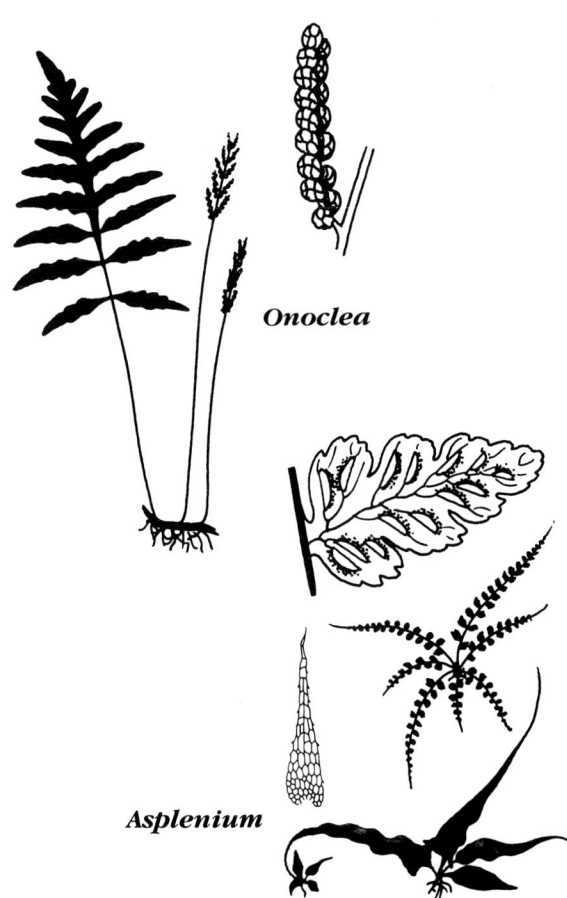

Onoclea

Asplenium

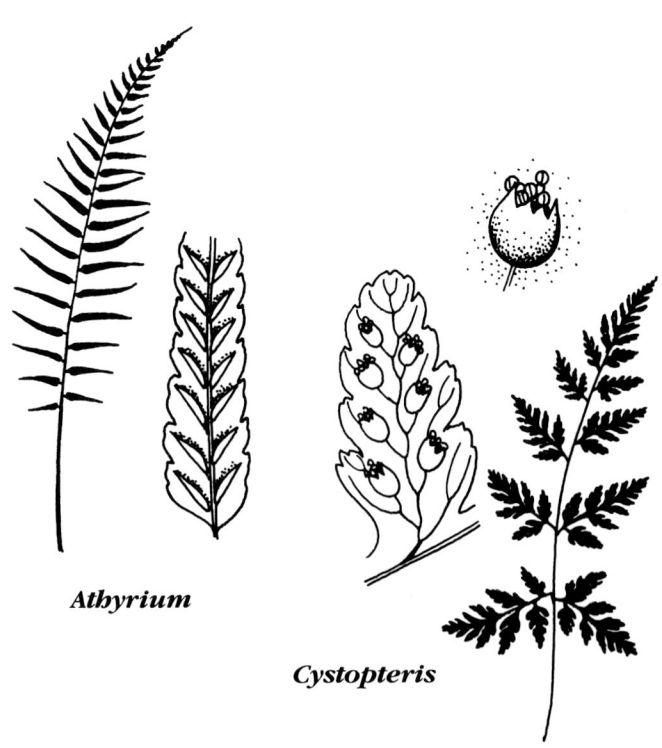

Athyrium

Cystopteris

28. Indusium cup-like, opening above and splitting into several segments; stipe pilose or scaly .... *Woodsia* (p. 237)
27. Indusium attached near center of sorus, peltate or reniform
    29. Indusium peltate; fronds pinnate ..... *Polystichum* (p. 197)
    29. Indusium reniform; fronds pinnate-pinnatifid to bipinnate-pinnatifid
        30. Fronds glabrous; rhizome with persistent stipe bases; indusium glabrous, eglandular .... *Dyropteris* (p. 103)
        30. Fronds puberulent; rhizome without persistent stipe bases; indusium hirtellous or glandular ciliolate ....
        .... *Thelypteris* (p. 221)

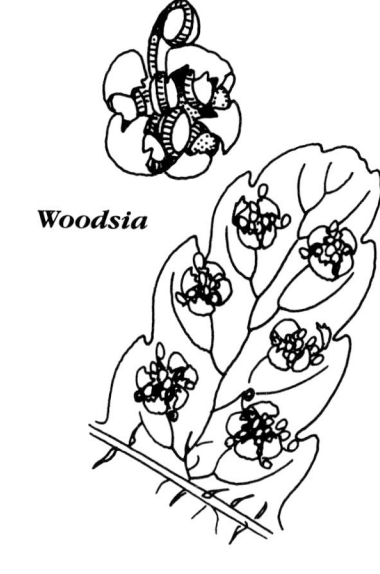

Woodsia

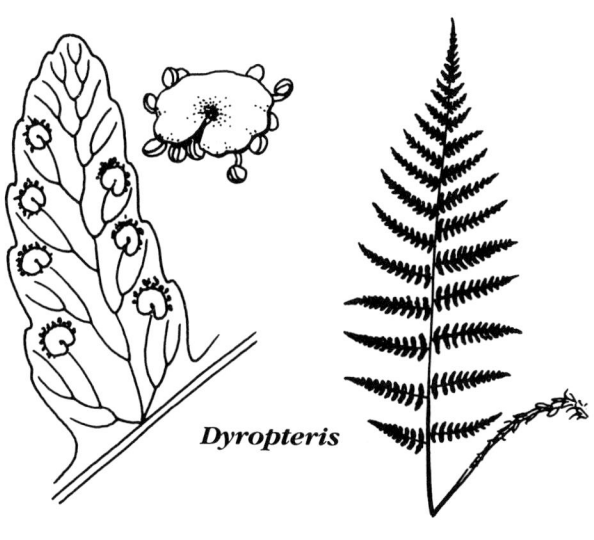

Dyropteris

Polystichum

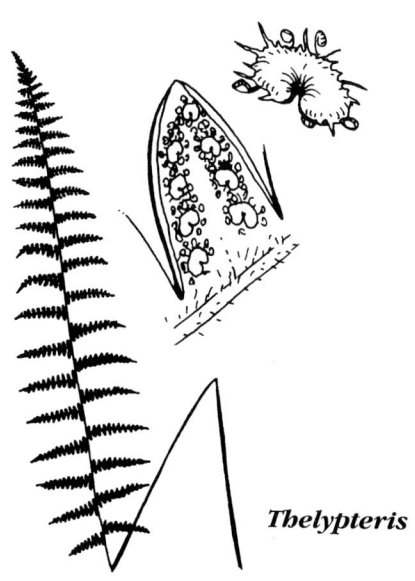

Thelypteris

9. County map of Arkansas

Description of Arkansas Pteridophytes

Adiantum L. Maidenhair Ferns

Rhizome creeping; scales light brown, linear-lanceolate. Fronds bipinnate or tripinnate, glabrous; stipe and rachis lustrous, reddish brown to purplish black; pinnules or segments flabellate to rhombic, stipitate; veins forked, free. Sori borne along distal edge of pinnule or segment on underside of reflexed marginal flap; flap lunate to elongate-reniform.

A mainly tropical genus of over 200 species.

Key to the species of *Adiantum* in Arkansas

1. Fronds erect; stipe dichotomizing at apex into recurving, secund rachises; blade flabellate to reniform .... 1. *A. pedatum* (p. 26)
1. Fronds weakly ascending to pendulous; stipe continuous at apex into flexuous rachis; blade lanceolate to deltoid . 2. *A. capillus-veneris* (p. 28)

1. *Adiantum pedatum* L.

COMMON NAME: Northern Maidenhair Fern

Fronds deciduous, erect, bipinnate, up to 50 cm tall; stipe dichotomizing at apex into recurving secund rachises; blade flabellate to reniform, horizontally flattened, up to 30 cm long and 40 cm wide; pinnules flabellate to deltoid with distal margins crenate and incised to lobed.

HABITAT: Moist, shaded, rich woods; primarily Interior Highlands and Crowley's Ridge.

RANGE: North America.

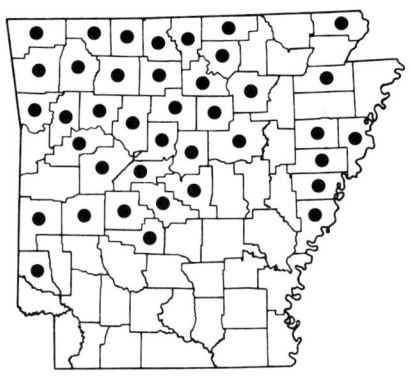

Adiantum pedatum

Baxter Co.: *Taylor 2682* (SIU). Benton Co.: *Demaree 4592* (SMU). Boone Co.: *Demaree s.n.* (UARK). Carroll Co.: *Palmer 4547* (MO). Clay Co.: *Richards 4402* (ARKSU). Cleburne Co.: *Demaree 30509* (SMU). Conway Co.: *Demaree 22793* (SMU). Craighead Co.: *Alliston 15* (ARKSU). Crawford Co.: *Taylor 1093* (SIU). Crittenden Co.: *Demaree 61080* (SMU). Cross Co.: *Lowman 344* (HXC). Faulkner Co.: *Demaree s.n.* (MO). Franklin Co.: *Johnson 527* (HXC). Fulton Co.: *Demaree 5372* (NY). Garland Co.: *Trelease s.n.* (MO). Hot Spring Co.: *Palmer 26589* (UARK). Independence Co.: *Demaree 17097* (MO). Izard Co.: *Matthews 91* (ARKSU). Johnson Co.: *D. Moore 450265* (UARK). Lee Co.: *Taylor 1186* (SIU). Logan Co.: *Palmer 24158* (MO). Madison Co.: *Key 265* (SMS). Marion Co.: *Palmer 4777* (MO). Montgomery Co.: *Taylor 2215* (SIU). Newton Co.: *Taylor 1221* (SIU). Perry Co.: *Demaree 35477* (SMU). Phillips Co.: *Demaree 19221* (SMU). Polk Co.: *Taylor 1067* (SIU). Pope Co.: *Taylor 1202* (SIU). Pulaski Co.: *Johnson 122* (HXC). St. Francis Co.: *Demaree 21539* (M). Saline Co.: *Demaree 23987* (SMU). Searcy Co.: *Taylor 2572* (SIU). Sevier Co.: *D. Moore 410371* (UARK). Stone Co.: *Taylor 1253b* (SIU). Van Buren Co.: *Taylor 25615* (SIU). Washington Co.: *Taylor 1102* (SIU). White Co.: *Johnson 457* (HXC). Yell Co.: *Buchholz 1077* (NY).

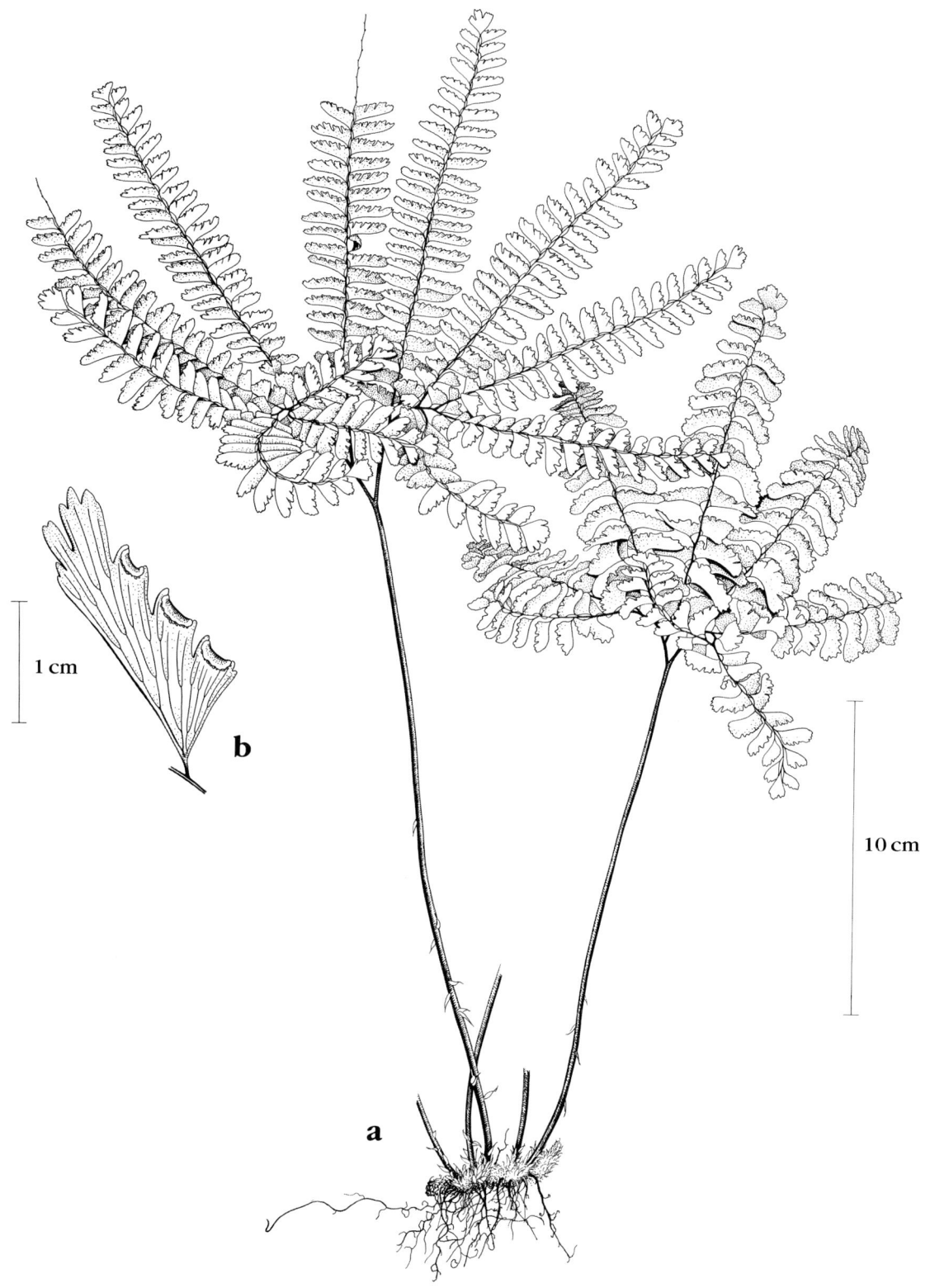

Adiantum pedatum
a. Habit; b. Lower surface of sporiferous pinnule.

2. *Adiantum capillus-veneris* L.

Adiantum modestum Underw.
Adiantum tricholepis f. *glabrum* Clute

COMMON NAME: Southern Maidenhair Fern

Fronds nearly evergreen, weakly ascending to pendulous, bipinnate or tripinnate, up to 70 cm long; blade lanceolate to deltoid, up to 40 cm long and 25 cm wide; rachis flexuous; pinnules or segments flabellate to rhombic, distal margins crenate to serrate and incised to lobed.

HABITAT: Moist to wet calcareous rock outcrops; principally in the Ozark Mountains but also on the limestone tufa at the base of Hot Springs Mountain, Hot Springs National Park, Garland County, and on basic igneous rocks near Magnet, Hot Spring County.

RANGE: Southern and west central United States, tropical and warm-temperate regions of the world.

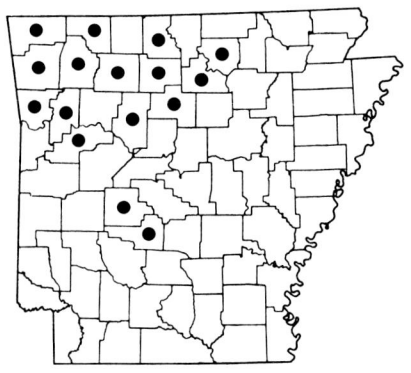

Adiantum capillus-veneris

Benton Co.: *Palmer 2940* (MO). Carroll Co.: *D. Moore 410188a* (UARK). Crawford Co.: *Moore 710274* (UARK). Franklin Co.: *Barber 2011* (UARK). Garland Co.: *Engelmann 19* (MO). Hot Spring Co.: *Demaree 19856* (MO). Izard Co.: *Taylor 12619* (SIU). Logan Co.: *D. Moore 480076* (UARK). Madison Co.: *Nelson 10873* (MO). Marion Co.: *Palmer 5985* (MO). Newton Co.: *Taylor 1218* (SIU). Pope Co.: *D. Moore 520755* (UARK). Searcy Co.: *Taylor 1239* (SIU). Stone Co.: *Taylor 1250* (SIU). Van Buren Co.: *Palmer 24203* (UARK). Washington Co.: *Palmer 23906* (MO).

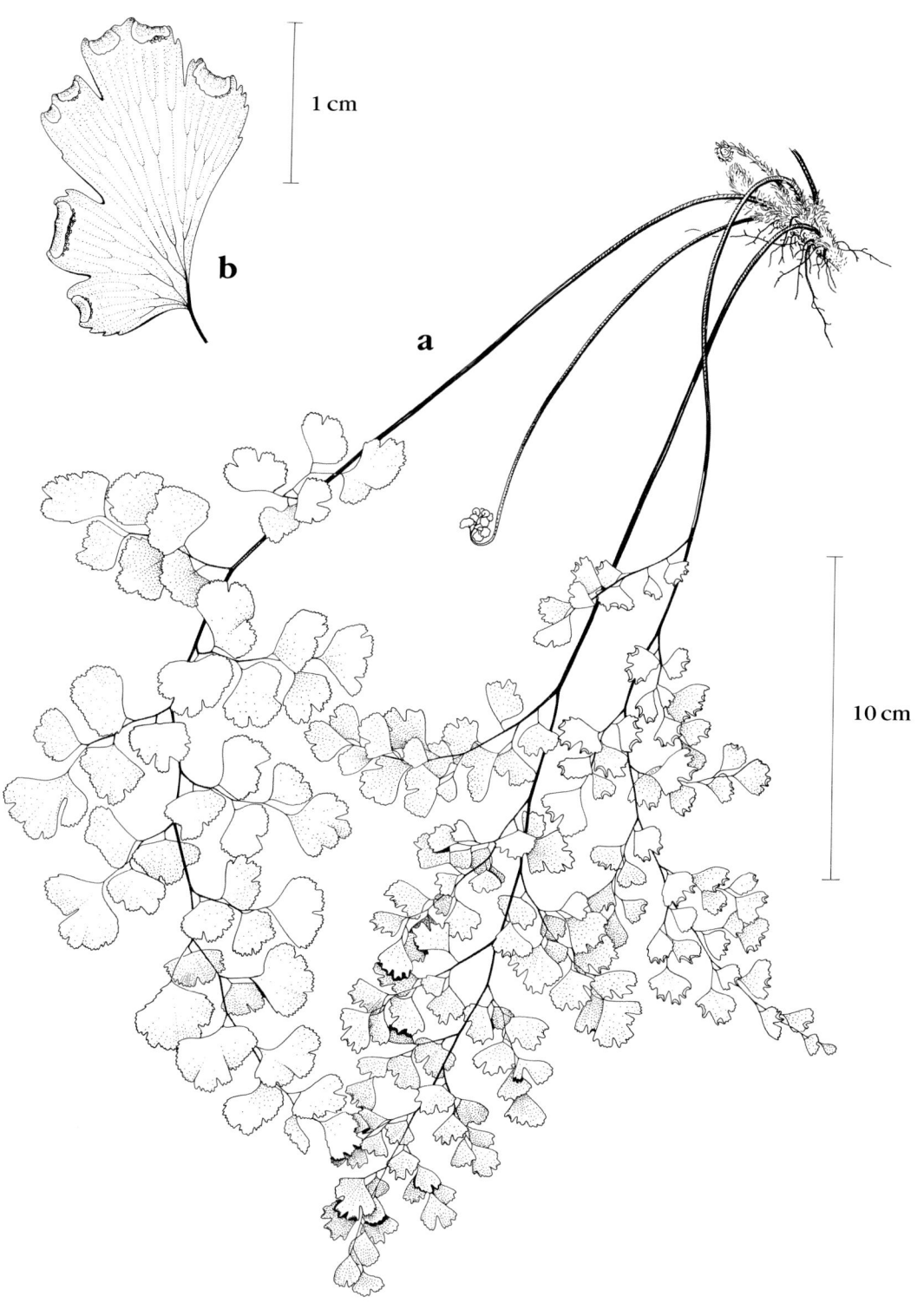

Adiantum capillus-veneris
a. Habit; b. Lower surface of sporiferous pinnule.

Asplenium L. Spleenworts

Rhizome short-creeping to erect; scales clathrate, linear to lanceolate. Fronds evergreen, simple to bipinnate-pinnatifid, glabrate; stipe and rachis green to black; veins simple or forked, free or reticulate. Sori elongate, straight or slightly curved, borne along veins; indusium unilateral.

A mostly tropical genus of nearly 700 species. A number of *Asplenium* species hybridize, producing sterile plants of intermediate morphology. Occasionally, chromosome doubling occurs and fertile plants are formed. Wagner (1954) describes how hybridization has played an important role in the evolution of certain species of *Asplenium*. Chromatographic studies by Smith and Levin (1963) support Wagner's proposed concept of "reticulate evolution in the genus."

Key to the species and hybrids of *Asplenium* in Arkansas

1. Fronds simple and unlobed except cordate-auriculate or occasionally hastate at base of blade; veins reticulate .. 1. *A. rhizophyllum* (p. 32)
1. Fronds pinnatifid, pinnate, or bipinnate; veins free or rarely reticulate
    2. Stipe green at least distally; rachis green throughout
        3. Fronds pinnatifid, occasionally pinnate for lowest pinna pair ....
           .... 2. *A. pinnatifidum* (p. 34)
        3. Fronds mostly bipinnate .... 3. *A. ruta-muraria* (p. 36)
    2. Stipe reddish brown to black; rachis reddish brown to black at least in lower part.
        4. Rachis reddish brown to black over 3/4 of its length
            5. Pinnae auriculate at base of upper margin, oblong to lanceolate
                6. Pinnae alternate, auricles overlapping rachis; rachis reddish brown to purplish black; fronds dimorphic .. 4. *A. platyneuron* (p. 38)
                6. Pinnae opposite or subopposite, auricles not overlapping rachis; rachis dark brown to black; fronds alike .. 5. *A. resiliens* (p. 42)
            5. Pinnae not auriculate, orbicular to ovate-oblong or flabellate ......
                .... 6. *A. trichomanes* (p. 44)
        4. Rachis reddish brown to dark brown up to 3/4 of its length
            7. Fronds pinnate above to bipinnate-pinnatifid below; spores normal
                .... 7. *A. bradleyi* (p. 46)
            7. Fronds pinnatifid above, pinnate below; spores abortive
8. Fronds usually pinnate less than 1/2 their blade length; blades often irregular in outline; pinnae subentire to crenulate; plants associated with *A. platyneuron* and *A. rhizophyllum* .... 8. *A.* X *ebenoides* (p. 48)
8. Fronds usually pinnate more than 1/2 their blade length; blades mostly regular in outline; pinnae crenulate to denticulate-serrulate; plants associated with *A. pinnatifidum*
    9. Blades tapering toward base, with lowest two pinna pairs shorter than the two pinna pairs above them; plants associated with *A. platyneuron*
       .... 9. *A.* X *kentuckiense* (p. 50)
    9. Blades not tapering toward base, with lowest two pinna pairs more or less equal to the two pinna pairs above them; plants associated with *A. bradleyi* .... 10. *A.* X *gravesii* (p. 52)

1. *Asplenium rhizophyllum* L.

Camptosorus rhizophyllus (L.) Link

COMMON NAME: Walking Fern

Fronds spreading, simple, up to 40 cm long; stipe green, brown near base; blade deltoid-attenuate to linear-lanceolate, up to 30 cm long and 3 cm or more wide at base, apex usually caudate and often proliferous, cordate-auriculate or occasionally hastate at base; veins reticulate, forming areolae along midrib, free toward margin.

HABITAT: Moist, shaded, limestone and sandstone outcrops; chiefly Ozark Mountains.

RANGE: Eastern North America.

Asplenium rhizophyllum is capable of forming extensive, matted, colonies through proliferation at the apices of its fronds. Although this species is often placed in the genus *Camptosorus*, it is here retained in *Asplenium* due to the close relationship evidenced by its ability to hybridize with other members of the genus *Asplenium*.

Considerable variation is found in leaf shape, especially in the form of the leaf base. Key (1976) reported the occurrence of forked fronds in several colonies of *A. rhizophyllum* in Newton County.

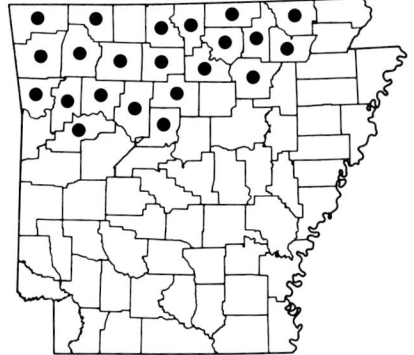

Asplenium rhizophyllum

Baxter Co.: *Taylor 1849* (SIU). Benton Co.: *Demaree 4616* (SMU). Carroll Co.: *Haas 1453* (UCA). Conway Co.: *Johnson 195* (HXC). Crawford Co.: *Redfearn 21086* (SMS). Franklin Co.: *Johnson 520* (HXC). Fulton Co.: *Wheeler 50* (F). Independence Co.: *Thomas 8494* (SMU). Izard Co.: *Barr s.n.* (UARK). Johnson Co.: *Redfearn 23826* (SMS). Lawrence Co.: *Taylor 1785* (SIU). Logan Co.: *Pyle 286* (APCR). Madison Co.: *Taylor 1994a* (SIU). Marion Co.: *D. Moore 380727* (UARK). Newton Co.: *Taylor 2696* (SIU). Pope Co.: *Taylor 1213* (SIU). Randolph Co.: *Demaree 26812* (SMU). Searcy Co.: *Taylor 2574* (SIU). Sharp Co.: *Demaree 25922* (SMU). Stone Co.: *Taylor 1246* (SIU). Van Buren Co.: *Palmer 24292* (UARK). Washington Co.: *Henbest 14* (UARK).

Asplenium rhizophyllum
a. Habit; b. Lower portion of sporiferous frond; c. Forked fronds.

2. *Asplenium pinnatifidum* Nutt.

Asplenosorus pinnatifidus (Nutt.) Mickel

COMMON NAME: Lobed Spleenwort

Fronds spreading, pinnatifid to occasionally pinnate below, up to 20 cm long; stipe green above, dark brown below; blade deltoid-lanceolate to linear-lanceolate, up to 15 cm long and 3 cm or more wide, apex usually attenuate to caudate and rarely proliferous; blade divisions deltoid-ovate to orbicular or occasionally oblong-lanceolate, decurrent; veins free, rarely reticulate.

HABITAT: Sheltered crevices of noncalcareous sandstone and novaculite outcrops; Interior Highlands.

RANGE: Eastern United States.

Asplenium pinnatifidum was reported for Arkansas by Lesquereux (1860) and by Harvey (1881) on "limestone cliffs." However, all currently known stations in Arkansas are either on sandstone or novaculite.

Wagner (1954) postulates that *Asplenium pinnatifidum,* a tetraploid, originated as a hybrid between *A. rhizophyllum* and *A. montanum,* a species found east of Arkansas, followed by chromosome doubling. In addition to cytological evidence, Wagner suggests the frequent appearance of irregular frond-forms as a further indication of hybrid origin (Wagner, 1962a).

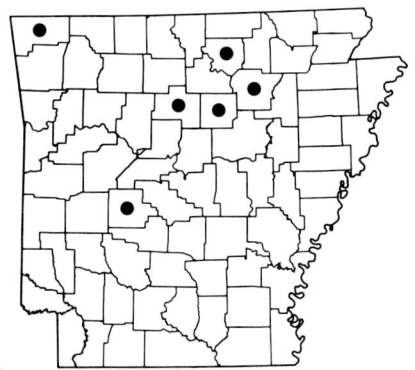

Asplenium pinnatifidum

Benton Co.: *Taylor 1123* (SIU). Cleburne Co.: *Johnson 435* (HXC). Garland Co.: *Taylor 2704* (SIU). Independence Co.: *D. Moore 61118* (UARK). Izard Co.: *Johnson 79054* (HXC). Van Buren Co.: *Johnson 437* (HXC).

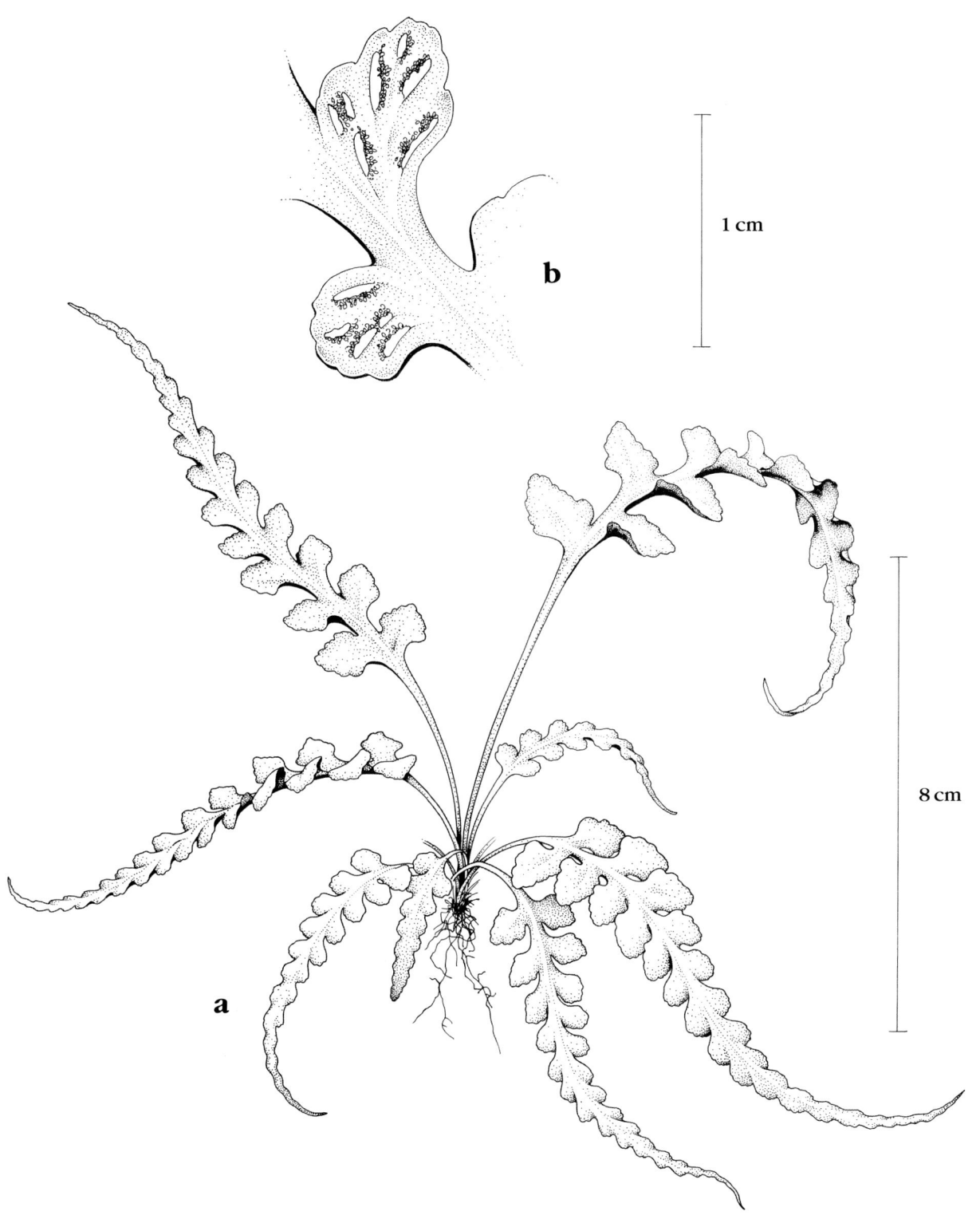

Asplenium pinnatifidum
a. Habit; b. Lower portion of sporiferous frond.

3. *Asplenium ruta-muraria* L.

Asplenium cryptolepis Fern.

COMMON NAME: Wall Rue Spleenwort

Fronds erect, mostly bipinnate, up to 12 cm tall; stipe green; blade deltoid-ovate to lanceolate, up to 6 cm long and 4 cm wide; pinnae alternate; pinnules flabellate or rhombic to elliptic, crenulate to crenate-incised along upper margin, cuneate at base; veins free.

HABITAT: "Limestone cliffs".

RANGE: Eastern North America, Europe, Asia.

Asplenium ruta-muraria was first reported from Arkansas in the list of Nuttall (1835). Lesquereux (1860) recorded this species from "limestone cliffs." Harvey (1881) also included *A. ruta-muraria* in his list, stating that he had specimens from Lesquereux said to have been collected in northeast Arkansas. Although no specimens have been located to confirm its presence in the state, *A. ruta-muraria* is included here on the basis of the above reports.

Asplenium ruta-muraria should be found in Arkansas. It has been collected from a number of counties in southeast Missouri including Stone, Ozark, Howell, Oregon, and Ripley Counties which border Arkansas to the north. In Missouri, *A. ruta-muraria* is found on north-and east-facing shaded limestone outcrops (Steyermark, 1963, p. 30). Similar sites occur in the Ozark Highlands of Arkansas.

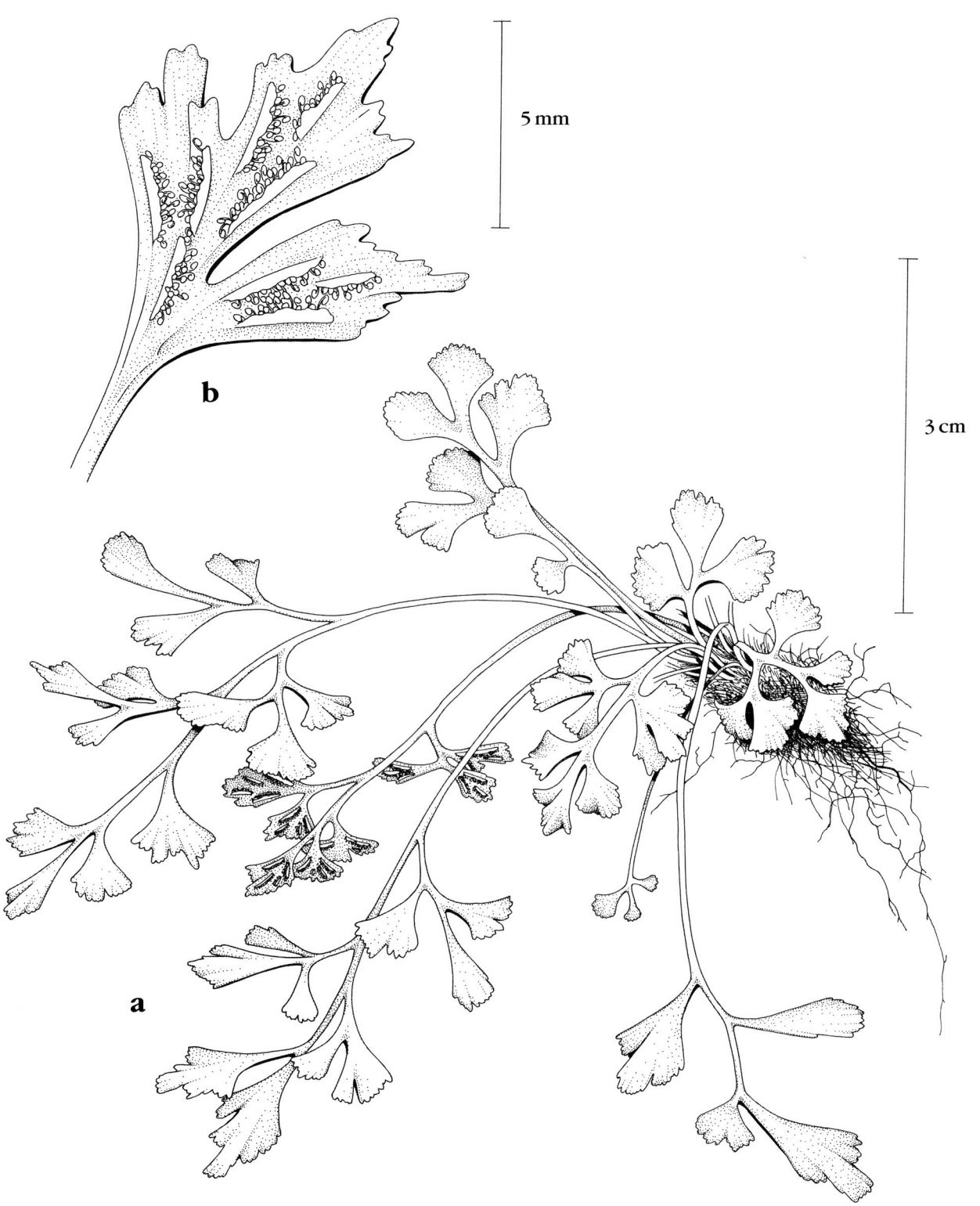

Asplenium ruta-muraria
a. Habit; b. Lower portion of sporiferous pinnule.

4. *Asplenium platyneuron* (L.) B.S.P.

Asplenium ebeneum Ait.

COMMON NAME: Ebony Spleenwort

Fronds erect or spreading, pinnate, dimorphic, up to 70 cm tall; fertile fronds more erect and larger than sterile fronds; stipe and rachis brittle, lustrous, reddish brown to purplish black; blade linear-oblong or linear-oblanceolate, up to 60 cm long and 8 cm wide; pinnae alternate, deep green, mostly oblong or oblong-lanceolate, usually crenulate to serrulate, sometimes serrate-incised, or rarely pinnatifid to pinnatisect, auriculate at base on upper margin, auricle overlapping rachis; veins free.

Asplenium platyneuron is one of the most common and widespread ferns in Arkansas. It is found nearly throughout the state but has seldom been collected in the Mississippi Alluvial Plain.

Because *A. platyneuron* is a common, attractive, and variable species over much of eastern North America, a number of varieties and forms have been recognized (Taylor, Mohlenbrock, and Burton, 1976). Two varieties and one form differing from typical plants have been noted in Arkansas material, but Wagner and Johnson (1981) doubt that these variations merit taxonomic distinction.

Key to variations of *Asplenium platyneuron* in Arkansas

1. Longest pinnae less than 3.5 cm long; blades up to 50 cm long
   2. Pinnae subentire to crenulate or serrulate .... 4a. var. *platyneuron*
   2. Pinnae doubly serrate to deeply incised, or pinnatifid to pinnatisect
      3. Pinnae doubly serrate to deeply incised, all or nearly all of the pinnae cut less than 4/5 of the way to the midrib . 4b. var. *incisum*
      3. Pinnae pinnatifid to pinnatisect, all or nearly all of the pinnae cut more than 4/5 of the way to the midrib ....
      .... f. *hortonae*
1. Longest pinnae greater than 3.5 cm long; blades up to 70 cm long ....
   .... 4c. var. *bacculum-rubrum*

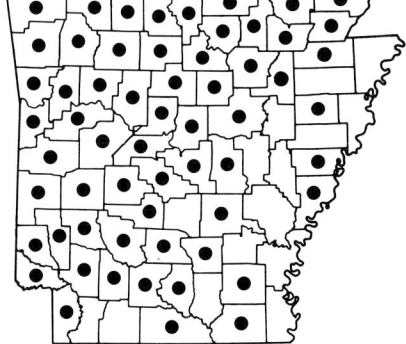

Asplenium platyneuron

Ashley Co.: *Demaree 16368* (SMU). Baxter Co.: *Taylor 2677* (SIU). Benton Co.: *D. Moore 460177* (UARK). Boone Co.: *Haas 2798* (UCA). Calhoun Co.: *Demaree 22666* (MO). Carroll Co.: *Palmer 6351* (MO). Clark Co.: *Taylor 2175* (SIU). Clay Co.: *Taylor 2661* (SIU). Cleburne Co.: *Taylor 1017* (SIU). Cleveland Co.: *Taylor 2736* (SIU). Conway Co.: *Demaree 23122* (SMU). Craighead Co.: *Demaree 3523* (NY). Crawford Co.: *Taylor 1126* (SIU). Cross Co.: *Akers 20* (HXC). Dallas Co.: *Taylor 1137* (SIU). Drew Co.: *Demaree 24348* (MO). Faulkner Co.: *Taylor 2609* (SIU). Franklin Co.: *Palmer 8160* (MO). Fulton Co.: *Taylor 2667* (SIU). Garland Co.:

4a. *Asplenium platyneuron* var. *platyneuron*

COMMON NAME: Ebony Spleenwort

This typical variety and var. *incisum* are the two most common kinds of Ebony Spleenwort found in Arkansas.

HABITAT: Moist to dry, rocky woods, hillsides, ravines, thickets, rock outcrops, stream banks, and roadsides.

RANGE: Eastern North America.

4b. *Asplenium platyneuron* var. *incisum* (Peck) B. L. Robins.

COMMON NAME: Serrate Ebony Spleenwort

This variety often occurs with var. *platyneuron* and the two varieties freely intergrade.

HABITAT: Moist to dry, rocky woods, hillsides, ravines, thickets, rock outcrops, stream banks, and roadsides.

RANGE: Eastern North America.

Palmer 23106 (MO). Greene Co.: *Richards 5488* (ARKSU). Hempstead Co.: *Palmer 10512* (MO). Hot Spring Co.: *Demaree 15610* (SMU). Howard Co.: *McSwain 43E69* (UARK). Independence Co.: *Demaree 17067* (MO). Izard Co.: *Taylor 2136* (SIU). Jackson Co.: *Richards 6203* (ARKSU). Jefferson Co.: *Locke 1223* (UARK). Johnson Co.: *Taylor 1087* (SIU). Lawrence Co.: *Taylor 1787* (SIU). Lee Co.: *McDaniel 804* (ARKSU). Little River Co.: *Johnson 475* (HXC). Logan Co.: *Taylor 1032* (SIU). Lonoke Co.: *Clark 665* (HXC). Madison Co.: *Taylor 2005* (SIU). Marion Co.: *Palmer 4747* (MO). Miller Co.: *Taylor 1172* (SIU). Montgomery Co.: *Taylor 2843* (SIU). Nevada Co.: *D. Moore 420470* (UARK). Newton Co.: *Taylor 2700* (SIU). Ouachita Co.: *Hoiberg 351* (SMU). Perry Co.: *Demaree 54546* (SMU). Phillips Co.: *Palmer 25162* (UARK). Pike Co.: *Johnson 177* (HXC). Polk Co.: *Taylor 1061* (SIU). Pope Co.: *Taylor 1204* (SIU). Pulaski Co.: *Palmer 23002* (UARK). Randolph Co.: *Taylor 2087* (SIU). Saline Co.: *Demaree 23031* (SMU). Scott Co.: *Taylor 1058* (SIU). Searcy Co.: *Taylor 1853* (SIU). Sebastian Co.: *Taylor 2721* (SIU). Sevier Co.: *Taylor 2164* (SIU). Sharp Co.: *Demaree 27332* (SMU). Stone Co.: *Taylor 1248* (SIU). Union Co.: *Taylor 1163* (SIU). Van Buren Co.: *Nelson 482* (SIU). Washington Co.: *Buchholz s.n.* (US). White Co.: *Johnson 217* (HXC). Yell Co.: *Taylor 1192* (SIU).

Asplenium platyneuron f. *hortonae* (Davenp.) L. B. Smith is a striking, sporadic, sterile plant. In Arkansas, it has been collected from a mossy, rock ledge on Petit Jean Mountain, Conway County by Dwight Moore (*Moore 480355* UARK) on 26 July 1948.

4c. *Asplenium platyneuron* var. *bacculum-rubrum* (Featherm.) Fern.

COMMON NAME: Jagged Ebony Spleenwort

This variety is a robust, mainly southern plant which has coarsely serrate-incised pinnae that are typically longer than 3.5 cm. Specimens characteristic of this variety have been collected in Boone, Cleburne, Johnson, Lee, Polk, Pulaski, Stone, and Van Buren Counties.

HABITAT: Rocky, open woods.

RANGE: Southeastern United States.

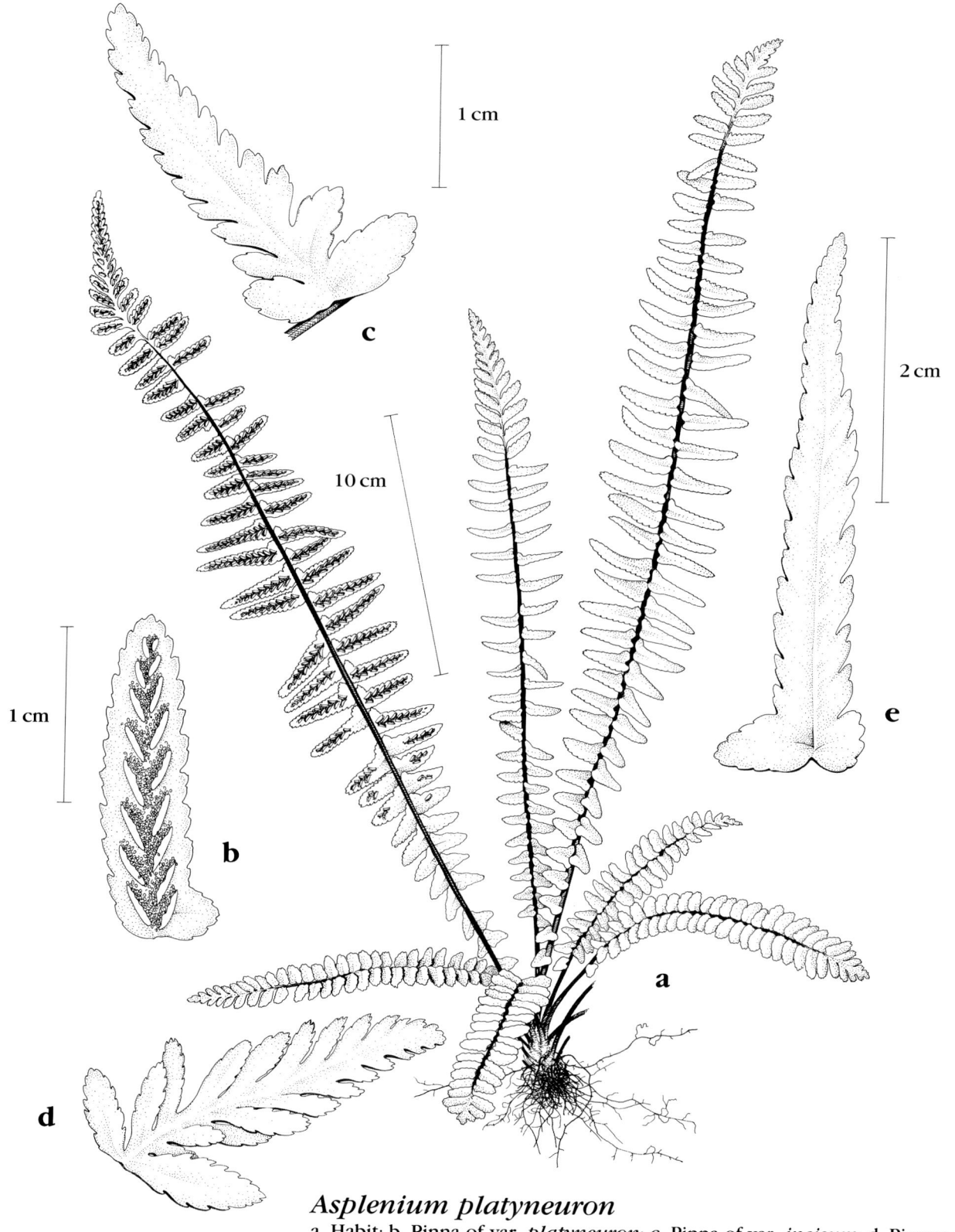

Asplenium platyneuron
a. Habit; b. Pinna of var. *platyneuron*; c. Pinna of var. *incisum*; d. Pinnae of f. *hortonae*; e. Pinna of var. *bacculum-rubrum*.

5. *Asplenium resiliens* Kunze

Asplenium parvulum Mart. & Gal.

COMMON NAME: Black-stemmed Spleenwort

Fronds erect-spreading, pinnate, alike, up to 30 cm long; stipe and rachis wiry, lustrous, dark brown to black; blade linear-lanceolate to linear-oblong, up to 25 cm long and 3 cm wide; pinnae opposite or subopposite, often slightly deflexed, grayish green, mostly oblong, subentire to crenulate or bluntly denticulate-serrulate, auriculate at base on upper margin, auricle not overlapping rachis; veins free.

HABITAT: Shaded crevices in limestone, dolomite, and chert outcrops, primarily in the Ozark Mountains but also on the limestone tufa at the base of Hot Springs Mountain, Hot Springs National Park, Garland County.

RANGE: Southern North America, West Indies, Central and South America.

Asplenium resiliens is an apogamous triploid normally producing 32 diploid spores per sporangium (Wagner, 1966).

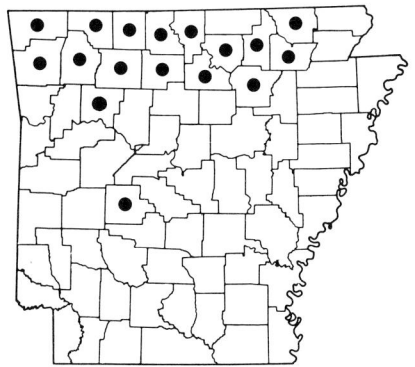

Asplenium resiliens

Baxter Co.: *Taylor 1840* (SIU). Benton Co.: *Demaree 4654* (F). Boone Co.: *Palmer 6907* (MO). Carroll Co.: *Palmer 29314* (MO). Garland Co.: *Engelmann 10* (MO). Independence Co.: *Demaree 28594* (SMU). Izard Co.: *Demaree 17039* (SMU). Johnson Co.: *Johnson 79033* (HXC). Lawrence Co.: *Taylor 1788* (SIU). Madison Co.: *Haas 1437* (UCA). Marion Co.: *Palmer 43872* (MO). Newton Co.: *Taylor 2698* (SIU). Randolph Co.: *Demaree 26813* (SMU). Searcy Co.: *Taylor 1243* (SIU). Sharp Co.: *Demaree 26434* (SMU). Stone Co.: *Taylor 1244* (SIU). Washington Co.: *Demaree 2797* (UARK).

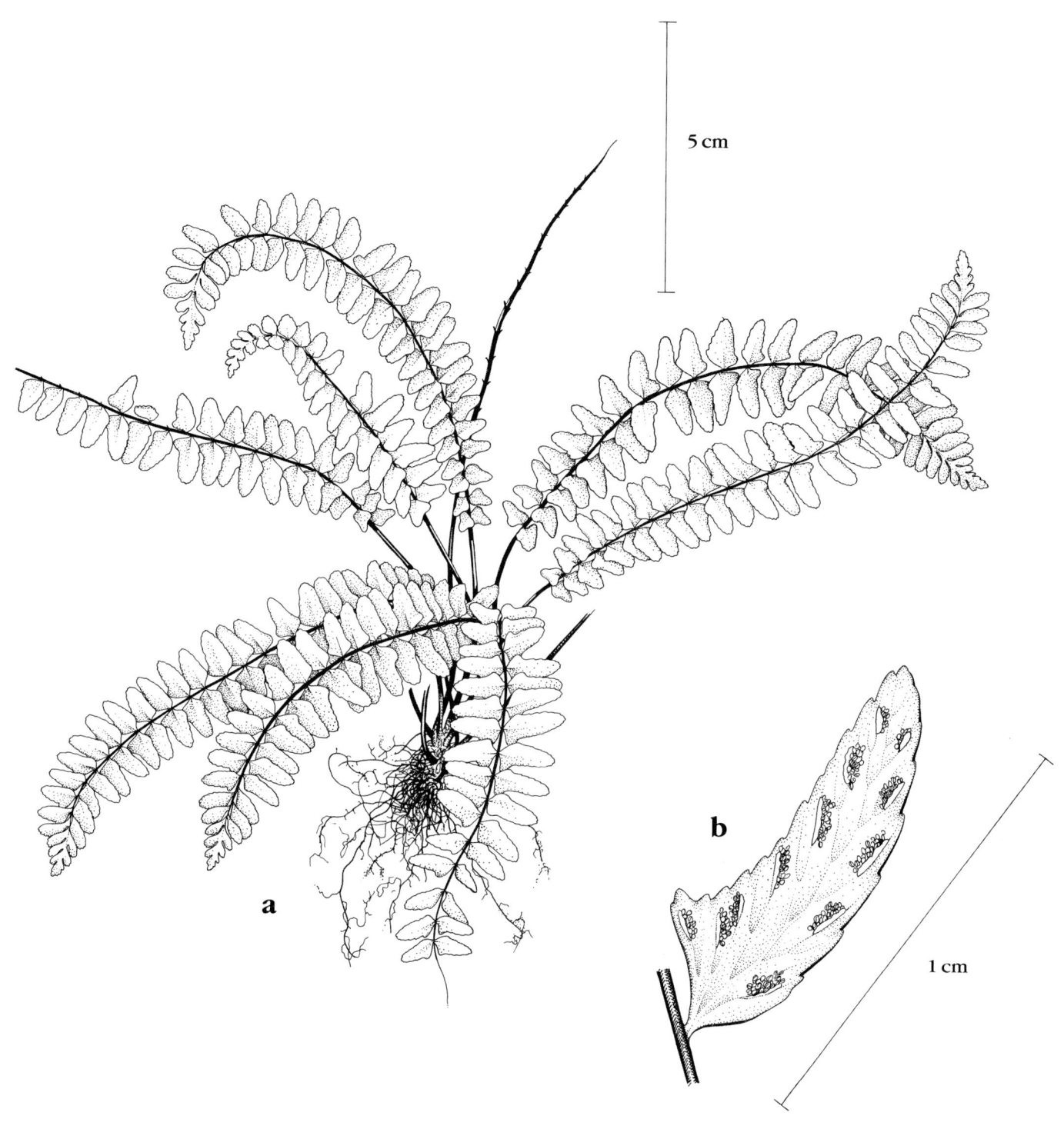

Asplenium resiliens
a. Habit; b. Lower surface of sporiferous pinna.

6. *Asplenium trichomanes* L.

Asplenium melanocaulon Willd.

COMMON NAME: Maidenhair Spleenwort

Fronds spreading, pinnate, up to 20 cm long; stipe and rachis wiry, lustrous, dark reddish brown; blade linear-oblong, up to 18 cm long and 1.5 cm wide; pinnae opposite or subopposite, deep green, orbicular to ovate-oblong or flabellate, crenulate, often cuneate at base, not auriculate; veins free.

HABITAT: Shaded, moist crevices in rock outcrops; Interior Highlands.

RANGE: North America, Europe, Asia.

In North America, *Asplenium trichomanes* exists as a sexual diploid, a sexual tetraploid, and a sterile triploid. These three cytotypes are distinguished most readily by the size and shape of their spores. Diploid plants occur mostly on sandstone rocks and have spores averaging about 30 µm in diameter, while tetraploid plants are found on calcareous rocks and have spores approximately 41 µm in diameter (Moran, 1982). Triploid plants produce shriveled, aborted spores and are thought to represent hybrids between diploid and tetraploid plants. At present, only diploid plants are known from Arkansas.

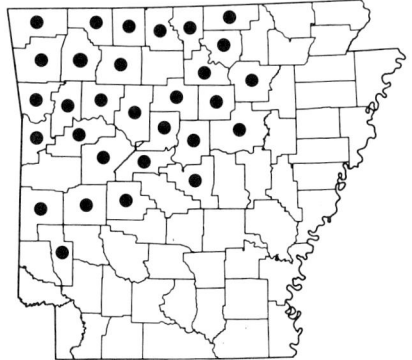

Asplenium trichomanes

Baxter Co.: *Taylor 2685* (SIU). Benton Co.: *Taylor 1117* (SIU). Boone Co.: *Demaree 3246* (NY). Carroll Co.: *Palmer 5615* (MO). Cleburne Co.: *Palmer 6952* (MO). Conway Co.: *Demaree 23123* (MO). Crawford Co.: *Taylor 1098* (SIU). Faulkner Co.: *Buchholz 1995* (UARK). Franklin Co.: *Taylor 1128* (SIU). Fulton Co.: *Palmer 14691* (MO). Garland Co.: *Palmer 23105* (UARK). Howard Co.: *Kellogg s.n.* (MO). Independence Co.: *Demaree 17099* (MO). Izard Co.: *Demaree 3275* (UARK). Johnson Co.: *Redfearn 238147* (SMS). Logan Co.: *Taylor 1031* (SIU). Madison Co.: *Davis 1503* (UARK). Marion Co.: *Taylor 1232* (SIU). Montgomery Co.: *J. Moore 3154* (UCA). Newton Co.: *Redfearn 23102* (SMS). Perry Co.: *Redfearn 24135* (SMS). Polk Co.: *J. Moore s.n.* (UARK). Pope Co.: *Robinette 2789* (UCA). Pulaski Co.: *Owens s.n.* (US). Sebastian Co.: *Taylor 2720* (SIU). Stone Co.: *D. Moore 450518* (UARK). Van Buren Co.: *Taylor 2561* (SIU). Washington Co.: *Demaree 3007* (UARK). White Co.: *Johnson 453* (HXC). Yell Co.: *Taylor 1194* (SIU).

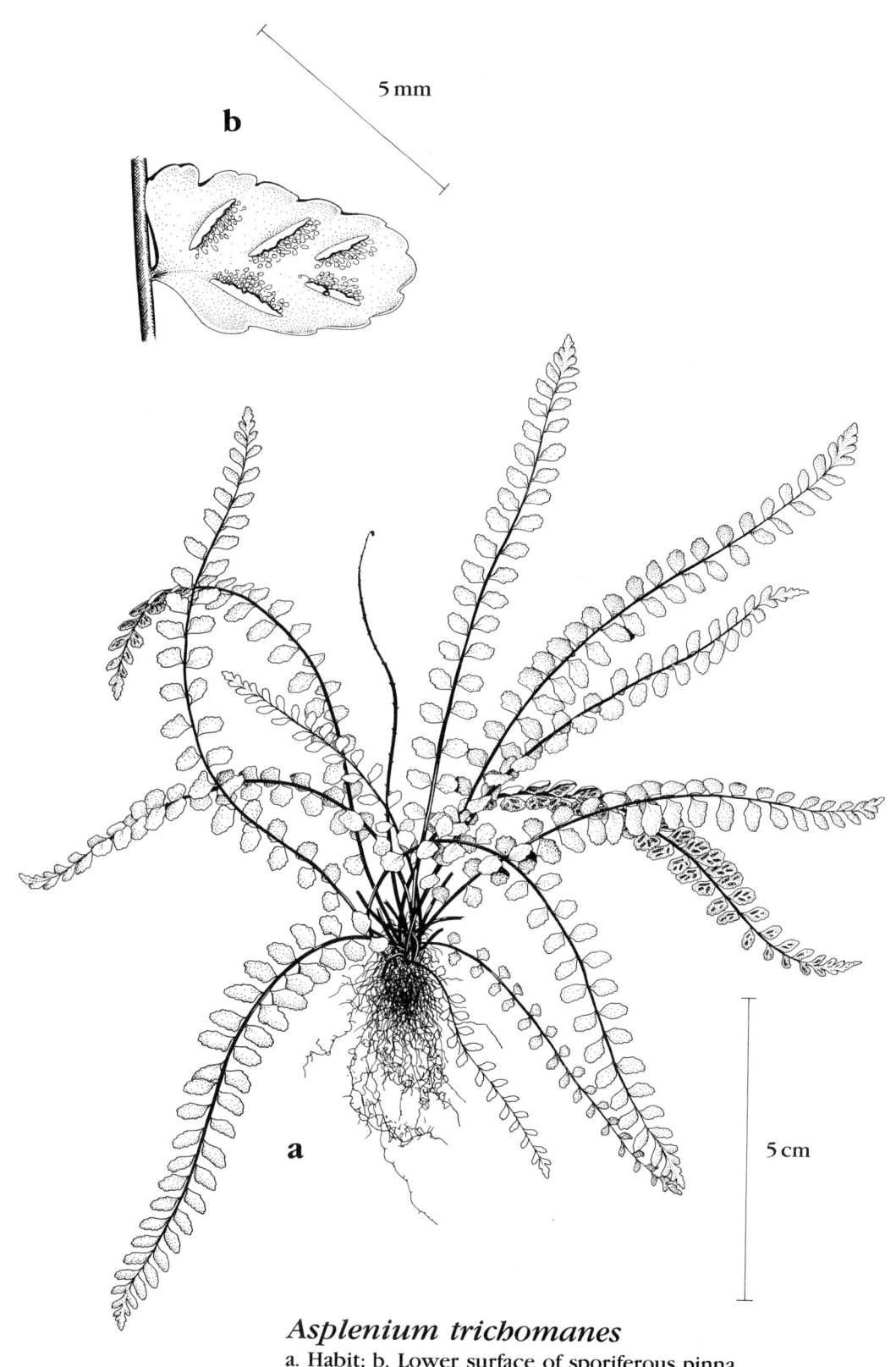

Asplenium trichomanes
a. Habit; b. Lower surface of sporiferous pinna.

7. *Asplenium bradleyi* D. C. Eat.

Asplenium X *stotleri* Wherry

COMMON NAME: Bradley's Spleenwort

Fronds erect-spreading, pinnate to bipinnate-pinnatifid, up to 25 cm long; stipe wiry, lustrous, dark brown; blade lanceolate to oblong-lanceolate, up to 20 cm long and 4 cm wide; rachis lustrous, dark brown from one-third to three fourths its length, green toward apex; pinnae deltoid-ovate to oblong-lanceolate, normally serrate and often lobed to pinnatisect, usually auriculate at base on upper margin; veins free.

HABITAT: Sandstone and novaculite outcrops; chiefly Interior Highlands.

RANGE: Eastern United States.

Wagner (1954) postulates that *Asplenium bradleyi*, a tetraploid, originated as a hybrid between *A. montanum*, a species found east of Arkansas, and *A. platyneuron*, followed by chromosome doubling.

A comparison of *A.* X *stotleri* from West Virginia and specimens of *A. bradleyi* collected at Blanchard Springs, Stone County by Donald Farrar indicates that *A.* X *stotleri* is merely a round-lobed form of *A. bradleyi* (Wagner and Wagner, 1969).

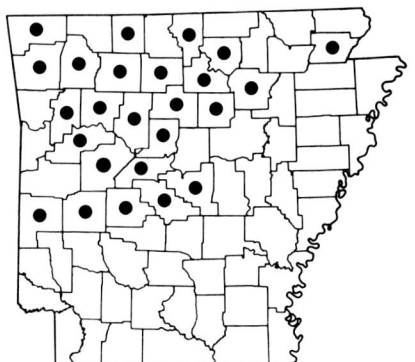

Asplenium bradleyi

Baxter Co.: *Culwell 3188* (UCA). Benton Co.: *D. Moore 41096* (UARK). Boone Co.: *Redfearn 23716* (SMS). Cleburne Co.: *Johnson 468* (HXC). Conway Co.: *D. Moore 470468* (UARK). Franklin Co.: *Redfearn 21149* (SMS). Garland Co.: *D. Moore 46-092* (UARK). Greene Co.: *Demaree 26704* (SMU). Independence Co.: *Coville 161* (US). Izard Co.: *Demaree 23437* (SMU). Johnson Co.: *Redfearn 23834* (SMS). Logan Co.: *Haas 135* (MO). Madison Co.: *Taylor 2004* (SIU). Montgomery Co.: *Johnson 180* (HXC). Newton Co.: *Taylor 2699* (SIU). Perry Co.: *Redfearn 23982* (SMS). Polk Co.: *D. Moore & McWilliam 56197* (UARK). Pope Co.: *Taylor 1216* (SIU). Pulaski Co.: *Hasse s.n.* (NY). Saline Co.: *Redfearn 24325* (SMS). Searcy Co.: *Redfearn 23721* (SMS). Stone Co.: *Taylor 2902* (SIU). Van Buren Co.: *Demaree 4757* (SIU). Washington Co.: *D. Moore 340680* (UARK). Yell Co.: *Taylor 4368* (SIU).

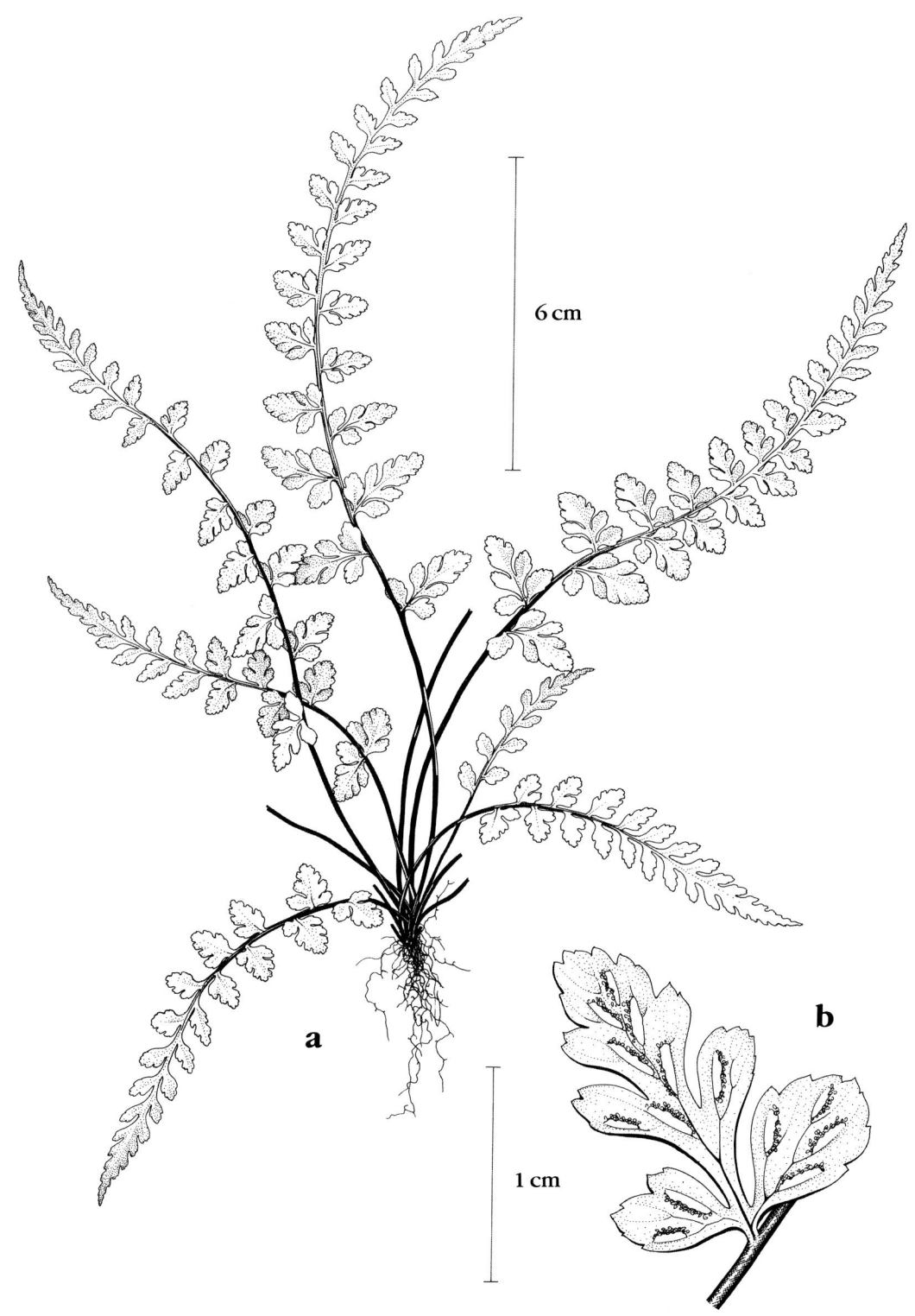

Asplenium bradleyi
a. Habit; b. Lower surface of sporiferous pinna.

8. *Asplenium* X *ebenoides* R. R. Scott

Asplenium platyneuron X *Camptosorus rhizophyllus*
Asplenosorus ebenoides (R. R. Scott) Wherry

COMMON NAME: Scott's Spleenwort

Fronds spreading, pinnatifid above, pinnate below usually for less than one-half blade length, up to 30 cm long; stipe wiry, lustrous, reddish brown to dark brown; blade often irregular in outline, deltoid-lanceolate to oblong-lanceolate, up to 20 cm long and 4 cm or more wide, apex acuminate to caudate and occasionally proliferous; rachis lustrous, reddish brown about one-half to two-thirds its length, green toward apex; pinnae or blade divisions quite variable in outline, deltoid-ovate to oblong or deltoid-attenuate, subentire to crenulate; veins free or occasionally reticulate. Spores abortive.

HABITAT: Johnson Co.: shaded boulder face; Haw Creek Falls Recreation Area; W of Fort Douglas; *Johnson 79028* (HXC).

RANGE: Eastern United States, within the sympatric range of *Asplenium platyneuron* and *A. rhizophyllum*.

On 4 June 1979, David Johnson discovered this hybrid growing, as it typically does, with its parent species *Asplenium platyneuron* and *A. rhizophyllum*. This hybrid was also reported along Lee Creek, Crawford County (Moore, 1940b) but a voucher specimen has not been located.

Asplenium X *ebenoides* has long been known to be a hybrid between *A. platyneuron* and *A. rhizophyllum* (Slosson, 1902). The fronds of this sporadic plant are often conspicuously irregular in outline and vary considerably in size and form even on the same plant. Normally a sterile diploid, this hybrid has doubled its chromosome number to produce a fertile tetraploid population at Havana Glen, Hale Co., Alabama (Wagner, 1954).

Asplenium X *ebenoides*

Johnson Co.: *Johnson 79028* (HXC).

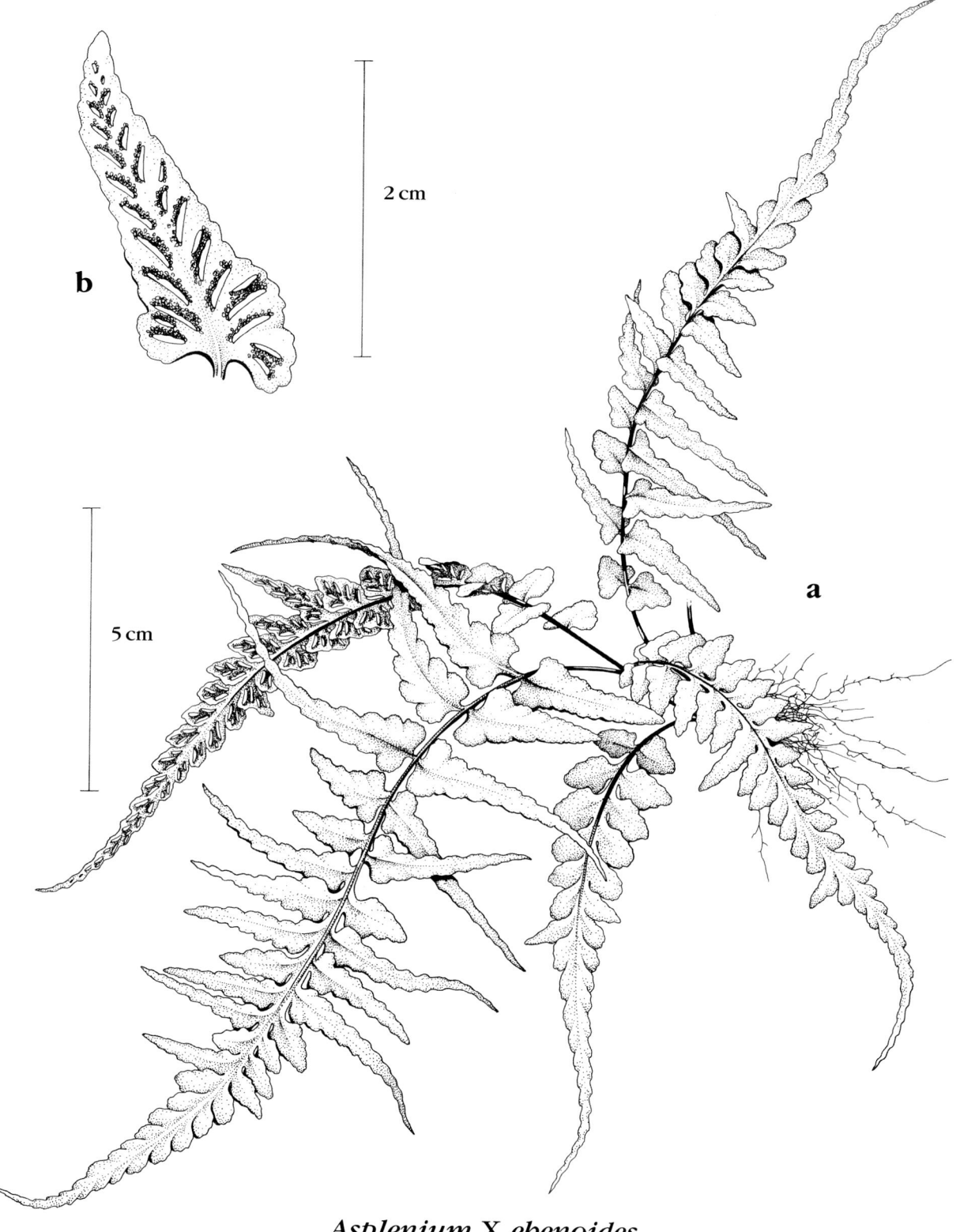

Asplenium X *ebenoides*
a. Habit; b. Lower surface of sporiferous pinna.

9. *Asplenium* X *kentuckiense* McCoy

Asplenium pinnatifidum X *platyneuron*

COMMON NAME: Kentucky Spleenwort

Fronds erect-spreading, pinnatifid above, pinnate below usually for more than one-half blade length, up to 30 cm long; stipe lustrous, reddish brown to purplish black; blade oblong-lanceolate to linear-lanceolate, up to 20 cm long and 6 cm or more wide, attenuate to apex, tapering toward base, with lowest two pinna pairs shorter than the two pinna pairs above them; rachis lustrous, reddish brown about one-third to two-thirds its length, green toward apex; pinnae or blade divisions deltoid-ovate to oblong or deltoid-attenuate, crenulate to denticulate-serrulate; veins free. Spores abortive.

HABITAT: Benton Co.: sandstone outcrop; Pea Ridge National Military Park; *Moore 430114* (MO).

RANGE: Eastern United States, within the sympatric range of its putative parents *Asplenium pinnatifidum* and *A. platyneuron*.

Asplenium X *kentuckiense*, a rare, sporadic plant, is a hybrid, probably between *A. pinnatifidum* and *A. platyneuron* (Smith et al., 1961). The only known Arkansas location, cited above, was discovered by Dwight Moore on 20 June 1943 (Moore, 1947).

Asplenium X kentuckiense

Benton Co.: *D. Moore 430114* (MO).

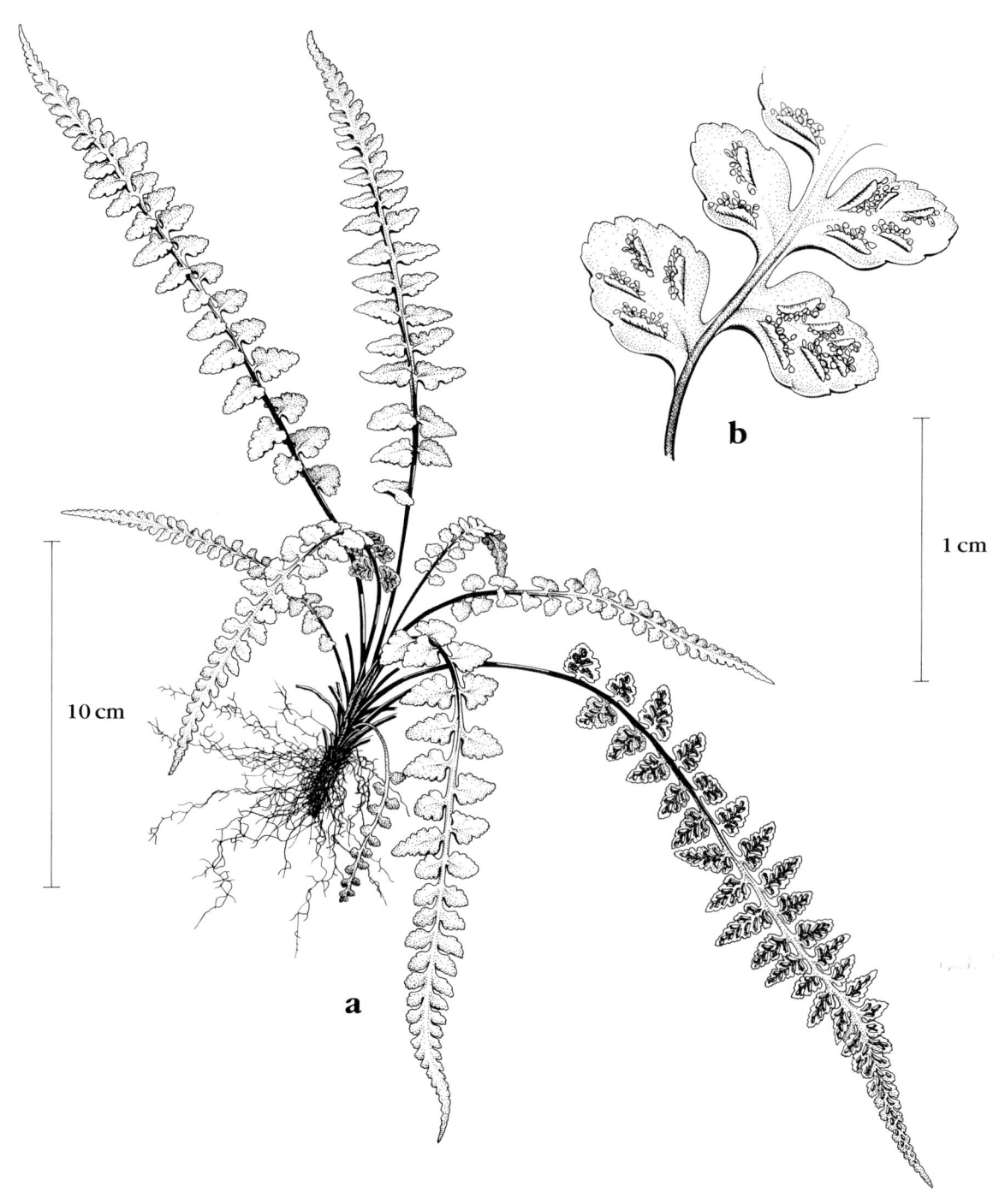

Asplenium X *kentuckiense*
a. Habit; b. Lower surface of sporiferous pinna.

10. *Asplenium* X *gravesii* Maxon

Asplenium bradleyi X *pinnatifidum*

COMMON NAME: Graves' Spleenwort

Fronds spreading, pinnatifid above, pinnate below usually for more than one-half blade length, up to 15 cm long; stipe dark brown; blade oblong-lanceolate to linear lanceolate, up to 12 cm long and 3 cm or more wide, attenuate to apex, most often not tapering toward base, with lowest two pinna pairs more or less equal to the two pinna pairs above them; rachis green or occasionally brown up to one-third its length; pinnae deltoid-ovate to oblong-lanceolate, serrate, often lobed at base; veins free. Spores abortive.

HABITAT: Garland Co.: novaculite outcrop; Hot Springs National Park; *Werth 39K8* (SIU).

RANGE: Eastern United States, within the sympatric range of *Asplenium bradleyi* and *A. pinnatifidum*.

Asplenium X *gravesii* is a rare, sporadic hybrid between *A. bradleyi* and *A. pinnatifidum* (Wagner and Darling, 1957). The only known Arkansas location was discovered by Charles Werth on 10 August 1979 (Werth and Taylor, 1980).

Asplenium X *gravesii*

Garland Co.: *Werth 39K8* (SIU).

Asplenium X *gravesii*
a. Habit; b. Lower surface of sporiferous pinna.

Athyrium Roth Lady Ferns, Glade Ferns

Rhizome creeping; scales brown, not latticed, lanceolate. Fronds deciduous, erect-spreading, pinnate to tripinnate, glabrate to pilose; stipe green to stramineous, sometimes reddish tinted, scaly at least toward base; blade deltoid-lanceolate to elliptic, veins simple or forked, free. Sori elliptic to linear-elongate, straight or slightly curved along anterior side of vein or recurved to reflexed across and along both sides of vein; indusium unilateral. A largely temperate genus of about 300 species.

Key to the species of *Athyrium* in Arkansas

1. Fronds bipinnate to bipinnate-pinnatifid; sori often recurved or reflexed across and along both sides of vein .... 1. *A. filix-femina* (p. 56)
1. Fronds pinnate or pinnate-pinnatifid; sori straight or slightly curved along anterior side of vein
    2. Fronds pinnate; rachis scaleless and sparsely pilose .... 2. *A. pycnocarpon* (p. 58)
    2. Fronds pinnate-pinnatifid; rachis scaly and pilose .... 3. *A. thelypterioides* (p. 60)

1. *Athyrium filix-femina* (L.) Roth subsp. *asplenioides* (Michx.) Hulten

Nephrodium asplenioides Michx.
Athyrium asplenioides (Michx.) A. A. Eat.
Asplenium asplenioides (Michx.) Chapm.
Athyrium filix-femina var. *asplenioides* (Michx.) Farw.

COMMON NAME: Southern Lady Fern

Fronds alike, bipinnate to bipinnate-pinnatifid, up to 1 m tall; stipe and rachis green to stramineous, often reddish tinted, glabrate; blade deltoid-lanceolate to lanceolate or elliptic-lanceolate, up to 60 cm long and 30 cm wide; pinnae oblong-lanceolate, divided to incised and serrate, decurrent. Sori elliptic to elongate, straight or slightly curved along anterior side of vein or recurved to reflexed across and along both sides of vein; indusium glandular-ciliolate.

HABITAT: Moist woodlands, stream banks, roadsides, and marshy areas around ponds and lakes.

RANGE: Southeastern United States.

Athyrium filix-femina subsp. *asplenioides* occurs throughout the state but has seldom been collected in the Mississippi Alluvial Plain. It is most common in the West Gulf Coastal Plain where large robust plants often occur on disturbed sites.

There has been disagreement among various pteridologists as to the proper status of this taxon. In the past, it has been treated both as a variety and as a species. The subspecific rank suggested by Liew (1972) as a result of his numerical taxonomic studies of *Athyrium* in North America is followed here.

According to Liew, subsp. *asplenioides* is distinguished from the more northeastern ranging subsp. *angustum* by the absence of stipitate glands on the rachis and costae, and by having blackish spores with a reticulate perine. In addition, the blade of subsp. asplenioides is generally broadest near its base. Subsp. angustum (Willd.) Clausen, which has stipitate glands on the rachis, yellowish spores with a smooth to papillate perine, and blades which usually taper toward the base, was reported from Hot Springs National Park, Garland County, by Scully (1939). The occurrence of subsp. *angustum* in this region is dubious and Scully's material might have been confused with a tapered blade form of subsp. *asplenioides.*

The tapered blade form of subsp. *asplenioides,* distinguished as f. *ellipticum* by Wherry, has "the blade narrowed below so as to approach an elliptic outline" (Wherry, 1948). In Arkansas, it appears that this form is scarcely justifiable, for fronds assignable to f. *ellipticum* may be found in nearly every population of subsp. *asplenioides.* Elliptical blades have been noted particularly in juvenile plants and in early, spring foliage.

The striking, highly dissected f. *subtripinnatum,* which has pinnules that are deeply cut into oblong divisions, was collected in Pike County by Delzie Demaree on 7 October 1932 (F 1420306). Additional collections from Harrisburg, Poinsett County; Sand Gap (Pelsor), Pope County; and Grassy Lake, Hempstead County were reported by Moore (1940b).

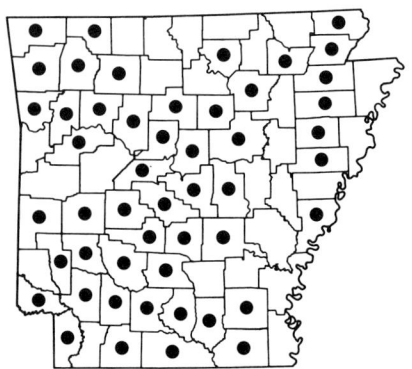

Athyrium filix-femina

Ashley Co.: *Taylor 1876* (SIU). Benton Co.: *Buchholz s.n.* (UARK). Bradley Co.: *Locke 547* (UARK). Calhoun Co.: *Demaree 22107* (MO). Carroll Co.: *Palmer 3813* (NY). Clark Co.: *Taylor 2177* (SIU). Clay Co.: *Rosen 90* (UARK). Cleburne Co.: *Taylor 1014* (SIU). Columbia Co.: *Taylor 1167* (SIU). Conway Co.: *Demaree 37230* (SMU). Craighead Co.: *Demaree 3569* (MO). Crawford Co.: *Moore 710287* (UARK). Cross Co.: *Palmer 31665* (UARK). Dallas Co.: *Miller 682* (UARK). Drew Co.: *Demaree 22101* (SMU). Faulkner Co.: *Buchholz s.n.* (UARK). Franklin Co.: *D. Moore 340684* (UARK). Garland Co.: *Taylor 2555* (SIU). Grant Co.: *Taylor 2723* (SIU). Greene Co.: *Demaree 26695* (SMU). Hempstead Co.: *Taylor 1177* (SIU). Hot Spring Co.: *Palmer 26592* (UARK). Howard Co.: *D. Moore 410263* (UARK). Independence Co.: *Demaree 17099* (SMU). Izard Co.: *Demaree 23512* (SMU). Jefferson Co.: *Demaree 24069* (MO). Johnson Co.: *D. Moore 450273* (UARK). Lawrence Co.: *Demaree 520965* (SIU). Little River Co.: *Palmer 8353* (MO). Logan Co.: *Taylor 1038* (SIU). Lonoke Co.: *Clark 663* (HXC). Madison Co.: *Davis 1504* (UARK). Miller Co.: *Palmer 10530* (MO). Montgomery Co.: *Taylor 1072* (SIU). Nevada Co.: *Bush 694* (MO). Newton Co.: *D. Moore 480752* (UARK). Ouachita Co.: *D. Moore 490652* (UARK). Perry Co.: *J. Moore 6616* (UCA). Phillips Co.: *Palmer 25146* (UARK). Pike Co.: *Taylor 2169* (SIU). Poinsett Co.: *Demaree 3667* (SMU). Polk Co.: *Taylor 1069* (SIU). Pope Co.: *Robinette 2795* (UCA). Pulaski Co.: *Demaree 8899* (SMU). St. Francis Co.: *Clark 613* (HXC). Saline Co.: *Demaree 23034* (MO). Union Co.: *Taylor 1160* (SIU). Van Buren Co.: *Palmer 24294* (MO). Washington Co.: *Hite 23* (UARK). White Co.: *Johnson 458* (HXC).

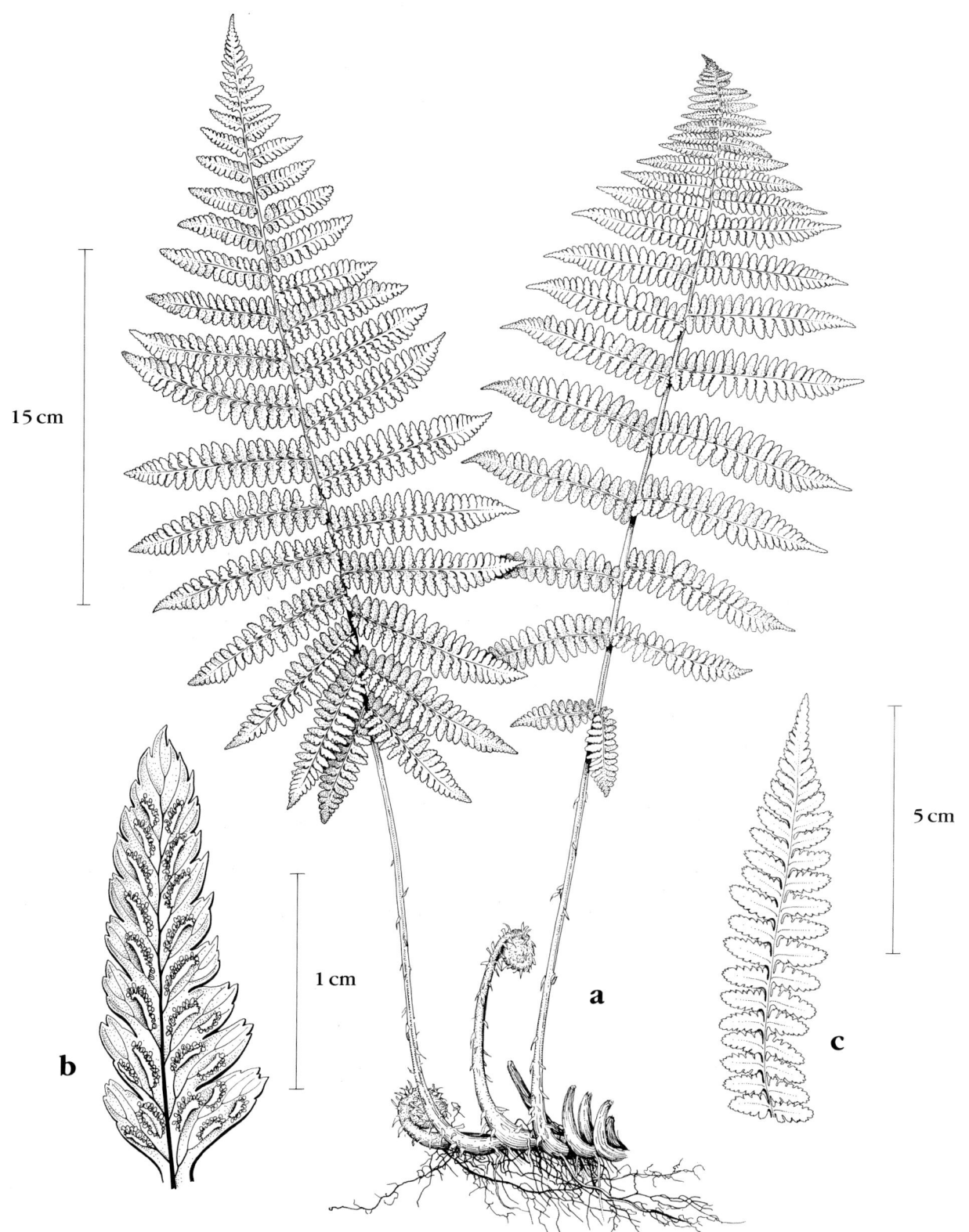

Athyrium filix-femina subsp. *asplenioides*
a. Habit; b. Lower surface of sporiferous pinna; c. Pinna.

2. *Athyrium pycnocarpon* (Spreng.) Tidest.

Asplenium angustifolium Michx.
Asplenium pycnocarpon Spreng.
Diplazium angustifolium (Michx.) Butters
Homalosorus pycnocarpus (Spreng.) Small
Diplazium pycnocarpon (Spreng.) Broun

COMMON NAME: Narrow-leaved Glade Fern

Fronds slightly dimorphic, pinnate, up to 1 m tall; stipe and rachis green, sparsely pilose; blade lanceolate to elliptic, up to 70 cm long and 20 cm wide; pinnae linear-lanceolate to ovate-lanceolate, subentire to serrulate; fertile pinnae usually narrower than sterile pinnae. Sori linear-elongate, straight or slightly curved along anterior side of vein; indusium glabrous.

HABITAT: Rocky slopes and ravines in moist, rich woods; primarily in the Ozark Mountains.

RANGE: Eastern North America.

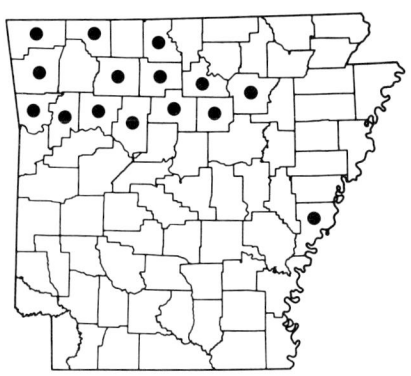

Athyrium pycnocarpon (Spreng.)

Benton Co.: *Demaree 4494* (SMU). Carroll Co.: *Palmer 3813* (US). Cleburne Co.: *Babb 1596* (ARKSU). Crawford Co.: *Taylor 1097* (SIU). Franklin Co.: *Davis 1357* (UARK). Independence Co.: *Thomas 8568* (NLU). Johnson Co.: *Redfearn 18927* (SMS). Marion Co.: *D. Moore 410516* (UARK). Newton Co.: *Taylor 2694* (SIU). Phillips Co.: *Clark 446* (HXC). Pope Co.: *Tucker 3545* (APCR). Searcy Co.: *D. Moore 350149* (UARK). Stone Co.: *Graham 373* (APCR). Van Buren Co.: *Palmer 24302* (UARK). Washington Co.: *Palmer 27037* (MO).

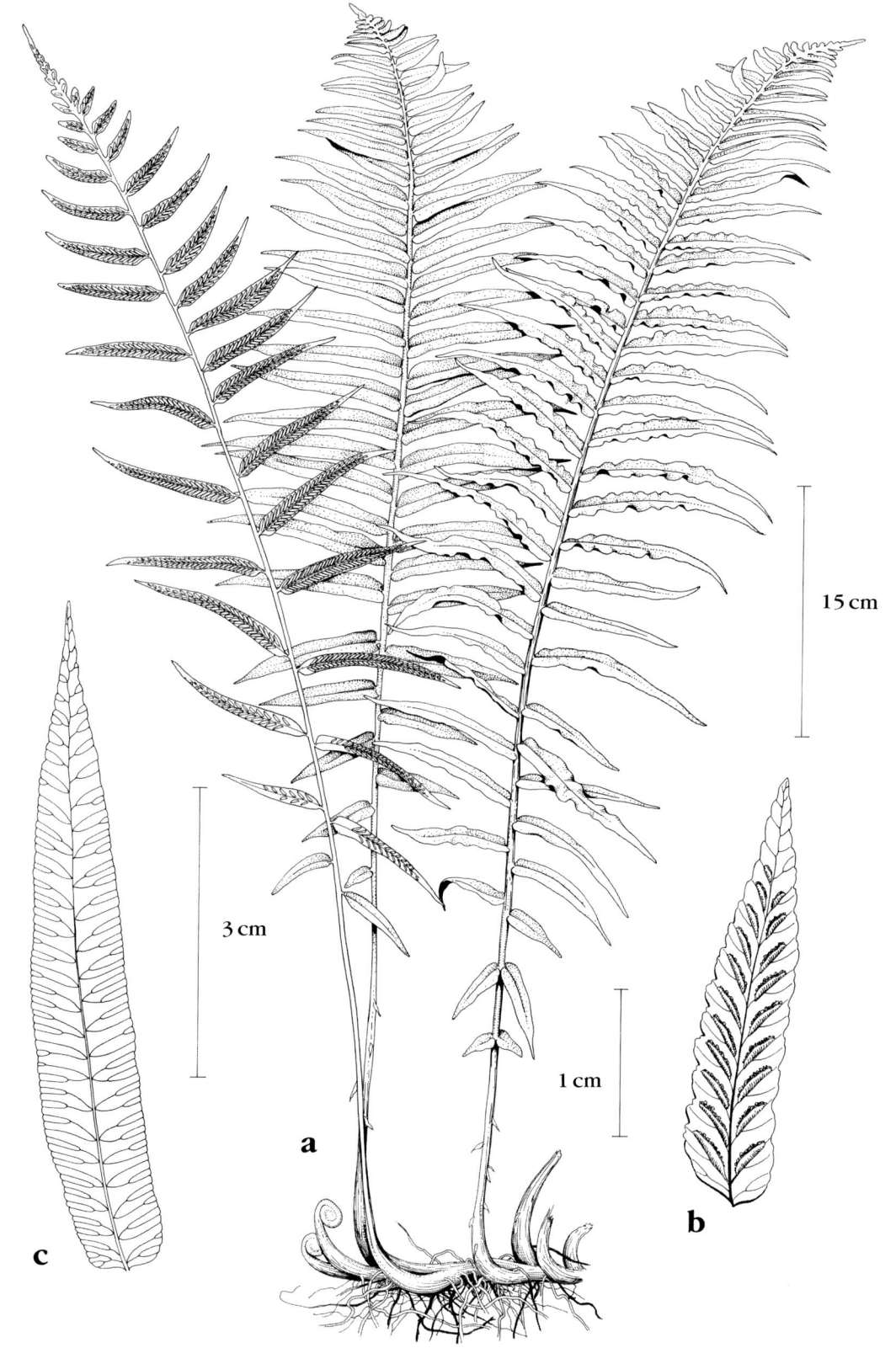

Athyrium pycnocarpon
a. Habit; b. Lower surface of sporiferous pinna; c. Pinna.

3. *Athyrium thelypterioides* (Michx.) Desv.

Asplenium acrostichoides Sw.
Asplenium thelypterioides Michx.
Diplazium acrostichoides (Sw.) Butters

COMMON NAME: Silvery Glade Fern

Fronds alike, pinnate-pinnatifid, up to 1 m tall; stipe and rachis green to stramineous, and scaly, pilose; blade lanceolate to elliptic, up to 70 cm long and 20 cm wide; pinnae linear-lanceolate, deeply pinnatifid, serrate or crenate. Sori linear-elongate, straight or slightly curved along anterior side of vein; indusium glabrous.

HABITAT: Moist, rich woods near streams and on shaded slopes.

RANGE: Eastern North America, Asia.

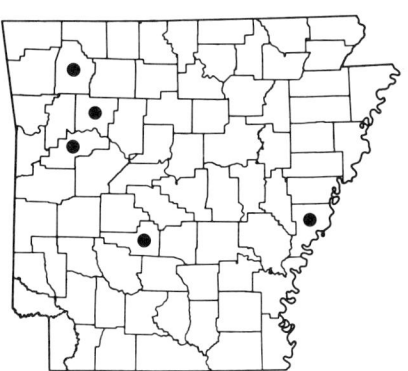

Athyrium thelypterioides (Michx.)

Hot Spring Co.: *Redfearn 24143* (SMS). Johnson Co.: *Johnson 47* (HXC). Logan Co.: *D. Moore 420124* (SMU). Madison Co.: *Davis 1506* (UARK). Phillips Co.: *Akers 42* (HXC).

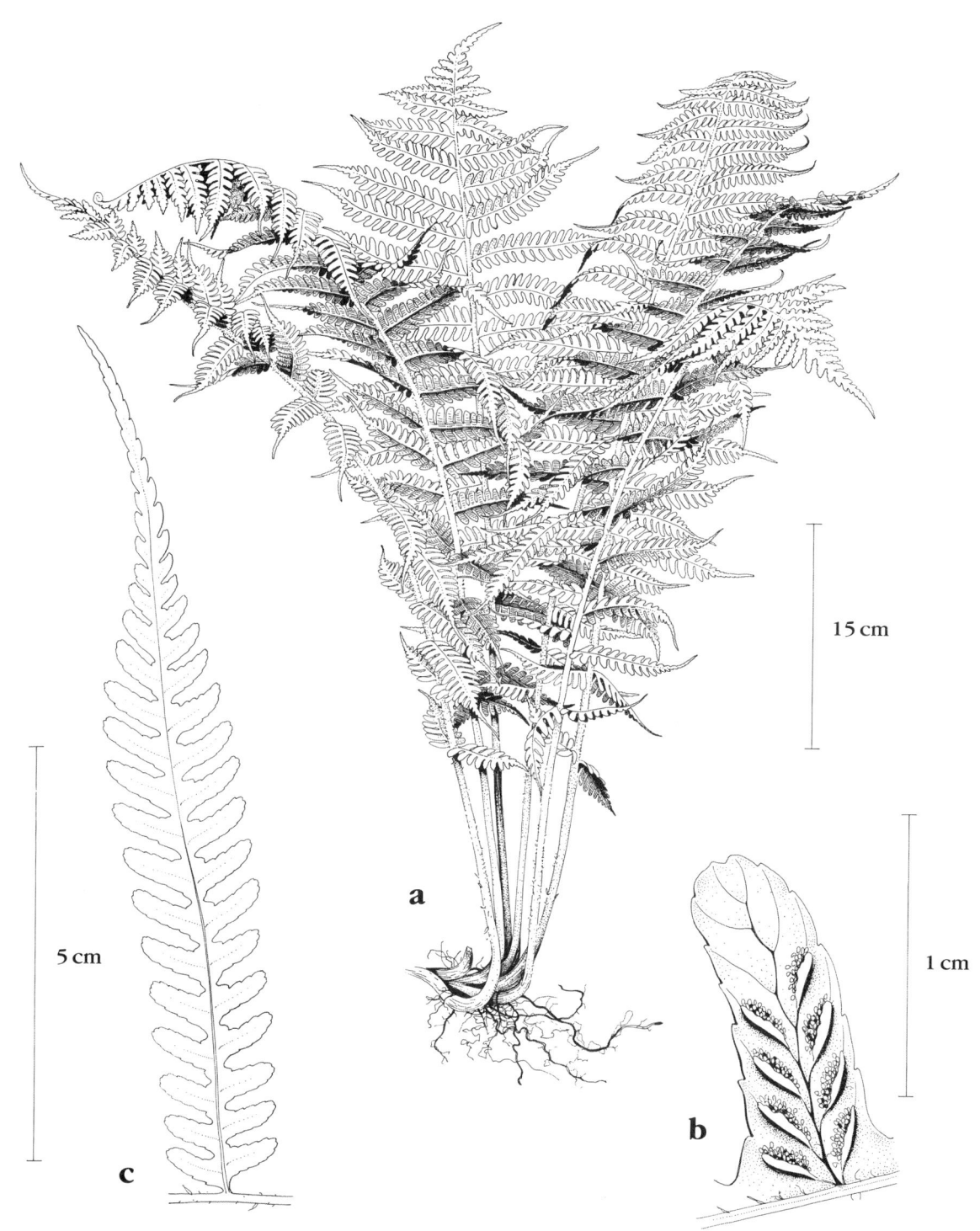

Athyrium thelypterioides
a. Habit; b. Lower surface of sporiferous pinna division; c. Pinna

Azolla Lam. Mosquito Fern

Azolla is a genus of six species found in temperate and tropical regions.

1. *Azolla mexicana* Presl.

COMMON NAME: Mosquito Fern

Plants aquatic, free-floating, spreading, usually occurring as circular to reniform individuals less than 3 cm across. Rhizome horizontal, hyaline or light green to violet green; roots filiform, unbranched, generally borne at junctions of dichotomies. Leaves numerous, distichous, alternate, two-lobed, with upper lobe aerial and lower lobe floating; aerial lobes deep green to violet brown, suborbicular to ovate, up to 1.2 mm long, papillose, margins hyaline; floating lobes hyaline to light green, often rose tinged along apical margin, suborbicular to ovate-oblong, up to 1.8 mm long, one cell thick. Sporocarps borne on the floating lobes, usually in pairs, dimorphic; microsporocarp subglobose to ovoid, up to 2 mm long, containing numerous, globose, long-stalked microsporangia; microsporangium usually containing 4 globose massulae; massula bearing numerous, usually septate glochidia with terminal retrorse hooks; megasporocarp reddish brown toward apex, obpyriform, up to 0.7 mm long, filled with one, ovoid megasporangium; megasporangium white, conical, containing three abortive megaspores distally, one functional megasporie proximally.

HABITAT: Floating on still waters of lakes, ponds, creeks, and ditches or occasionally stranded along their exsiccated margins.

RANGE: Central and western North America, Central and South America.

Distinctions are not clear between the North American species of *Azolla*. Bates and Brown (1981) state that megaspore ornamentation provides the only suitable means for identification. Svenson (1944) uses the characteristics listed in the following table to contrast three New World taxa of *Azolla* which could occur in Arkansas.

TABLE I

Character	A. caroliniana	A. filiculoides	A. mexicana
	Contrasting Characters for *Azolla caroliniana*, *A. filiculoides*, and *A. mexicana*, after Svenson (1944)		
Glochidia	not septate	rarely with 1 or 2 septa	many septate
Plants	0.5-1 cm in diam.	frequently 2-6 cm long	1-1.5 cm in diam.
Leaf length	0.5 mm	1 mm	upper lobes 0.7 mm
Range	Eastern United States and the West Indies	Guatemala to Alaska; Andean and southern South America; occasionally introduced in the eastern United States, Hawaii, and Europe	Mexico and of scattered occurrence in the lowlands southward to French Guiana and Bolivia, northward to Utah and British Columbia, and eastward to Wisconsin and Illinois.

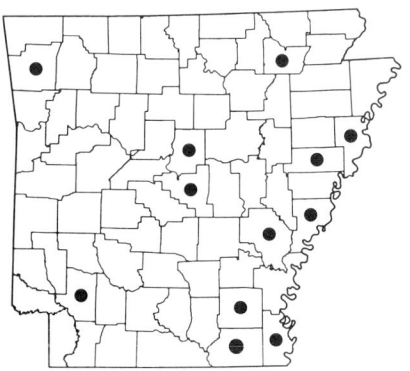

***Azolla mexicana* Presl.**

Arkansas Co.: *Taylor 1858* (SIU). Ashley Co.: *Shepherd s. n.* (LRU). Chicot Co.: *Taylor 1869* (SIU). Conway Co.: *Johnson 478* (HXC). Crawford Co.: *Peck 82-693* (LRU). Crittenden Co.: *Taylor 2822* (SIU). Desha Co.: *Peck 82-730* (LRU). Drew Co.: *Demaree 17625* (SMU). Faulkner Co.: *Engelmann 127* (MO). Hempstead Co.: *Taylor 1180* (SIU). Jefferson Co.: *Locke 2133* (UARK). Johnson Co.: *Peck 82-780* (LRU). Lawrence Co.: *McNalty 652* (ARKSU). Lee Co.: *Peck 82-720* (LRU). Lincoln Co.: *Peck 82-770* (LRU). Logan Co.: *Peck 82-661* (LRU). Lonoke Co.: *Peck 82-761* (LRU). Mississippi Co.: *Peck 82-710* (LRU). Monroe Co.: *Peck 82-735* (LRU). Perry Co.: *Peck 82768* (LRU). Phillips Co.: *Richards 4793* (ARKSU). Pope Co.: *Peck 82-771* (LRU). Prairie Co.: *Peck 82-740* (LRU). Pulaski Co.: *Engelmann 126* (MO). St. Francis Co.: *McDaniel 1097* (NY). Sebastian Co.: *Peck 82-655* (LRU). Washington Co.: *D. Moore 4184* (UARK).

Godfrey, Reinert, and Houk (1961) have questioned the use of septate versus non-septate glochidia to separate *A. filiculoides* from *A. caroliniana* and Correll and Correll (1972, pp. 58-61) allow plants to 1 cm in diameter having glochidia rarely with 1 or 2 septa to be identified as *A. caroliniana*.

Nearly all the Arkansas collections of *Azolla* represented in herbaria are sterile and have been identified as *A. caroliniana*. Examination of this material reveals that mature plants are normally greater than 1 cm in diameter and invariably possess at least some upper leaf lobes 0.7 mm long or longer.

Based primarily on distribution patterns and vegetative characters, which are the only ones consistently available on Arkansas material, it seems most reasonable to place Arkansas specimens tentatively with *A. mexicana* pending further studies. It may be that more than one taxon is represented in the state.

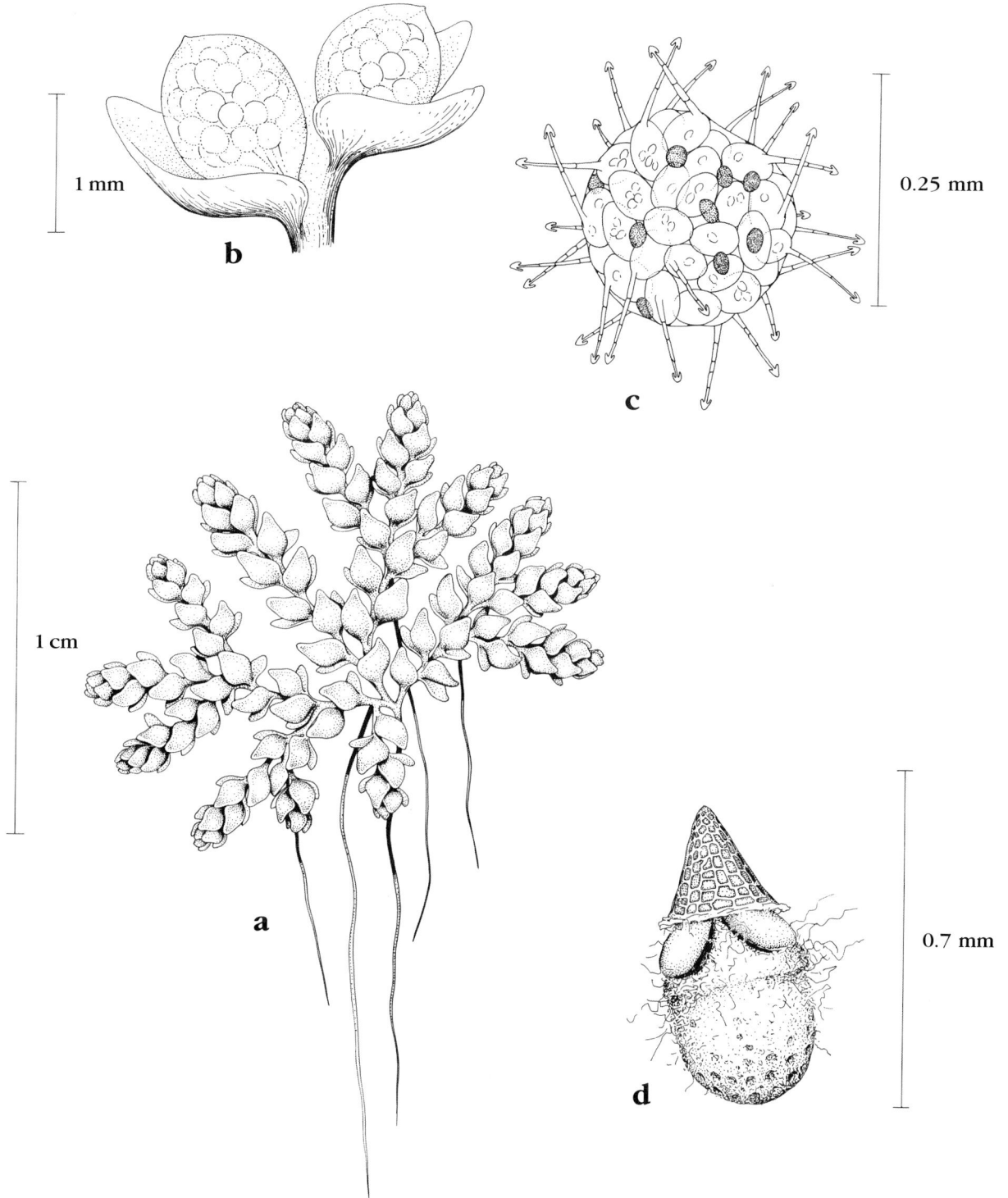

Azolla mexicana
a. Habit; b. Position of two microsporocarps containing numerous microsporangia; c. Microspore massula bearing glochidia; d. Megasporocarp (megasporangium).

Botrychium Sw. Grape Ferns

Rhizome subterranean, erect, brownish-yellow to dark brown, suberous-fleshy, scaleless, roots spreading, brownish yellow to dark brown, cord-like. Fronds deciduous or evergreen, solitary, erect, bud for the next year ensheathed by stipe base; stipe fleshy, dividing into a dissected sterile blade and a branched, long-stalked fertile portion; blade deltoid to flabellate, spreading, papery to leathery; veins forked, free. Sporangia borne on branches of the fertile portion, globose, about 1 mm in diam., splitting transversely; spores light yellow, tetrahedral.

A genus of perhaps 40 species, mainly of temperate climates.

Key to the species of *Botrychium* in Arkansas

1. Blade papery, sessile; frond arising in late winter and spring, deciduous . . . . 1. *B. virginianum* (p. 68)
1. Blade leathery, petiolulate; frond arising in summer and fall, evergreen
    2. Ultimate divisions of the blade mostly flabellate or reniform, with their midveins obscure; sterile blade prostrate . 2. *B. lunarioides* (p. 70)
    2. Ultimate divisions of the blade mostly oblong, lanceolate, or oblong-lanceolate, with their midveins apparent; sterile blade elevated
        3. Ultimate division of the blade mostly oblong, apices mostly obtuse, bases cuneate . . . . 3. *B. biternatum* (p. 72)
        3. Ultimate divisions of the blade lanceolate, apices mostly acute, bases truncate or obtuse . . . . 4. *B. dissectum* (p. 74)

1. *Botrychium virginianum* (L.) Sw.

Osmunda virginiana L.
Osmundopteris virginiana (L.) Small

COMMON NAME: Rattlesnake Fern

Frond arising in spring, deciduous, up to 60 cm tall; stipe up to 30 cm long; blade elevated, deltoid, bipinnate to tripinnate, up to 25 cm long and 30 cm wide, papery, sessile; ultimate divisions mostly ovate to lanceolate, midveins apparent, apices obtuse or acute, lobed to pinnatifid, serrate to incised, bases truncate to cuneate.

HABITAT: Moist to dry woodlands and thickets.

RANGE: Widespread in North America, Europe, Asia.

Botrychium virginianum is the most common and widespread member of the genus in Arkansas, probably occurring in every county of the state. Young plants will often have a small potato-like gametophyte still attached to the stem just below ground level, affording a good opportunity to find this rarely observed structure.

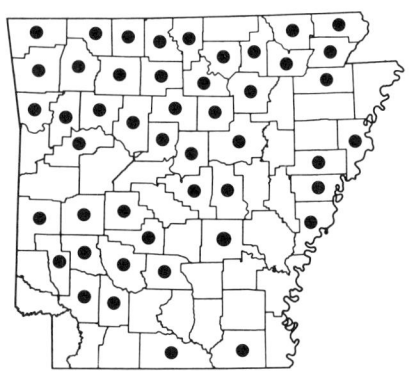

Botrychium virginianum (L.) Sw.

Ashley Co.: *Taylor 1875* (SIU). Baxter Co.: *Taylor 2675* (SIU). Benton Co.: *Taylor 1124* (SIU). Boone Co.: *Demaree s.n.* (UARK). Carroll Co.: *Palmer 4443* (MO). Clark Co.: *Taylor 2178* (SIU). Clay Co.: *Hartsoe 374* (SMU). Cleburne Co.: *Babb 338* (ARKSU). Conway Co.: *J. Moore 1086* (UARK). Craighead Co.: *Richards 5332* (ARKSU). Crawford Co.: *Moore 710233* (UARK). Crittenden Co.: *Browne 62123* (MEM). Dallas Co.: Taylor 1133 (SIU). Faulkner Co.: *Haas 1496* (UCA). Franklin Co.: *D. Moore 30025* (UARK). Garland Co.: *Palmer 24553* (MO). Greene Co.: *Demaree 3932* (SMU). Hempstead Co.: *Bush 1364* (NY). Hot Spring Co.: *D. Moore 451096* (UARK). Howard Co.: *McSwain 43E77* (UARK). Independence Co.: *Demaree 26732* (SMU). Izard Co.: *Matthews 125* (ARKSU). Jefferson Co.: *Locke 2231* (UARK). Johnson Co.: *D. Moore 45027* (UARK). Lawrence Co.: *Taylor 2596* (SIU). Lee Co.: *Taylor 1183* (SIU). Logan Co.: *Haas 1495* (UCA). Lonoke Co.: *Clark 672* (HXC). Madison Co.: *D. Moore 460146* (UARK). Marion Co.: *Taylor 1234* (SIU). Montgomery Co.: *Taylor 2838* (SIU). Nevada Co.: *D. Moore 450105* (UARK). Newton Co.: *D. Moore 32504* (UARK). Phillips Co.: *Taylor 2829* (SIU). Pike Co.: *Lindley & Lindley s.n.* (UARK). Polk Co.: *Lodewyks 195* (MO). Pope Co.: *Taylor 1207* (SIU). Pulaski Co.: *Redfearn 25934* (SMS). Randolph Co.: *Taylor 2100* (SIU). St. Francis Co.: *Demaree 4349* (NY). Searcy Co.: *Taylor 1852* (SIU). Sharp Co.: *Demaree 27719* (SMU). Stone Co.: *Taylor 1262* (SIU). Union Co.: *D. Moore 68109* (UARK). Van Buren Co.: *Taylor 2566* (SIU). Washington Co.: *D. Moore 50008* (UARK). White Co.: *Johnson 456* (HXC).

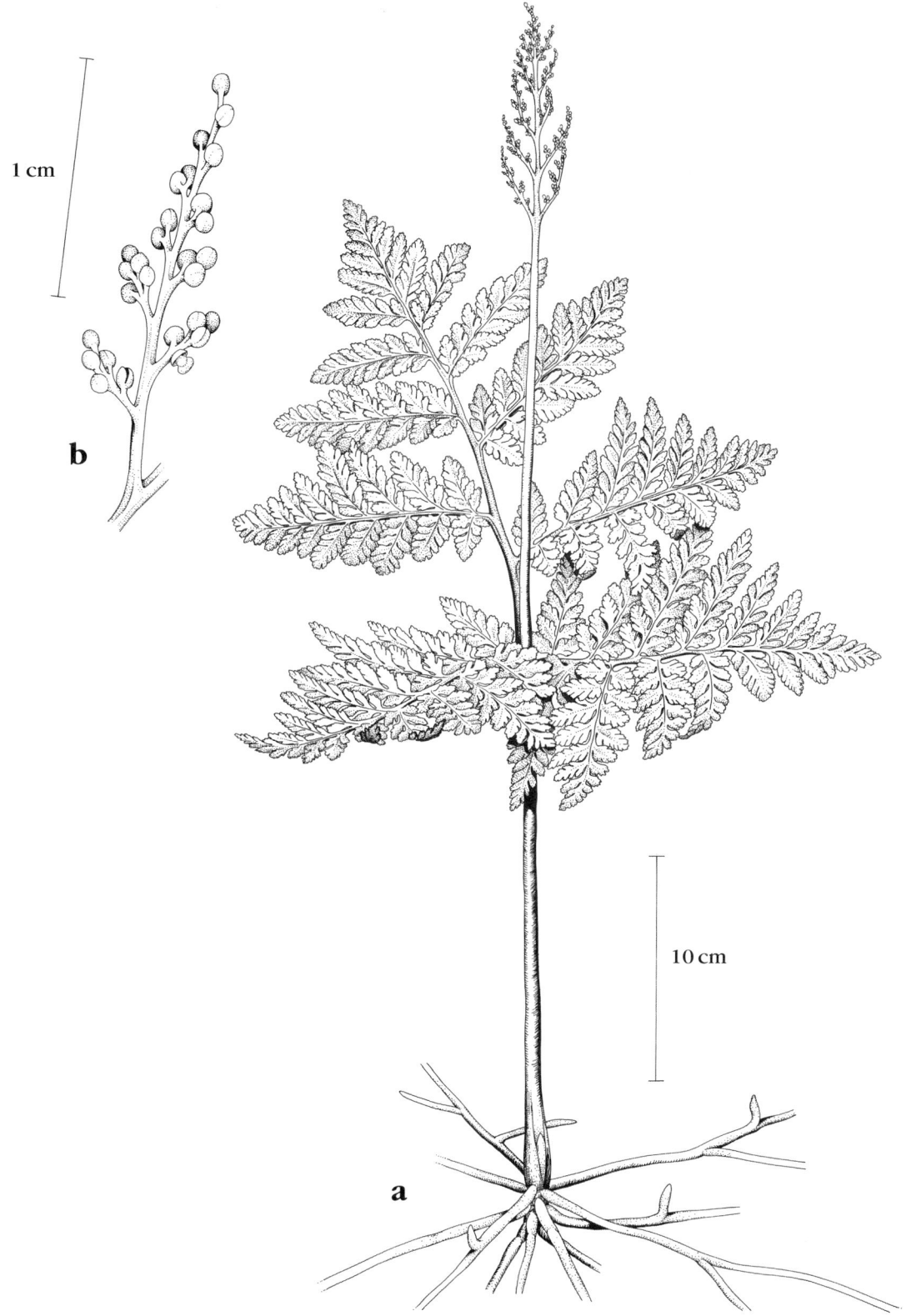

Botrychium virginianum
a. Habit; b. Fertile branches bearing sporangia.

2. *Botrychium lunarioides* (Michx.) Sw.

Botrypus lunarioides Michx.
Botrychium fumarioides Willd.
Botrychium ternatum var. *lunarioides* D. C. Eat.

COMMON NAME: Winter Grape Fern

Frond arising in fall, evergreen, up to 12 cm tall; stipe up to 1.5 cm long; blade prostrate, deltoid to flabellate, bipinnate to tripinnate, up to 8 cm long and 10 cm wide, leathery, petiolule up to 2.5 cm long; ultimate divisions mostly flabellate or reniform, midveins obscure, apices obtuse, often lobed, crenulate or denticulate, bases truncate to cuneate.

HABITAT: Cemeteries and church yards in the West Gulf Coastal Plain. Howard Co.: County Line Missionary Baptist Church Cemetery; W of Nashville; *Thomas 28147* (NLU). Lafayette Co.: Forest Grove Baptist Church Cemetery; off Hwy. 53; N of Walker Creek; *Thomas 34005* (NLU). Sevier Co.: Coulter Memorial Garden; Locksburg; *Thomas 28139* (NLU). Union Co.: Olive Branch Methodist Church Yard; SE of New Caledonia; *Taylor 2638* (SIU).

RANGE: Southeastern United States.

Dale Thomas (1978) is responsible for the known records of *Botrychium lunarioides* in Arkansas. His first collections of this species in the state were made from the Sevier and Howard County locations on 26 March 1972.

The relatively small size and low profile of this species make it extremely difficult to discern from the surrounding vegetation.

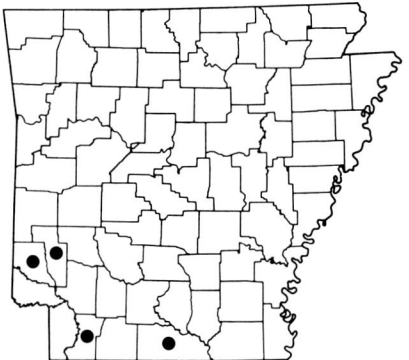

Botrychium lunarioides (Michx.) Sw.

Howard Co.: *Thomas 28147* (NLU). Lafayette Co.: *Thomas 34005* (NLU). Sevier Co.: *Thomas 28139* (NLU). Union Co.: *Taylor 2638* (SIU).

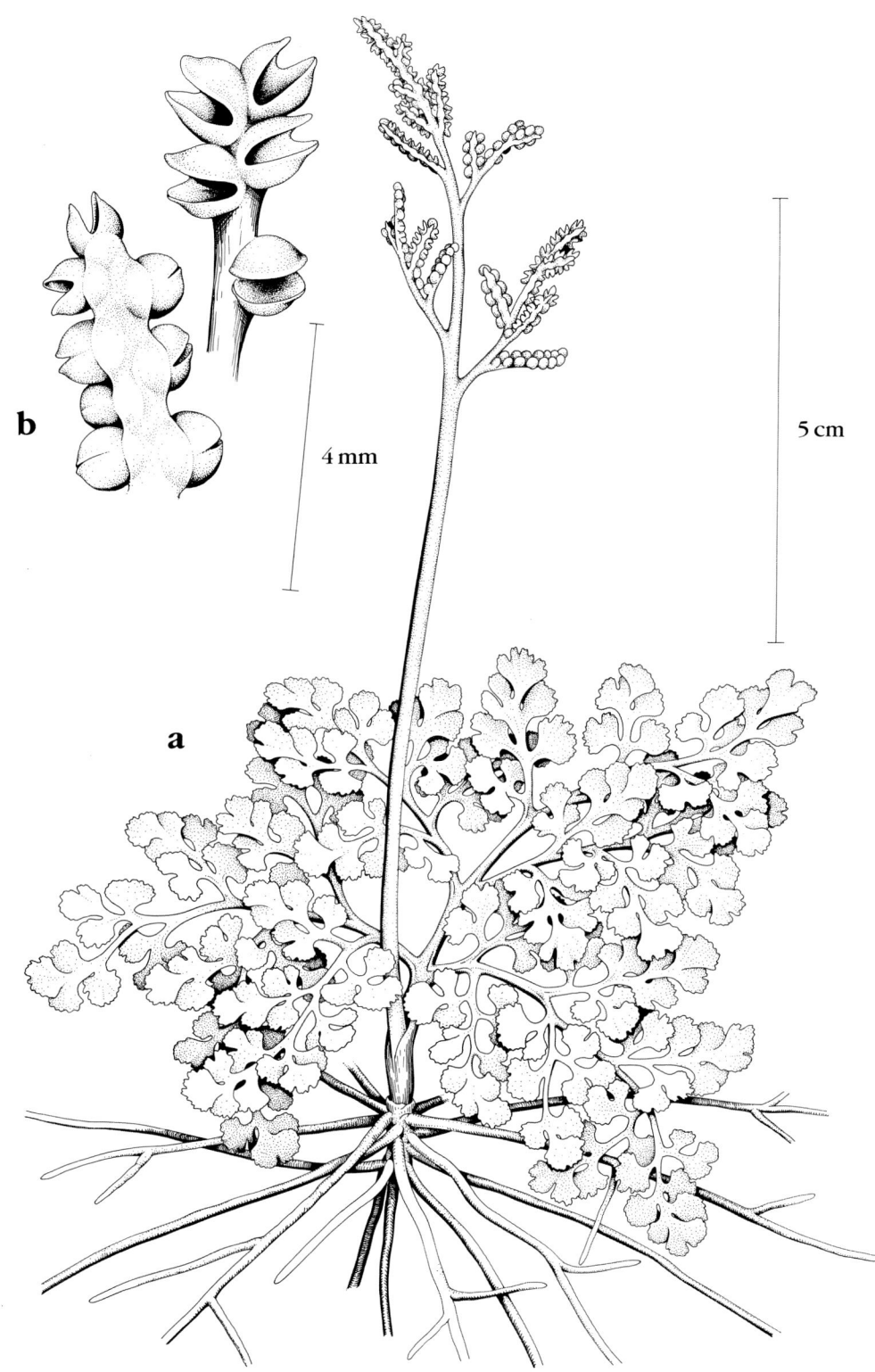

Botrychium lunarioides
a. Habit; b. Fertile branches bearing sporangia.

3. *Botrychium biternatum* (Sav.) Underw.

Osmunda biternata Sav.
Botrychium tenuifolium Underw.
Botrychium obliquum tenuifolium (Underw.) Gilbert
Botrychium dissectum var. *tenuifolium* (Underw.) Farw.

COMMON NAME: Sparse-lobed Grape Fern

Frond arising in summer and fall, evergreen, up to 40 cm tall, stipe up to 7 cm long; blade elevated, sometimes becoming bronze colored in winter, deltoid, mostly bipinnate to bipinnate-pinnatifid, up to 18 cm long and 20 cm wide, papery; petiolule up to 10 cm long; ultimate divisions mostly oblong, midveins apparent, apices mostly obtuse, sometimes lobed to pinnatifid, uniformly denticulate to serrulate, bases cuneate.

HABITAT: Moist to dry open woods, thickets, and low wet areas.

RANGE: Southeastern United States.

Some Arkansas material of *Botrychium biternatum* closely resembles *B. dissectum* var. *obliquum*. In fact, there do not appear to be any stable characters which will always clearly distinguish these two taxa. At their opposite extremes of variation they are relatively easy to recognize, yet some Arkansas specimens seem to be intermediate, leading one to question separation at the species level. Reducing *B. biternatum* in rank to reflect a closer relationship to *B. dissectum* would require several new combinations since the epithet *biternatum* has priority over the epithet *dissectum*. Until good biosystematic evidence is available to support such a change, it does not seem sound to generate additional synonymy (Wagner, 1961).

Generally, the sterile blade of *Botrychium biternatum* is thinner, less dissected, and has blunter terminal segments with finer and more uniform marginal teeth than *B. dissectum*. There also appears to be a tendency for *B. dissectum* to sporulate and have its aerial parts become senescent before *B. biternatum*. Green sporiferous specimens of *B. biternatum* can be found in late December and early January. By this time, *B. dissectum* is normally found to have bronzed or yellowish sterile blades and shriveled sporangia.

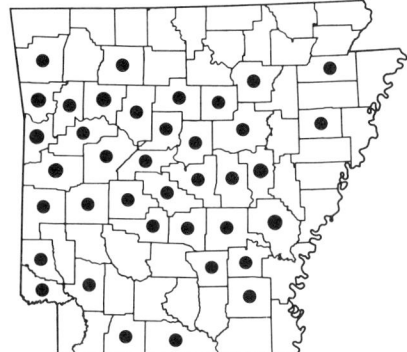

Botrychium biternatum

Arkansas Co.: *Peck 82-750* (LRU). Cleburne Co.: *Johnson 398* (HXC). Cleveland Co.: *Miller 764* (UARK). Columbia Co.: *D. Moore 420478* (UARK). Conway Co.: *J. Moore 1233* (UARK). Craighead Co.: *Watkins s.n.* (UARK). Crawford Co.: *Peck 82-651* (LRU). Cross Co.: *Lowman 260* (HXC). Drew Co.: *Palmer 44224* (MO). Faulkner Co.: *Johnson 470* (HXC). Franklin Co.: *Barber 420* (UARK). Garland Co.: *Taylor 2862* (SIU). Grant Co.: *Demaree 87193* (SMU). Hempstead Co.: *Palmer 8980* (MO). Hot Spring Co.: *D. Moore 400085* (UARK). Independence Co.: *Thomas 34313* (NLU). Jefferson Co.: *Locke 1216A* (UARK). Johnson Co.: *Peck 82-698* (LRU). Lincoln Co.: *Thomas 34392* (NLU). Little River Co.: *D. Moore 5621* (UARK). Logan Co.: *Pyle 557* (UARK). Lonoke Co.: *Clark 673* (HXC). Montgomery Co.: *Taylor 2219* (SIU). Newton Co.: *Johnson 463* (HXC). Perry Co.: *Johnson 133* (HXC). Polk Co.: *Taylor 2548* (SIU). Pope Co.: *Johnson 289* (HXC). Prairie Co.: *Peck 82-741* (LRU). Pulaski Co.: *Merrill 1217* (UARK). Saline Co.: *D. Moore 50171* (UARK). Scott Co.: *Peck 82-682* (LRU). Sebastian Co.: *Peck 82-668* (LRU). Sevier Co.: *D. Moore 401102* (UARK). Union Co.: *Taylor 2640* (SIU). Van Buren Co.: *Johnson 100* (HXC). Washington Co.: *Hartsoe 370* (SMU). White Co.: *Thomas 34166* (NLU). Yell Co.: *Demaree 67357* (SIU).

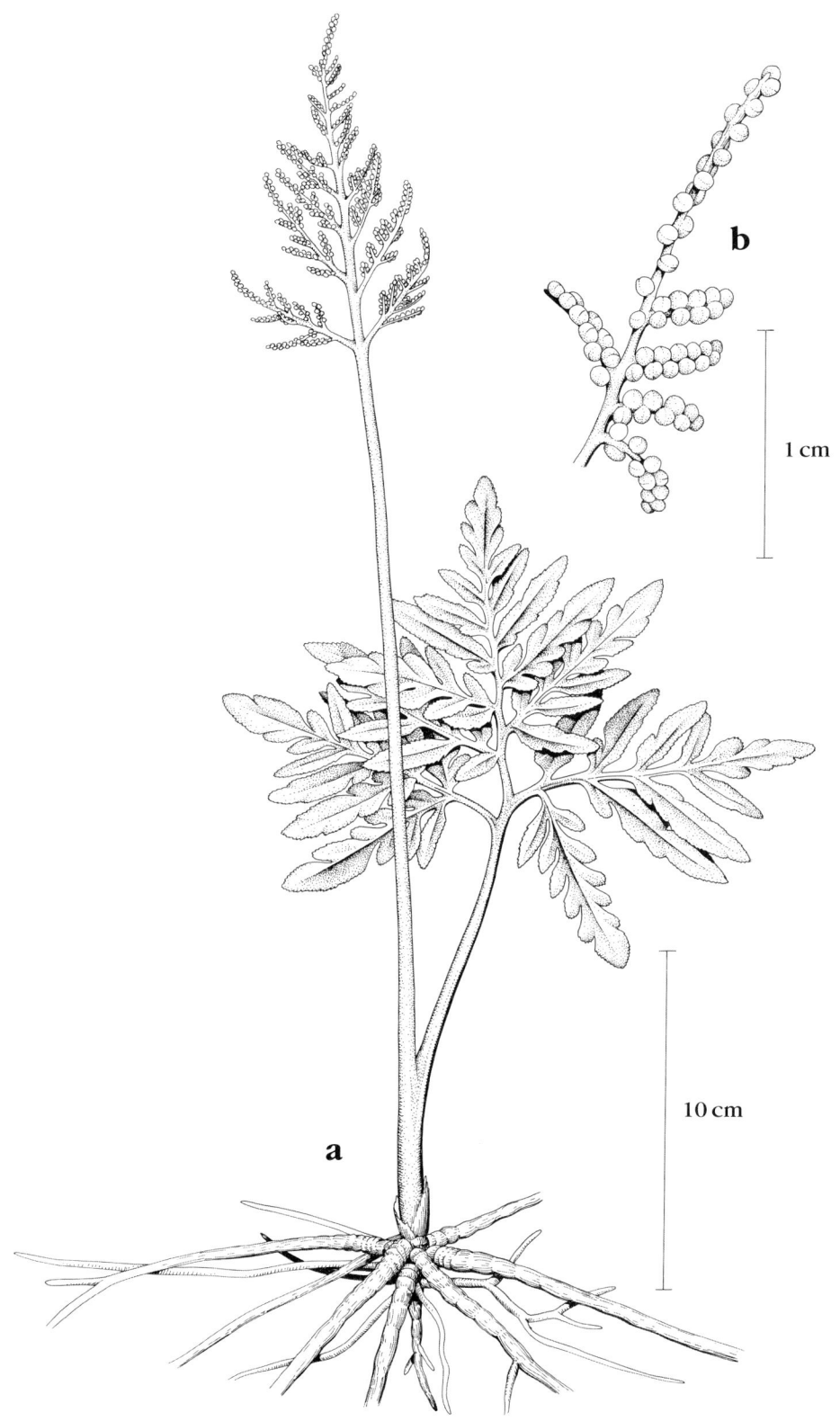

Botrychium biternatum
a. Habit. b. Fertile branches bearing sporangia.

4. *Botrychium dissectum* Spreng.

COMMON NAME: Grape Fern

Frond arising in summer and fall, evergreen, up to 40 cm tall; stipe up to 5 cm long; blade elevated, becoming bronze colored in autumn, deltoid, mostly bipinnate-pinnatifid to tripinnate, up to 16 cm long, and 18 cm wide, leathery; petiolule up to 10 cm long; ultimate divisions mostly lanceolate, midveins apparent, apices mostly acute, often lobed to pinnatifid, irregularly serrulate or incised to lacerate, bases truncate to obtuse.

Botrychium dissectum, a common species in the northeastern United States, has only a scattered occurrence in Arkansas where it nears the southwestern limit of its range. Two intergrading varieties of *B. dissectum* have been collected in the state.

Key to the varieties of *Botruchium dissectum* in Arkansas

1. Margins of the ultimate divisions incised to lacerate . 4a. var. *dissectum*
1. Margins of the ultimate divisions crenulate to serrulate . . . .
. . . . 4b. var. *obliquum*

4a. *Botrychium dissectum* Spreng. var. *dissectum*

***Botrychium lunarioides* var. *dissectum* Gray**
***Botrychium obliquum* var. *dissectum* (Spreng.) Prantl**
***Botrychium dissectum* var. *typicum* Clausen**

COMMON NAME: Cut-leaved Grape Fern

HABITAT: Newton Co.: mesic ravine in Lost Valley State Park; *Thompson 907* (SMS). Washington Co.: low, open woods near Farmington; *D. Moore 330309* (MO).

RANGE: Eastern North America.

The Dwight Moore collection of *B. dissectum* var. *dissectum* from Washington County was made on 15 November 1933. It includes plants of var. *obliquum* and an intermediate form. Ralph Thompson's collections of *B. dissectum* from Lost Valley State Park, Newton Co. also include both var. *dissectum* and var. *obliquum* (Thompson, 1975).

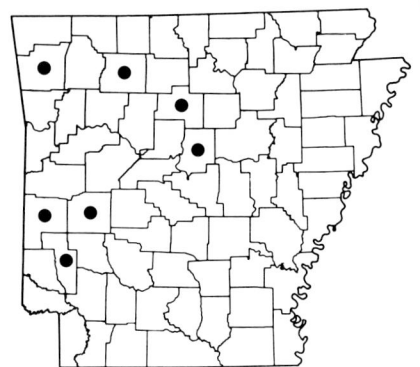

Botrychium dissectum

Faulkner Co.: *Taylor 2606* (SIU). Howard Co.: *Kellogg s.n.* (MO). Montgomery Co.: *J. Moore & McWilliam s.n.* (UARK). Newton Co.: *Thompson 906* (UARK). Polk Co.: *D. Moore 510021* (UARK). Van Buren Co.: *Demaree 4755* (UARK). Washington Co.: *D. Moore 330309* (UARK).

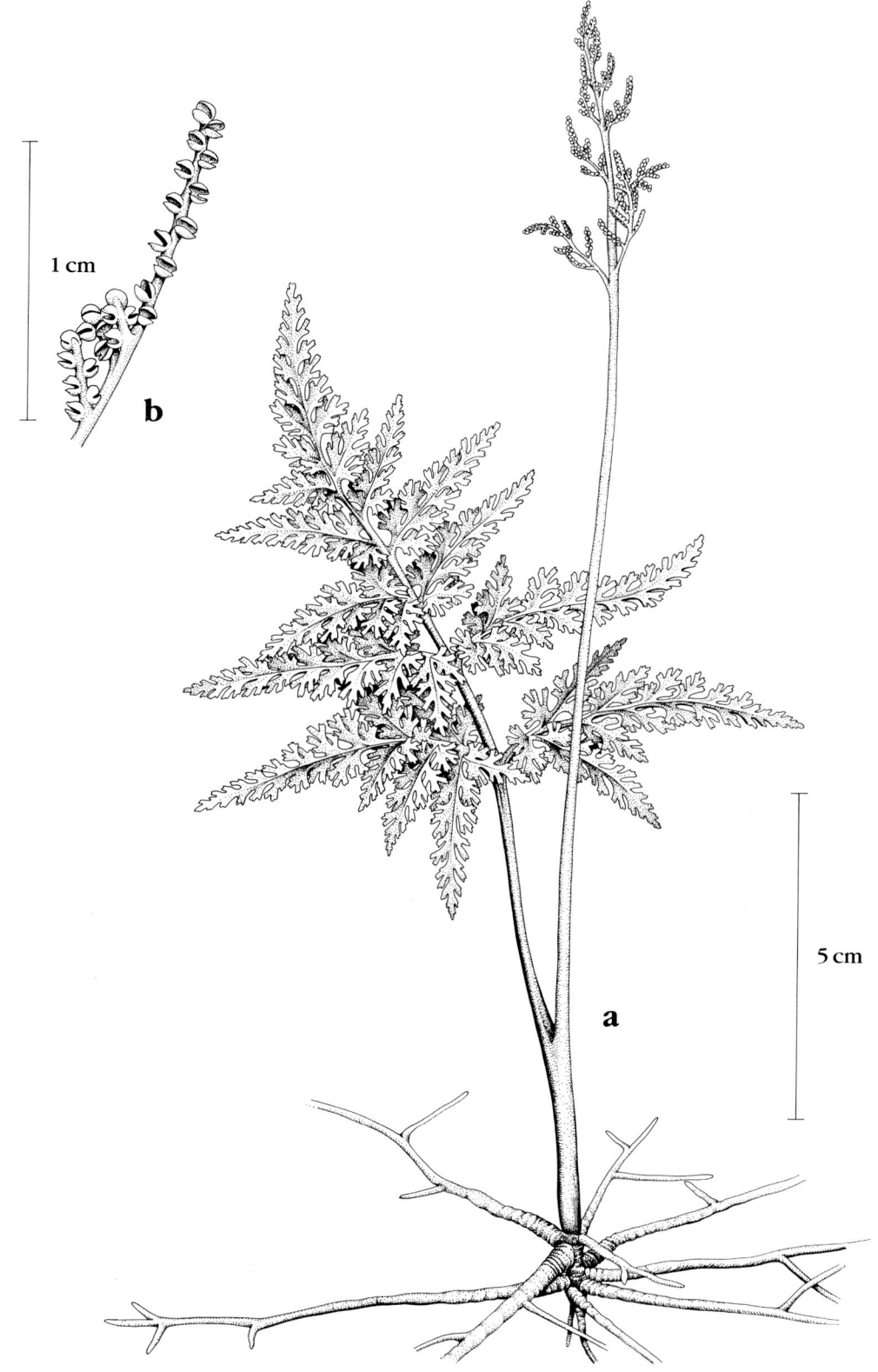

***Botrychium dissectum* var. dissectum**
a. Habit; b. Fertile branches bearing sporangia.

4b. *Botrychium dissectum* Spreng. var. *obliquum* (Muhl.) Clute

Botrychium obliquum **Muhl.**
Botrychium lunarioides **var.** *obliquum* **(Muhl.) Gray**
Botrychium ternatum **var.** *obliquum* **(Muhl.) D. C. Eat.**

COMMON NAME: Coarse-lobed Grape Fern

HABITAT: Rich, moist, open woodlands and thickets.

RANGE: Eastern North America.

As mentioned under the preceding species, some Arkansas species of *Botrychium dissectum* var. *obliquum* closely resemble plants of *B. biternatum*. Generally, the sterile blade of *Botrychium dissectum* var. *obliquum* is thicker, more dissected, and has sharper pointed terminal segments with slightly coarser and more irregular marginal teeth. Autumnal bronzing of the blade is also characteristic of *B. dissectum*.

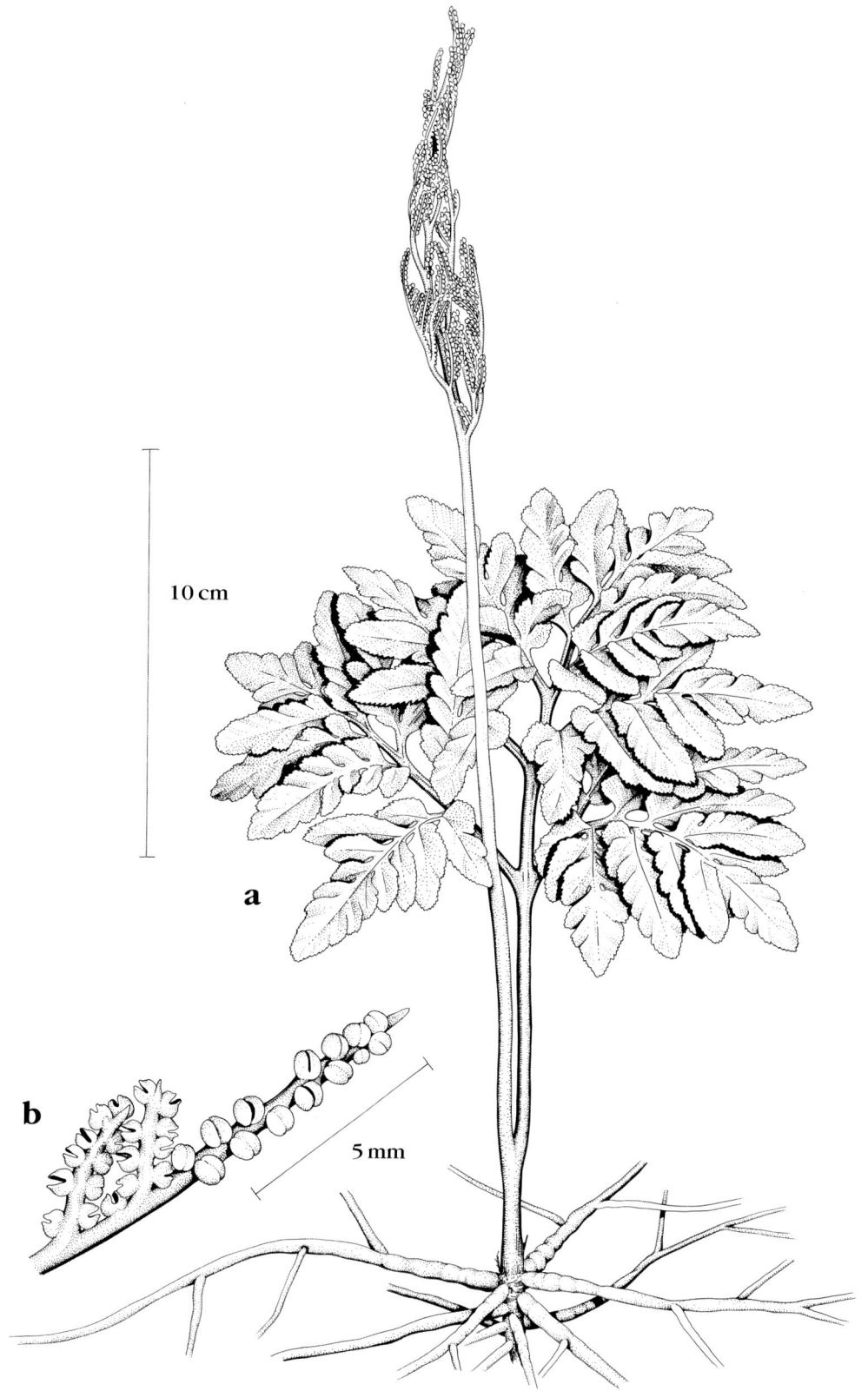

Botrychum dissectum* var. *obliquum
a. Habit; b. Fertile branches bearing sporangia.

Cheilanthes Sw. Lip Ferns

Rhizome short-creeping to erect; scales linear-subulate. Fronds evergreen, tufted, erect-spreading, bipinnate to tripinnate, pilose, lanuginose or glabrate; stipe and rachis wiry, reddish brown to black; blade lanceolate; ultimate divisions of mature fronds under 1 cm long; veins forked, free. Sori marginal, partly covered by revolute margins of pinnules or segments.

A genus of temperate and tropical regions containing about 125 species. In Arkansas, the Lip Ferns generally occupy exposed habitats that can become quite dry. While there is ample moisture, the fronds remain fully expanded, but during dry periods, the fronds curl up until adequate moisture is again available.

Key to the species of *Cheilanthes* in Arkansas

1. Stipe and rachis tomentose to lanuginose; hairs of stipe and rachis mixed with scales
    2. Rachis scales less than 0.15 mm wide; pinnules brownish-gray lanuginose below .... 1. *C. tomentosa* (p. 80)
    2. Rachis scales more than 0.15 mm wide; pinnules reddish brown lanuginose below .... 2. *C. eatonii* (p. 82)
1. Stipe and rachis glabrate, hispidulous or pilose to villous, scaleless except at stipe base
    3. Blade glabrate to sparsely short-pilose below . 3. *C. alabamensis* (p. 84)
    3. Blade pilose to lanuginose below
        4. Blade pilose to villous below; stipe and rachis hispidulous ......
           .... 4. *C. lanosa* (p. 86)
        4. Blade tomentose to lanuigonse below; stipe and rachis glabrate to pilose .... 5. *C. feei* (p. 88)

1. *Cheilanthes tomentosa* Link

Cheilanthes lanosa sensu Fern.

COMMON NAME: Woolly Lip Fern

Fronds bipinnate-pinnatifid to tripinnate up to 50 cm long; stipe and rachis white to reddish brown lanuginose, bearing white to reddish brown linear-subulate scales up to 1.5 mm wide; blade oblong-lanceolate to linear-lanceolate, up to 35 cm long and 7 cm wide, pilose to tomentose above, brownish gray lanuginose below; segments obovate to elliptic, up to 3 mm long.

HABITAT: Sandstone, shale, dolomite, limestone, chert, and novaculite outcrops; Interior Highlands.

RANGE: Southern United States, northern Mexico.

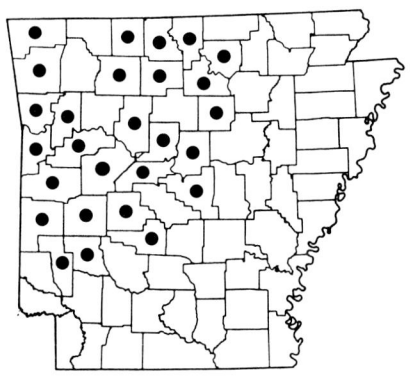

Cheilanthes tomentosa

Baxter Co.: *D. Moore 541021* (UARK). Benton Co.: *Demaree 2911* (SMU). Boone Co.: *D. Moore 490379* (UARK). Cleburne Co.: *Taylor 1026* (SIU). Conway Co.: *D. Moore 480368* (UARK). Crawford Co.: *Palmer 26423* (UARK). Faulkner Co.: *Taylor 2601* (SIU). Franklin Co.: *Palmer 8140* (MO). Garland Co.: *Harvey 83* (MO). Hot Spring Co.: *Demaree 16534* (SMU). Howard Co.: *Kellogg s.n.* (MO). Izard Co.: *Demaree 3285* (SMU). Logan Co.: *Palmer 23207* (UARK). Marion Co.: *Johnson 98* (HXC). Montgomery Co.: *Demaree 34158* (SMU). Newton Co.: *D. Moore 32488* (UARK). Perry Co.: *Redfearn 24134* (SMU). Pike Co.: *Roberts 27* (UARK). Polk Co.: *J. Moore 3139* (UCA). Pope Co.: *D. Moore 520746* (UARK). Pulaski Co.: *Palmer 22990* (UARK). Scott Co.: *D. Moore 430134* (UARK). Searcy Co.: *D. Moore 350152* (UARK). Sebastian Co.: *Taylor 2716* (SIU). Stone Co.: *D. Moore 470747* (UARK). Washington Co.: *Taylor 1114* (SIU). Yell Co.: *Taylor 4369* (SIU).

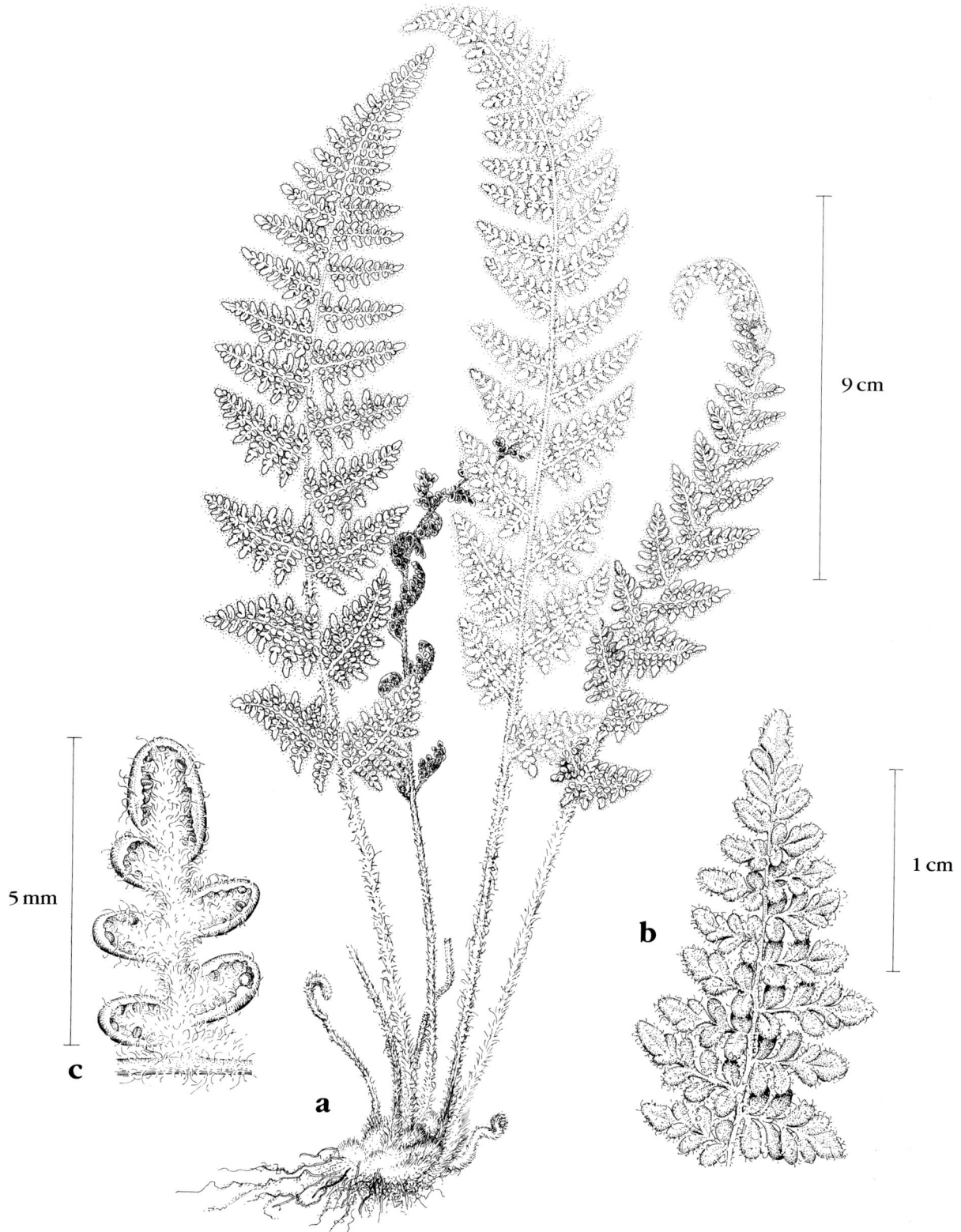

Cheilanthes tomentosa
a. Habit; b. Upper surface of pinna; c. Lower surface of sporiferous pinnule.

2. *Cheilanthes eatonii* Hooker & Baker

Cheilanthes castanea Maxon

COMMON NAME: Eaton's Lip Fern

Fronds bipinnate-pinnatifid to tripinnate, up to 40 cm long; stipe and rachis reddish brown tomentose, bearing reddish brown linear-subulate scales over 1.5 mm wide; blade oblong-lanceolate to linear-lanceolate, up to 25 cm long and 5 cm wide, pilose above, reddish brown lanuginose below; segments obovate to elliptic, up to 3.5 mm long.

HABITAT: Baxter Co.: "rock outcrops; Norfork;" *Moore 451026* (UARK). Benton Co.: *E. N. Plank s.n.* (NY).

RANGE: Southwestern United States and Virginia, northern Mexico.

Unknowingly, *Cheilanthes eatonii* was collected by E. N. Plank in 1899 and by Dwight Moore in 1945. For many years these two collections remained incompletely or incorrectly identified. Possibly because *C. eatonii* resembles *C. tomentosa*, these specimens were overlooked. In 1979, David Johnson and Timothy Reeves correctly annotated these collections. Arkansas localities of *C. eatonii* with accurate habitat data are needed as there is little information on the occurrence of this species in the state.

Branner and Coville (1891) reported *C. eatonii* "in clefts in the rocks at Mountain Park, Big Rock, near Little Rock." Coville's specimen of *C. eatonii* was found to be *C. tomentosa* (Buchholz, 1924).

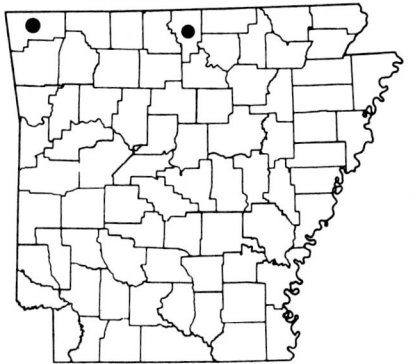

Cheilanthes eatonii

Baxter Co.: *D. Moore 451026* (UARK). Benton Co.: *Plank s. n.* (NY).

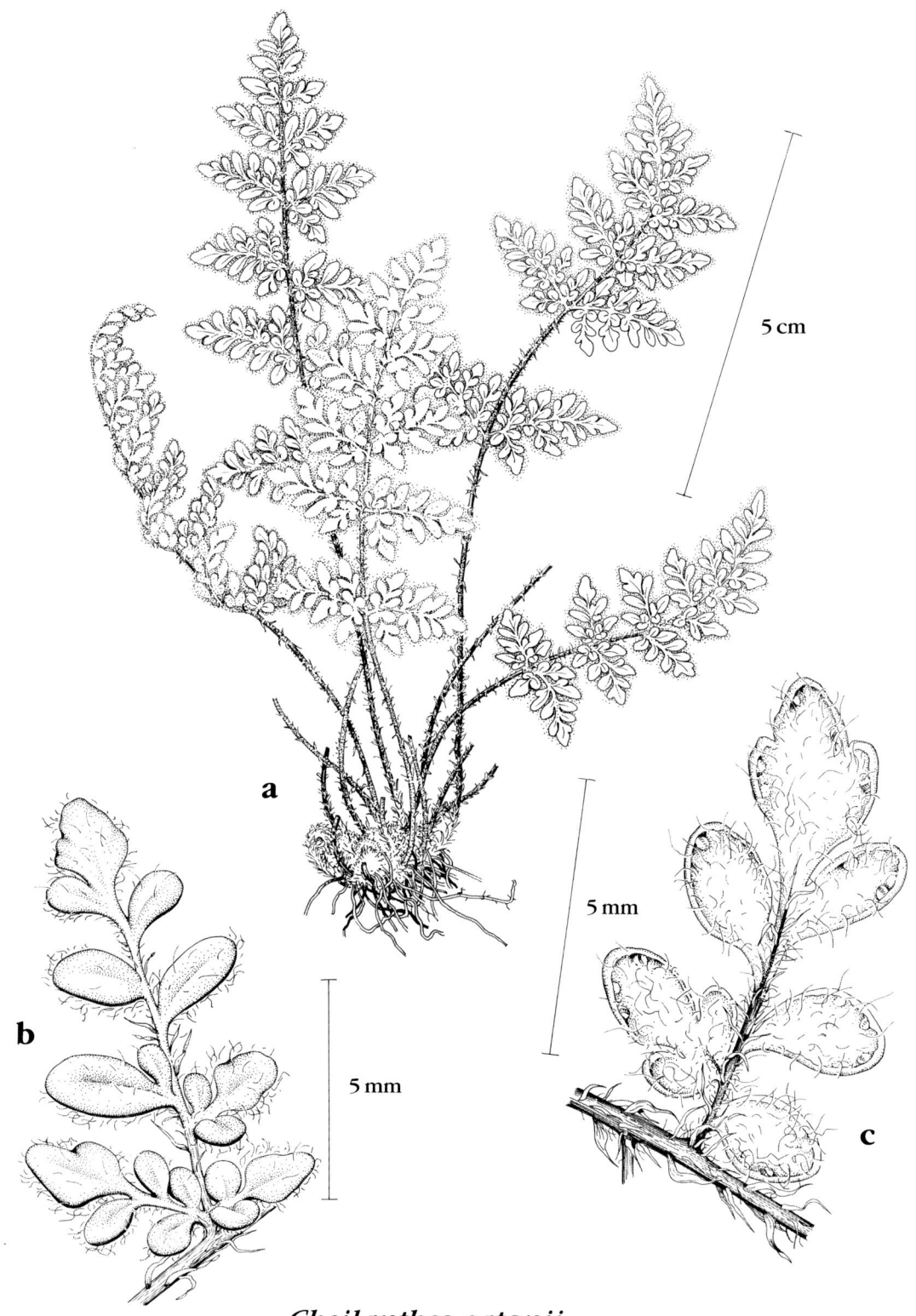

Cheilanthes eatonii
a. Habit; b. Upper surface of pinna: c. Lower surface of sporiferous pinna.

3. *Cheilanthes alabamensis* (Buckl.) Kunze

Pteris alabamensis Buckl.

COMMON NAME: Alabama Lip Fern

Fronds bipinnate to bipinnate-pinnatifid, up to 40 cm long; stipe and rachis dark reddish purple to black, glabrate or with scattered appressed and crisped hairs; blade lanceolate, up to 25 cm long and 6 cm wide, glabrate to sparsely short-pilose; pinnules ovate-oblong, up to 1 cm long, entire to divided.

HABITAT: Limestone or dolomite outcrops; primarily Ozark Mountains. Particularly robust plants of *Cheilanthes alabamensis* are found on the shaded, west-facing, limestone tufa at the base of Hot Springs Mountain, Hot Springs National Park, Garland County.

RANGE: Southern United States, northern Mexico, Jamaica.

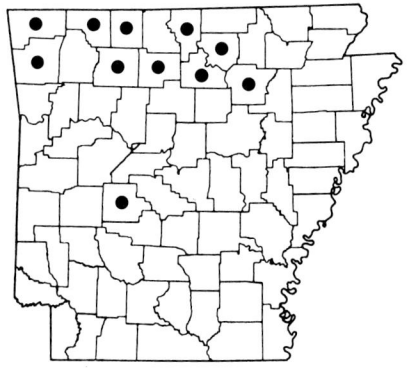

Cheilanthes alabamensis

Baxter Co.: *Taylor 2674* (SIU). Benton Co.: *Palmer 24739* (MO). Boone Co.: *Palmer 6905* (MO). Carroll Co.: *Leonard 115* (UARK). Garland Co.: *Engelmann s.n.* (MO). Independence Co.: *Thomas 7720* (NLU). Izard Co.: *Demaree 3264* (UARK). Newton Co.: *Taylor 1219* (SIU). Searcy Co.: *Taylor 2583* (SIU). Stone Co.: *D. Moore 470697* (UARK). Washington Co.: *Taylor 1111* (SIU).

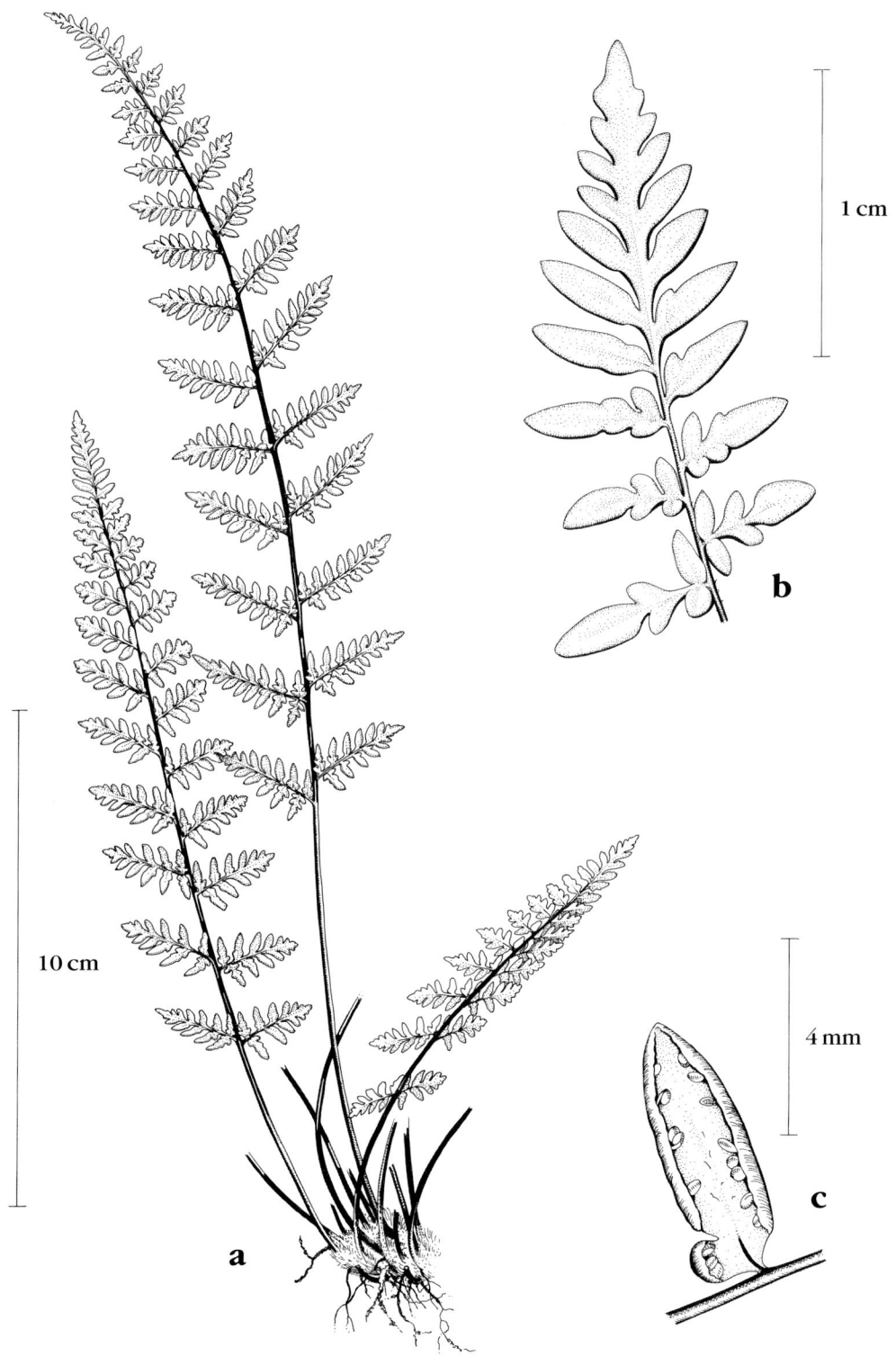

Cheilanthes alabamensis
a. Habit; b. Upper surface of pinna; c. Lower surface of sporiferous pinnule.

4. *Cheilanthes lanosa* (Michx.) D. C. Eat.

Nephrodium lanosum Michx.
Adiantum vestitum Spreng.
Cheilanthes vestita (Spreng.) Sw.

COMMON NAME: Hairy Lip Fern

Fronds bipinnate-pinnatifid, up to 40 cm long; stipe and rachis dark reddish brown, hispidulous; blade narrowly oblong-lanceolate, up to 30 cm long and 6 cm wide, sparsely hairy above, pilose to villous below; pinnules ovate to ovate-oblong, up to 1 cm long, lobed to divided.

HABITAT: Sandstone, shale, dolomite, chert, novaculite, and occasionally limestone outcrops; chiefly Interior Highlands.

RANGE: Eastern United States.

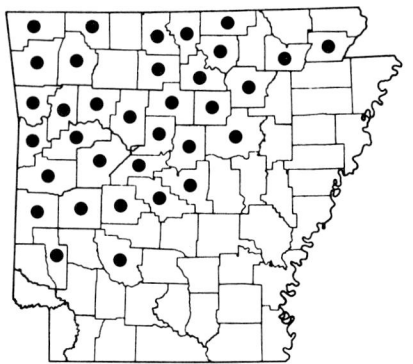

Cheilanthes lanosa

Baxter Co.: *Taylor 1844* (SIU). Benton Co.: *Taylor 1118* (SIU). Carroll Co.: *Palmer 4454* (MO. Clark Co.: *Taylor 2189* (SIU). Cleburne Co.: *Taylor 1023* (SIU). Conway Co.: *Tucker 3509* (APCR). Crawford Co.: *D. Moore 710221* (UARK). Faulkner Co.: *Taylor 2607* (SIU). Franklin Co.: *Taylor 1127* (SIU). Fulton Co.: *Palmer 29131* (MO). Garland Co.: *Taylor 2227 (SIU). Greene Co.: Richards 5489* (ARKSU). Howard Co.: *Kellogg s.n.* (MO). Independence Co.: *Thomas 16443* (NLU). Izard Co.: *Palmer 35550* (MO). Johnson Co.: *Taylor 1091* (SIU). Lawrence Co.: *Taylor 2594* (SIU). Logan Co.: *Palmer 24191* (UARK). Madison Co.:*Redfearn 26788* (SMS). Marion Co.:*Johnson 91* (HXC). Montgomery Co.: *D. Moore 32975* (UARK). Perry Co.: *Owens s.n.* (US). Polk Co.: *J. Moore 3148* (UCA). Pope Co.: *Snider 23* (APCR). Pulaski Co.: *Buchholz 576* (UARK). Saline Co.: *Demaree 230171* (MO). Scott Co.: *D. Moore 430135* (UARK). Searcy Co.: *Taylor 1238* (SIU). Sebastian Co.:*Taylor 2718* (SIU). Stone Co.: *Taylor 2125* (SIU). Van Buren Co.: *Johnson 102* (HXC). Washington Co.: *Taylor 1113* (SIU). White Co.: *Demaree 26934* (SMU). Yell Co.: *Taylor 1198* (SIU).

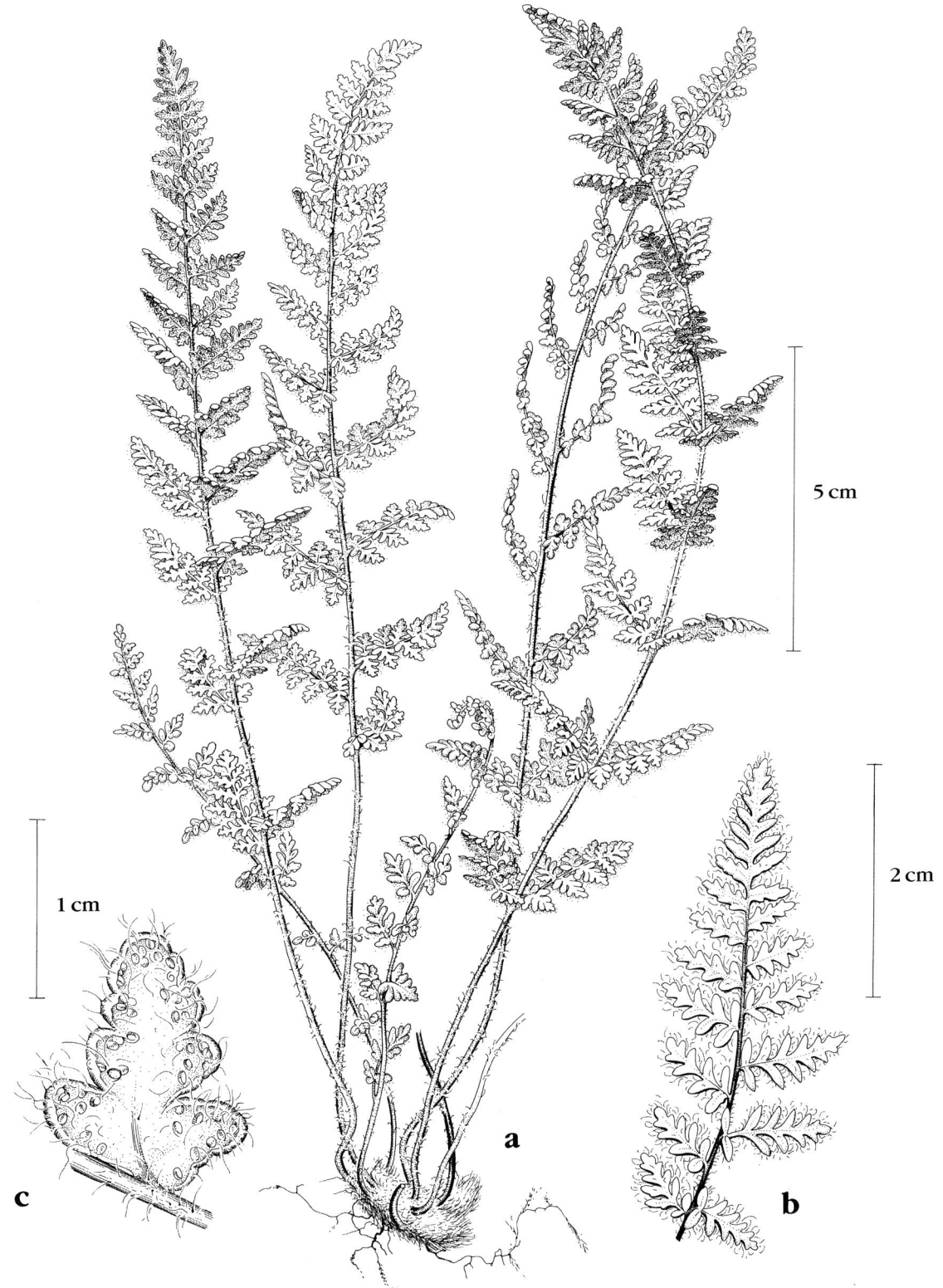

Cheilanthes lanosa
a. Habit; b. Upper surface of pinna; c. Lower surface of sporiferous pinnule.

5. *Cheilanthes feei* Moore

Cheilanthes lanuginosa Hook.

COMMON NAME: Slender Lip Fern

Fronds bipinnate-pinnatifid to tripinnate, up to 20 cm long; stipe and rachis dark reddish brown to purplish black, pilosulous, becoming glabrate with age; blade ovate-lanceolate, up to 10 cm long and 3.5 cm wide, villous above, lanuginose below; segments suborbicular to broadly elliptic, up to 2 mm long.

HABITAT: Limestone, dolomite, or calcareous sandstone outcrops; primarily Ozark Mountains but it also has been collected in Hot Springs, apparently from the limestone tufa near the base of Hot Springs Mountain, Hot Springs National Park, Garland County.

RANGE: Central and western United States.

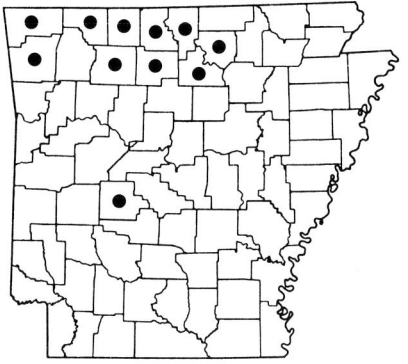

Cheilanthes feei

Baxter Co.: *Taylor 2681* (SIU). Benton Co.: *Demaree 4975* (UARK). Boone Co.: *Palmer 6906* (MO). Carroll Co.: *Trelease 4/20799* (MO). Garland Co.: *Letterman s.n.* (MO). Izard Co.: *Demaree 17038* (MO). Marion Co.: *D. Moore 410522* (UARK). Newton Co.: *D. Moore 350103* (UARK). Searcy Co.: *D. Moore 350150* (UARK). Stone Co.: *Tucker 6904* (APCR). Washington Co.: *Demaree s.n.* (SMU).

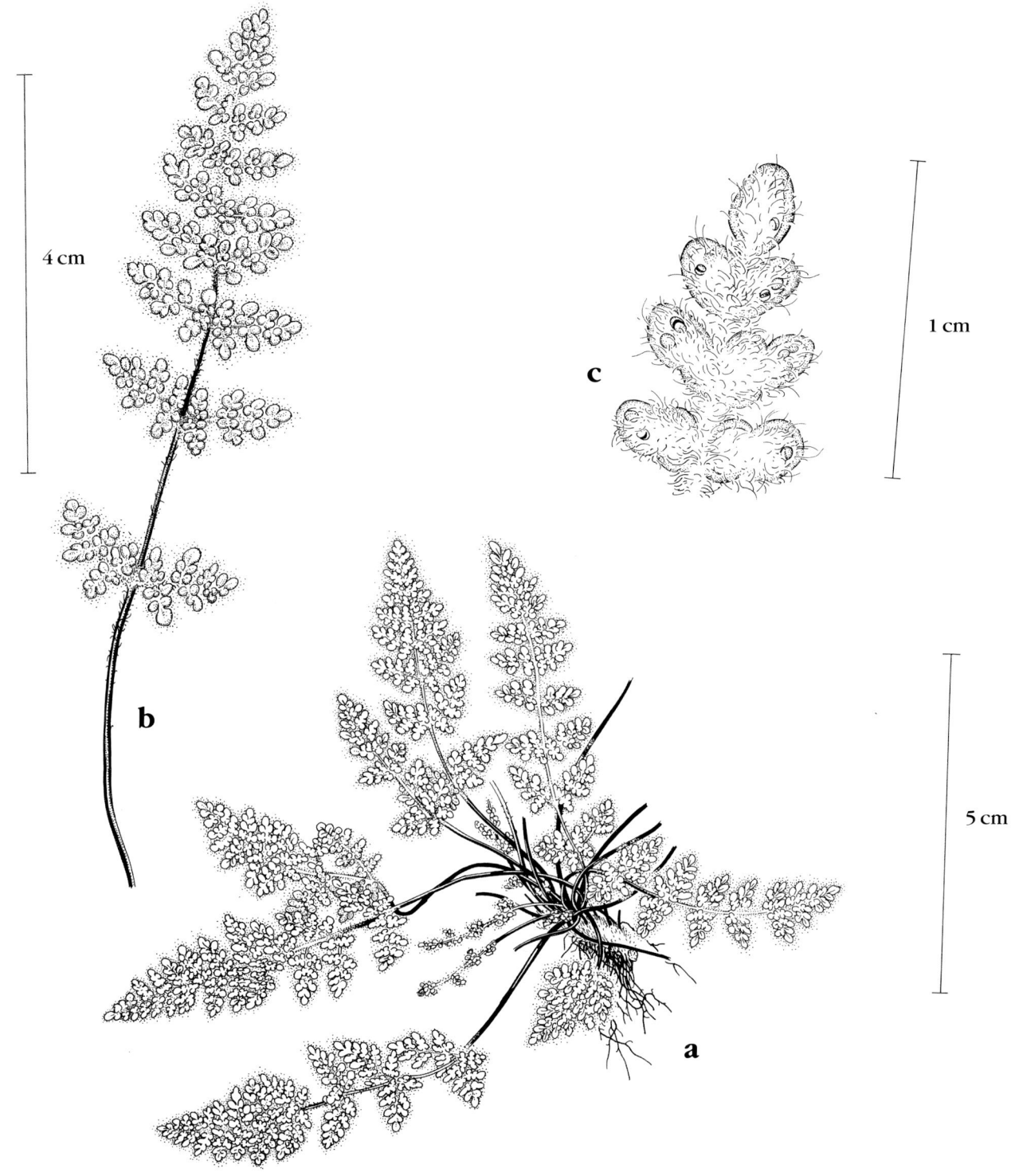

Cheilanthes feei
a. Habit; b. Upper surface of frond; c. Lower surface of sporiferous pinna.

Cystopteris Bernh. Fragile Ferns, Bladder Ferns

Rhizome creeping; scales mostly near rhizome apex, concolorous, brown, lanceolate. Fronds delicate, deciduous, pinnate-pinnatifid to bipinnate-pinnatifid, glabrate; stipe and rachis green to stramineous; stipe virtually scaleless; blade ovate-lanceolate to deltoid-attenuate, pinnae or pinnules lobed to pinnatifid, serrate or serrate-emarginate to serrulate, with veins simple or forked, free, reaching the margins. Sori round, borne on veins; indusium delicate, pocket-like, apex arching over sorus, opening along edge toward pinna margin.

Cystopteris is a mainly temperate genus of about 10 species. It has been monographed by Blasdell (1963).

Key to the species of *Cystopteris* in Arkansas

1. Plants of rich, forest floor soils; rhizome protruding up to 5 cm beyond current season's fronds; veins of pinnae or pinnules mostly ending in teeth; rachis and pinnae not bulbiferous .... 1. *C. protrusa* (p. 92)
1. Plants of rock outcrops; rhizome not extending beyond current season's fronds; veins of pinnae or pinnules mostly ending in emarginations at tips of teeth or in sinuses between teeth, rachis and pinnae often bulbiferous
   2. Blade deltoid-attenuate, mostly long tapering; upper pinnae or segments toward blade apex not strongly ascending, more or less perpendicular to rachis; bulblets globose, 2-3 lobed . 2. *C. bulbifera* (p. 94)
   2. Blade deltoid-ovate to lanceolate, apex acuminate; upper pinnae or segments toward blade apex strongly ascending, oblique to rachis; bulblets clavate, unlobed, scaly .... 3. *C. tennesseensis* (p. 96)

1. *Cystopteris protrusa* (Weatherby) Blasdell

Cystopteris fragilis var. *protrusa* Weatherby

COMMON NAME: Southern Fragile Fern

Rhizome extended and long-creeping, partly covered by old stipe bases, protruding up to 5 cm beyond current season's fronds. Fronds appearing in early spring, erect to erect-spreading, up to 45 cm long, eglandular, not bulbiferous; blade ovate-lanceolate, up to 25 cm long and 12 cm wide, acuminate; pinnae or segments toward blade apex strongly ascending, oblique to rachis; lower pinnae deltoid, petiolulate; lower basal pinnules stipitate, pinnatifid with 3-4 sinuses per side; veins of pinnae or pinnules mostly ending in teeth.

HABITAT: Moist, shaded, humus-rich, loam soils of woodlands; Interior Highlands and Crowley's Ridge.

RANGE: Eastern United States.

Blasdell (1963) elevated this taxon to the rank of species and this treatment now appears to have wide acceptance. *Cystopteris protrusa* possesses a long-creeping rhizome with distinct internodes that normally extends well beyond the current season's fronds. The rhizome of *C. fragilis* is more compact, has very short and indistinct internodes, and does not extend beyond the current season's fronds. Arkansas collections which include rootstocks and are identified as *C. fragilis*, are clearly referable to *C. protrusa* on the basis of their rhizome morphology. In North America, *Cystopteris fragilis* ranges to the north and west of Arkansas.

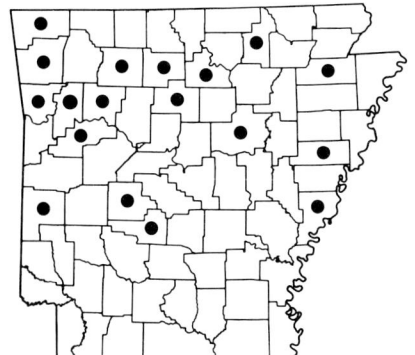

Cystopteris protrusa

Benton Co.: *Demaree 6517* (UARK). Craighead Co.: *Richards 6346* (ARKSU). Crawford Co.: *Taylor 1100* (SIU). Franklin Co.: *Johnson 528* (HXC). Garland Co.: *D. Moore 480192* (UARK). Hot Spring Co.: *Palmer 29708* (UARK). Johnson Co.: *Johnson 48* (HXC). Logan Co.: *Taylor 1047* (SIU). Newton Co.: *D. Moore 480225* (UARK). Phillips Co.: *Lowman 98* (HXC). Polk Co.: *Taylor 1065* (SIU). St. Francis Co.: *Johnson 441* (HXC). Searcy Co.: *D. Moore 350143* (UARK). Sharp Co.: *Demaree 27712* (SMU). Stone Co.: *D. Moore 510354* (UARK). Van Buren Co.: *Johnson 152* (HXC). Washington Co.: *Hite 24* (UARK). White Co.: *Johnson 221* (HXC).

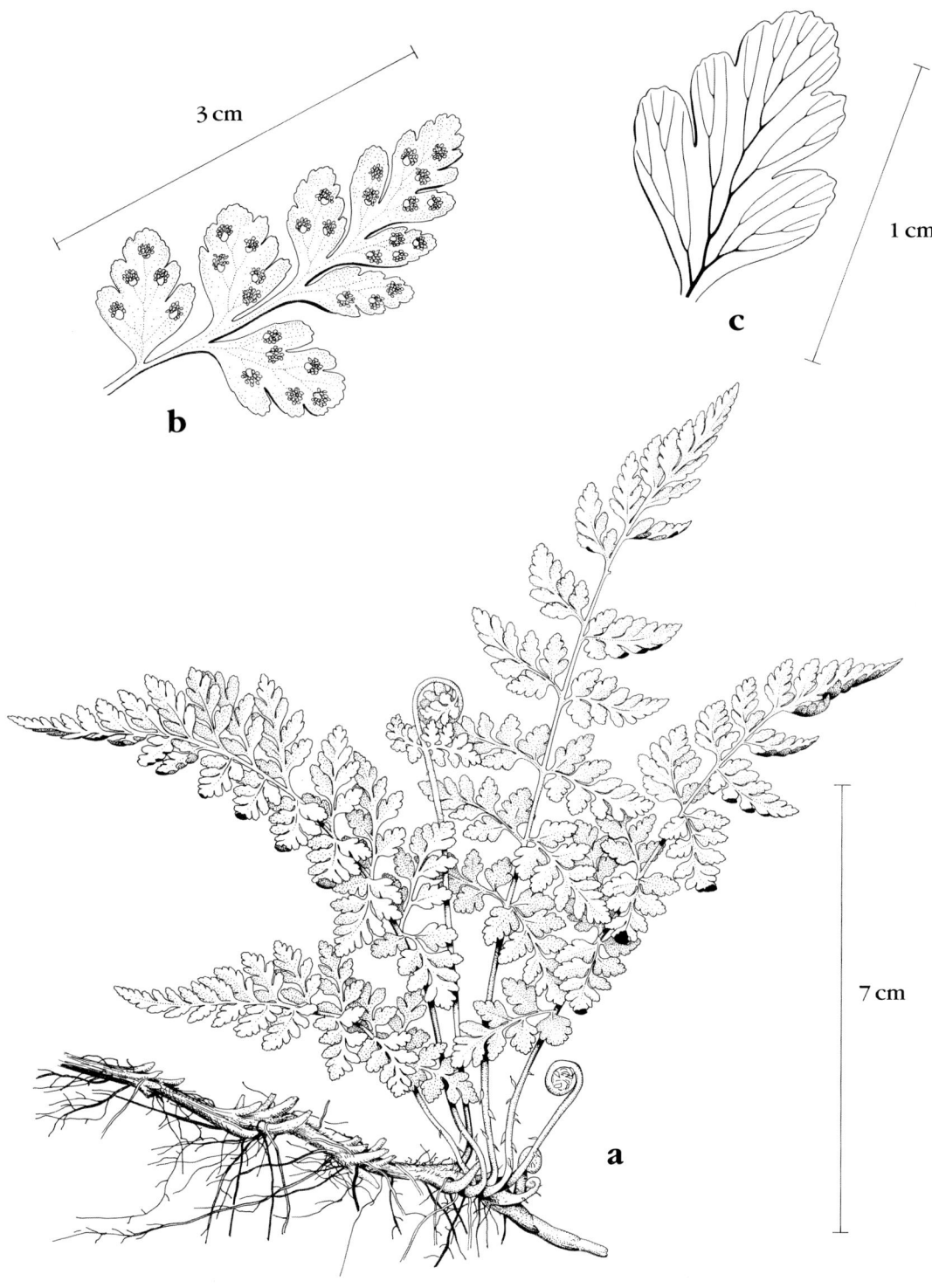

Cystopteris protrusa
a. Habit; b. Lower surface of pinna with sori; c. Pinnule venation.

2. *Cystopteris bulbifera* (L.) Bernh.

Polypodium bulbiferum L.

COMMON NAME: Bulblet Bladder Fern

Rhizome compact and short-creeping, densely covered with old stipe bases, not protruding beyond current season's fronds. Fronds erect-spreading to pendulous, up to 1 m or more long, minutely stipitate glandular below; stipe often pinkish or purplish tinted; blade deltoid-attenuate, up to 1 m long and 15 cm wide, long-attenuate to apex; rachis and pinnae often bulbiferous on lower surface toward apex at base of pinnae; bulblets globose, 2-3 lobed; pinnae or lobes toward blade apex not strongly ascending, more or less perpendicular to rachis; lower pinnae oblong-lanceolate; upper pinnae often bulbiferous on lower surface along midveins; lower basal pinnules sessile, pinnatifid, with 5-7 sinuses per side; veins of pinnae or pinnules ending in sinuses between teeth.

HABITAT: Moist, shaded outcrops of limestone, dolomite, calcareous sandstone and shale; primarily Ozark Mountains.

RANGE: Eastern North America, southwestern United States.

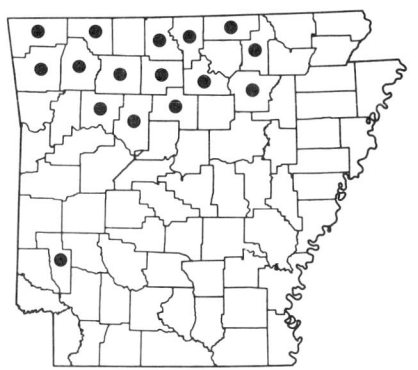

Cystopteris bulbifera

Baxter Co.: *D. Moore 510522* (UARK). Benton Co.: *Demaree 4897* (F). Carroll Co.: *D. Moore 58218* (UARK). Fulton Co.: *Wheeler 13* (F). Howard Co.: *Kellogg s.n.* (MO). Independence Co.: *Thomas 8302* (NLU). Johnson Co.: *Redfearn 23832* (SMS). Madison Co.: *Palmer 24796* (MO). Marion Co.: *Palmer 4780* (MO). Newton Co.: *Taylor 2693* (SIU). Pope Co.: *Key 383* (SMS). Searcy Co.: *Taylor 2579* (SIU). Sharp Co.: *Demaree 26436* (SMU). Stone Co.: *Taylor 2899* (SIU). Van Buren Co.: *Palmer 25192* (MO). Washington Co.: *Palmer 27033* (MO).

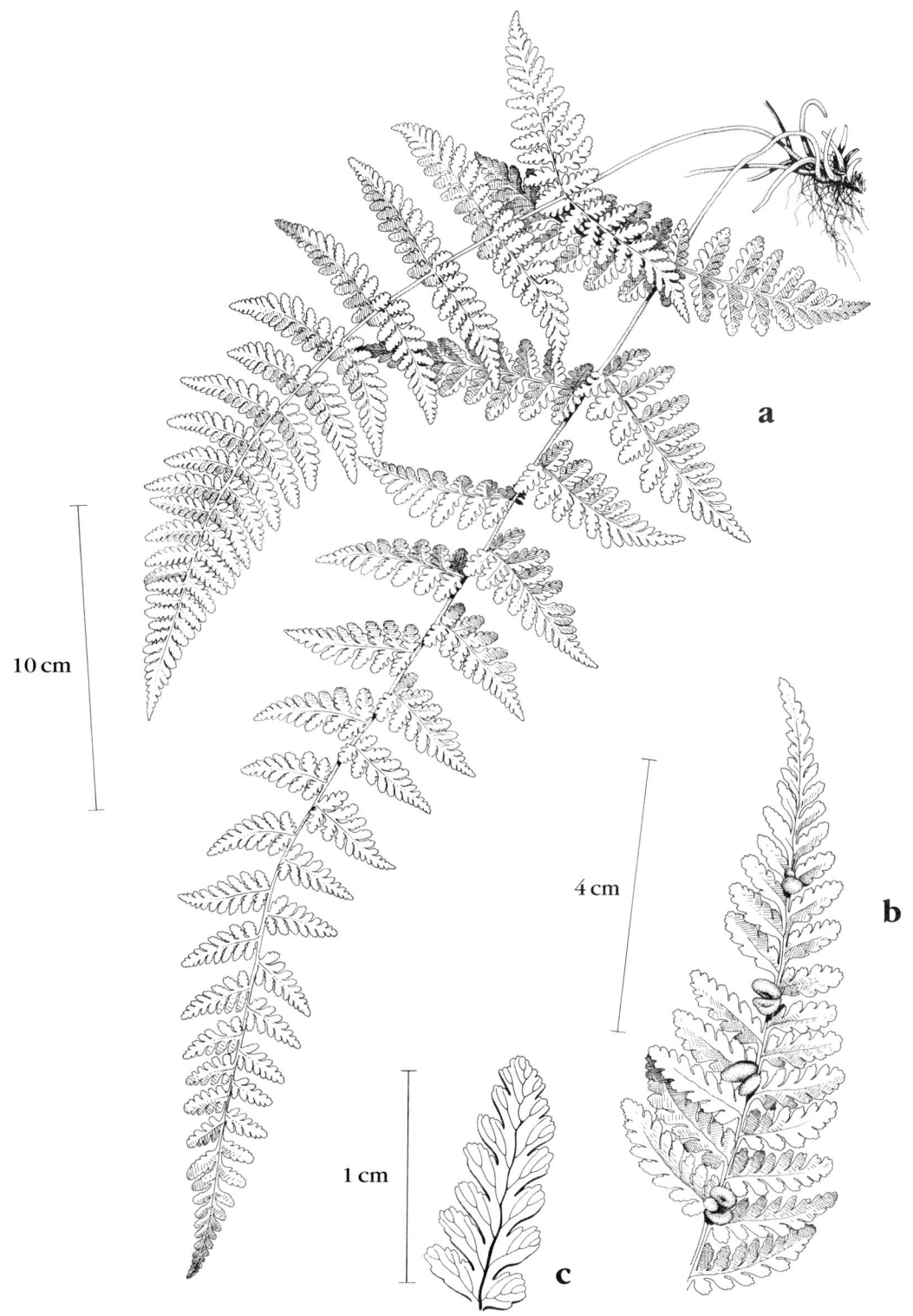

Cystopteris bulbifera
a. Habit; b. Lower surface of frond apex with bulblets; c. Pinnule venation.

3. *Cystopteris tennesseensis* Shaver

Cystopteris fragilis f. *simulans* Weatherby
Cystopteris fragilis var. *simulans* (Weatherby) McGregor
Cystopteris fragilis var. *tennesseensis* (Shaver) McGregor

COMMON NAME: Tennessee Bladder Fern

Rhizome compact and typically short-creeping, covered with old stipe bases, rarely protruding slightly beyond current season's fronds; fronds erect to erect-spreading, up to 80 cm long, usually minutely stipitate glandular below; blade deltoid-ovate to lanceolate, up to 50 cm long, and 18 cm wide, acuminate; rachis often bulbiferous on lower surface at base of pinnae; bulblets clavate, unlobed, scaly; pinnae or segments toward blade apex strongly ascending, oblique to rachis; lower pinnae deltoid to ovate; upper pinnae rarely bulbiferous on lower surface along midveins; lower basal pinnules mostly stipitate, pinnatifid, with 4-6 sinuses per side; veins of pinnae or pinnules mostly ending in emarginations at the tips of teeth or in sinuses between teeth.

HABITAT: Moist, shaded outcrops of limestone, sandstone, dolomite, and shale; Interior Highlands.

RANGE: Mainly central United States.

Cystopteris tennesseensis, a plant more common than generally recognized, is evidently an allopolyploid combining the characters of its putative parents *C. bulbifera* and *C. protrusa* (Blasdell, 1963). Features similar to *C. bulbifera* include fronds that are usually broadest at the base, glandular, and which frequently bear bulblets. Like *C. protrusa*, *C. tennesseensis* bears strongly ascending pinnae or segments toward the frond apex. In Arkansas, *C. tennesseensis* also seems to accept a somewhat intermediate habitat. Sometimes occurring on sandstone outcrops or rarely even in the humus-rich soils at the base of outcrops, it has the saxicolous habitat of *C. bulbifera* but it does not appear to have as strong a requirement for a calcareous substrate.

Spore size is a useful character for distinguishing *C. tennesseensis* from *C. bulbifera* and *C. protrusa*. Spore slides, from which you can measure spore size, can easily be made. Place a drop of 95% ethyl alcohol on a soriferous pinnule. Then, using a dissecting needle, scrape off spores and sporangia into a drop of water on a glass slide. Cover with a cover slip. The alcohol prevents dehiscence of the sporangia and aids in transfer of the spores (Robbin Moran, personal communication).

The spores of *C. tennesseensis*, a tetraploid, average 34-41 μm in diameter while those of *C. bulbifera* and *C. protrusa*, both diploids, average only 27-32 μm across.

Robbin Moran (personal communication) has recently detected what he believes to be a *C. tennesseensis* backcross to *C. bulbifera*. The plant in question, of intermediate morphology and bearing abortive spores, was collected along Cave Creek, NE of Chinn Springs, Independence Co., by Dale Thomas (*Thomas 8673* TENN) on 17 June 1968.

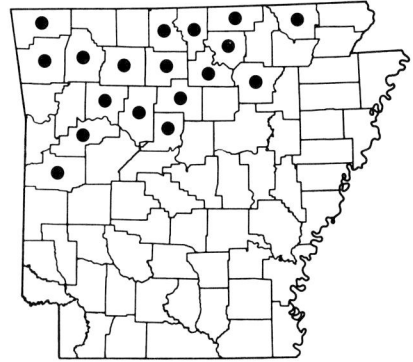

Cystopteris tennesseensis

Baxter Co.: *Taylor 2679* (SIU). Benton Co.: *Taylor 1122* (SIU). Conway Co.: *J. Moore 1089* (SMU). Fulton Co.: *Wheeler 39* (UARK). Independence Co.: *Thomas 7753* (NLU). Izard Co.: *Taylor 1267* (SIU). Johnson Co.: *Redfearn 23833* (SMS). Logan Co.: *Pyle 280* (APCR). Madison Co.: *Key 270* (SMS). Marion Co.: *Taylor 1235* (SIU). Newton Co.: *Redfearn 23479* (SMS). Pope Co.: *D. Moore 520756* (UARK). Randolph Co.: *Demaree 26816* (SMU). Scott Co.: *Demaree 54899* (UARK). Searcy Co.: *Taylor 1240* (SIU). Stone Co.: *Taylor 1245* (SIU). Van Buren Co.: *Demaree 4753* (UARK). Washington Co.: *Haas 1471* (UCA).

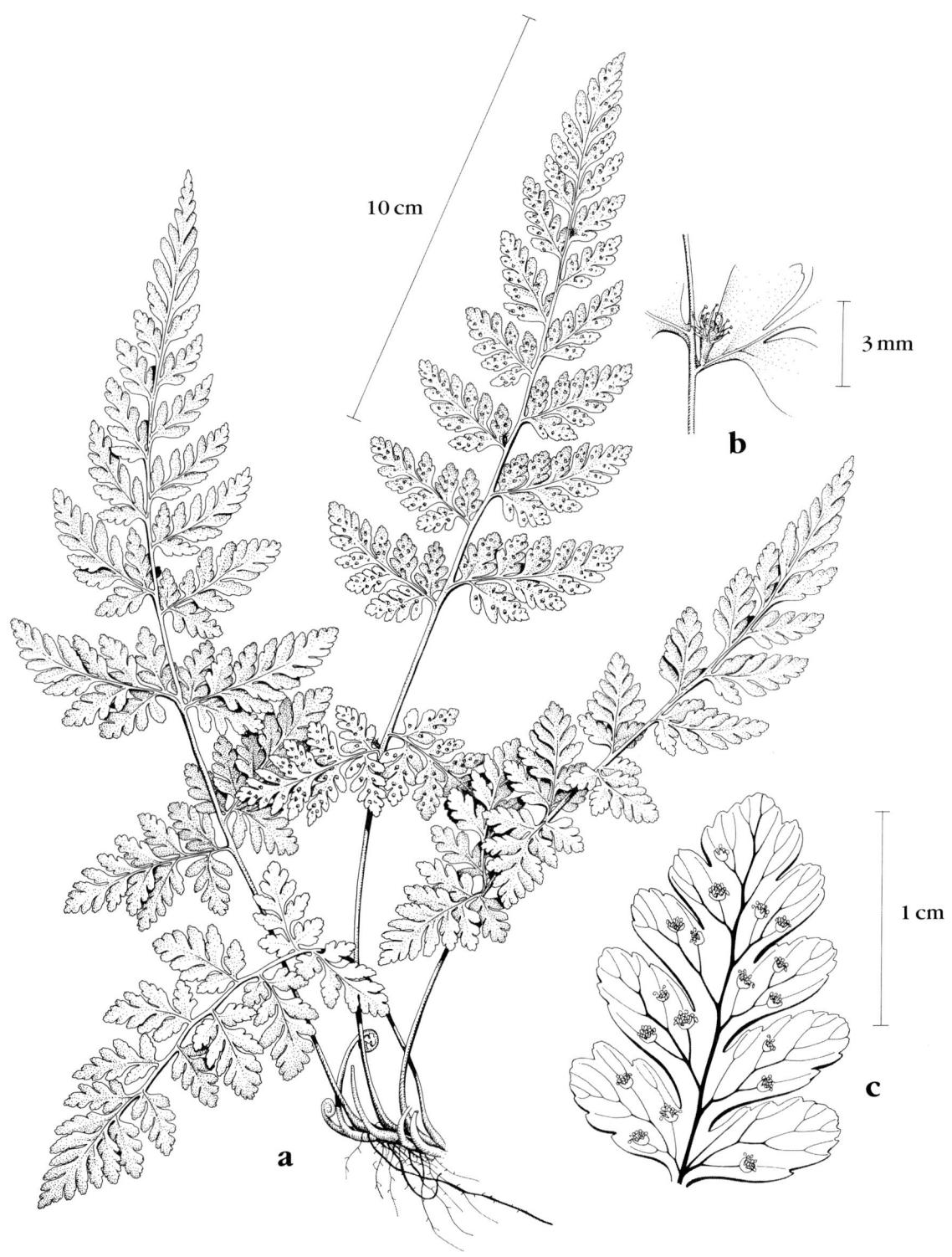

Cystopteris tennesseensis
a. Habit; b. Lower surface of pinna base with bulblet; c. Lower surface of pinna with sori.

Dennstaedtia Bernh. Hay-scented Fern

Dennstaedtia is a genus of about 70 species mainly found in wet tropical forests. For a review of the genus in America, see Tryon (1960).

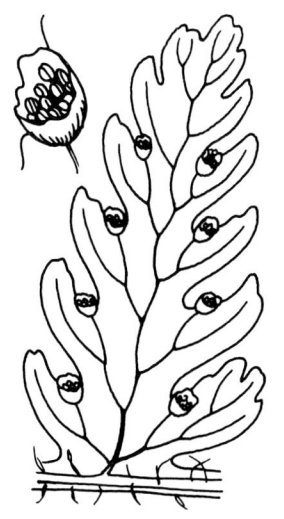

1. *Dennstaedtia punctilobula* (Michx.) Moore

Nephrodium punctilobula Michx.
Dicksonia punctilobula (Michx.) Gray

COMMON NAME: Hay-scented Fern

Rhizome creeping or climbing, hairy; scaleless. Fronds delicate, deciduous, erect or arching, bipinnate-pinnatifid, up to 80 cm long, bearing minute, pellucid, gland-tipped hairs releasing fragrance of fresh cut hay; stipe and rachis lustrous reddish brown to stramineous; blade lanceolate, up to 50 cm long and 20 cm wide, attenuate to apex; pinnules lobulate; veins simple or forked, free. Sori marginal, globose, at tips of basal lobules distal to pinnule base; indusium cupulate.

HABITAT: Crevices and ledges of moist, shaded, sandstone outcrops: Logan Co.: near summit on N side of Magazine Mountain *Taylor 1046* (SIU). Stone Co.: Blanchard Spring; *Moore 450729* (F); City Rock Bluff across the White River from Calico Rock; *Moore 490311* (F).

RANGE: Northeastern North America.

Dennstaedtia punctilobula was first collected in Arkansas from "Fern Cave" on Magazine Mountain by E. J. Palmer in October 1923 (Palmer, 1924). Dwight Moore collected it at Blanchard Springs on 23 June 1945, and at City Rock Bluff on 4 July 1949. This species was also reported near Pine Bluff, Jefferson County (Moore, 1940b), but voucher specimens have not been found.

Dennstaedtia punctilobula is common in pastures and rocky, open woods in the New England states but, in Arkansas, where it reaches the southwestern extent of its range, it is apparently restricted to moist, shaded sandstone outcrops. Arkansas plants of *D. punctilobula* are possibly relicts, survivors from a once wider distribution or from past southern migrations during Pleistocene glaciation.

Dennstaedtia punctilobula

Logan Co.: *Taylor 1046* (SIU). Stone Co.: *D. Moore 450729* (F) and *D. Moore 490311* (F).

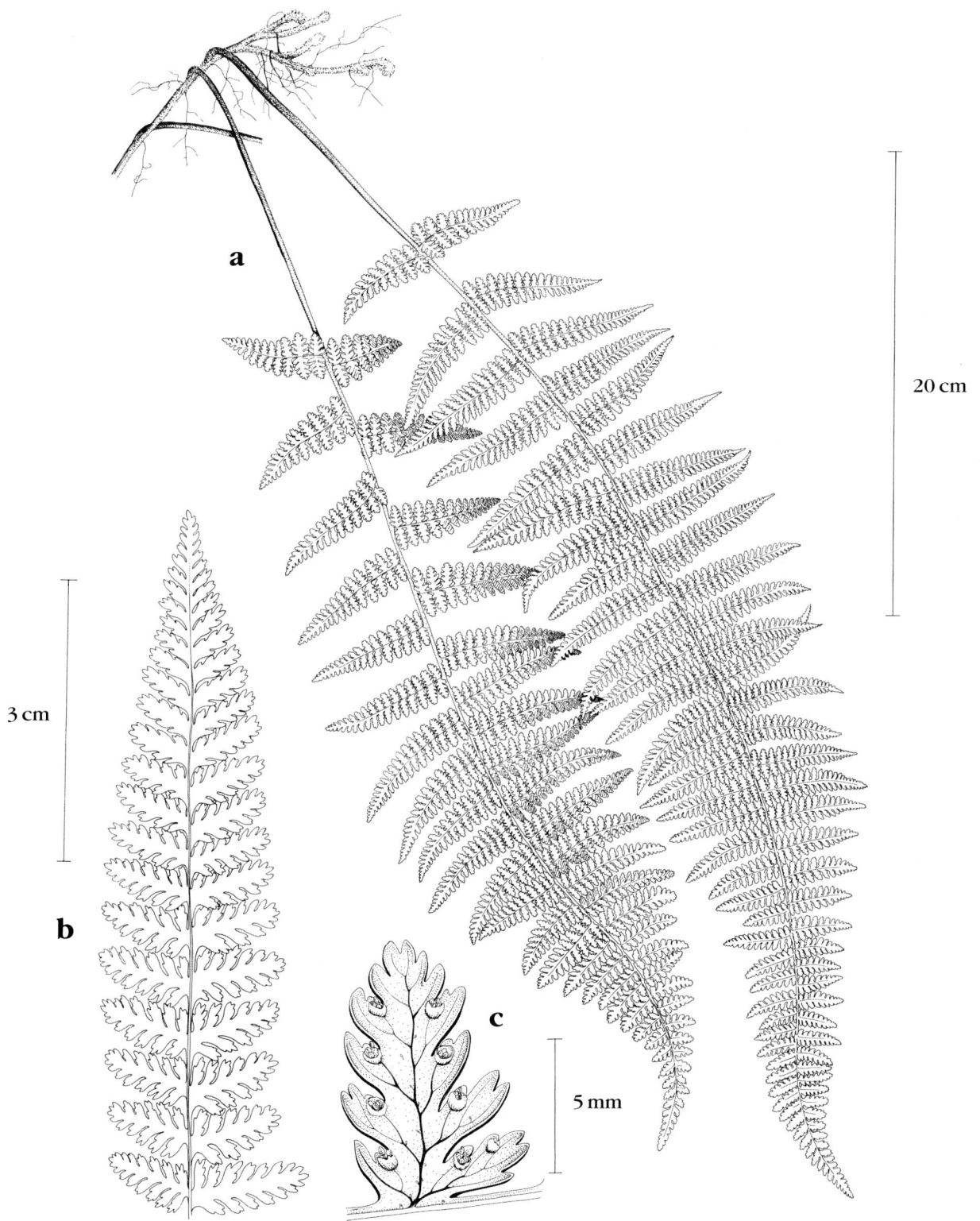

Dennstaedtia punctilobula
a. Habit; b. Pinna; c. Lower surface of pinnule with sori.

Dryopteris Adans. Wood Ferns

Rhizome creeping to erect, stout; scales brown, covering rhizome apex and stipe bases. Fronds erect to erect-spreading, pinnate-pinnatifid to bipinnate-pinnatifid, glabrous; stipe and rachis stramineous, scaly; blade ovate-lanceolate to lanceolate; pinnules or ultimate segments crenulate to serrulate, with veins forked, free, not reaching the margins. Sori round, borne on veins; indusium orbicular to reniform, attached at sinus.

A mostly temperate genus of about 150 species. Many species of *Dryopteris* are known for their tendency to form hybrids. These fascinating hybrids, more or less intermediate between their parents and a source of taxonomic confusion, have provided evidence for a proper interpretation of the genus. Cytological and chemotaxonomic studies by Manton and Walker (1953), Walker (1955, 1959, 1960, 1961, 1962a,b, 1969), Britton (1961), Scora and Wagner (1964), Wagner and Wagner (1965, 1966), Tryon and Britton (1966), Wagner, Wagner, and Hagenah (1969), Wagner (1971b), Widen and Britton (1971), Britton and Widen (1974), Widen, Britton, Wagner, and Wagner (1975), and others have contributed to an understanding of relationships within the genus.

Key to the species and hybrids of *Dryopteris* in Arkansas

1. Sori submarginal, near edges of pinnae; blade leathery . . . . 1. *D. marginalis* (p. 104)
1. Sori medial, away from edges of pinnae; blade papery
    2. Fronds bipinnate-pinnatifid; stipe scales ovate . . . . 2. *D. carthusiana* (p. 106)
    2. Fronds pinnate-pinnatifid to bipinnate; stipe scales lanceolate
        3. Pinnae segments serrulate with teeth apiculate; pinnae acuminate . . . . 3. *D. celsa* (p. 108)
        3. Pinna segments crenulate or serrulate with teeth acuminate or acute; pinnae attenuate to apex . . . . 4. *D. X leedsii* (p. 110)

1. *Dryopteris marginalis* (L.) Gray

Polypodium marginale L.
Aspidium marginale (L.) Sw.
Nephrodium marginale (L.) Michx.
Thelypteris marginalis (L.) Nieuw.

COMMON NAME: Marginal Wood Fern

Fronds pinnate-pinnatifid to bipinnate, up to 70 cm long; stipe scales light brown, lanceolate to linear-lanceolate; blade lanceolate, up to 50 cm long and 20 cm wide; pinnae lanceolate to oblong, leathery, attenuate to apex; pinna lobes or pinnules crenulate or serrulate with teeth mostly blunt. Sori submarginal; indusium firm, persisting.

HABITAT: Rich, rocky slopes and ravine woods, exposed or shaded outcrops; Interior Highlands.

RANGE: Eastern North America.

Two luxuriant forms of *Dryopteris marginalis* have been collected in Arkansas. Forma *tripinnatifida* (Clute) Weatherby, which has pinnules that are deeply lobed, has been found at Camp Albert Pike along the Little Missouri River, Montgomery County (*Taylor 1084* SIU). Forma *elegans* (J. Robins.) F.W. Gray, with the pinnules pinnatifid, long and overlapping the pinnules of adjacent pinnae, has been collected from Magnet Cove, Hot Spring County (*Demaree 19033a* NY).

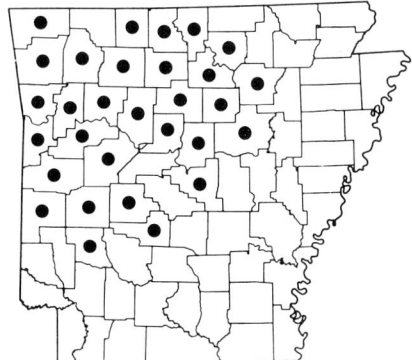

***Dryopteris marginalis* (L.)**

Baxter Co.: *Taylor 2689* (SIU). Benton Co.: *Taylor 1119* (SIU). Boone Co.: *Redfearn 12376* (SMS). Cleburne Co.: *Palmer 6964* (MO). Conway Co.: *Demaree 22792* (MO). Crawford Co.: *Redfearn 21082* (SMS). Faulkner Co.: *Buchholz 950* (UARK). Franklin Co.: *Stephens 10582* (NY). Garland Co.: *Taylor 2195* (SIU). Hot Spring Co.: *Demaree 19033a* (NY). Independence Co.: *D. Moore 450510* (UARK). Izard Co.: *Taylor 2132* (SIU). Johnson Co.: *Redfearn 18920* (SMS). Logan Co.: *Taylor 1039* (SIU). Madison Co.: *Taylor 1999* (SIU). Marion Co.: *D. Moore 41052* (UARK). Montgomery Co.: *Taylor 1085* (SIU). Newton Co.: *Redfearn 23587* (SMS). Perry Co.: *Johnson 481* (HXC). Pike Co.: *Demaree 9486* (SMU). Polk Co.: *Taylor 1060* (SIU). Pope Co.: *Taylor 1212* (SIU). Pulaski Co.: *Demaree 8477* (MO). Searcy Co.: *Spessard 149* (HXC). Scott Co.: *Taylor 271* (SIU). Sebastian Co.: *Palmer 33287* (NY). Stone Co.: *D. Moore 450610* (UARK). Van Buren Co.: *Taylor 2562* (SIU). Washington Co.: *Redfearn 14818* (SMS). White Co.: *Johnson 216* (HXC). Yell Co.: *Taylor 1195* (SIU).

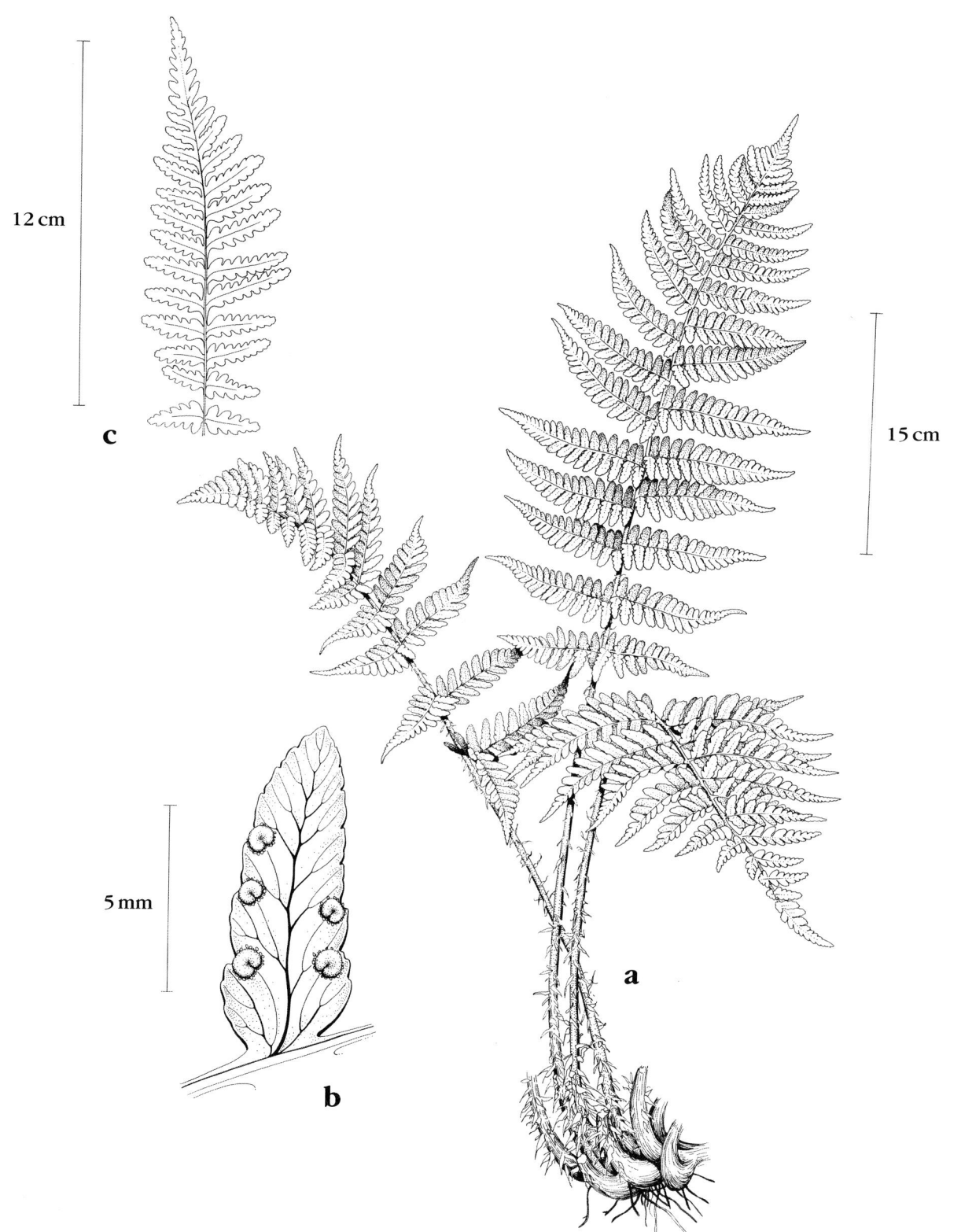

Dryopteris marginalis
a. Habit; b. Lower surface of pinnule with sori. c. Pinna of f. *tripinnatifida*.

2. *Dryopteris carthusiana* (Villars) H. P. Fuchs

Polypodium spinulosum O. F. Muell.
Polypodium carthusianum Villars
Aspidium spinulosum (O. F. Muell.) Sw.
Dryopteris spinulosa (O. F. Muell.) Watt
Dryopteris austriaca var. *spinulosa* (O. F. Muell.) Fiori

COMMON NAME: Spinulose Wood Fern

Fronds bipinnate-pinnatifid, up to 60 cm long; stipe scales light brown, ovate to lanceolate; blade ovate-lanceolate to lanceolate, up to 40 cm long and 20 cm wide; pinnae deltoid or lanceolate to oblong, papery, acuminate; pinnules serrulate with teeth apiculate or spinulose tipped. Sori medial; indusium thin, soon shriveling.

HABITAT: Stone Co.: rich, moist humus on a limestone outcrop sloping toward the entrance to a cave; *Taylor 2894* (SIU).

RANGE: Northern North America.

Lesquereux (1860) reported *Dryopteris carthusiana* from "woods" in Arkansas and, on the basis of that report, this species was included in the lists of Harvey (1881) and Branner and Coville (1891). Buchholz (1924) doubted the presence of *D. carthusiana* in Arkansas since he failed to locate any voucher material. Buchholz and Palmer (1926) listed this species as occurring on the north slope of Magazine Mountain, Logan County, based on a discovery by Dwight Moore in 1924. Attempts to find plants or voucher specimens from this locality have been unsuccessful.

The earliest vouchered collections of Arkansas *D. carthusiana* that have been found were made by Dwight Moore on 7 August 1960, and are from Stone County. The Stone County population consists of about 10 plants which are situated such that air venting from a cave opening provides them with a cool, moist, moderated environment.

Dryopteris carthusiana

Stone Co.: *Taylor 2894* (SIU).

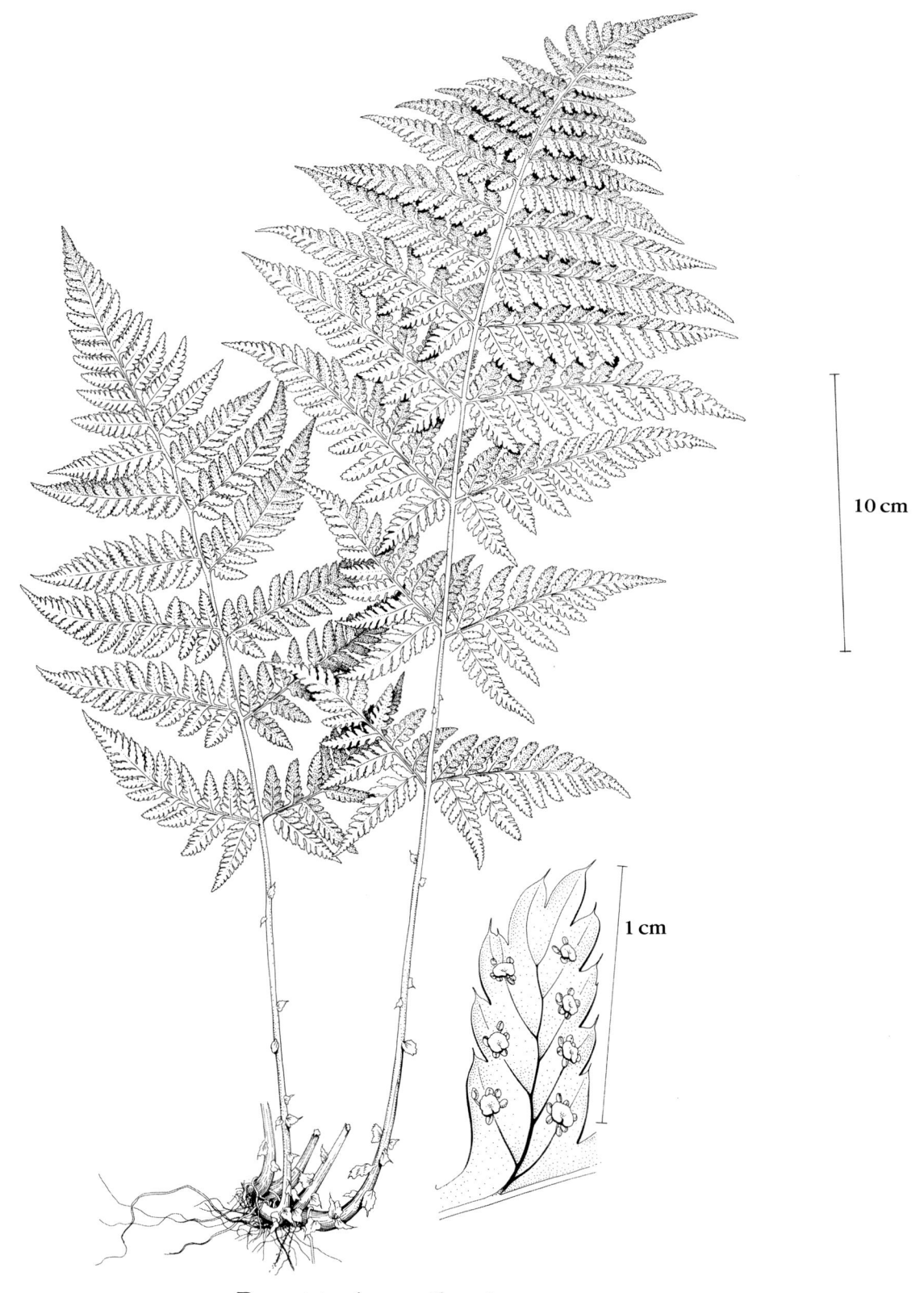

Dryopteris carthusiana
a. Habit; b. Lower surface of pinnule with sori.

3. *Dryopteris celsa* (W. Palmer) Small

Dryopteris goldiana var. *celsa* W. Palmer

COMMON NAME: Log Fern

Fronds pinnate-pinnatifid, up to 1 m long; stipe scales brown, with a dark medial band, lanceolate to linear-lanceolate; blade lanceolate, up to 70 cm long and 25 cm wide; pinnae lanceolate to oblong, thick-papery, acuminate; pinnae segments serrulate with teeth apiculate. Sori medial; indusium thin, soon shriveling.

HABITAT: Moist to wet shaded, rocky humus around springs in rich woods: Lawrence Co.: York Springs, S. of Imboden; *Marshall 9* (US). Montgomery Co.: wet humus near small spring off Hwy 8; *Taylor 2845* (SIU). Polk Co.: valley of Big Fork Creek on north side of Missouri Mountain; *D. Moore 520840* (MO).

RANGE: Eastern United States.

The first reported collection of *D. celsa* in Arkansas was made on 24 May 1925 by B. C. Marshall, who sent material to William Maxon in Washington, D. C. for identification.

Cytological evidence indicates that *D. celsa,* a tetraploid, originated as a hybrid between the diploids *D. goldiana* and *D. ludoviciana* followed by chromosome doubling (Walker, 1962a). Neither of these putative parents is known from Arkansas. *D. goldiana* ranges to the north and east of Arkansas and has been found in southeastern Missouri, while *D. ludoviciana,* a Coastal Plain species, occurs as far west as southeast Louisiana. Wagner and Wagner (1965), Wagner, Wagner, and Hagenah (1969), Thomas, Wagner, and Mesler (1973), and others have studied the occurrence and distribution of *D. celsa.* From these studies, it appears that the parent species could have been pushed into contact during glacial advance to provide the opportunity for hybridization. After retreat of the glaciers the ranges of the parents separated.

Dryopteris celsa

Lawrence Co.: *Marshall 9* (US). Montgomery Co.: *Taylor 2845* (SIU). Polk Co.: *D. Moore 520840* (MO).

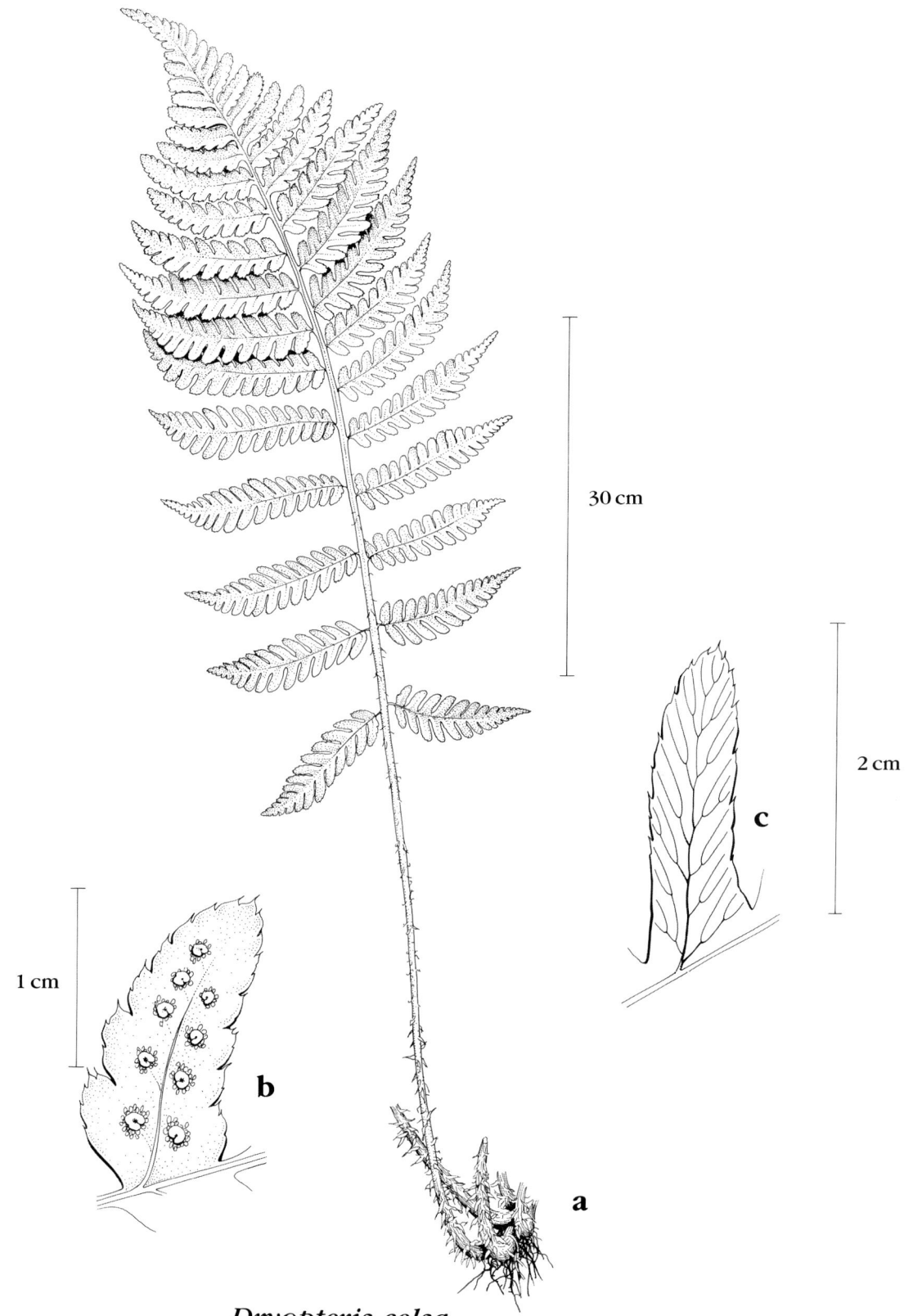

Dryopteris celsa
a. Habit; b. Lower surface of pinna lobe with sori; c. Pinna lobe.

4. *Dryopteris* X *leedsii* Wherry

Dryopteris celsa X *D. marginalis*

COMMON NAME: Leeds' Wood Fern

Fronds pinnate-pinnatifid to bipinnate, up to 1 m or more long; stipe scales brown, with a dark medial band, lanceolate to linear-lanceolate; blade lanceolate, up to 1 m long and 30 cm wide; pinnae lanceolate to oblong, thick-papery, attenuate to apex; pinna lobes or pinnules crenulate or serrulate with teeth acuminate or acute. Sori medial; indusium firm but shriveling.

HABITAT: Van Buren Co.: moist, wooded, rocky slope along the Middle Fork of the Little Red River near Shirley; *Taylor 2597* (SIU).

RANGE: Eastern United States, within the sympatric range of its putative parents *Dryopteris celsa* and *D. marginalis*.

Dryopteris X *leedsii* was originally found in Arkansas by E. J. Palmer near Shirley on 30 March 1928. Initially, it was identified as *Dryopteris cristata* (L.) Gray. Shortly after its discovery, the fern attracted considerable attention from a number of individuals, including J. K. Small, William Maxon, and Edgar Wherry. The main source of interest lay in the possibility that the plant might represent a new taxon. Later, this was, in fact, shown to be the case.

Additional collections of this plant from the Shirley location by Delzie Demaree on 4 November 1932, and by Dwight Moore on 3 November 1935, were later identified as *D. celsa* X ? and *D. celsa* X *marginalis* by F. W. Crane and as *D. separabilis* by J. K. Small. Apparently, the exact locality was lost to botanists after 1935, for several later attempts to relocate the plants were unsuccessful. On 18 August 1974, *D.* X *leedsii* was rediscovered at the Shirley locality (Wagner and Taylor, 1976).

D. X *leedsii* represents a hybrid between *D. celsa* and *D. marginalis* and cytogenetically it is a sterile triploid (Wagner and Wagner, 1966). This rare plant is known from only six localities in New York, Pennsylvania, Maryland, and Arkansas.

The Arkansas population of *D.* X *leedsii* is interesting for several reasons: first, because it is over 800 miles disjunct from the other known stations; second, because one of the parents, *D. celsa*, is missing at the locality; and third, because this same colony apparently has persisted on a rocky, wooded slope near Shirley for over half a century.

Dryopteris X leedsii

Van Buren Co.: *Taylor 2597* (SIU).

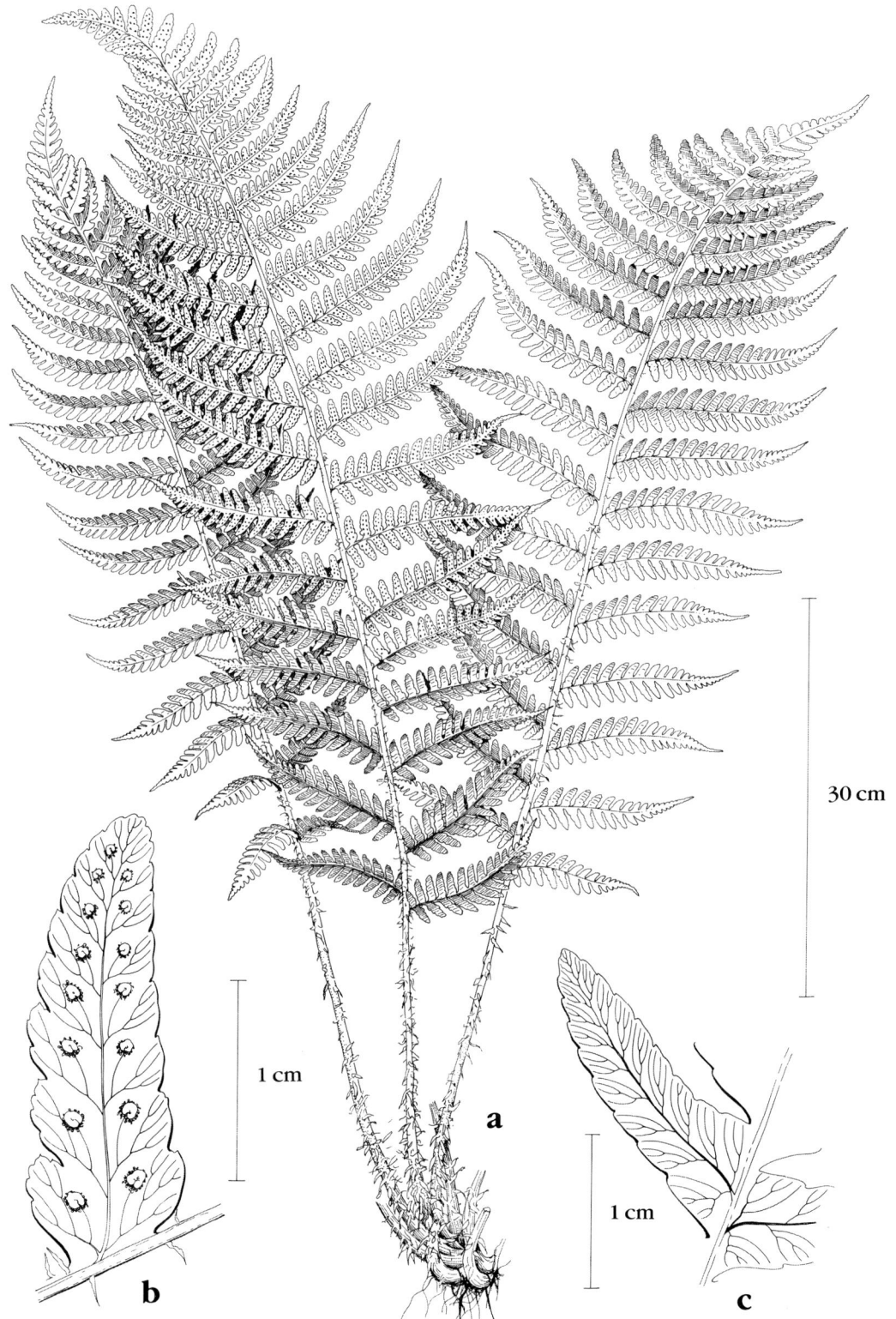

Dryopteris X *leedsii*
a. Habit; b. Lower surface of pinnule with sori; c. Portion of pinna.

Equisetum L. Horsetails, Scouring Rushes

Rhizome subterranean, long-creeping to erect. Aerial stems annual or perennial, erect, solitary to fastigiate, tubular, simple or branched, jointed, fluted; internodes in transection with a large central pith cavity, vallecular canals under each groove alternating with smaller carinal canals below each ridge, and cortical sclerenchyma extending some distance to the carinal canal; nodes each bearing a verticil of small, subulate leaves; leaves laterally connate below and forming a cylindrical leaf sheath; leaf apices persistent or deciduous, reddish brown to black, scarious margined, attenuate to apex. Branches, if present, normally verticillate from the nodes, slender, perforating the leaf sheath. Sporangiophores aggregated in a terminal, ovoid to cylindrical strobilus, each suspending 5-6 ovoid sporangia on the adaxial surface; sporangia dehiscing longitudinally on the side toward the sporangiophore axis; homosporous. Spores green, globose, each bearing 4 hygroscopic, linear-spatulate elaters.

A mainly temperate genus of 15 species. The most recent monographic studies on the genus are by Hauke (1963, 1979).

Key to the species and hybrids of *Equisetum* in Arkansas

1. Green aerial stems profusely branched; aerial stems dimorphic, with unbranched, light brown to grayish orange fertile stems appearing in early spring and soon withering .... 1. *E. arvense* (p. 114)
1. Green aerial stems unbranched except when old or injured; stems alike
    2. Leaf sheaths about as long as wide; internodes in transection show cortical sclerenchyma extending more than two-thirds the distance to the carinal canal; sporangia discharging numerous spores .... 2. *E. hyemale* (p. 116)
    2. Leaf sheaths longer than wide; internodes in transection show cortical sclerenchyma extending less than two-thirds the distance to the carinal canal
        3. Cones blunt at apex, discharging globose, green spores; leaf sheaths uniformly green .... 3. *E. laevigatum* (p. 118)
        3. Cones apiculate; sporangia containing aborted spores; leaf sheaths often black girdled on lower portion of stem . 4. *E. X ferrissii* (p. 120)

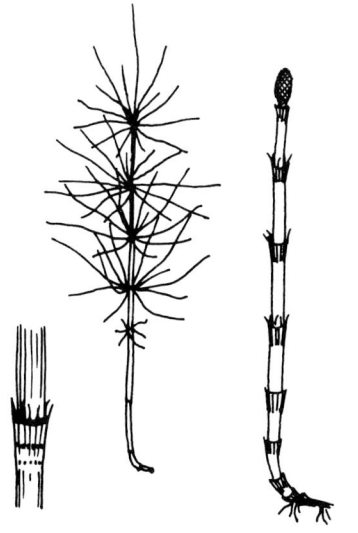

1. *Equisetum arvense* L.

COMMON NAME: Field Horsetail

Aerial stems annual, dimorphic. Sterile stems profusely branched, up to 60 cm tall and 4 mm in diam. Internodes in transection show cortical sclerenchyma usually extending less than one-fifth the distance to the carinal canal and a pith cavity less than one-half the diameter of the stem; leaf sheaths grayish green to dark brown or black toward rim, dark brown to black-girdled toward base, up to 1 cm long and 6 mm wide at rim, longer than wide; leaf apices persistent. Branches numerous at upper internodes, spreading, verticillate, 3-4 angled, up to 25 cm long and 1.2 mm in diam. Fertile stems appearing in early spring and soon withering, erect, light brown to grayish orange, unbranched, up to 25 cm long and 7 mm in diam.; leaf sheaths dark brown to black above, grayish yellow below, up to 2 cm long and 1.3 cm wide at apex, longer than wide. Strobilus up to 3.5 cm long, obtuse; sporangia discharging numerous spores.

HABITAT: Sandy or gravelly stream banks and roadsides.

RANGE: Widespread in North America, becoming rare south; Europe, Asia.

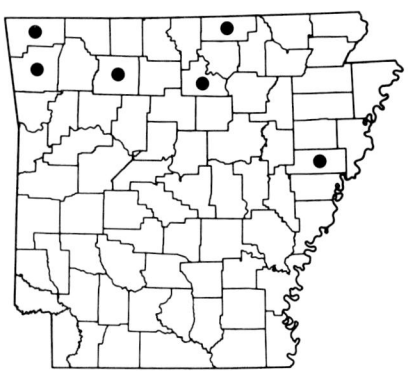

Equisetum arvense

Benton Co.: *D. Moore s.n.* (UARK). Fulton Co.: *Demaree 26821* (SMU). Newton Co.: *Smith 3180* (UARK). St. Francis Co.: *Demaree 22154* (NY). Stone Co.: *D. Moore 450615* (UARK). Washington Co.: *D. Moore 490105* (UARK).

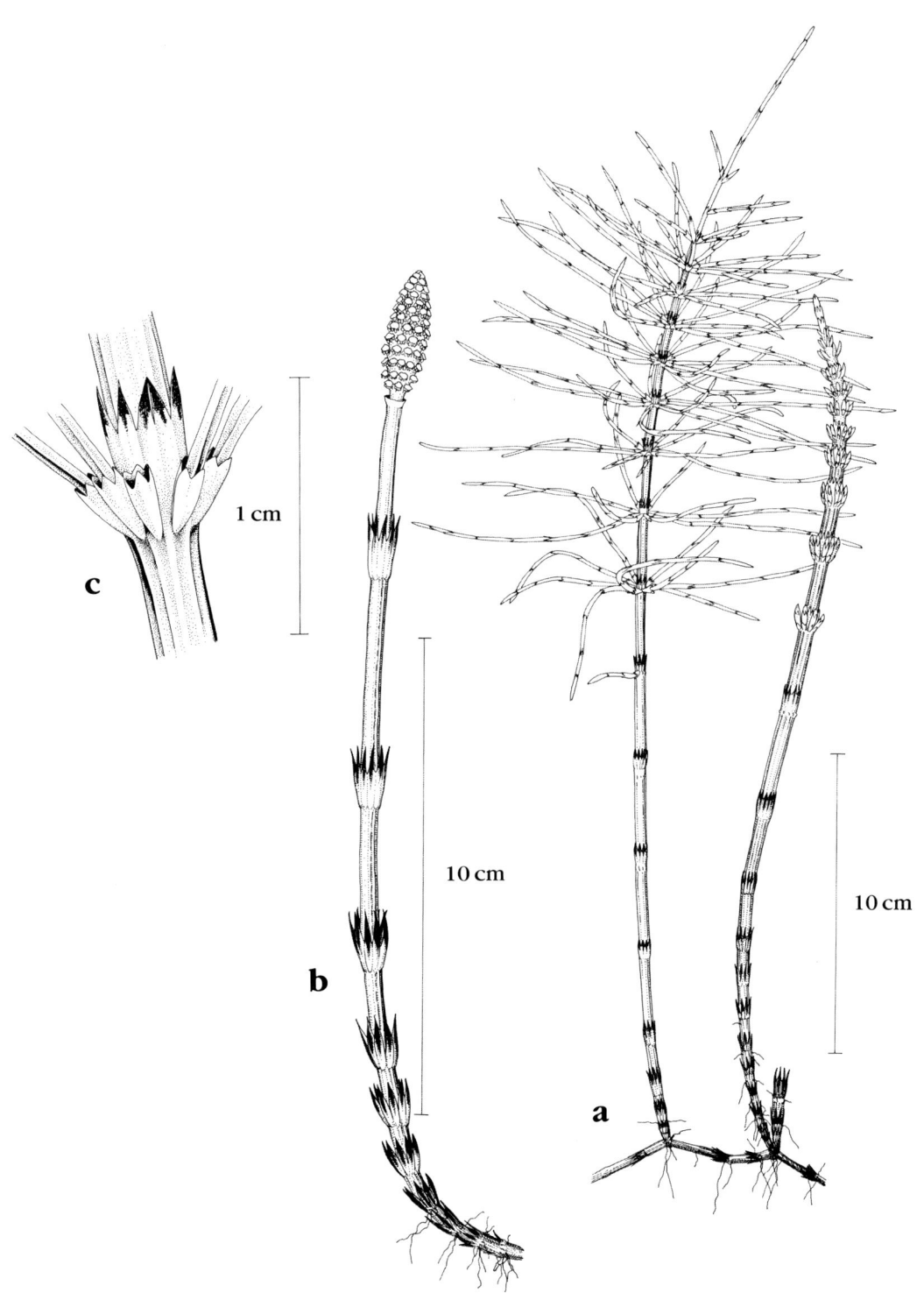

Equisetum arvense
a. Habit of sterile stems; b. Habit of fertile stems; c. Stem node.

2. *Equisetum hyemale* L. var. *affine* (Engelm.) A. A. Eat.

Equisetum praealtum Raf.
Equisetum robustum Engelm.
Equisetum hiemale var. *robustum* (A. Br.) A. A. Eat.
Equisetum hyemale var. *elatum* (Engelm.) Morton
Equisetum hyemale var. *pseudohyemale* (Farw.) Morton

COMMON NAME: Scouring Rush

Aerial stems evergreen, alike, unbranched except when old or injured, scabrid, to 3 m tall and 1.8 cm in diam.; internodes in transection show cortical sclerenchyma extending two-thirds to three-fourths the distance to the carinal canal and a pith cavity two-thirds or more the diameter of the stem; leaf sheaths grayish green to ash-gray, black rimmed, becoming medially black-girdled with age, up to 1.7 cm long and 2 cm wide at rim, about as long as wide; leaf apices mostly persistent. Strobilus up to 2.5 cm long, apiculate; sporangia discharging numerous spores.

HABITAT: Sandy or gravelly stream banks, roadside ditches, fence rows, edges of lakes, or generally disturbed, moist soil.

RANGE: Widespread in North America, south to Central America, Europe, Asia.

Due to the variability of *Equisetum hyemale* in America, this species has often been split into several taxa based on overall size of the plant, persistence of leaf apices, and form of the stem ridges. Arkansas material frequently has been considered to be either *E. praealtum* (*E. hyemale* var. *robustum or var. elatum*), a relatively large plant with tardily deciduous or persistent leaf apices, or *E. hyemale* var. *pseudohyemale* (or var. *affine*), a medium sized plant with promptly deciduous leaf apices. Hauke (1963) analyzed variation in American *E. hyemale* and found that each of the above three characters varies clinally and independently to the extent that he considers all American representatives to be *E. hyemale* var. *affine*. Study of Arkansas collections supports Hauke's conclusion.

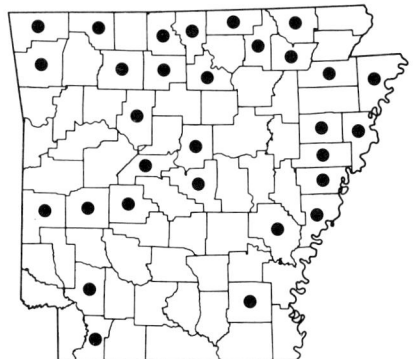

Equisetum hyemale var. *affine* (Engelm.) A. A. Eat.

Arkansas Co.: *D. Moore 480644* (UARK). Baxter Co.: *Demaree 23551* (SMU). Benton Co.: *Demaree 4631* (UARK). Carroll Co.: *Leonard 59* (UARK). Craighead Co.: *Demaree 30294* (PH). Cross Co.: *Demaree 3759* (UARK). Drew Co.: *D. Moore s.n.* (UARK). Faulkner Co.: *Haas 1503* (UCA). Fulton Co.: *D. Moore 470255* (UARK). Garland Co.: *Taylor 2559* (SIU). Hempstead Co.: *Buchholz 438* (UARK). Lafayette Co.: *Loche s.n.* (UARK). Lawrence Co.: *Carter 352* (UARK). Lee Co.: *Taylor 1188* (SIU). Marion Co.: *D. Moore 480731* (UARK). Mississippi Co.: *Bowers s.n.* (MEM). Montgomery Co.: *Taylor 2610* (SIU). Newton Co.: *D. Moore 32463* (UARK). Perry Co.: *Johnson 62* (HXC). Phillips Co.: *Taylor 1190* (SIU). Polk Co.: *McWilliam s.n.* (UARK). Pope Co.: *Tucker s.n.* (APCR). Pulaski Co: *Demaree 8567* (NY). Randolph Co.: *Riggs s.n.* (UARK). St. Francis Co.: *Demaree 7230* (UARK). Searcy Co.: *Clark 104* (HXC). Sharp Co.: *Demaree 26448* (SMU). Stone Co.: *Taylor 2900* (SIU). Washington Co.: *D. Moore 450851* (UARK).

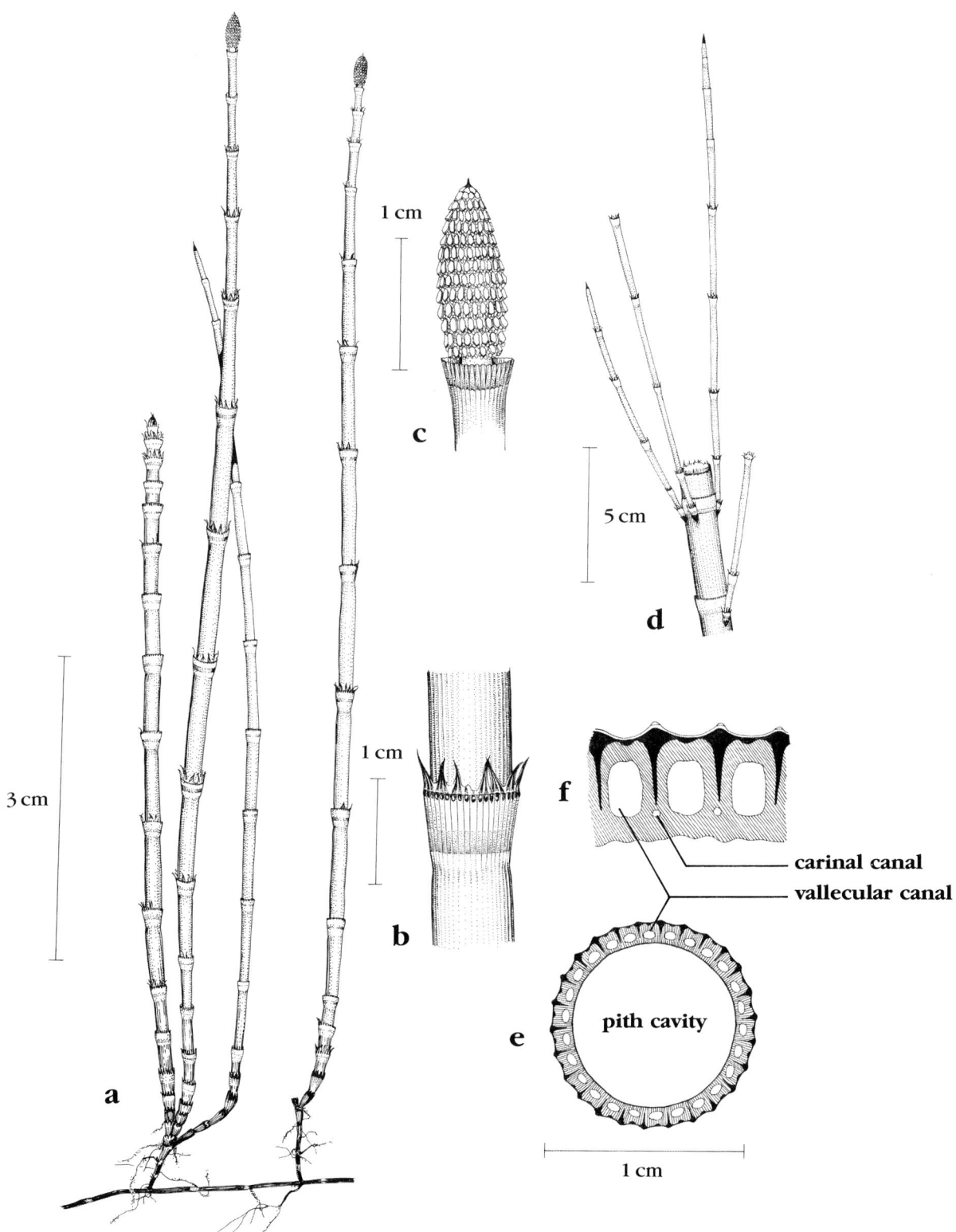

Equisetum hyemale* var. *affine
a. Habit; b. Leaf sheath; c. Strobilus; d. Injured stem with branches; e. Transection of stem; f. Transection of stem with cortical sclerenchyma in black.

3. *Equisetum laevigatum* A. Br.

COMMON NAME: Smooth Scouring Rush

Aerial stems annual, alike, unbranched except when old or injured, smooth, up to 1.5 m tall and 7 mm in diam.; internodes in transection show cortical sclerenchyma extending to one-third the distance to the carinal canal and a pith cavity three-fourths or more the diameter of the stem; leaf sheaths grayish green, black rimmed, up to 1.5 cm long and 0.9 mm wide at rim, longer than wide; leaf apices soon deciduous. Strobilus up to 2 cm long, blunt at apex; sporangia discharging numerous spores.

HABITAT: Sebastian Co.: grassy opening on the Arkansas River flood plain; *Peck 812-357* (LRU).

RANGE: Western and north central North America.

This species was first collected in Arkansas by James Peck who discovered a small colony of these plants near the Arkansas River on 6 September 1982.

Equisetum laevigatum

Sebastian Co.: *Peck 812-357* (LRU).

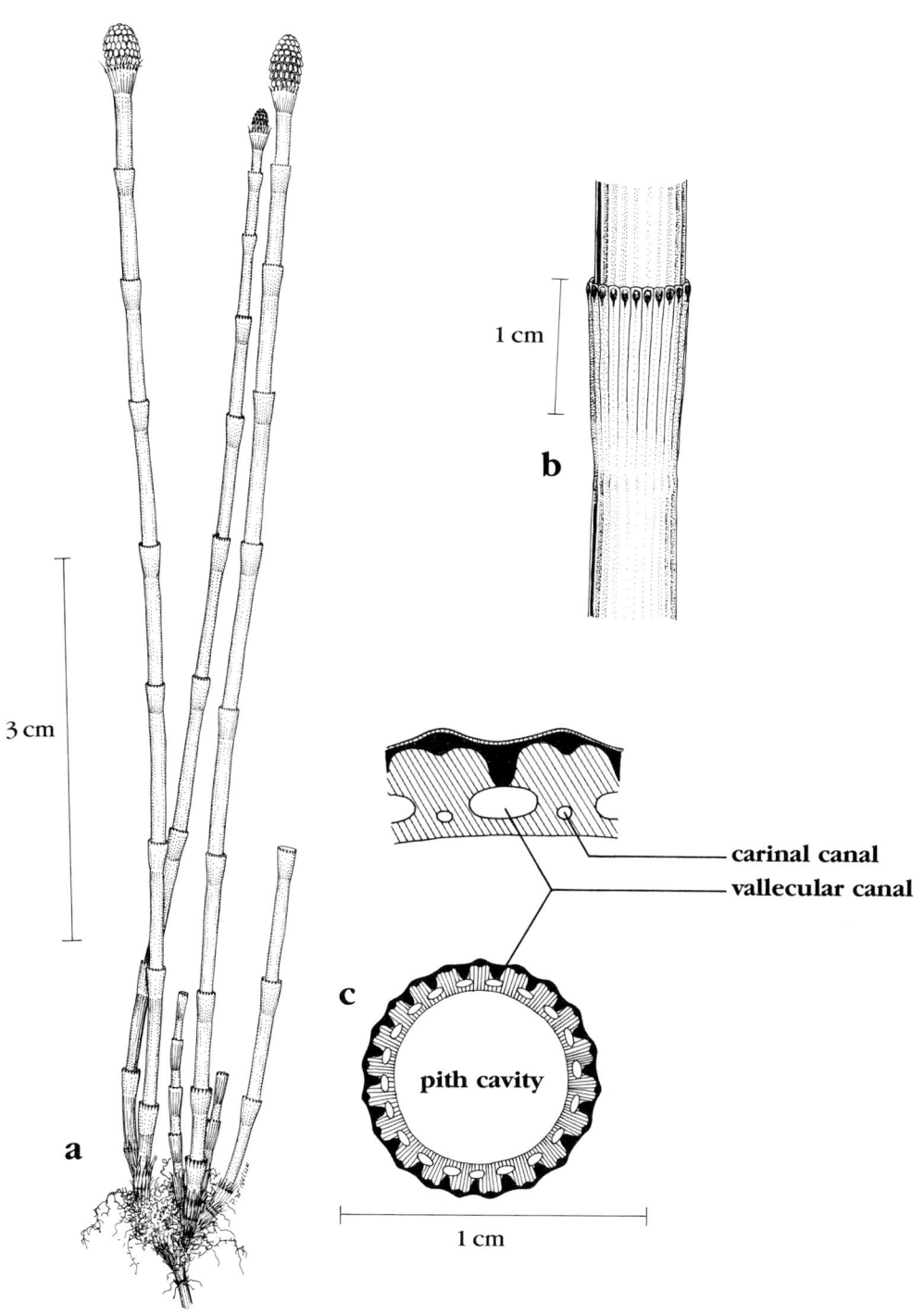

Equisetum laevigatum
a. Habit; b. Leaf sheath; c. Transection of stem; d. Transection of stem with cortical sclerenchyma in black.

4. *Equisetum* X *ferrissii* Clute

Equisetum laevigatum var. *elatum* Engelm.
Equisetum hiemale var. *intermedium* A. A. Eat.
Equisetum laevigatum Schaffner
Equisetum hyemale var. *affine* X *E. laevigatum*

COMMON NAME: Ferriss' Scouring Rush

Aerial stems partly evergreen, alike, unbranched except when old or injured, smooth to scabrid, up to 1.5 m tall and 1 cm in diam.; internodes in transection show cortical sclerenchyma extending one-third to two-thirds the distance to the carinal canal and a pith cavity three-fourths or more the diameter of the stem; leaf sheaths grayish green, black rimmed, lower ones becoming medially black-girdled with age, up to 1.5 cm long and 1.2 cm wide at rim, longer than wide; leaf apices mostly deciduous. Strobilus up to 2 cm long, apiculate; sporangia containing aborted spores.

HABITAT: Moist, sandy or calcareous soils along stream banks, railroad tracks, and roadsides.

RANGE: Widely scattered in northern and western US, southern Canada and northern Mexico.

Until Hauke's studies, most Arkansas collections of *Equisetum* X *ferrissii* were passing for *E. laevigatum*. *E.* X *ferrissii* approaches complete intermediacy between its putative parents and is often misidentified as either *E. hyemale* or *E. laevigatum*.

While the absence of spore discharge is a distinctive character for *E.* X *ferrissii*, to verify identification it is usually necessary to make transections of the stem internode and examine them for distribution of cortical sclerenchyma.

Transections can be easily made as follows. An approximately 5 mm² piece of stem tissue is removed from the internode region with a razor blade. This tissue is placed on a glass slide and soaked with water for a few minutes until soft. Then, with the epidermis side down, thin sections are cut off one end using a sharp razor blade. Sections are best studied at about 100X (Richard Hauke, personal communication).

In transection, the cortical sclerenchyma appears as aggregations of hyaline, thick-walled cells extending some distance from the epidermis toward the carinal canals. This distance will distinguish *E.* X *ferrissii*, *E. hyemale* var. *affine*, and *E. laevigatum*. In *E. hyemale* var. *affine* the cortical sclerenchyma generally extends two-thirds to three-fourths the distance to the carinal canal, in *E. laevigatum* usually less than one-third this distance, and in *E.* X *ferrissii* one-third to two-thirds the distance.

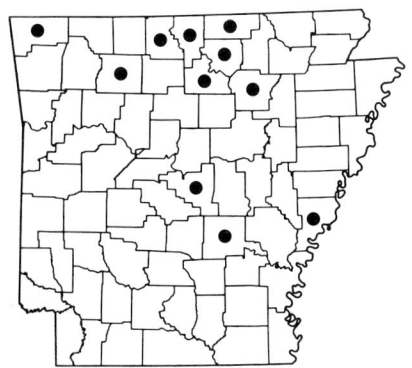

Equisetum X *ferrissii*

Baxter Co.: *D. Moore 450742* (UARK). Benton Co.: *D. Moore 400255* (UARK). Fulton Co.: *D. Moore 330167* (UARK). Independence Co.: *Thomas 9056* (NLU). Izard Co.: *Taylor 1272* (SIU). Jefferson Co.: *Locke 978* (UARK). Marion Co.: *D. Moore 480731* (UARK). Newton Co.: *D. Moore 650* (UARK). Phillips Co.: *Demaree 15219* (SMU). Pulaski Co.: *Merrill 513* (UARK). Stone Co.: *D. Moore 451190* (UARK).

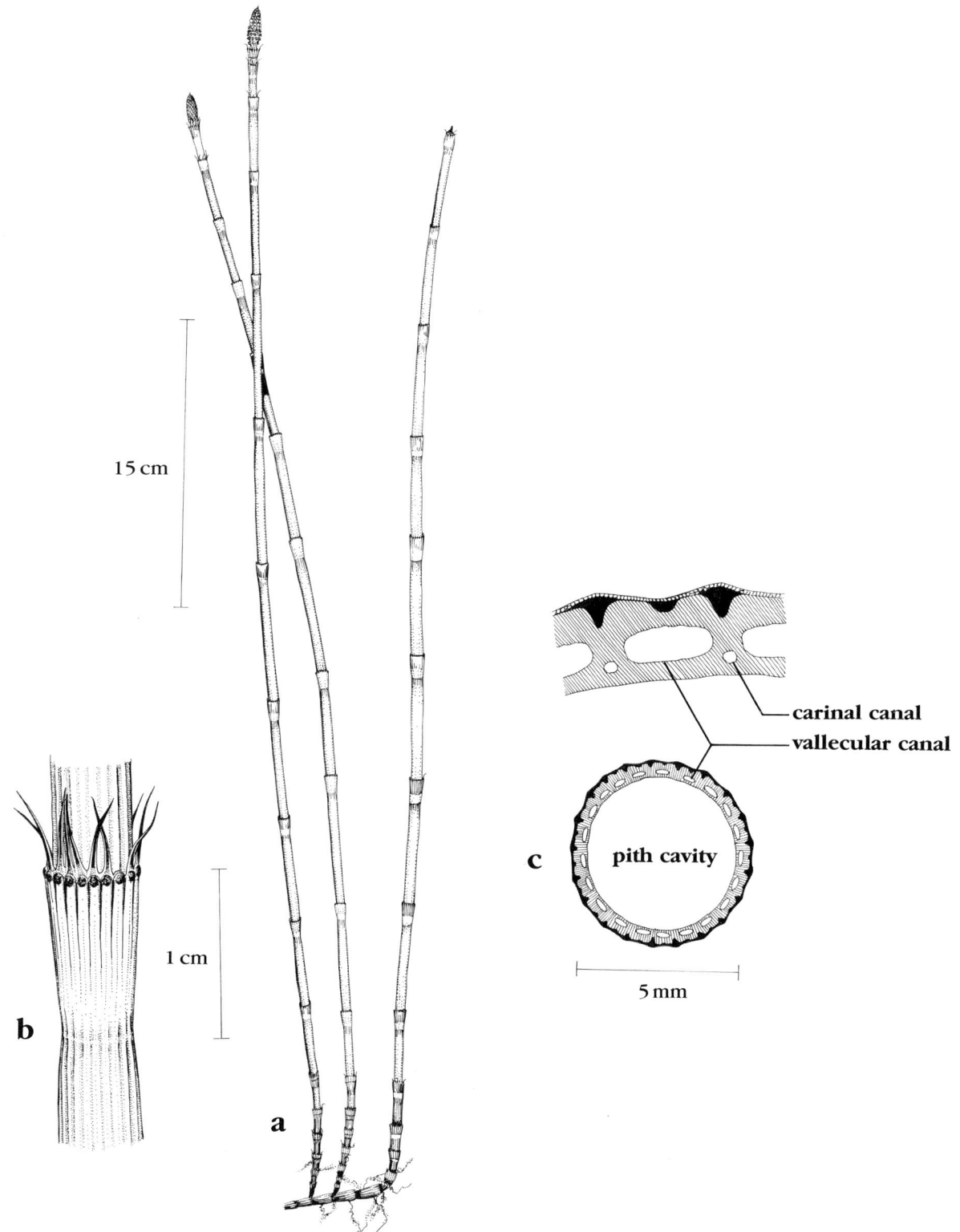

Equisetum* X *ferrissii
a. Habait; b. Leaf sheath; c. Transection of stem; d. Transection of stem with cortical sclerenchyma in black

Isoetes L. Quillworts

Corm two-lobed, bearing a cluster of spirally arranged linear leaves or sporophylls above, and simple or dichotomously branched roots arising across each lobe from central groove below. Sporophylls deciduous, ligulate, simple, erect-spreading, slender, four-chambered above, flattened and expanded toward base; ligule deltoid, about 1 mm long; velum narrow to broad. Sporangia adaxial, basal, solitary, oblong, heterosporous; megaspores numerous in megasporangium, white, tetrahedral-globose; microspores numerous in microsporangium, ash gray or olive, tetrahedral-ovoid.

A cosmopolitan genus of about 150 species. *Isoetes* has been monographed by Engelmann (1882) and by Pfeiffer (1922). Reed (1965) and Boom (1979, 1982) have studied the genus in the southeastern United States.

The grass-like or rush-like habit of *Isoetes* makes it difficult to discern from surrounding vegetation and it is easily overlooked in the field. In addition, the Arkansas species are usually only found in the spring or early summer because the warmer and drier conditions of summer cause the sporophylls to wither.

Careful attention to habitat and megaspore size will usually serve to distinguish the two known Arkansas species. However, the presence of somewhat intermediate forms may confuse identification. Intermediate material has caused some investigators to question the recognition of two species. Examination of the spores using the scanning electron microscope has revealed that the spore surfaces of *Isoetes melanopoda* consistently differ from those of *I. butleri* (Taylor, Mohlenbrock, and Murphy, 1975). *Isoetes melanopoda* possesses echinate megaspores and microspores while *I. butleri* has arachnoid megaspores and tuberculate microspores. These differences support maintaining *I. melanopoda* and *I. butleri* as separate species.

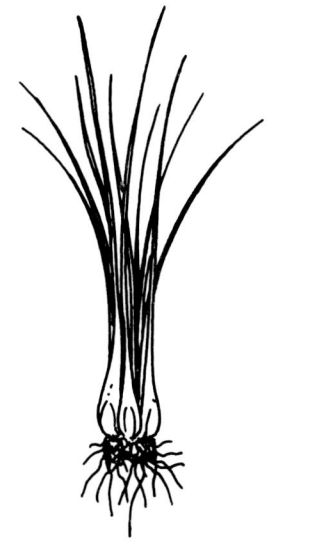

Key to the species of *Isoetes* in Arkansas

1. Plants of noncalcareous soils; megaspores 280-480 µm in diam., echinate; microspores ash gray, echinate; sporangium brown-punctate .... 1. *I. melanopoda* (p. 124)
1. Plants of calcareous soils; megaspores 480-640 µm in diam., arachnoid; microspores olive, tuberculate; sporangium hyaline or faintly brown-lineolate .... 2. *I. butleri* (p. 126)

1. *Isoetes melanopoda* Gay & Dur.

COMMON NAME: Black-based Quillwort

Plants mostly monoecious. Sporophylls pale or lustrous black toward base, up to 40 cm long and 1.5 mm wide at middle; ligule deltoid-subulate; velum narrow to broad, covering up to one-half of the sporangium. Sporangia brown-punctate, up to 1.5 cm long; megaspores 280-480 µm in diam., echinate; microspores ash gray, 20-30 µm long, echinate.

HABITAT: Seasonally moist to wet woods, meadows, fields, margins of ponds, roadside ditches, and vernally saturated soil pockets on sandstone, shale, or igneous rock outcrops.

RANGE: Central United States, locally east to New Jersey.

The pale-based form, *Isoetes melanopoda* f. *pallida* (Engelm.) Clute, is often found growing with the typical black-based form.

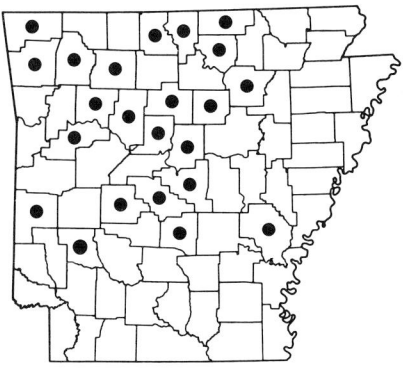

Isoetes melanopoda

Arkansas Co.: *D. Moore 510225* (UARK). Baxter Co.: *J. Moore 5677* (UCA). Benton Co.: *D. Moore 400259* (UARK). Cleburne Co.: *Taylor 1011* (SIU). Conway Co.: *Demaree 23119* (MO). Faulkner Co.: *Taylor 2006* (SIU). Fulton Co.: *D. Moore 330226* (UARK). Garland Co.: *Palmer 24921* (UARK). Grant Co.: *Locke 2513* (UARK). Independence Co.: *D. Moore 450503* (APCR). Izard Co.: *Taylor 2117* (SIU). Johnson Co.: *D. Moore 380015* (UARK). Logan Co.: *Taylor 1043* (SIU). Madison Co.: *D. Moore 32320* (UARK). Marion Co.: *D. Moore 390302* (UARK). Newton Co.: *D. Moore 301818* (UARK). Pike Co.: *Taylor 4669* (SIU). Polk Co.: *J. Moore 3147* (UCA). Pope Co.: *Taylor 2703* (SIU). Pulaski Co.: *Demaree 18801* (MO). Saline Co.: *D. Moore 480157* (UARK). Van Buren Co.: *Johnson 296* (HXC). Washington Co.: *Palmer 24755* (MO).

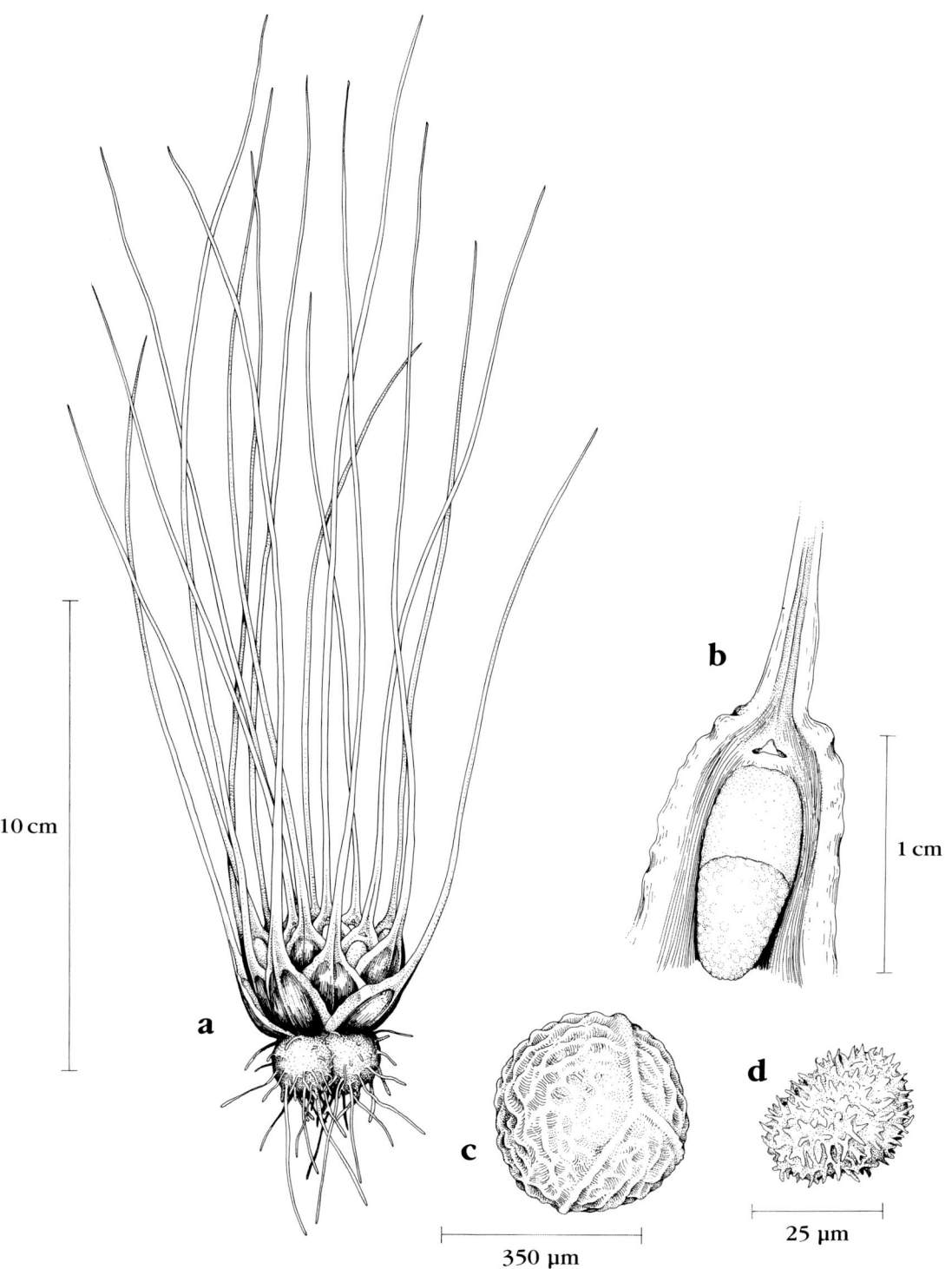

Isoetes melanopoda
a. Habit; b. Adaxial side of sporophyll base with megasporangium; c. Megaspore; d. Microspore.

2. *Isoetes butleri* Engelm.

COMMON NAME: Butler's Quillwort

Plants mostly dioecious. Sporophylls pale or brown toward base, up to 20 cm long and 0.9 mm wide at middle; ligule elongate, cordate; velum very narrow. Sporangia hyaline or faintly brown-lineolate, up to 7 mm long; megaspores 480-640 µm in diam., arachnoid; microspores olive, 27-37 µm long, tuberculate.

HABITAT: Seasonally moist to wet calcareous soils of limestone glades and dolomite, calcareous shale, or chalk outcrops.

RANGE: Uplands of south central and southeastern U.S.

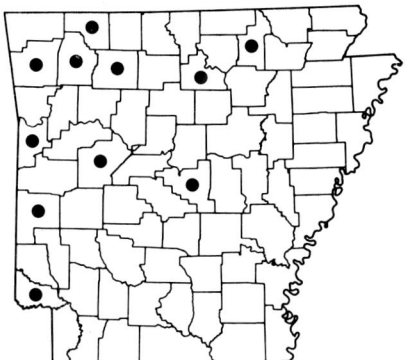

Isoetes butleri

Carroll Co.: *Bush 1350* (MO). Little River Co.: *D. Moore 50040* (UARK). Madison Co.: *Haas 1519* (UCA). Newton Co.: *Taylor 1228* (SIU). Polk Co.: *J. Moore 3147* (UCA). Pulaski Co.: *Harper 17* (PH). Sebastian Co.: *D. Moore 490016* (UARK). Sharp Co.: *Hartsoe 333* (SMU). Stone Co.: *D. Moore 470698* (UARK). Washington Co.: *D. Moore 531861* (UARK). Yell Co.: *Buchholz s.n.* (UARK).

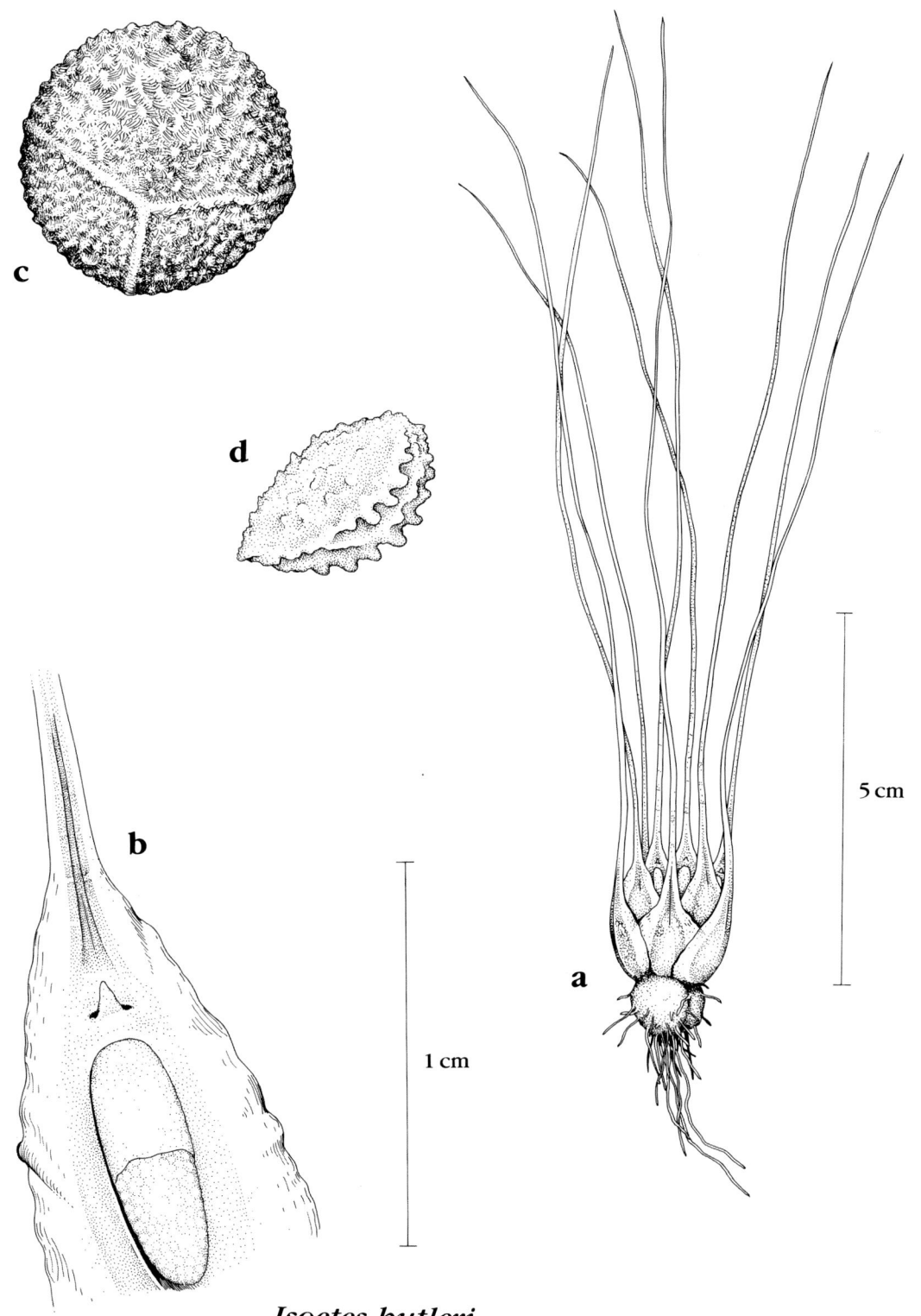

Isoetes butleri
a. Habit; b. Adaxial side of sporophyll base with megasporangium; c. Megaspore; d. Microspore.

Lorinseria J. Smith Net-veined Chain Fern

The genus *Lorinseria* includes only the following species.

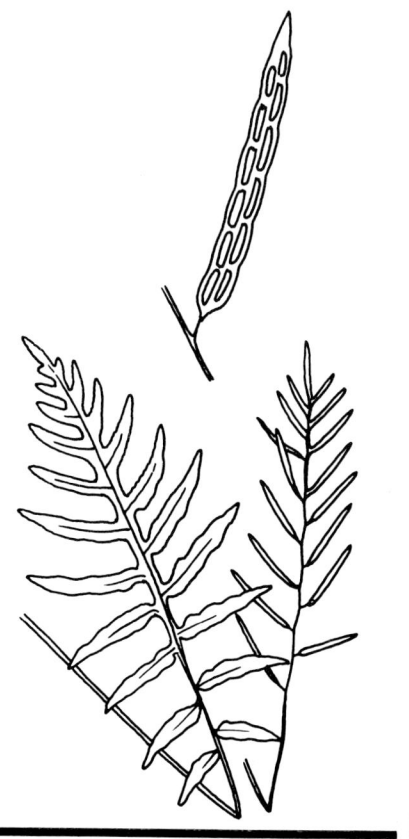

1. *Lorinseria areolata* (L.) Pres.

Acrostichum areolatum L.
Woodwardia angustifolia J. Smith
Woodwardia areolata (L.) Moore

COMMON NAME: Net-veined Chain Fern

Rhizome long-creeping; scales deltoid-ovate to lanceolate. Fronds deciduous, deeply pinnatifid to pinnate, dimorphic; sterile fronds erect-spreading, up to 60 cm long; stipe reddish brown to stramineous; blade deltoid-ovate to lanceolate, up to 40 cm long and 25 cm wide; veins reticulate, forming several series of linear to oblong areoles along midveins; rachis green to stramineous; blade divisions alternate, linear-lanceolate to oblong-lanceolate, serrulate; fertile fronds erect, usually longer than the sterile fronds, up to 70 cm tall; stipe and rachis lustrous purplish red to reddish brown; blade ovate-oblong, up to 30 cm long and 20 cm wide, leathery; pinnae or blade divisions spreading, linear. Sori linear to elongate, borne on veins bordering outer edge of areoles; indusium firm, persistent, attached by its outer margin, opening toward midvein.

HABITAT: Moist to wet woods, along streams, marshy areas, roadside ditches, occasionally on sandstone outcrops; primarily Ouachita Mountains and West Gulf Coastal Plain.

RANGE: Eastern North America.

A frond of *Lorinseria areolata* collected in Pike County by Delzie Demaree (*Demaree 9785* HXC) has the blade abnormally expanded so that it is more or less intermediate between a fertile and sterile frond. This intermediate condition has been described as *f. obtusilobata* by Waters (1903, p. 128).

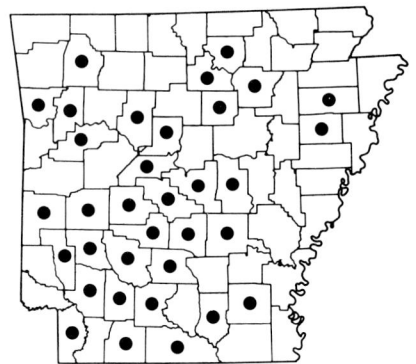

Lorinseria areolata (L.)

Bradley Co.: *Demaree 18381* (MO). Cleburne Co.: *Johnson 436* (HXC). Clark Co.: *Taylor 2180* (SIU). Columbia Co.: *Taylor 1170* (SIU). Conway Co.: *Culwell 3328* (UCA). Crawford Co.: *D. Moore 66121* (APCR). Cross Co.: *Richards 3963* (ARKSU). Dallas Co.: *Taylor 2733* (SIU). Drew Co.: *D. Moore 420045* (UARK). Franklin Co.: *Barber 1026* (UARK). Garland Co.: *Taylor 2556* (SIU). Grant Co.: *Demaree 57196* (SIU). Hempstead Co.: *Taylor 1176* (SIU). Hot Spring Co.: *D. Moore 440088* (UARK). Howard Co.: *McSwain 43 E128* (UARK). Independence Co.: *Johnson 302* (HXC). Izard Co.: *Demaree 22436* (MO). Jefferson Co.: *Demaree 24294* (SMU). Logan Co.: *D. Moore 510073* (UARK). Lonoke Co.: *Clark 662* (HXC). Madison Co.: *Taylor 4274* (SIU). Miller Co.: *Taylor 1908* (SIU). Montgomery Co.: *Taylor 1079* (SIU). Nevada Co.: *Pule 587* (UARK). Ouachita Co.: *D. Moore 490668* (UARK). Perry Co. *J. Moore 6603* (UCA). Pike Co.: *Taylor 2910* (SIU). Poinsett Co.: *Pyle 587* (UARK). Polk Co.: *Taylor 2552* (SIU). Pope Co.: *Tucker 16079* (APCR). Pulaski Co.: *Demaree 8478* (SMU). Saline Co.: *Haas 1435* (UCA). Stone Co.: *Tucker 3581* (APCR). Union Co.: *Demaree 19408* (SMU). Yell Co.: *Taylor 4367* (SIU).

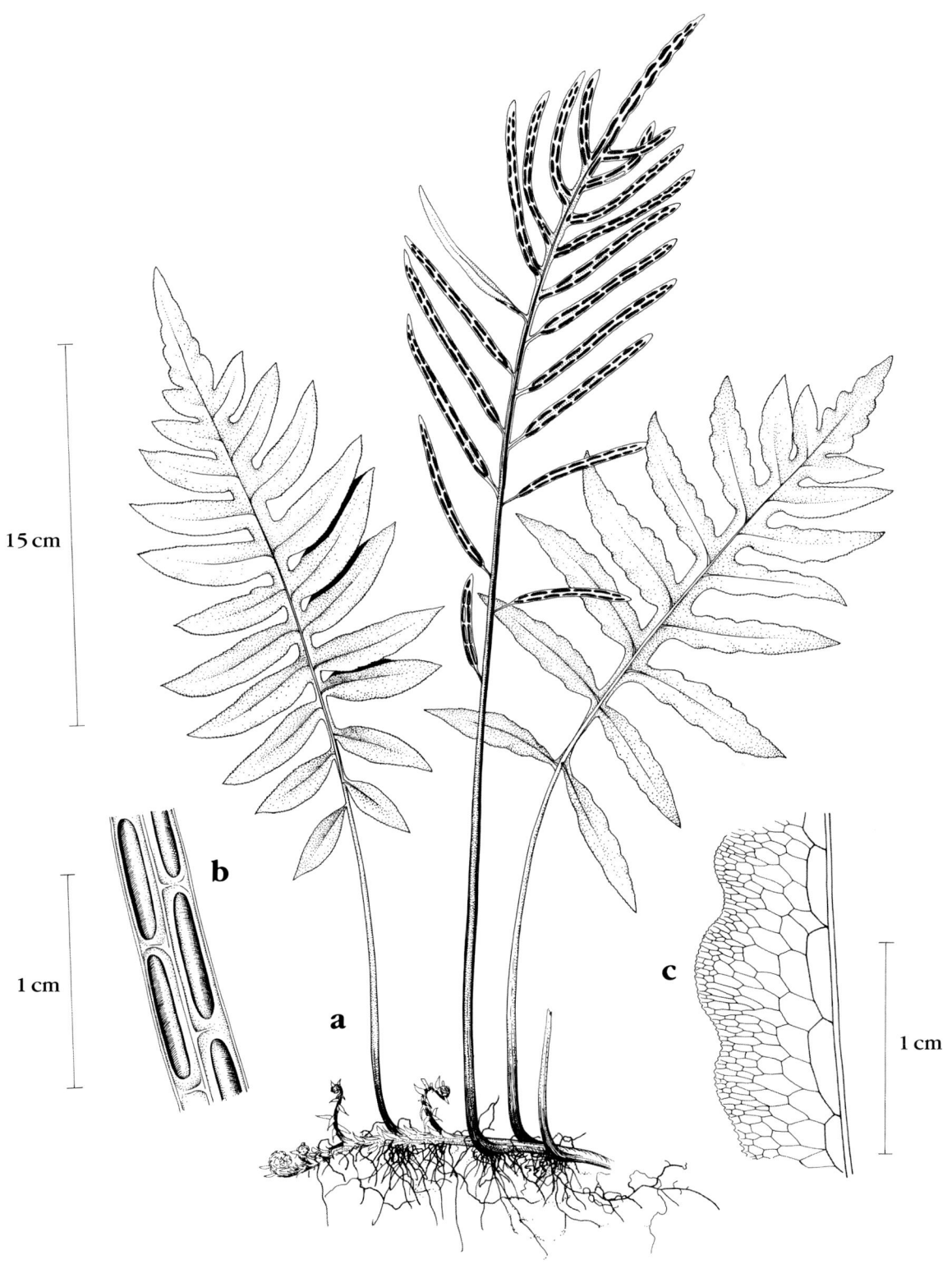

Lorinseria areolata
a. Habit; b. Portion of fertile pinna with sori; c. Portion of sterile frond.

Lycopodium L. Clubmosses

Stems prostrate or decumbent to erect, clothed with small, scale-like leaves; roots adventitious, borne on lower side of prostrate or reclining segment of stem. Leaves numerous, spirally arranged, eligulate, simple, linear-subulate or linear-oblanceolate, with a single, unbranched vein. Sporophylls aggregated in a terminal cylindric strobilus or grouped in subterminal cauline zones; sporangia at base of sporophyll, solitary, splitting transversely, homosporous. Spores numerous, pallid to yellow, tetrahedral.

A genus of nearly 400 species found in both temperate and tropical regions. For a review of the North American species of *Lycopodium,* see Beitel (1979).

Key to the species of *Lycopodium* in Arkansas

1. Branches dimorphic, with sterile branches prostrate and fertile branches erect; leaves ascending or appressed, linear-subulate, broadest below middle; sporophylls aggregated in a terminal, cylindric strobilus .... 1. *L. appressum* (p. 134)
1. Branches alike, decumbent or ascending; leaves spreading, linear-oblanceolate, broadest above middle; sporophylls grouped in subterminal, cauline zones .... 2. *L. lucidulum* (p. 136)

1. *Lycopodium appressum* (Chapm.) Lloyd and Underw.

Lycopodium inundatum var. *bigelovii* Tuckerm.
Lycopodium inundatum var. *appressum* Chapm.
Lycopodium alopecuroides var. *appressum* Chapm.

COMMON NAME: Southern Clubmoss

Plants deciduous. Stems dimorphic; sterile branches prostrate, long-creeping, up to 40 cm long, rooting frequently and throughout; leaves ascending, linear-subulate, broadest below the middle, up to 12 mm long and 1.5 mm wide, glabrous or sparsely ciliolate, attenuate to apex, entire or denticulate; fertile branches erect, up to 30 cm tall and 3 mm in diam.; leaves ascending to appressed, imbricate, up to 5 mm long and 0.8 mm wide, attenuate to apex, entire. Strobilus cylindric, up to 7 cm long; sporangia subglobose; spores tetrahedral-globose, 45-56 µm in diam., rugulate.

HABITAT: Moist to wet, sandy, disturbed soil along streams and railroad tracks, at edges of lakes, in open pine woods, waste ground, and sandy bogs; West Gulf Coastal Plain.

RANGE: Gulf and Atlantic coastal plain states and western Kentucky, West Indies.

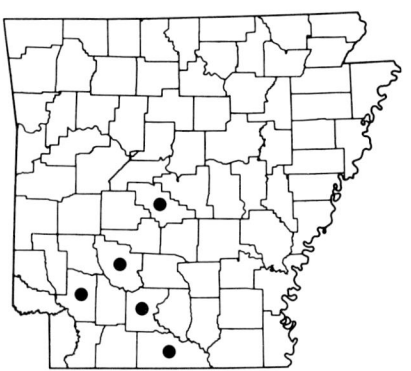

Lycopodium appressum (Chapm.) Lloyd

Clark Co.: *Taylor 2172* (SIU). Hempstead Co.: *D. Moore 490062* (UARK). Ouachita Co.: *Taylor 2627* (SIU). Saline Co.: *Young 1513* (UCA). Union Co.: *D. Moore 6264* (APCR).

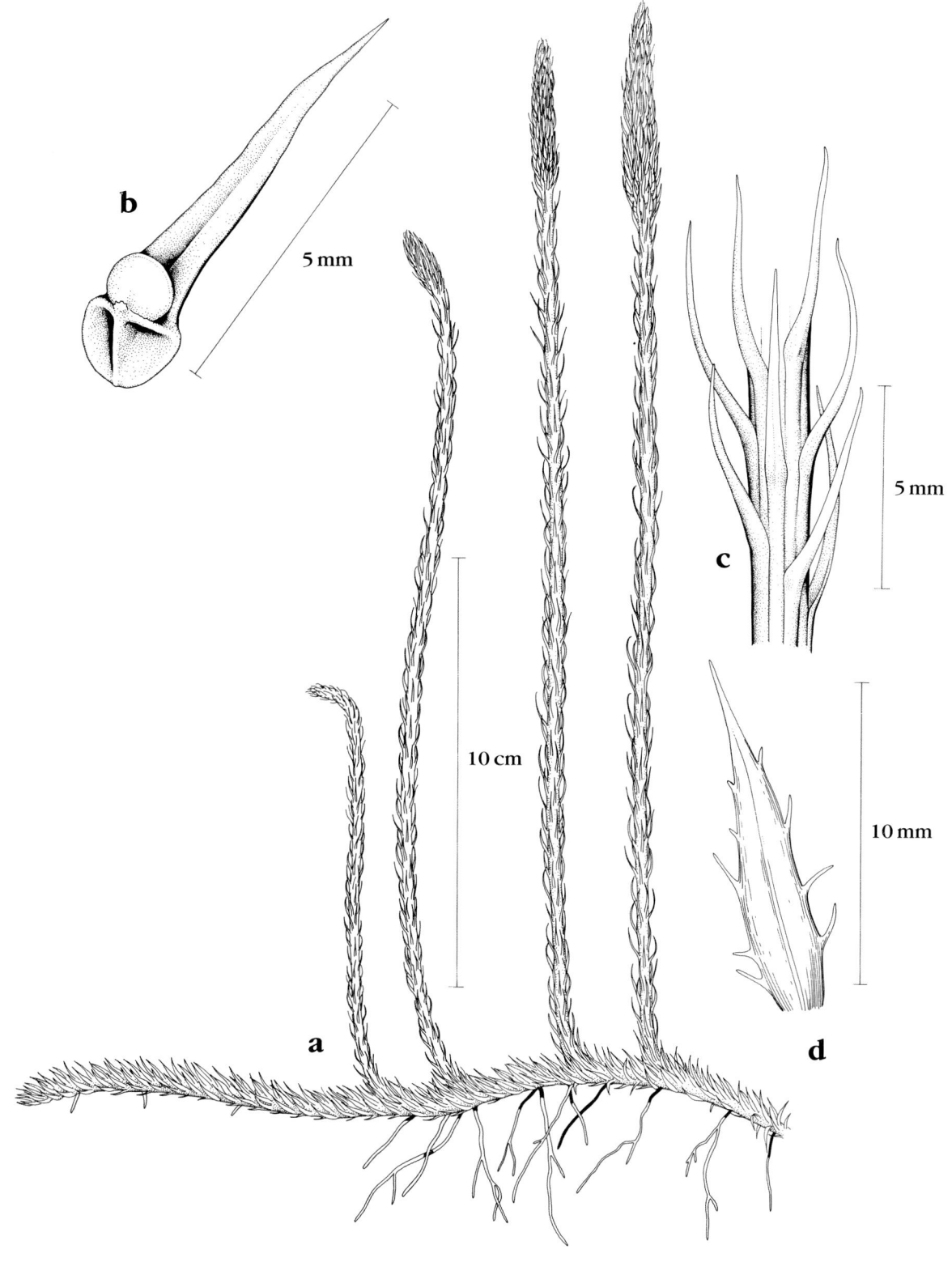

Lycopodium appressum
a. Habit; b. Adaxial side of sporophyll with sporangium; c. Portion of erect branch below strobilus; d. Leaf from prostrate branch.

2. *Lycopodium lucidulum* Michx.

COMMON NAME: Shining Clubmoss

Plants evergreen. Stems alike, decumbent to ascending, up to 30 cm long, rooting frequently where reclining; leaves spreading or reflexed, lustrous, linear-oblanceolate, up to 12 mm long, and 2.5 mm wide, glabrous, acuminate, subentire to serrulate toward apex, often gemmiparous in upper leaf axils. Sporophylls grouped in subterminal, cauline zones, lanceolate, slightly smaller than sterile leaves; sporangia reniform; spores tetrahedral with sides concave, 23-32 µm in diam., foveolate.

HABITAT: Franklin Co.: lower talus slope; Spy Rock Hollow; *Redfearn 21148* (SMS). Madison Co.: tributaries to Mulberry Creek; *Redfearn 18553* (SMS). Newton Co.: narrow ravine along upper reaches of Terrapin Branch; *Redfearn & Weber 27493* (SMS).

RANGE: Eastern North America.

Frank Bowers and Paul Redfearn (1967) first collected *Lycopodium lucidulum* in Arkansas on 27 January 1966 at Spy Rock Hollow. Since then, additional stations in Madison and Newton Counties have been found.

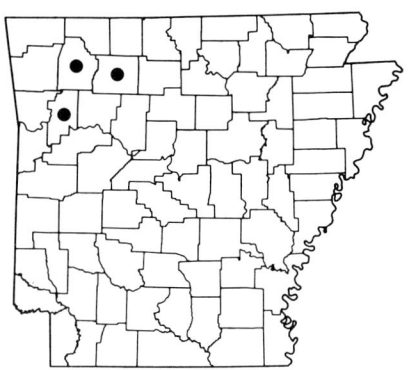

Lycopodium lucidulum

Franklin Co.: *Redfearn 21148* (SMS). Madison Co.: *Redfearn 18553* (SMS). Newton Co.: *Redfearn & Weber 27493* (SMS).

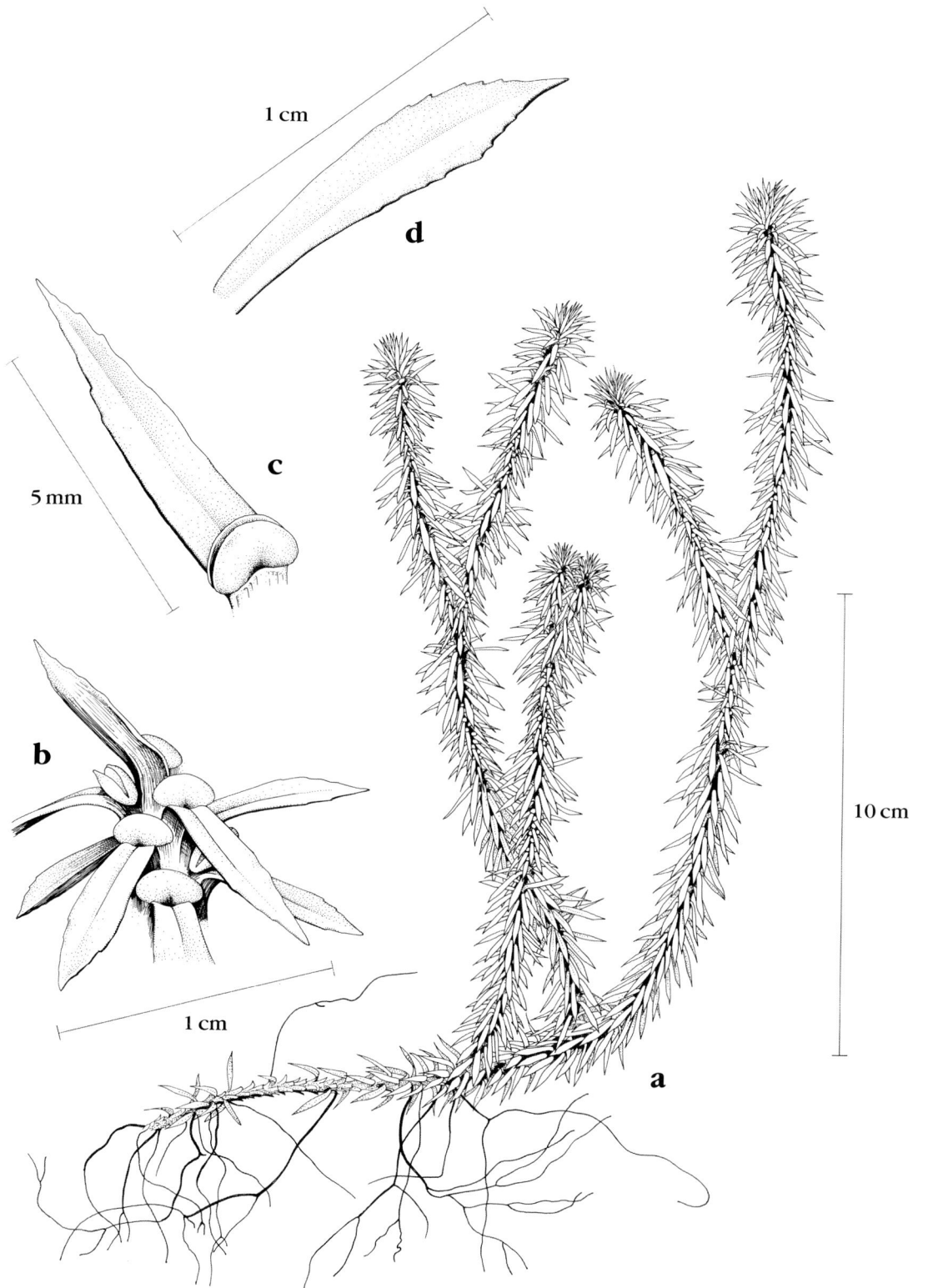

Lycopodium lucidulum
a. Habit; b. Portion of stem with sporophylls; c. Adaxial side of sporophyll with sporangium; d. Leaf.

Lygodium Sw. Climbing Ferns

A largely tropical genus of about 40 species.

1. *Lygodium japonicum* (Thunb.) Sw.

COMMON NAME: Japanese Climbing Fern

Rhizome slender, long-creeping, bearing brown to black hairs. Fronds climbing and twining or trailing, bipinnate to tripinnate up to 2 m or more long, pubescent; stipe and rachis green to stramineous; pinnae dimorphic; veins forked, usually free, stipitate; lower pinnae diverging into pinnule pair with interposed abortive bud; sterile pinnules deltoid to ovate-lanceolate, up to 25 cm long and 20 cm wide; segments ovate to linear-lanceolate, often lobed, serrulate; fertile pinnules deltoid to ovate, up to 20 cm long and 15 cm wide; fertile segments deltoid to ovate-lanceolate or flabellate. Sori borne in a double row on digitate projections along margins of pinnules or segments; indusium laterally attached.

HABITAT: Ashley Co.: base of slope in lumbered, mixed pine-hardwood forest; along timber access road ca. 10 mi NE of Hamburg; *Meyer s. n.* (UARK). Union Co.: roadside opening, pine-oak woods ca. 3 mi N of El Dorado; *Thomas s.n.* (LRU).

RANGE: Naturalized in the southeastern United States, native to eastern Asia.

Lygodium japonicum was collected by Charles Meyer on 14 November 1981 from the above locality, where numerous plants were found. This collection is the first documented report of naturalized *Lygodium* in Arkansas. These plants approximate the northwesternmost naturalized population in North America. Plants from Sebastian County are vouchered at UARK but are not naturalized since they were collected from a yard in Ft. Smith.

Lygodium japonicum

Ashley Co.: *Meyer s. n.* (UARK). Union Co.: *Thomas s. n.* (LRU).

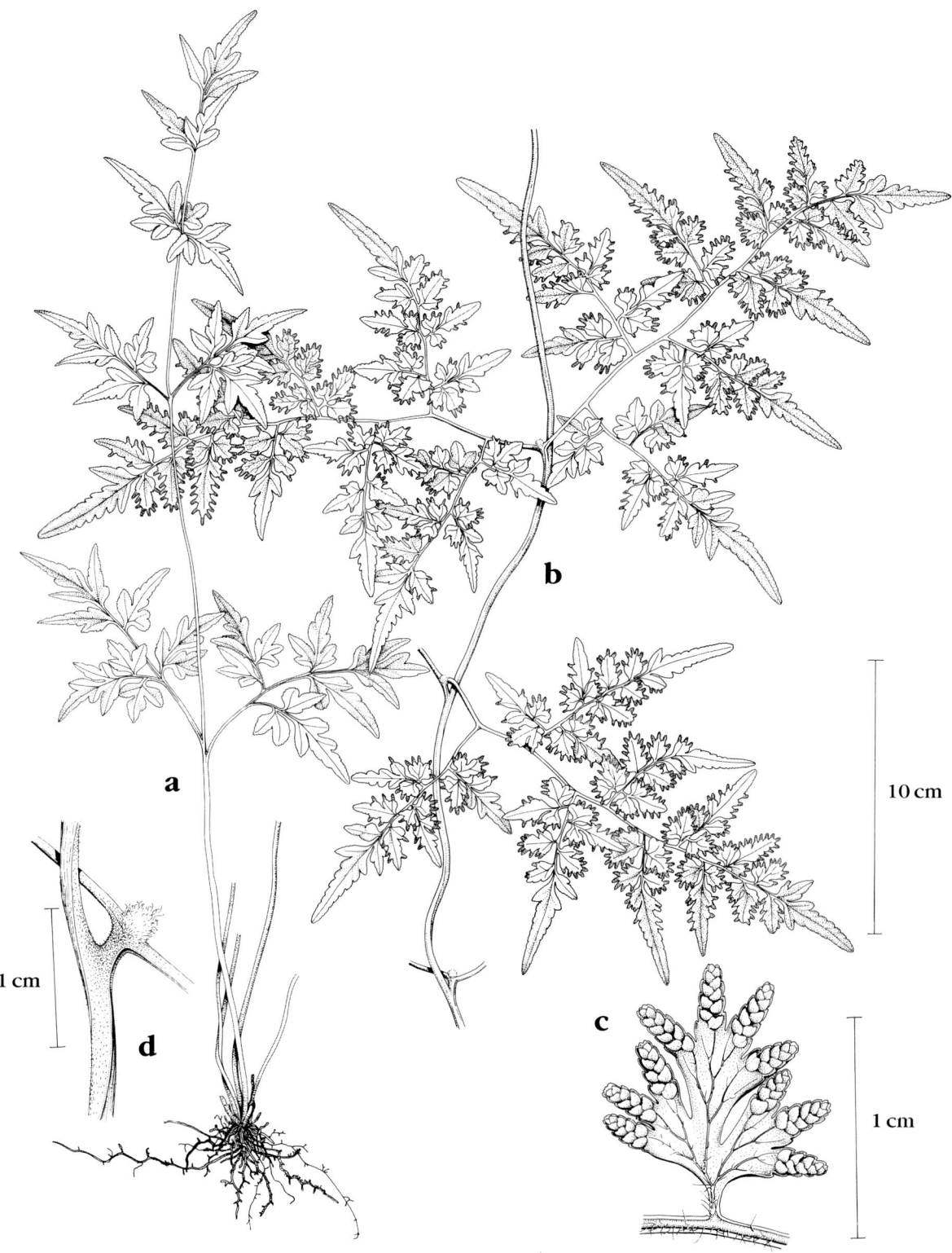

Lygodium japonicum
a. Habit; b. Portion of frond with sporiferous pinnae; c. Lower surface of sporiferous segment; d. Base of lower pinna with interposed abortive bud.

Marsilea L. Water Clovers

Anchored aquatics with creeping, slender branching rhizomes. Fronds erect or ascending, deciduous, with four subopposite pinnae at apex of each stipe, appearing like four-leaf clover; stipes slender; pinnae cuneate to flabellate; veins forked, free and reticulate. Sporocarps solitary near base of frond, borne on erect or ascending stalks, subglobose to ovoid up to 8 mm long and 6 mm wide, punctate, strigillose, bearing two knob-like excrescences above insertion of stalk, bivalvate, releasing numerous sori on a gelatinous sorophore, heterosporous; sori bearing megasporangia medially and microsporangia laterally; megaspores solitary in megasporangium, white ovoid; microspores numerous in microsporangium, white, tetrahedral globose.

A genus of about 60 species in both temperate and tropical regions. The most recent monographic study on *Marsilea* is by Gupta (1962·), who dealt primarily with the Indian species.

The *Marsilea vestita* var. *mucronata*-*M. uncinata* complex in Arkansas is in need of study. The presence of intermediate material and the small number of collections available for examination pose a problem in developing descriptions which will serve to clearly distinguish these two taxa.

Key to the species of *Marsilea* in Arkansas

1. Pinnae pilose or strigose below; sporocarp stalk usually shorter than or equal to the length of the sporocarp, borne on rhizome at or near stipe base; sporocarp with upper excrescence mostly blunt and straight, containing 12-22 sori . . . . 1. *M. vestita* (p. 144)
1. Pinnae sparsely strigillose below; sporocarp stalk longer than the length of the sporocarp, borne on frond at least slightly above stipe base; sporocarp with upper excrescence mostly acute, curved or hooked, containing 26-28 sori . . . . 2. *M. uncinata* (p. 146)

1. *Marsilea vestita* Hook & Grev. var. *mucronata* (A. Br.) Baker

Marsilea mucronata A. Br.

COMMON NAME: Hairy Water Clover

Rhizome nodes and apices often with conspicuous tufts of reddish brown, linear scales. Stipes up to 15 cm long; pinnae up to 1.5 cm long and 1.6 mm wide, glabrate to sparsely strigose above, pilose to strigose below. Sporocarps ovoid, with upper excrescence mostly blunt and straight, containing 12-22 sori; stalk borne on rhizome at or near stipe base, up to 8 mm long, usually shorter than or equal to the length of the sporocarp.

HABITAT: Bradley Co.: temporary pools in hard pan of open, savanna-like area, ca. 7 mi. SE of Warren; *Demaree 18969* (MO).

RANGE: Southern and midwestern North America.

The Hairy Water Clover was collected from the above locality by Dwight Moore on 11 April 1936, and by Delzie Demaree on 24 April 1939. Apparently, plants have not been collected from the site since that time.

The seasonally wet habitat of this taxon, which becomes parched by the summer sun, differs from the more uniformly moist habitat of the following species.

Marsilea vestita

Bradley Co.: *Demaree 18969* (MO).

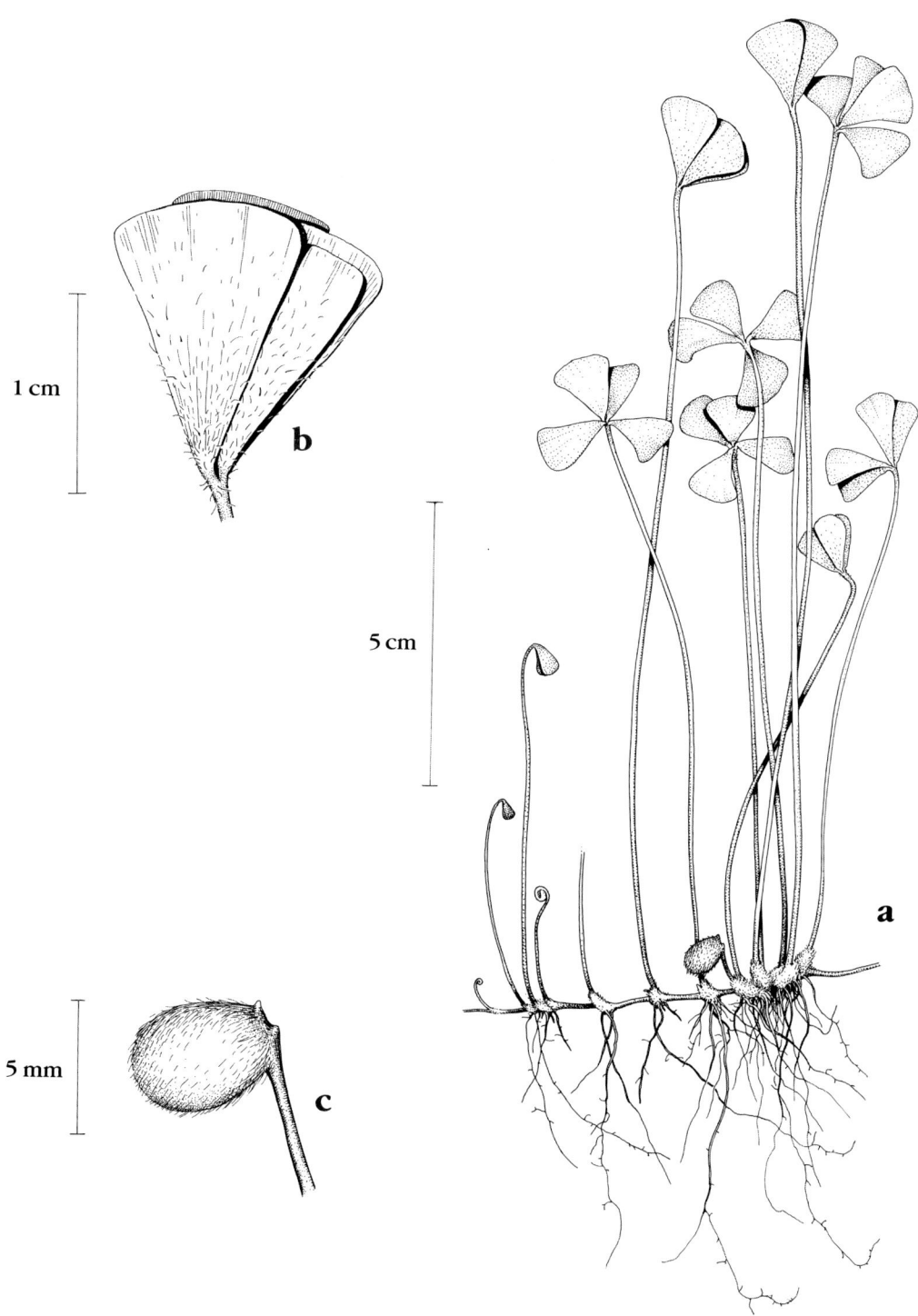

Marsilea vestita var. *mucronata*
a. Habit; b. Lower surface of pinnae; c. Sporocarp.

2. *Marsilea uncinata* A. Br.

Marsilea vestita var. *uncinata* (A. Br.) Baker

COMMON NAME: Hook-spined Water Clover

Rhizome nodes and apices without conspicuous tufts of reddish brown scales. Stipes up to 25 cm long; pinnae up to 2.5 cm long and 2.5 cm wide, glabrate above, sparsely strigillose below. Sporocarps subglobose to ovoid, with upper excrescence usually acute and curved or hooked, containing 26-28 sori; stalk borne on frond at least slightly above stipe base, up to 3 cm long, longer than the length of the sporocarp.

HABITAT: Along edges of ponds, streams, or in wet depressions.

RANGE: South central United States.

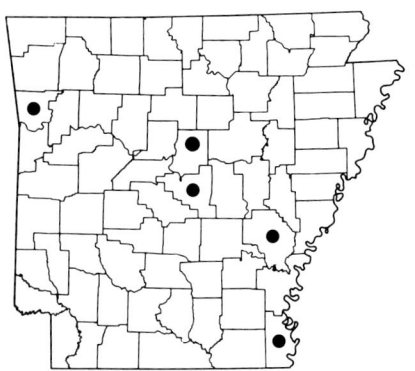

Marsilea uncinata A. Br.

Arkansas Co.: *Taylor 1863* (SIU). Chicot Co.: *McDaniel 20043* (SIU). Crawford Co.: *Barber s.n.* (APCR). Faulkner Co.: *Johnson 643* (HXC). Pulaski Co.: *Engelmann 33* (MO).

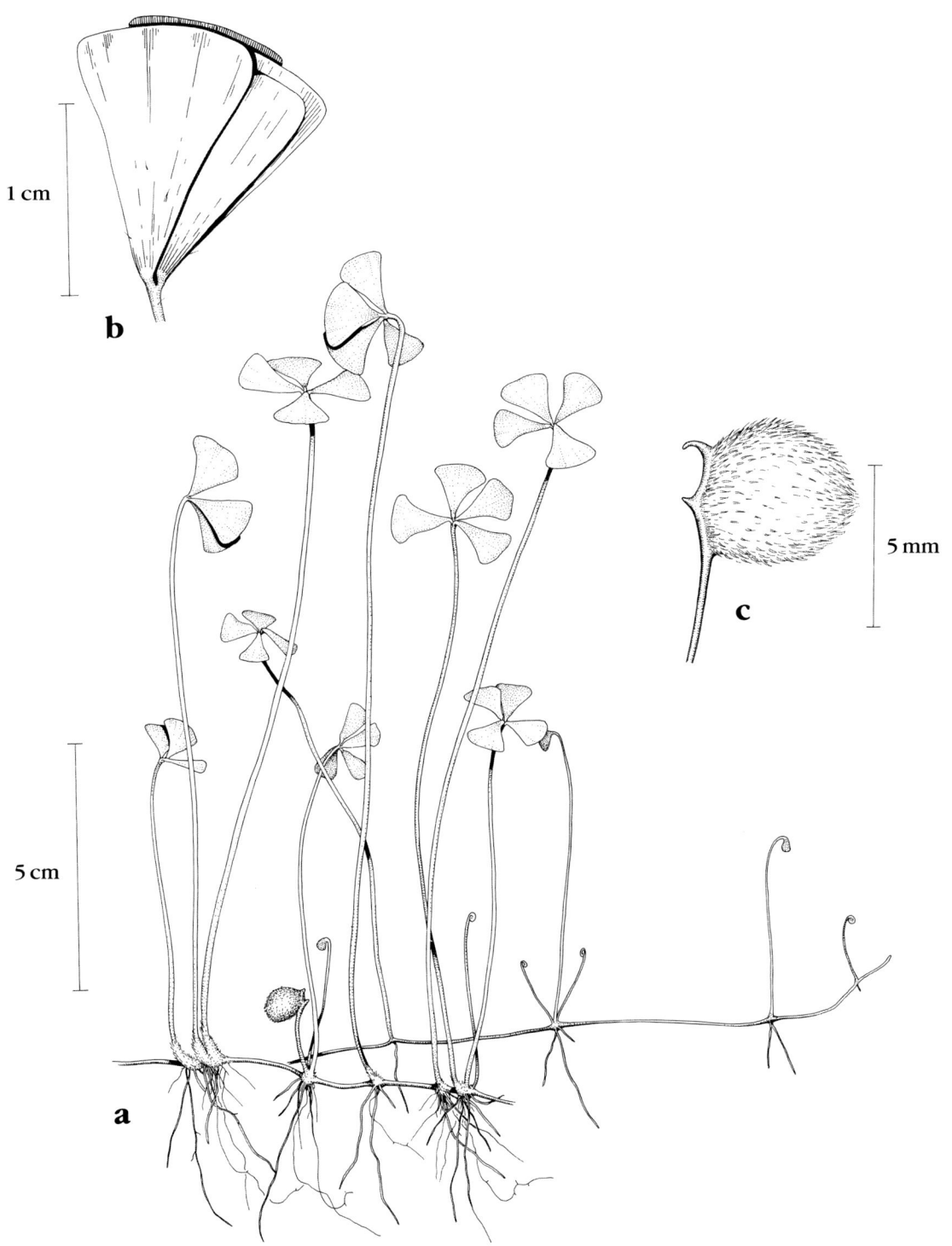

Marsilea uncinata
a. Habit; b. Lower surface of segments; c. Sporocarp.

Notholaena R. Br. Cloak Ferns

Notholaena, if recognized as a genus separate from *Cheilanthes*, contains perhaps 60 species found mainly in arid regions of the world. *Notholaena* is retained here out of convenience because the single Arkansas species appears distinct from the species of *Cheilanthes* found in the state.

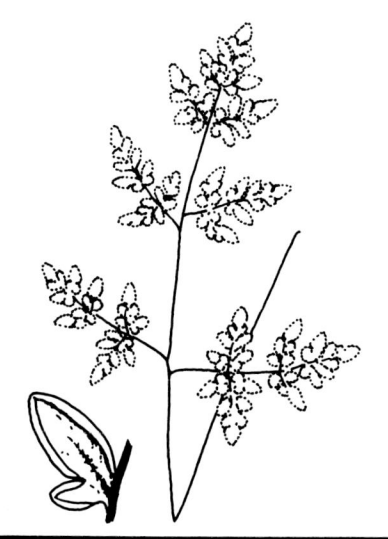

1. *Notholaena dealbata* (Pursh) Kunze

Cheilanthes dealbata Pursh
Pellaea dealbata (Pursh) Prantl

COMMON NAME: Powdery Cloak Fern

Rhizome short-creeping to erect; scales densely covering rhizome, linear-lanceolate. Fronds evergreen, tufted, erect-spreading, bipinnate to tripinnate, up to 15 cm long, glabrous; stipe and rachis wiry, reddish brown; blade deltoid-ovate, up to 8 cm long, and 5 cm wide; pinnules or segments white-powdery below, orbicular to ovate-oblong, up to 4 mm long; veins forked, free. Sori marginal, naked or covered partly by recurved margins of the pinnules or segments.

HABITAT: Dry limestone and dolomite outcrops; Ozark Mountains.

RANGE: Central United States.

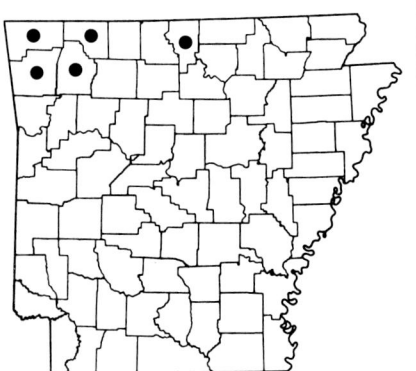

Notholaena dealbata (Pursh) Kunze

Baxter Co.: *Palmer 5951* (MO). Benton Co.: *Palmer 37190* (MO). Carroll Co.: *Palmer 4538* (MO). Madison Co.: *Nelson 10861* (MO). Washington Co.: *Taylor 1109* (SIU).

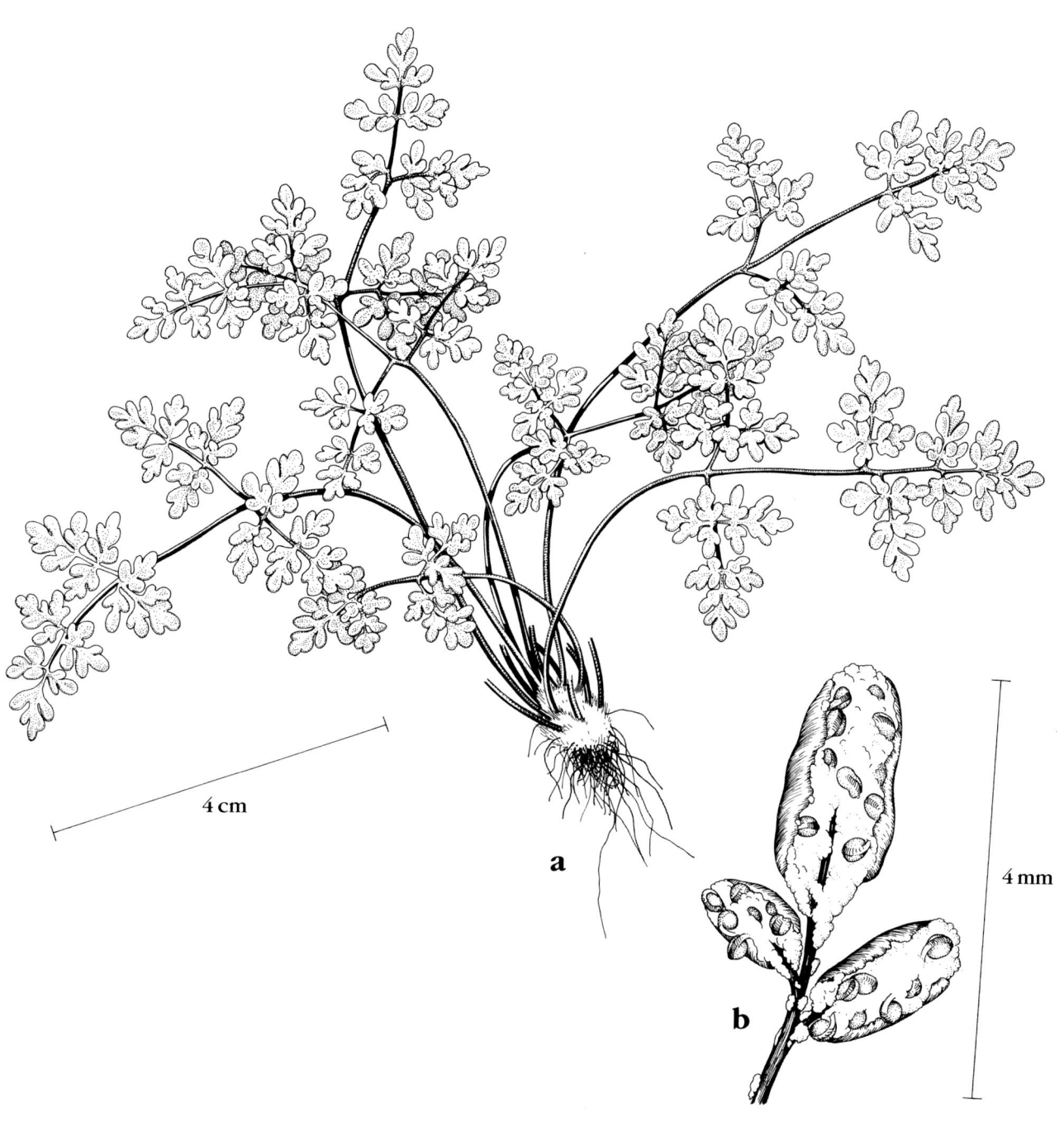

Notholaena dealbata
a. Habit; b. Lower surface of segments.

Onoclea L. Sensitive Fern

The genus *Onoclea* includes only the following species.

1. *Onoclea sensibilis* L.

COMMON NAME: Sensitive Fern

Rhizome long-creeping; scales sparse, ovate to lanceolate. Fronds dimorphic; sterile fronds deciduous, erect, pinnatifid to pinnate-pinnatifid, up to 1 m tall; stipe and rachis green to stramineous; blade deltoid-ovate, up to 45 cm long and 35 cm wide; rachis winged at least above; blade segments opposite or subopposite, elliptic-lanceolate to oblong-lanceolate, lobed or cleft, margins entire; veins reticulate, forming a series of linear to oblong areoles along midribs; fertile fronds persistent through following year, rigidly erect, bipinnate, usually shorter than the sterile fronds, up to 70 cm tall; blade oblong-lanceolate, up to 18 cm long and 4 cm wide, leathery; pinnae strongly ascending and much contracted; pinnules dark brown when mature, inrolled, forming globose structures about 3-4 mm in diam. which contain sporangia. Sori round, borne on the ends of free veins; indusium ephemeral, basal; sporangia opening early in year; spores green, globose.

HABITAT: Moist to wet soil along margins of streams and lakes, in wet meadows, woods, roadside ditches, and around springs.

RANGE: Eastern and central North America.

Onoclea sensibilis f. *obtusilobata* (Schkuhr) Gilb. has fronds somewhat intermediate in form between normal sterile and fertile leaves. In Arkansas, it was collected by F. L. Harvey without location (UARK 13) and by Dwight Moore at Crowley's Ridge State Park, Greene County *(Moore 480680* UARK). This sporadic form occurs as a result of disturbance to the developing leaves caused by mechanical injury, late spring frosts, drought, transplantation, fire, etc. (Beitel, Wagner, and Walter, 1981).

Onoclea sensibilis L.

Ashley Co.: *Taylor 1888* (SIU). Benton Co.: *Pyle s.n.* (UARK). Bradley Co.: *Demaree 23832* (SMU). Calhoun Co.: *Hoiberg 307* (SMU). Clark Co.: *Demaree 21920* (SMU). Clay Co.: *Demaree 4140* (NY). Cleburne Co.: *Babb 977* (ARKSU). Columbia Co.: *Johnson 33* (HXC). Conway Co.: *J. Moore 5* (UARK). Craighead Co.: *Demaree 7038* (SMU). Crawford Co.: *Taylor 1095* (SIU). Cross Co.: *D. Moore 420380* (UARK). Faulkner Co.: *Spencer 52* (HXC). Garland Co.: *Palmer 24933* (UARK). Franklin Co.: *Davis 444* (UARK). Greene Co.: *Demaree 26661* (SMU). Hempstead Co.: *Taylor 1175* (SIU). Independence Co.: *Johnson 500* (HXC). Johnson Co.: *Redfearn 23828* (SMS). Lawrence Co.: *Taylor 2595* (SIU). Lee Co.: *Davis 331* (ARKSU). Little River Co.: *Taylor 2141* (SIU). Marion Co.: *Thomas 16197* (SMU). Montgomery Co.: *Taylor 2210* (SIU). Nevada Co.: *D. Moore 410340* (UARK). Newton Co.: *Redfearn 27519* (SMS). Ouachita Co.: *Demaree 61376* (SMU). Perry Co.: *J. Moore 3318* (UCA). Phillips Co.: *Palmer 25128* (UARK). Pike Co.: *Demaree 9974* (MO). Poinsett Co.: *Demaree 3671* (SMU). Polk Co.: *J. Moore 3150* (ARKSU). Pope Co.: *Redfearn 17341* (SMS). Pulaski Co.: *Johnson 114* (HXC). St. Francis Co.: *Lowman 372* (HXC). Saline Co.: *Demaree 35157* (SIU). Searcy Co.: *Taylor 2577* (SIU). Sevier Co.: *Johnson 150* (HXC). Union Co.: *Taylor 1160* (SIU). Van Buren Co.: *Haas 1477* (ARKSU). Washington Co.: *Buchholz 1010* (UARK). White Co.: *Johnson 210* (HXC). Woodruff Co.: *Johnson 442* (HXC).

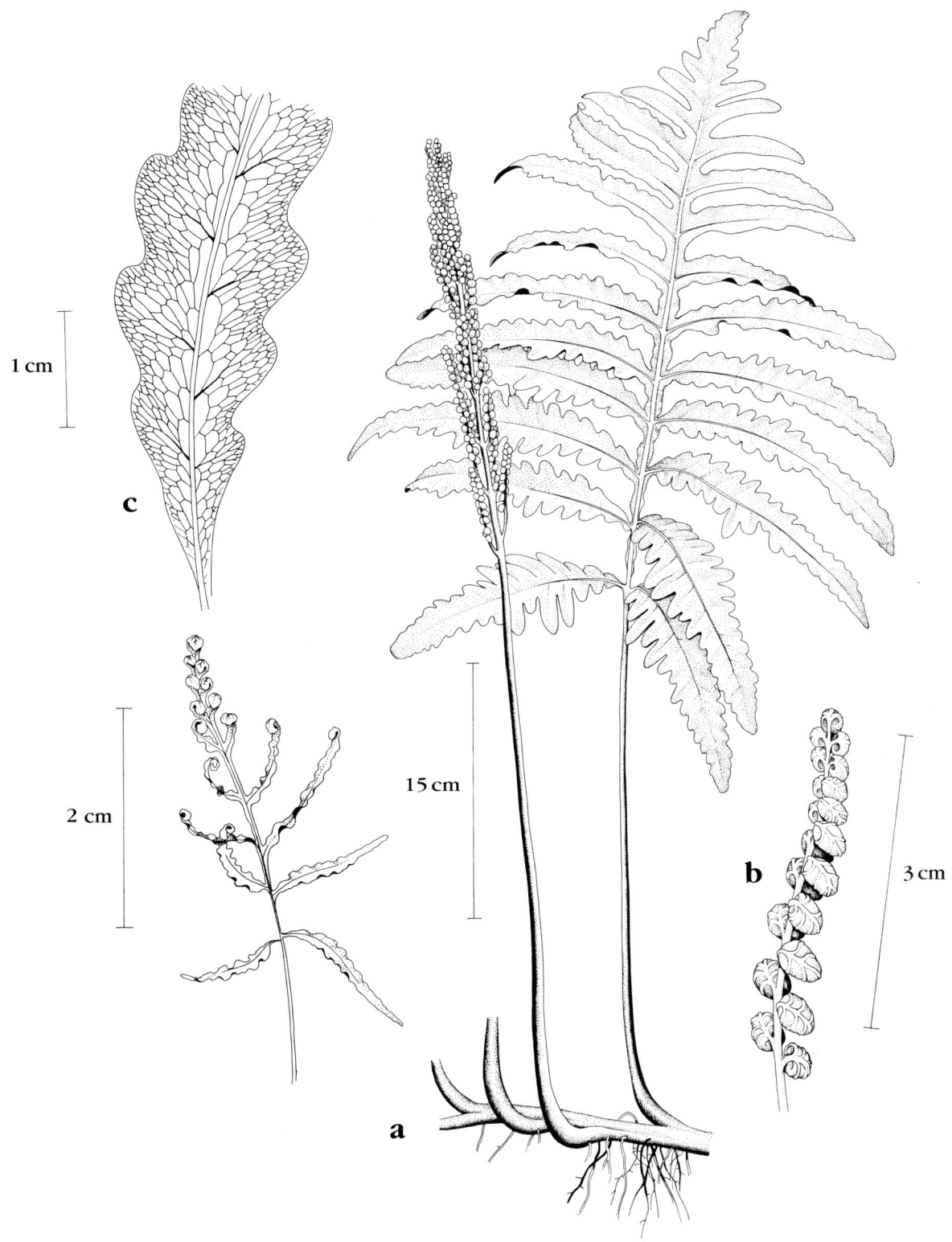

Onoclea sensibilis
a. Habit; b. Fertile pinnules; c. Portion of sterile pinna.

Ophioglossum L. Adder's-tongue Ferns

Stem subterranean, erect, brownish yellow to dark brown, suberous-fleshy, scaleless, roots spreading, brownish yellow to dark brown, cord-like. Fronds (leaves) deciduous, one to several produced per growing season, erect, buds for next year free from stipe base; stipe fleshy, dividing into a simple sterile blade and an unbranched, long-stalked fertile portion; blade ovate or lanceolate to elliptic, ascending or spreading, papery to leathery; veins forked, free or reticulate. Sporangia borne in two rows, embedded in the axis of the fertile segments, globose to ovoid, 1-2 mm in diam., splitting transversely; spores light yellow, tetrahedral.

A genus of about 30 species, mainly of temperate climates. The most recent monographic treatment of the family is by Clausen (1938). Plants of *Ophioglossum* are inconspicuous and easily overlooked in the field. This is particularly true of the smaller species which are often concealed by the surrounding vegetation. In addition, most species are rather ephemeral, appearing in spring when moisture is plentiful but withering and becoming dormant during drier seasons of the year.

Key to the species of *Ophioglossum* in Arkansas

1. Stem conspicuously globose-bulbous . 1. *O. crotalophoroides* (p. 158)
1. Stem subcylindric to cylindric-bulbous
    2. Sterile blade with veins forming areoles that contain anastomosing veinlets which themselves often form secondary areoles .... 2. *O. engelmannii* (p. 160)
    2. Sterile blade with veins forming areoles that may contain free-ending or anastomosing veinlets but which themselves do not form secondary areoles
        3. Sterile blade usually less than 2 cm long; rhizome often cylindric-bulbous .... 3. *O. nudicaule* (p. 162)
        3. Sterile blade usually greater than 2 cm long; rhizome cylindric
            4. Leaves usually solitary; apex of sterile blade obtuse; roots rarely proliferous .... 4. *O. vulgatum* (p. 164)
            4. Leaves usually several per growing season; apex of sterile blade acute; roots often proliferous ..... 5. *O. petiolatum* (p. 166)

1. *Ophioglossum crotalophoroides* Walt.

Ophioglossum bulbosum Michx.
Ophioglossum pusillum Nutt.
Ophioglossum vulgatum var. *crotalophoroides* (Walt.) D. C. Eat.

COMMON NAME: Bulbous Adder's-tongue Fern

Stem conspicuously globose-bulbous. Leaves usually several per growing season, up to 10 cm tall; sterile blade ovate to elliptic, up to 3.5 cm long and 2.5 cm wide, apex obtuse to acuminate, base obtuse to cordate; veins forming areoles mostly without included veinlets; fertile portion bearing up to 10 sporangia in each row.

HABITAT: Sandy, well drained, open soil in lawns, meadows, cemeteries, pastures, and roadsides.

RANGE: Southeastern United States, tropical America.

Ophioglossum crotalophoroides was first collected in Arkansas by Dwight Moore on 12 April 1945 in a low, open meadow 1½ miles south of Prescott, Nevada County (Moore, 1950). At the time of its collection, this was the northernmost station recorded for this species. Since then a number of additional populations have been reported (Moore, 1951, 1957, 1958; J. Moore and Hartsoe, 1955; Thomas, 1978). This species has been collected as far north as southeastern Missouri (Thomas, Marx, and Lawson, 1974).

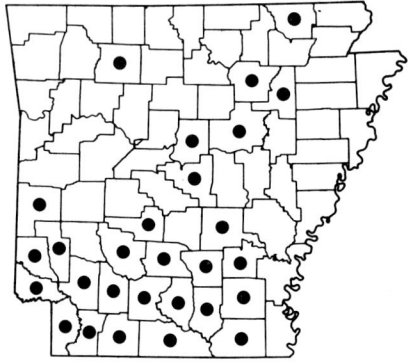

Ophioglossum crotalophoroides

Ashley Co.: *Thomas 27300* (NLU). Bradley Co.: *Thomas 27912* (NLU). Calhoun Co.: *Lawson 256* (NLU). Clark Co.: *Lawson 74* (NLU). Cleveland Co.: *Thomas 4399* (NLU). Columbia Co.: *D. Moore 5771* (UARK). Dallas Co.: *Lawson 226* (NLU). Drew Co.: *Thomas 26904* (NLU). Faulkner Co.: *Taylor 2009* (SIU). Hempstead Co.: *D. Moore 53155* (UARK). Hot Spring Co.: *Thomas 34114* (NLU). Howard Co.: *D. Moore 5772* (UARK). Independence Co.: *Thomas 38584* (NLU). Jackson Co.: *Thomas 34219* (NLU). Jefferson Co.: *Thomas 34132* (NLU). Lafayette Co.: *Thomas 27954* (NLU). Lincoln Co.: *Thomas 34141* (NLU). Little River Co.: *Thomas 27954* (NLU). Miller Co.: *Thomas 34011* (NLU). Nevada Co.: *D. Moore 450039* (UARK). Newton Co.: *Thompson 1015* (SMS). Ouachita Co.: *Taylor 2625* (SIU). Polk Co.: *Thomas 34106* (NLU). Pulaski Co.: *Thomas 34377* (NLU). Randolph Co.: *Thomas 34239* (NLU). Sevier Co.: *Taylor 2641* (SIU). Union Co.: *Taylor 2629* (SIU). White Co.: *Thomas 34159* (NLU).

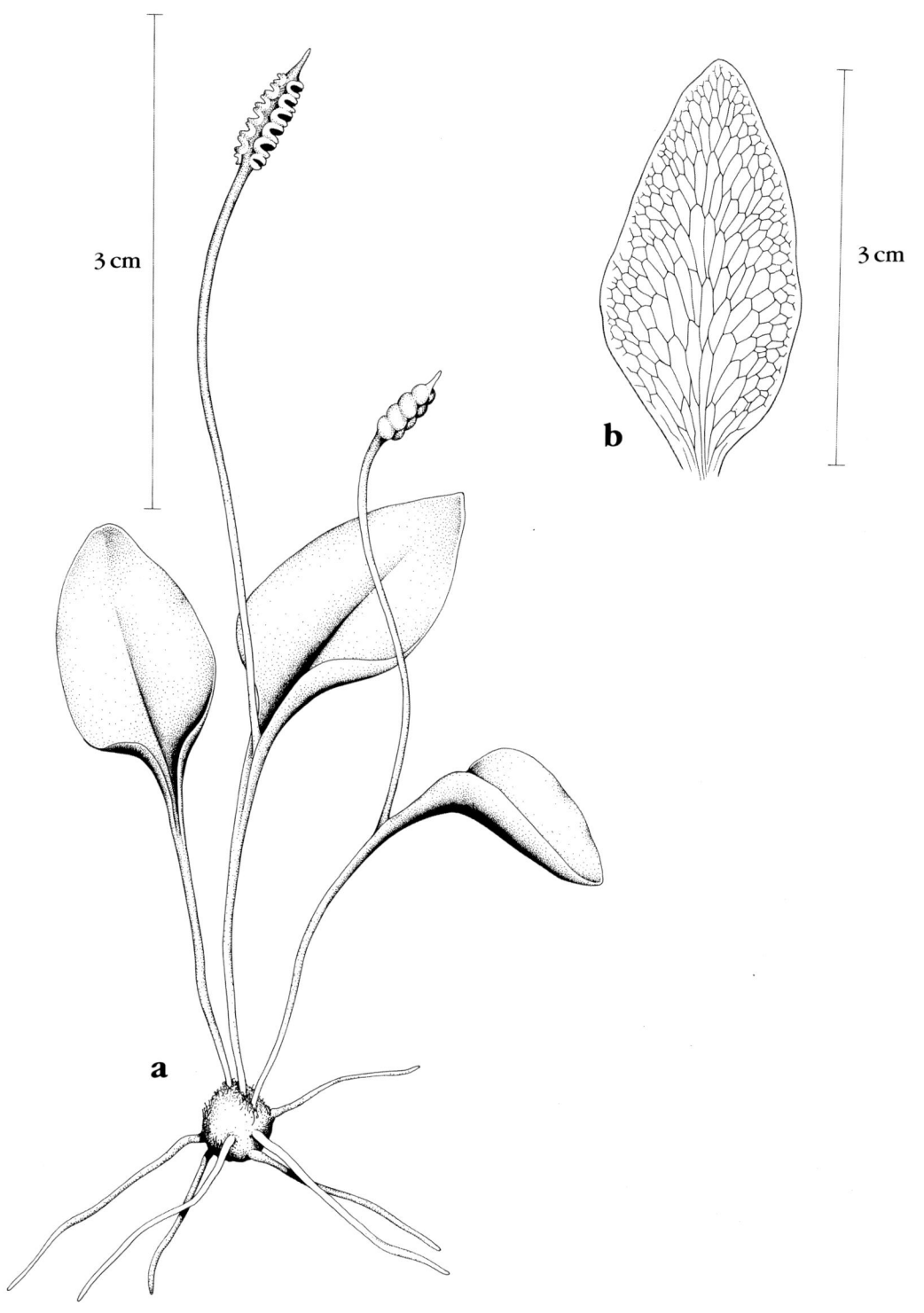

Ophioglossum crotalophoroides
a. Habit; b. Blade venation.

2. *Ophioglossum engelmannii* Prantl

Ophioglossum vulgatum f. *engelmannii* (Prantl) Clute
Ophioglossum vulgatum var. *engelmannii* (Prantl) Clute

COMMON NAME: Limestone Adder's-tongue Fern

Stem cylindric; roots often proliferous. Leaves one to several per growing season, up to 20 cm tall; sterile blade elliptic to oblong, up to 10 cm long and 3.5 cm wide, apex obtuse to acute, apiculate, base cuneate to obtuse; veins forming areoles containing free-ending veinlets or anastomosing veinlets which themselves often form secondary areoles; fertile portion bearing up to 30 sporangia in each row.

HABITAT: Seasonally moist to wet calcareous soils on limestone glades, in open woods, and on chalk outcrops.

RANGE: Southern United States, Mexico.

Ophioglossum engelmannii is normally found in the spring, since by summer its fronds have usually shriveled. New fronds may emerge in the fall if there is adequate moisture.

Ophioglossum engelmannii is probably more abundant in the Ozarks of Arkansas and Missouri than anywhere else in its range (Palmer, 1932). Once found, plants in a population of *O. engelmannii* are often observed in scattered clusters. Moore (1940b) attributed this clustered habit to root proliferation which he found to be a common form of reproduction in Arkansas plants of this species.

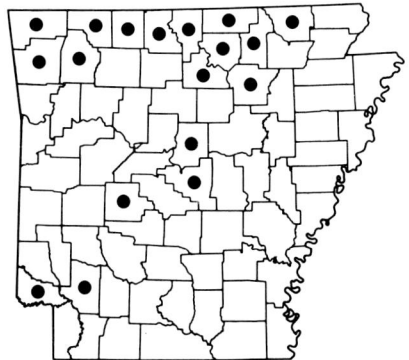

Ophioglossum engelmannii

Baxter Co.: *Palmer 14333* (MO). Benton Co.: *Palmer 17199* (MO). Boone Co.: *Demaree s.n.* (UARK). Carroll Co.: *D. Moore 350435* (MO). Faulkner Co.: *Taylor 2010* (SIU). Fulton Co.: *D. Moore 520391* (UARK). Garland Co.: *Haas 1492* (UCA). Hempstead Co.: *Palmer 5376* (MO). Independence Co.: *Thomas 8926* (NLU). Izard Co.: *Taylor 2107* (SIU). Little River Co.: *D. Moore 50036* (UARK). Madison Co.: *D. Moore 450406* (UARK). Marion Co.: *D. Moore 520332* (APCR). Pulaski Co.: *D. Moore 330069* (UARK). Randolph Co.: *Taylor 2086* (SIU). Sharp Co.: *D. Moore 520382* (UARK). Stone Co.: *Taylor 1259* (SIU). Washington Co.: *Palmer 23300* (MO).

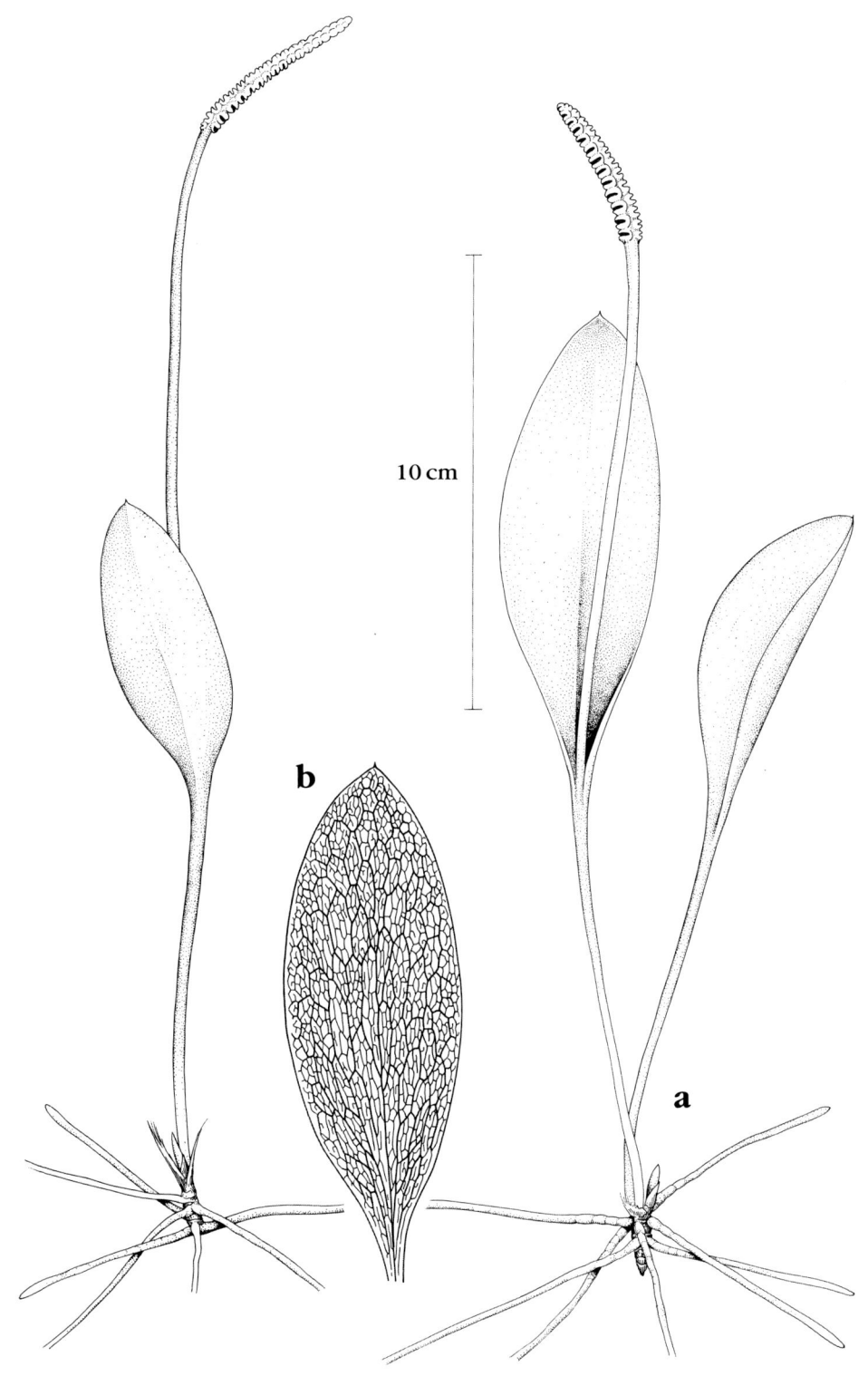

Ophioglossum engelmannii
a. Habit; b. Blade venation.

3. *Ophioglossum nudicaule* L. f. var. *tenerum* (Prantl) Clausen

Ophioglossum tenerum Prantl

COMMON NAME: Least Adder's-tongue Fern

Stem cylindric-bulbous; roots numerous, up to 0.8 mm in diam. Leaves one to several per growing season, up to 10 cm tall; sterile blade ovate to elliptic or lanceolate, up to 2 cm long and 1 cm wide, apex acute, base cuneate to obtuse; veins forming areoles containing free-ending veinlets; fertile portion bearing up to 12 sporangia in each row.

HABITAT: Cemeteries and church yards in the West Gulf Coastal Plain: Ashley Co.: Carter Cemetery; off Hwy. 82; *Thomas 27299* (NLU); Antioch Methodist Church Cemetery; off Hwy. 81; *Thomas 27903* (NLU). Hempstead Co.: Shover Springs Baptist Church Cemetery, Shover Springs; *Thomas 27951* (NLU). Nevada Co.: White's Chapel Baptist Church Yard; E of Bodcaw; *Thomas 27947* (NLU). Union Co.: Harper Springs Cemetery; S of Huttig; *Thomas 27400* (NLU); cemetery in pine woods along Hwy. 275; S of Strong; *Taylor 2630* (SIU).

RANGE: Southeastern United States, tropical America, Africa, Asia, Australia.

Ophioglossum nudicaule var. *tenerum* was first collected in Arkansas by Dale Thomas at the Carter Cemetery site on 23 January 1972. He has since located the five other Arkansas stations for this species (Thomas, 1978).

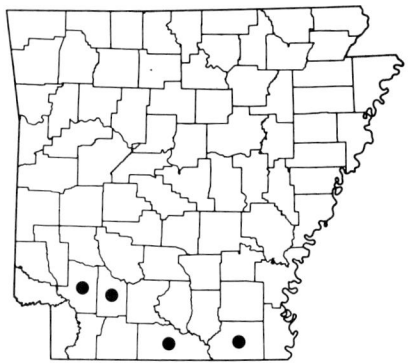

***Ophioglossum nudicaule* L. f. var. *tenerum* (Mett. ex Prantl) Clausen**

Ashley Co.: *Thomas 27903* (NLU). Hempstead Co.: *Thomas 27951* (NLU). Nevada Co.: *Thomas 27947* (NLU). Union Co.: *Taylor 2630* (SIU).

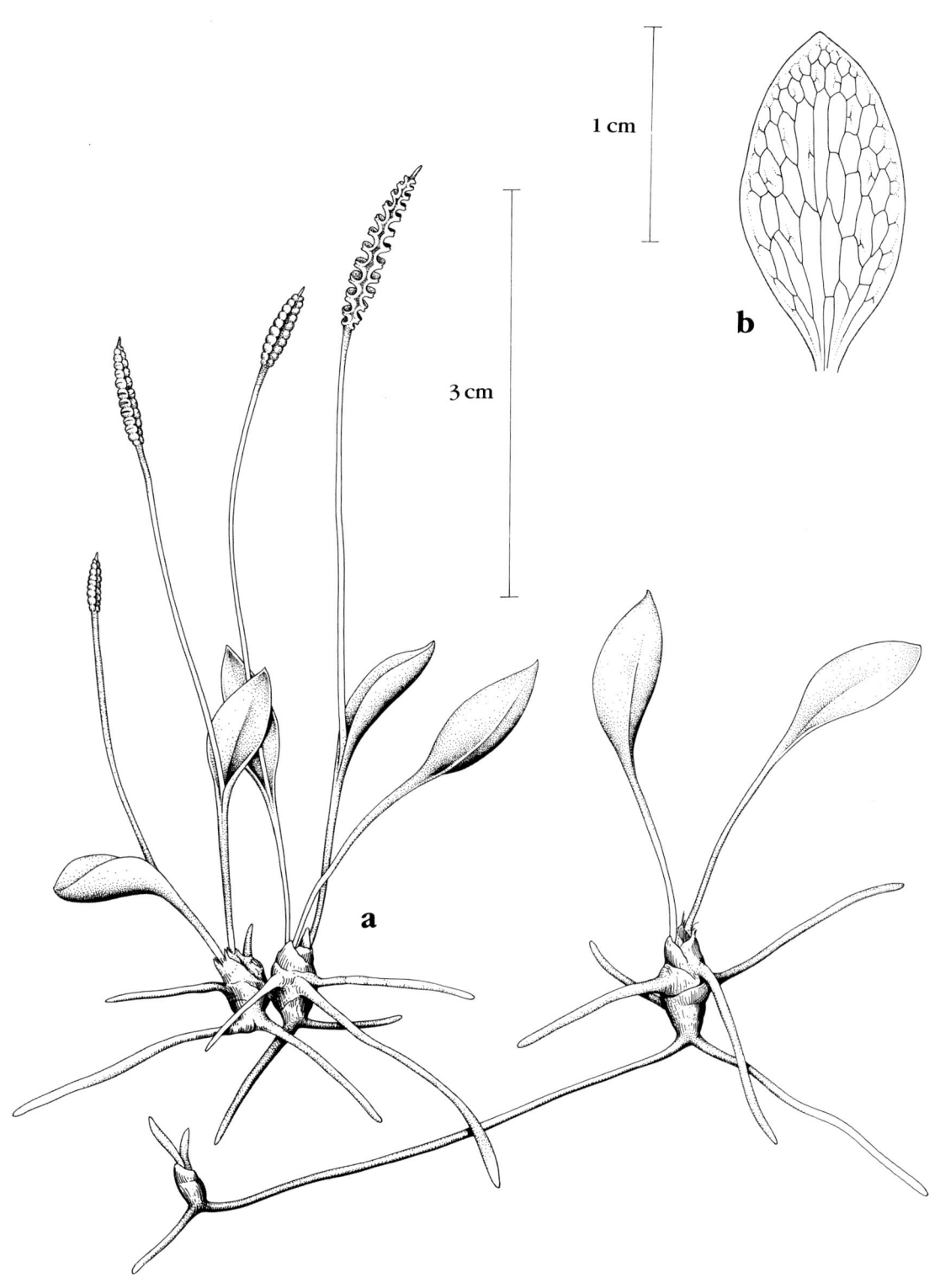

Ophioglossum nudicaule var. *tenerum*
a. Habit; b. Blade venation.

4. *Ophioglossum vulgatum* L. var. *pycnostichum* Fern.

Ophioglossum pycnostichum (Fern.) Love & Love

COMMON NAME: Southern Adder's-tongue Fern

Stem cylindric; roots rarely proliferous. Leaves usually solitary, up to 20 cm tall; base with a persistent, brown, leathery sheath up to 8 mm long; sterile blade ovate to ovate-lanceolate, up to 10 cm long and 4 cm wide, apex obtuse, base cuneate to truncate; veins forming areoles containing free ending veinlets; fertile portion bearing up to 30 sporangia in each row.

HABITAT: Moist, open woods, alluvial woodlands, and swamps.

RANGE: Mainly southeastern United States.

The southern variety of *Ophioglossum vulgatum*, var. *pycnostichum*, differs from the more northern var. *pseudopodum* in having a lustrous, dark green, ovate sterile blade and a brown, leathery, persistent basal sheath. Variety *pseudopodum* has a dull, pale green, mostly elliptic sterile blade and a light brown, membranous, ephemeral sheath (Wagner, 1971a). Arkansas plants are somewhat variable with regard to shape of the sterile blade but all appear to possess the persistent basal sheath.

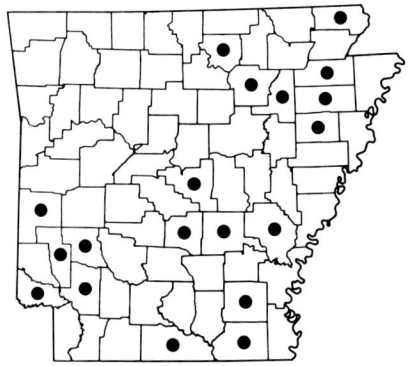

Ophioglossum vulgatum

Arkansas Co.: *Kellogg s.n.* (MO). Ashley Co.: *Thomas 34123* (NLU). Clay Co.: *Hartsoe s.n.* (UARK). Craighead Co.: *Richards 6209* (ARKSU). Cross Co.: *Clark 683* (HXC). Drew Co.: *Thomas 34129* (NLU). Grant Co.: *D. Moore 50095* (UARK). Hempstead Co.: *Kellogg s.n.* (MO). Howard Co.: *D. Moore 5680* (UARK). Independence Co.: *Thomas 38606* (NLU). Izard Co.: *J. Moore 5680* (UCA). Jackson Co.: *Richards 6197* (ARKSU). Jefferson Co.: *Locke 1734* (UARK). Little River Co.: *D. Moore 5620* (UARK). Pike Co.: *Lindley & Lindley s.n.* (NLU). Poinsett Co.: *Kellogg s.n.* (MO). Polk Co.: *J. Moore 3140* (UCA). Pulaski Co.: *Lowman s.n.* (HXC). Union Co.: *Thomas 35321* (NLU).

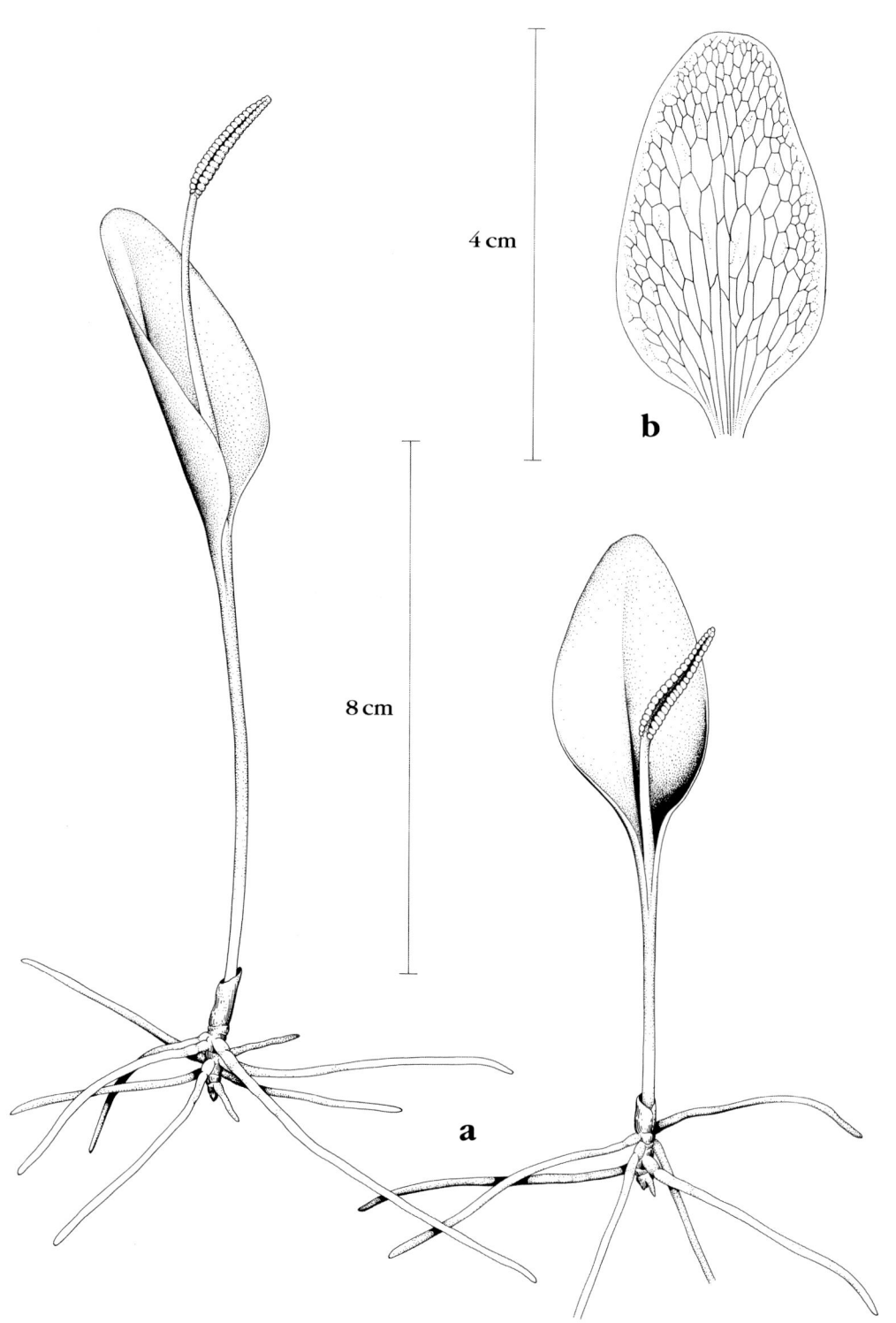

Ophioglossum vulgatum* var. *pycnostichum
a. Habit; b. Blade venation.

5. *Ophioglossum petiolatum* Hook.

Ophioglossum floridanum E. P. St. John

COMMON NAME: Stalked Adder's-tongue Fern

Rhizome cylindric; roots few, long, fleshy, up to 1.2 mm in diam., often proliferous. Fronds usually several per growing season, up to 20 cm tall; sterile blade ovate to ovate-lanceolate, apex acute, base obtuse to truncate; veins forming areoles often without included veinlets; fertile portion bearing up to 30 sporangia in each row.

HABITAT: Cemeteries and yards; West Gulf Coastal Plain and Mississippi Alluvial Plain. Dallas Co.: Oakland Cemetery, Fordyce; *Lawson 227* (NLU). Jefferson Co.: yard beside building at Pine Bluff Arsenal; *Thomas 44091* (NLU). Union Co.: Olive Branch Methodist Church Yard; SE of New Caledonia; *Taylor 2637* (SIU). White Co.: Union Church Yard; Antioch; *Thomas 34184* (NLU).

RANGE: Southeastern United States, pantropical.

Dale Thomas first collected *Ophioglossum petiolatum* in Arkansas at the Olive Branch Methodist Church Yard on 27 March 1972. Since then he has located other stations cited above (Thomas, 1978). This species has been collected as far north as southeastern Missouri (Thomas, Marx, and Lawson, 1974).

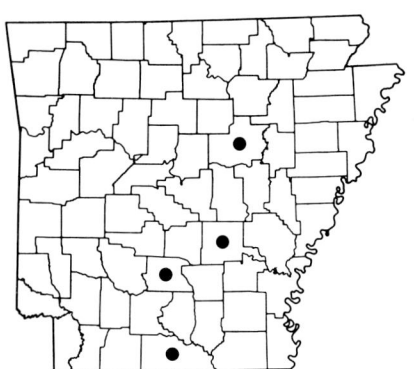

Ophioglossum petiolatum

Dallas Co.: *Thomas 27918* (NLU). Jefferson Co.: *Thomas 44091* (NLU). Union Co.: *Taylor 2637* (SIU). White Co.: *Thomas 34184* (NLU).

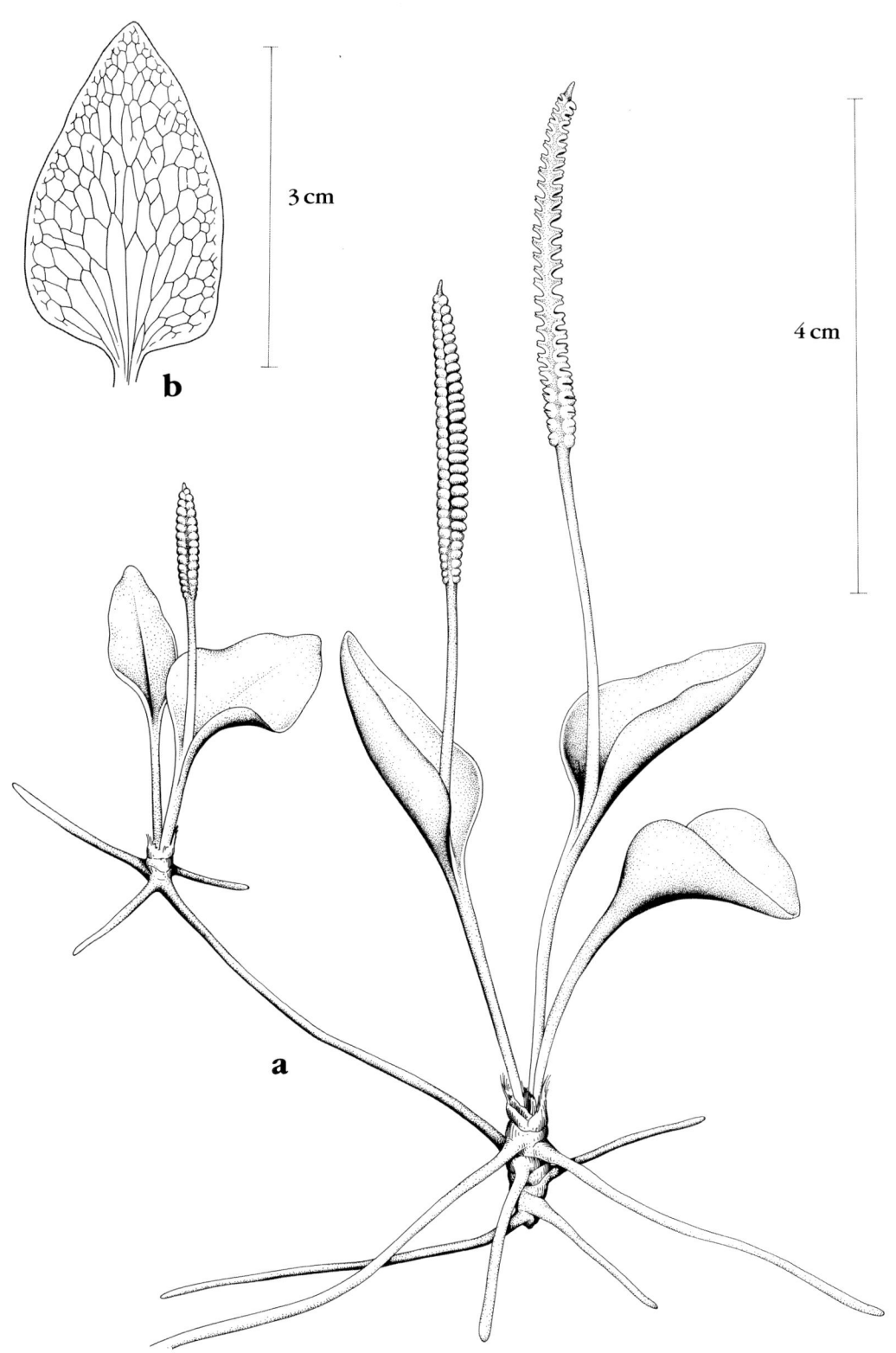

Ophioglossum petiolatum
a. Habit; b. Blade venation.

Osmunda L. Royal Ferns

Rhizome creeping, stout, covered by old stipe bases and wiry, fibrous roots, scaleless. Fronds dimorphic, deciduous, erect or erect spreading, pinnate-pinnatifid or bipinnate; stipe and rachis mostly green to stramineous, stipe base flattened and sheathing rhizome; veins forked, free, reaching the margin. Sporangia densely clustered on separate fertile fronds or on reduced fertile pinnae of otherwise vegetative fronds, globose, splitting longitudinally; spores green, tetrahedral, globose.

A genus of 14 species occurring mainly in temperate and subtropical regions.

Key to the species of *Osmunda* in Arkansas

1. Fronds bipinnate; pinnules serrulate .... 1. *O. regalis* (p. 170)
1. Fronds pinnate-pinnatifid; ultimate segments entire
    2. Fronds with a tuft of hairs at base of each pinna; fertile pinnae borne on a completely separate frond; .... 2. *O. cinnamomea* (p. 172)
    2. Fronds without a tuft of hairs at base of each pinna; fertile pinnae borne near middle of frond .... 3. *O. claytoniana* (p. 174)

1. *Osmunda regalis* L. var. *spectabilis* (Willd.) Gray

Osmunda spectabilis Willd.

COMMON NAME: Royal Fern

Fronds erect-spreading, bipinnate, up to 1.5 m long; stipe and rachis green to stramineous; blade obate to obate-oblong, up to 1.2 m long and 60 cm wide; pinnae dimorphic; sterile pinnae subopposite, sterile pinnules alternate, oblong, obtuse, serrulate; fertile pinnae typically borne at apex of frond.

HABITAT: Swamps, marshes, moist woods, seeps, wet depressions, stream banks, edges of lakes, and around springs.

RANGE: Eastern North America, tropical America.

Osmunda regalis var. *spectabilis* is widespread in Arkansas but appears to be most common in the West Gulf Coastal Plain where it is often associated with *O. cinnamomea*.

Osmunda regalis var. *spectabilis* f. *anomala* (Farw.) Harris, which differs from the typical form in having sterile pinnules borne in the fertile segment of the frond, has been collected in Clay, Green, Polk, and Washington Counties.

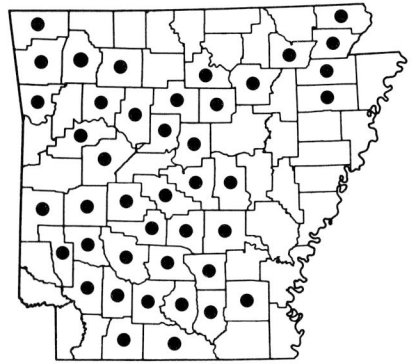

Osmunda regalis L. var. *spectabilis*

Benton Co.: *Plank s.n.* (NY). Bradley Co.: *Locke 1091* (UARK). Calhoun Co.: *Demaree 22108* (MO). Clark Co.: *Taylor 2182* (SIU). Clay Co.: *Richards 5046* (ARKSU). Cleburne Co.: *Taylor 1025* (SIU). Cleveland Co.: *Taylor 1140* (SIU). Columbia Co.: *Taylor 1158* (SIU). Conway Co.: *J. Moore 928* (UARK). Craighead Co.: *Demaree 5056* (UCA). Crawford Co.: *D. Moore 710286* (UARK). Dallas Co.: *Taylor 2734* (SIU). Drew Co.: *Demaree 22417* (MO). Faulkner Co.: *D. Moore 52236* (UARK). Franklin Co.: *Barber s.n.* (UARK). Garland Co.: *Palmer 24949* (MO). Grant Co.: *Taylor 2726* (SIU). Greene Co.: *Demaree 4065* (SMU). Hempstead Co.: *Taylor 1167* (SIU). Hot Spring Co.: *Demaree 14784A* (SMU). Howard Co.: *McSwain 43E127* (UARK). Independence Co.: *Johnson 304* (HXC). Jefferson Co.: *Demaree 24300* (MO). Johnson Co.: *Redfearn 23839* (SMS). Lawrence Co.: *Wheeler 54* (F). Logan Co.: *D. Moore 480041* (UARK). Lonoke Co.: *Clark 667* (HXC). Montgomery Co.: *Taylor 2208* (SIU). Nevada Co.: *D. Moore 450091* (UARK). Newton Co.: *Johnson 465* (HXC). Ouachita Co.: *Demaree 16846* (MO). Pike Co.: *Demaree 9539* (MO). Poinsett Co.: *Pyle 588* (UARK). Polk Co.: *Palmer 12625* (MO). Pope Co.: *D. Moore 350269* (UARK). Pulaski Co.: *Taylor 2542* (SIU). Saline Co.: *Haas 2485* (UCA). Stone Co.: *Thomas 8355* (NLU). Union Co.: *Taylor 1157* (SIU). Van Buren Co.: *D. Moore 350438* (UARK). Washington Co.: *Hite 29* (UARK). Yell Co.: *Buchholz 1088* (UARK).

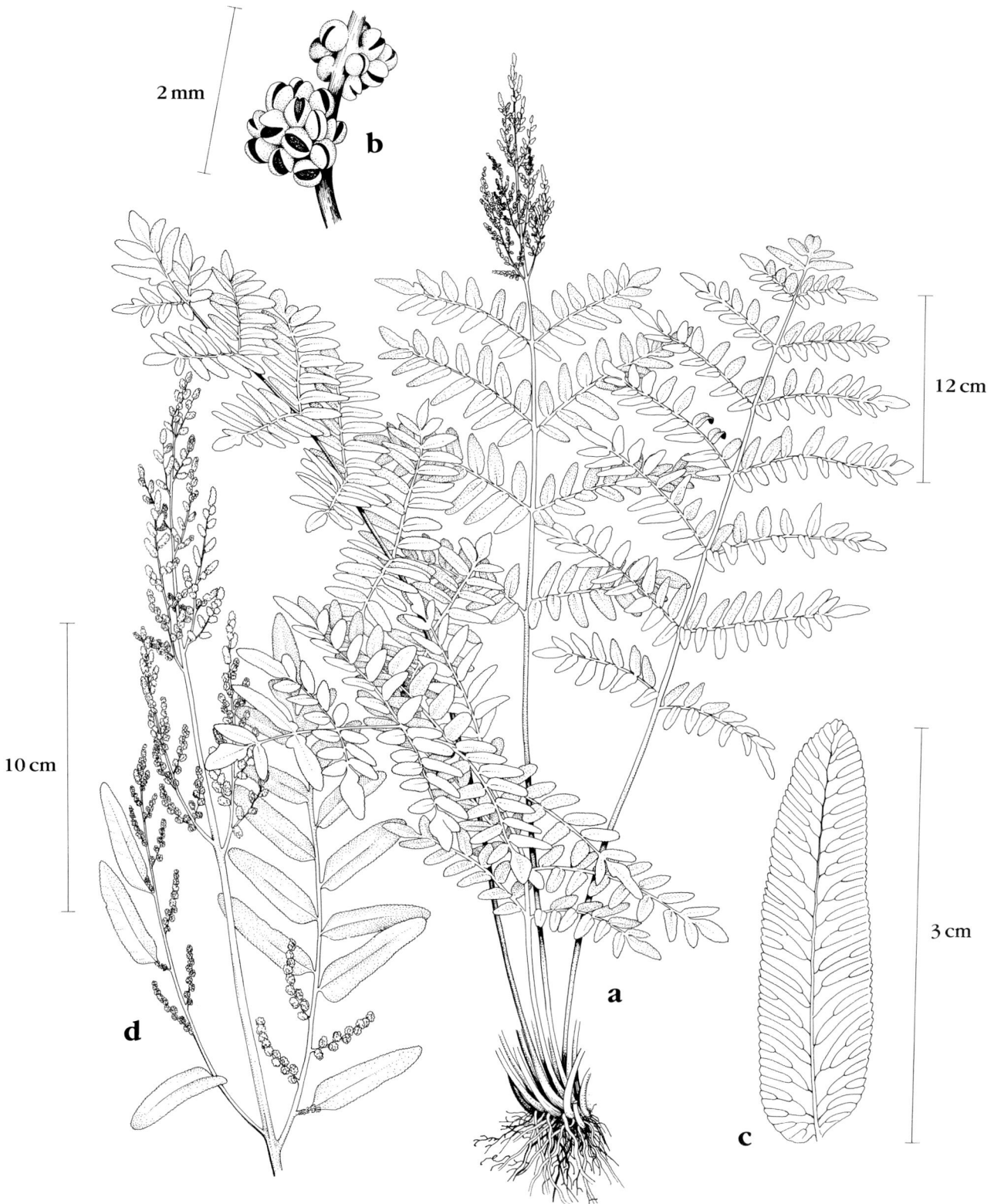

Osmunda regalis var. *spectabilis*
a. Habit; b. Sporangia; c. Pinnule; d. f. *anomala*, portion of frond.

2. *Osmunda cinnamomea* L.

COMMON NAME: Cinnamon Fern

Fronds dimorphic; sterile fronds erect-spreading, pinnate-pinnatifid, up to 1.2 m long; blade lanceolate to oblong-lanceolate, up to 1 m long and 30 cm wide, acuminate; pinnae opposite or subopposite, lanceolate to oblong-lanceolate, glabrate, acuminate, with a tuft of hairs persisting below at base; pinna lobes oblong, obtuse, sparsely ciliolate, with sinuses between them wide enough so that lobe edges do not usually overlap; fertile fronds surrounded by sterile fronds, erect, bipinnate, up to 1.3 m tall, brown-tomentose; fertile pinnae strongly ascending, oblong-lanceolate, soon withering.

HABITAT: Swamps, marshes, moist woods, seeps, wet depressions, stream banks, edges of lakes, around springs, and on wet rock ledges.

RANGE: Eastern North America, Mexico, West Indies.

Osmunda cinnamomea is widely distributed in Arkansas but, like *O. regalis* var. *spectabilis,* it appears to be most common in the West Gulf Coastal Plain.

Osmunda cinnamomea f. *frondosa* (Torr. & Gray) Britton, which differs from the typical form in having sterile pinnae toward the base of the fertile frond, was collected by E. J. Palmer (MO 945740) on 27 May 1926 from a sandy, open woods near Malvern, Hot Spring County.

Osmunda cinnamomea

Bradley Co.: *Locke 2026* (UARK). Benton Co.: *Demaree 4885* (UARK). Calhoun Co.: *Demaree 16908* (SMU). Clark Co.: *Taylor 2182* (SIU). Clay Co.: *Rosen 99* (HXC). Cleburne Co.: *Babb 281* (ARKSU). Cleveland Co.: *Demaree 23309* (MO). Columbia Co.: *Taylor 1898* (SIU). Conway Co.: *D. Moore s.n.* (UARK). Crawford Co.: *D. Moore 710288* (UARK). Cross Co.: *D. Moore 420368* (UARK). Drew Co.: *Demaree 28816* (SMU). Faulkner Co.: *Johnson 490* (HXC). Franklin Co.: *Hartsoe s.n.* (UARK). Garland Co.: *Taylor 2560* (SIU). Grant Co.: *Taylor 2724* (SIU). Greene Co.: *Demaree 26659* (SMU). Hempstead Co.: *Bush 5724* (MO). Hot Spring Co.: *Palmer 8103* (MO). Howard Co.: *McSwain 43E126* (UARK). Independence Co.: *Johnson 301* (HXC). Izard Co.: *Demaree 24435* (SMU). Jefferson Co.: *Demaree 24054* (SMU). Lafayette Co.: *Fassett 20907* (F). Logan Co.: *D. Moore 480082* (UARK). Lonoke Co.: *Clark 666* (HXC). Madison Co.: *Davis 1499* (UARK). Montgomery Co.: *Taylor 2207* (SIU). Nevada Co.: *D. Moore 450091A* (UARK). Newton Co.: *Redfearn 27509* (SMS). Ouachita Co.: *D. Moore 4505* (UARK). Perry Co.: *Robertson s.n.* (APCR). Pike Co.: *Demaree 9543* (MO). Polk Co.: *D. Moore 480559* (UARK). Pope Co.: *D. Moore 350368* (UARK). Pulaski Co.: *Taylor 2541* (SIU). Saline Co.: *Haas 1489* (UCA). Sevier Co.: *D. Moore 400181* (UARK). Stone Co.: *D. Moore 450520* (UARK). Union Co.: *Taylor 1155* (SIU). Van Buren Co.: *Palmer 25175* (MO).

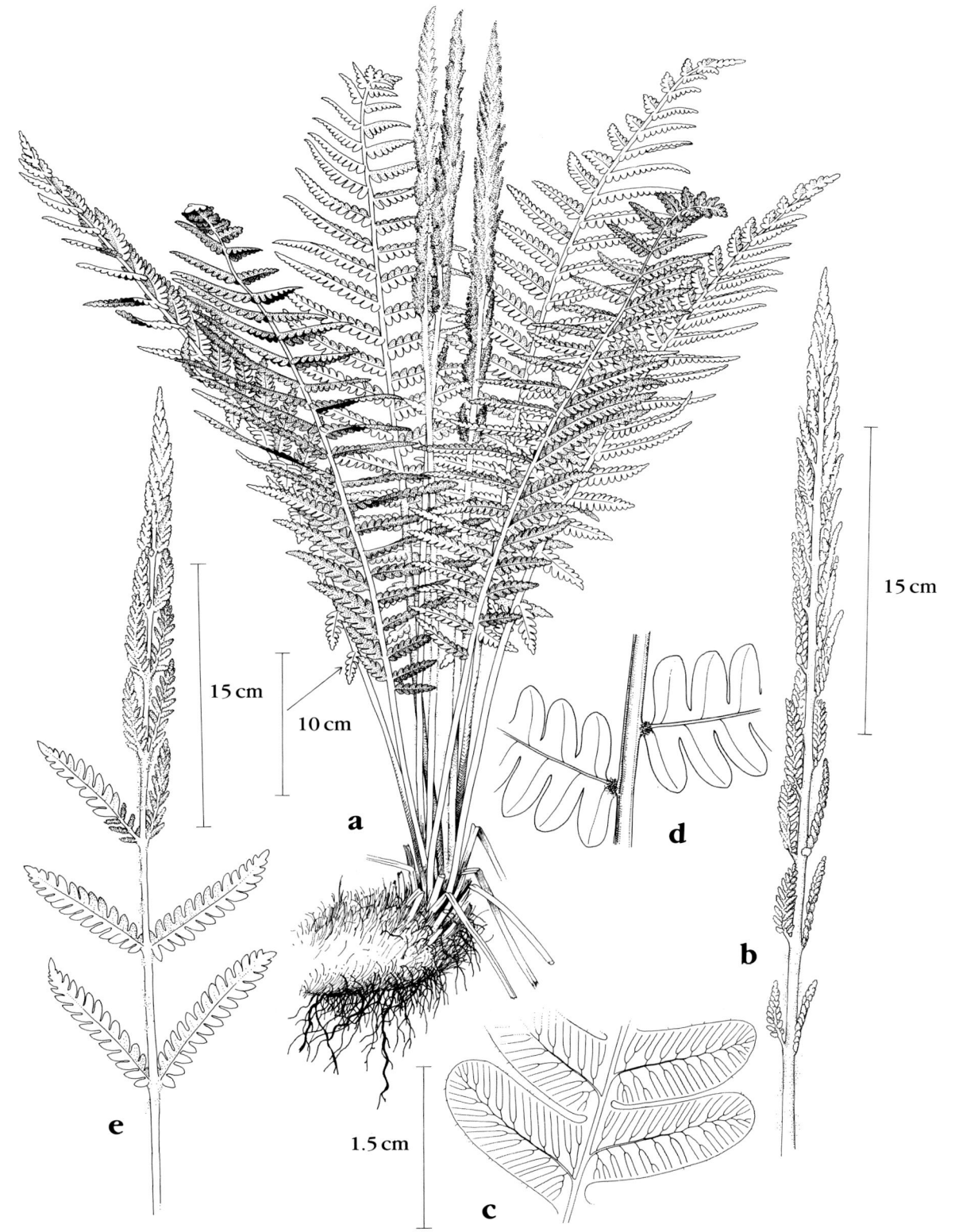

Osmunda cinnamomea
a. Habit; b. Portion of sporiferous frond; c. Portion of pinna: d. Basal portion of pinnae; e. f. *frondosa*, portion of frond.

3. *Osmunda claytoniana* L.

COMMON NAME: Interrupted Fern

Fronds erect-spreading, pinnate-pinnatifid, up to 1.2 m long; blade lanceolate to oblong-lanceolate, up to 1 m long and 30 cm wide, abruptly acuminate or obtuse; pinnae dimorphic; sterile pinnae alternate or subopposite, lanceolate to oblong-lanceolate, crisped-puberulent along midrib and veins below, glabrate above, abruptly acuminate or obtuse, without a tuft of hairs persisting below at base; pinna lobes oblong, obtuse, not ciliolate, with sinuses between them narrow enough so that lobe edges often overlap; fertile pinnae borne near middle of frond, strongly ascending, oblong-lanceolate, soon withering.

HABITAT: Pope Co.: Alder thicket above a persistent spring; W of Pelsor; *Moore 4191* (UARK). Stone Co.: vicinity of Blanchard Springs Caverns; *Taylor 1251* (SIU).

RANGE: Eastern North America, eastern Asia.

Osmunda claytoniana, a common species in the northeastern United States, reaches the southwestern extent of its range in Arkansas. The two Arkansas populations possibly represent relict populations reflecting a once wider distribution or past southern migrations of this species during Pleistocene glaciation.

Osmunda claytoniana was known to occur in Arkansas 10 years before it was collected by botanists. In June 1926, John Buchholz stopped at a hotel in Freeman Springs in northern Pope County where he noticed a vase containing fronds of *O. claytoniana*. Inquiring about these fronds, he was told that they had been gathered near a spring at Sand Gap (Pelsor). Buchholz and Dwight Moore subsequently made several unsuccessful attempts to locate these plants. On 12 June 1936, Moore finally located the population (Moore, 1940b). The Stone County population was discovered by Dwight Moore on 18 June 1945.

Osmunda claytoniana L.

Pope Co.: *D. Moore 4191* (UARK). Stone Co.: *Taylor 1251* (SIU).

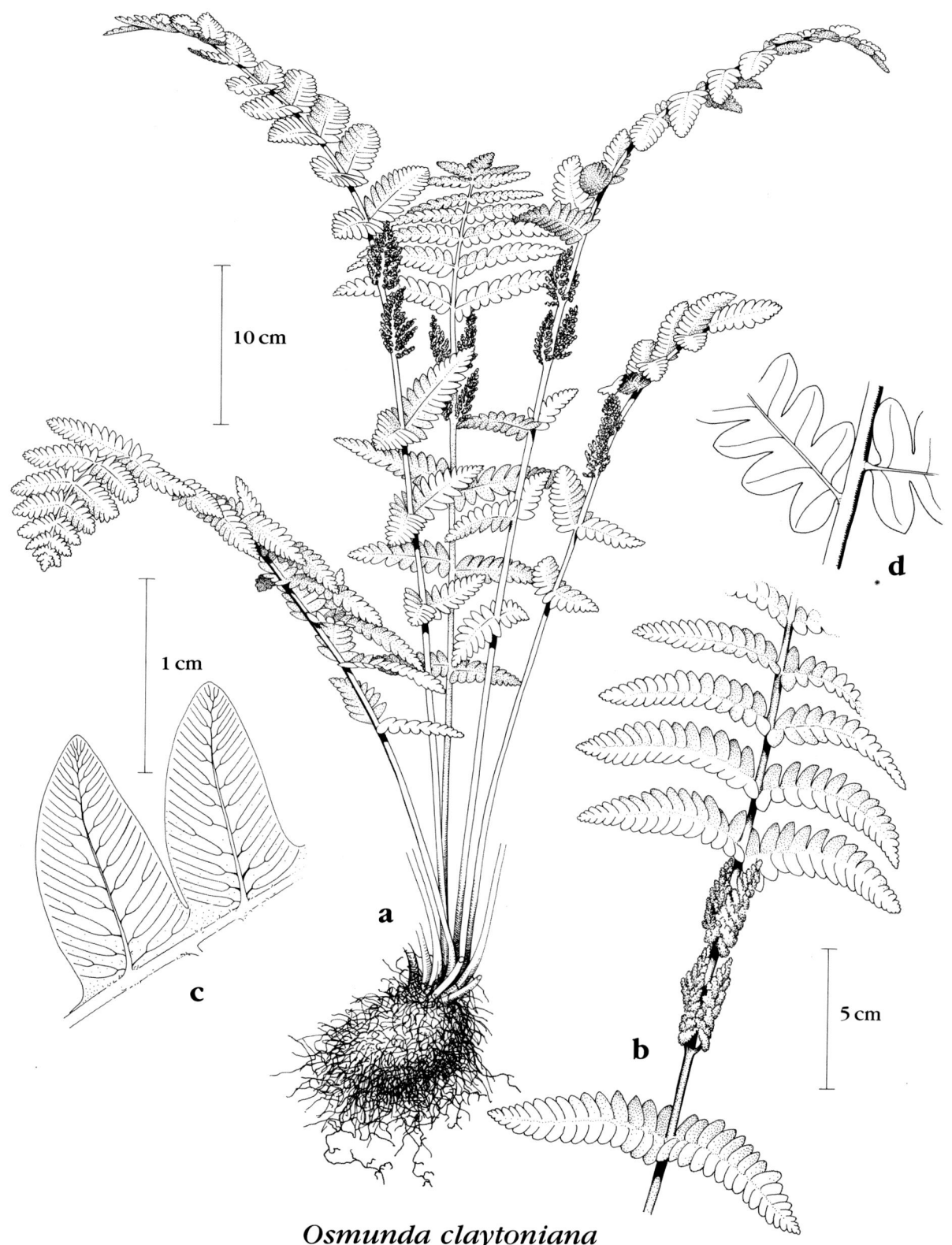

Osmunda claytoniana
a. Habit; b. Sporiferous pinnae; c. Portion of pinna; d. Basal portion of pinnae.

Pellaea Link Cliff Brakes

Rhizome short-creeping to erect. Fronds evergreen, tufted, erect to erect-spreading, pinnate to tripinnate; stipe and rachis wiry, reddish brown to purplish black; ultimate divisions of mature fronds over 1 cm long; veins forked, free. Sori marginal, partly covered by revolute margins of pinnae, pinnules, or segments.

A genus of about 80 species found mainly in arid temperate and subtropical regions. Tryon (1957) revised the genus *Pellaea* section *Pellaea*.

Key to the species of *Pellaea* in Arkansas

1. Stipe and rachis scabrid with appressed and crisped hairs; apical parts of the frond, pinnae, and pinnules stalked with blades not decurrent . . . . 1. *P. atropurpurea* (p. 178)
1. Stipe and rachis glabrate; apical parts of the frond and pinnae decurrent with blades often basally connate to adjacent lateral divisions . . . . 2. *P. glabella* (p. 180)

1. *Pellaea atropurpurea* (L.) Link

Pteris atropurpurea L.
Allosorus atropurpureus (L.) Presl

COMMON NAME: Purple-stemmed Cliff Brake

Rhizome scales white to reddish brown with age. Fronds pinnate to tripinnate, up to 50 cm tall, slightly dimorphic; fertile fronds usually more erect, larger, and bearing narrower pinnae or pinnules than sterile fronds; stipe and rachis scabrid with appressed and crisped hairs; blade deltoid to lanceolate, up to 30 cm long and 15 cm wide; apical parts of the frond, pinnae, and pinnules stalked with blades not decurrent; ultimate divisions deep green, ovate to linear-lanceolate, up to 5 cm long.

HABITAT: Limestone, dolomite, or calcareous sandstone outcrops; most common in the Ozark Mountains.

RANGE: Eastern to west central United States, south to Guatemala.

Pellaea atropurpurea is an apogamous triploid. It produces 32 unreduced spores per sporangium (Tryon and Britton, 1958). Each spore is capable of producing a sporophyte without fertilization during the gametophyte generation. Apogamy removes the need for water droplets in reproduction and is therefore adventageous to ferns that occur in dry habitats.

An aberrant form of *P. atropurpurea* in which the pinnae or ultimate segments repeatedly fork was collected by Dwight Moore near West Fork, Washington County, on 30 September 1934. Moore's specimens (MO 1860929, UARK 340687) are referable to f. *cristata* (Trel.) Clute.

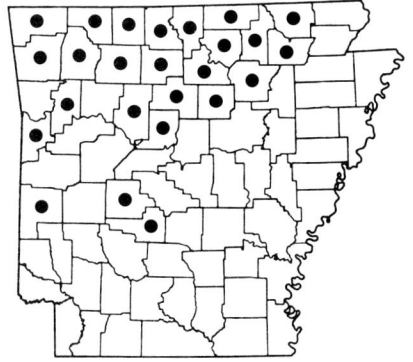

Pellaea atropurpurea

Baxter Co.: *Taylor 1842* (SIU). Benton Co.: *Demaree 2908* (SMU). Boone Co.: *Palmer 6904* (MO). Carroll Co.: *Palmer 4424* (MO). Cleburne Co.: *Taylor 1020* (SIU). Conway Co.: *J. Moore 1262* (UARK). Franklin Co.: *Barber 448* (UARK). Fulton Co.: *Demaree 5370* (UARK). Garland Co.: *Taylor 2225* (SIU). Hot Spring Co.: *Demaree 15567* (SMU). Independence Co.: *Trelease s.n.* (MO). Izard Co.: *Taylor 1270* (SIU). Lawrence Co.: *Taylor 1789* (SIU). Madison Co.: *Taylor 1995* (SIU). Marion Co.: *Taylor 1231* (SIU). Newton Co.: *Taylor 1217* (SIU). Polk Co.: *J. Moore s.n.* (UARK). Pope Co.: *D. Moore 52074* (UARK). Randolph Co.: *Taylor 1802* (SIU). Searcy Co.: *Taylor 1242* (SIU). Sebastian Co.: *Taylor 2719* (SIU). Sharp Co.: *Taylor 1809* (SIU). Stone Co.: *Taylor 1247* (SIU). Van Buren Co.: *Palmer 25171* (UARK). Washington Co.: *Taylor 1112* (SIU).

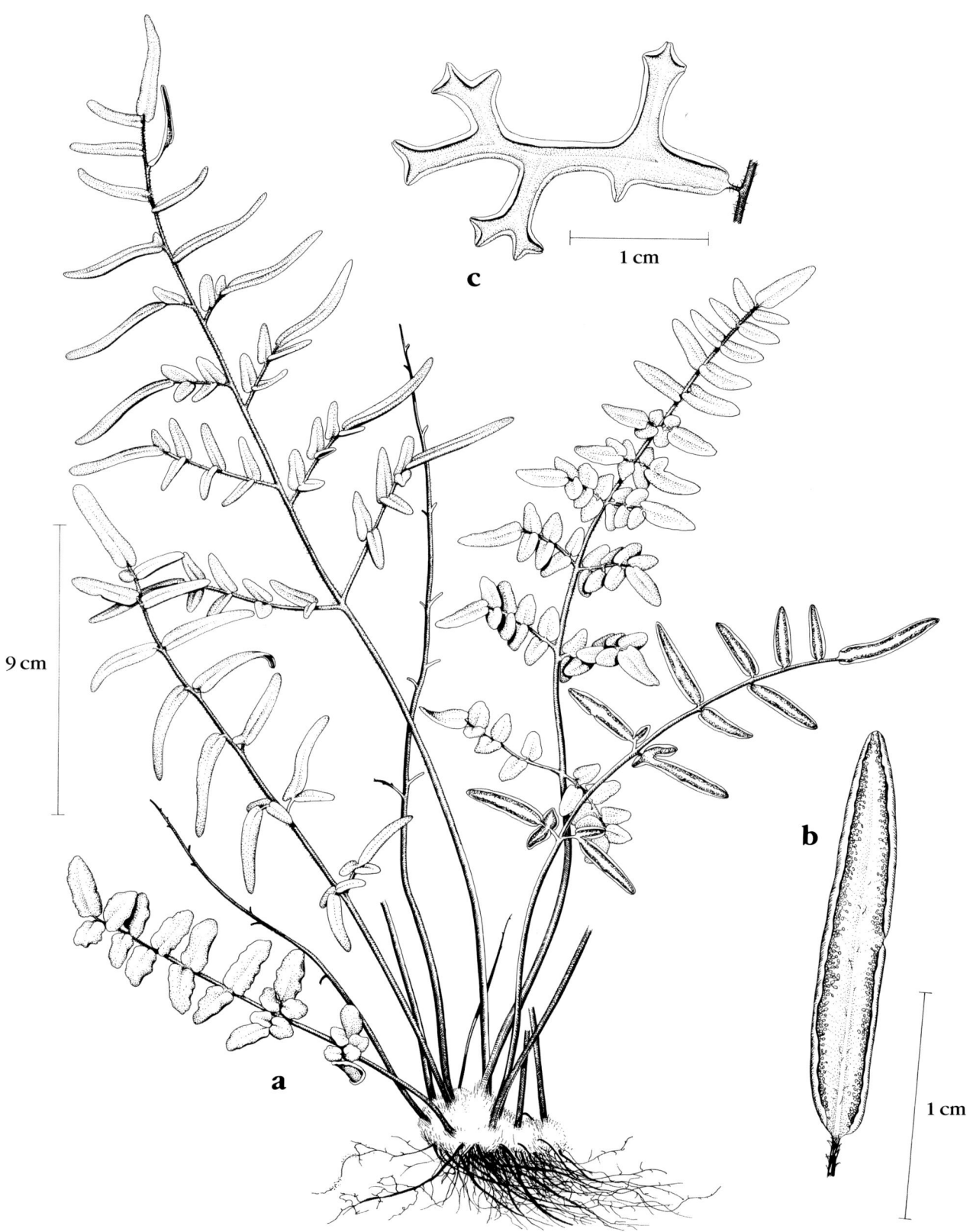

Pellaea atropurpurea
a. Habit; b. Lower surface of sporiferous pinna; c. f. *cristata*, pinna.

2. *Pellaea glabella* Kuhn

Pellaea atropurpurea var. *bushii* Mack. & Bush
Pellaea atropurpurea f. *glabella* (Kuhn) Clute

COMMON NAME: Smooth Cliff Brake

Rhizome scales orange-red to reddish brown with age. Fronds pinnate to bipinnate, up to 25 cm long, uniform; stipe and rachis glabrate; blade linear-oblong to oblong-lanceolate, up to 18 cm long and 6 cm wide; apical parts of the frond and pinnae decurrent, with blades often basally connate to adjacent pinnae or pinnules; ultimate divisions grayish green, usually with a bluish cast, elliptic to oblong-lanceolate, up to 2 cm long.

HABITAT: Limestone, dolomite, or calcareous sandstone outcrops; chiefly in the Ozark Mountains.

RANGE: Eastern North America.

Tryon (1957) recognizes three varieties of this species based on differences in frond size, pinnae form, and number of spores per sporangium. Varieties *occidentalis* and *simplex* are more western plants and do not occur in Arkansas. Variety *glabella,* the taxon found in Arkansas, is usually an apogamous tetraploid with 32 spores per sporangium, but Wagner, Farrar, and Chen (1965) have reported sexual, diploid specimens of var. *glabella* in Missouri. These diploid plants contained 64 spores in each sporangium.

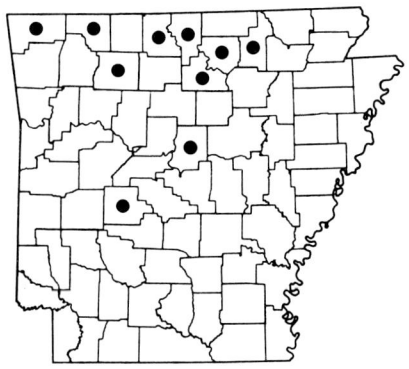

Pellaea glabella

Baxter Co.: *Taylor 1841* (SIU). Benton Co.: *D. Moore 4000284* (UARK). Carroll Co.: *D. Moore 410184* (UARK). Faulkner Co.: *Lane 241* (UARK). Garland Co.: *Engelmann s.n.* (MO). Izard Co.: *Taylor 1271* (SIU). Marion Co.: *Demaree s.n.* (SMU). Newton Co.: *Taylor 2697* (SIU). Sharp Co.: *Johnson 485* (HXC). Stone Co.: *Taylor 2898* (SIU).

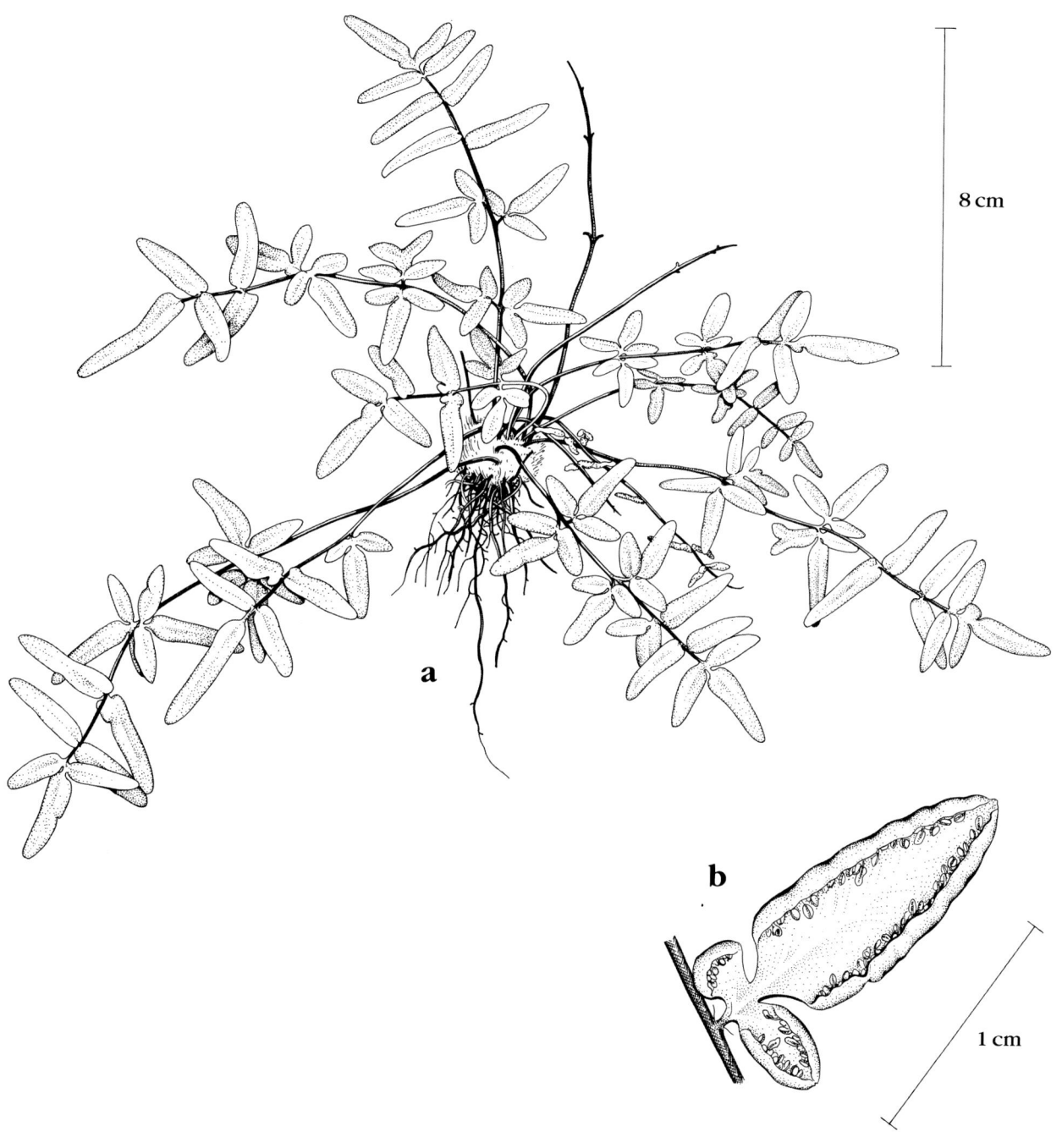

Pellaea glabella
a. Habit; b. Lower surface of sporiferous pinna.

Phegopteris Beech Ferns

According to Holttum (1969), this is a genus of three species related to and sometimes included in *Thelypteris*. Two species of *Phegopteris* occur in eastern North America and one is found in southeast Asia.

1. *Phegopteris hexagonoptera* (Michx.) Fee

Polypodium hexagonopterum Michx.
Dryopteris hexagonoptera (Michx.) C. Chr.
Thelypteris hexagonoptera (Michx.) Weatherby

COMMON NAME: Broad Beech Fern

Rhizome long creeping, slender, brown, pilosulous; scales lanceolate, often ciliolate. Fronds deciduous, erect-spreading bipinnatifid, up to 60 cm long; stipe stramineous, glabrate; blade broadly deltoid, up to 30 cm long and 35 cm wide; rachis green to stramineous, winged throughout, pilosulous, bearing lanceolate scales; blade divisions elliptic-lanceolate to oblong-lanceolate, pilosulous and minutely stipitate glandular below and along midvein above, ciliolate; veins forked, reaching the margins, sparsely scaly below; lowest pair of divisions recurved; pinna divisions entire to lobed. Sori submarginal; indusium absent.

HABITAT: Moist, sandy soil on slopes and in ravines of rich woods; Interior Highlands, West Gulf Coastal Plain, and Crowley's Ridge.

RANGE: Eastern North America.

Phegopteris hexagonoptera (Michx.) Fee

Ashley Co.: *Taylor 1877* (SIU). Benton Co.: *D. Moore 410010* (UARK). Bradley Co.: *Demaree 21022* (MO). Carroll Co.: *Palmer 4471* (MO). Clark Co.: *Taylor 2176* (SIU). Clay Co.: *Bush 2616* (MO). Cleburne Co.: *Smith 1494* (UARK). Conway Co.: *Tucker 7157* (APCR). Craighead Co.: *Demaree 3576* (MO). Cross Co.: *Palmer 31663* (UARK). Drew Co.: *Palmer 44223* (SMU). Faulkner Co.: *Buchholz 946* (UARK). Franklin Co.: *Johnson 521* (HXC). Garland Co.: *Palmer 29210* (UARK). Greene Co.: *Demaree 4002* (SMU). Hempstead Co.: *Bush 5713* (NY). Hot Spring Co.: *Wherry s.n.* (PH). Howard Co.: *McSwain 43E80* (UARK). Independence Co.: *Demaree 17080* (SMU). Izard Co.: *Thomas s.n.* (NLU). Jefferson Co.: *Stewart 20* (UARK). Johnson Co.: *Redfearn 18929* (SMS). Lawrence Co.: *Taylor 1793* (SIU). Lee Co.: *Taylor 1185* (SIU). Logan Co.: *Palmer 23236* (MO). Madison Co.: *Key 267* (SMS). Marion Co.: *Johnson 92* (HXC). Montgomery Co.: *Taylor 1075* (SIU). Newton Co.: *Taylor 1220* (SIU). Perry Co.: *Demaree 20145* (MO). Phillips Co.: *Taylor 1190a* (SIU). Pike Co.: *Redfearn 24472* (SMS). Poinsett Co.: *Emig 58* (MO). Polk Co.: *Taylor 1066* (SIU). Pope Co.: *Taylor 1203* (SIU). Pulaski Co.: *Haase s.n.* (NY). St. Francis Co.: *Demaree 7234* (UARK). Saline Co.: *Palmer 10549* (MO). Searcy Co.: *Taylor 2582* (SIU). Stone Co.: *Taylor 1254* (SIU). Union Co.: *Taylor 1153* (SIU). Van Buren Co.: *Palmer 24291* (UARK). Washington Co.: *Taylor 1103* (SIU). White Co.: *Johnson 460* (HXC).

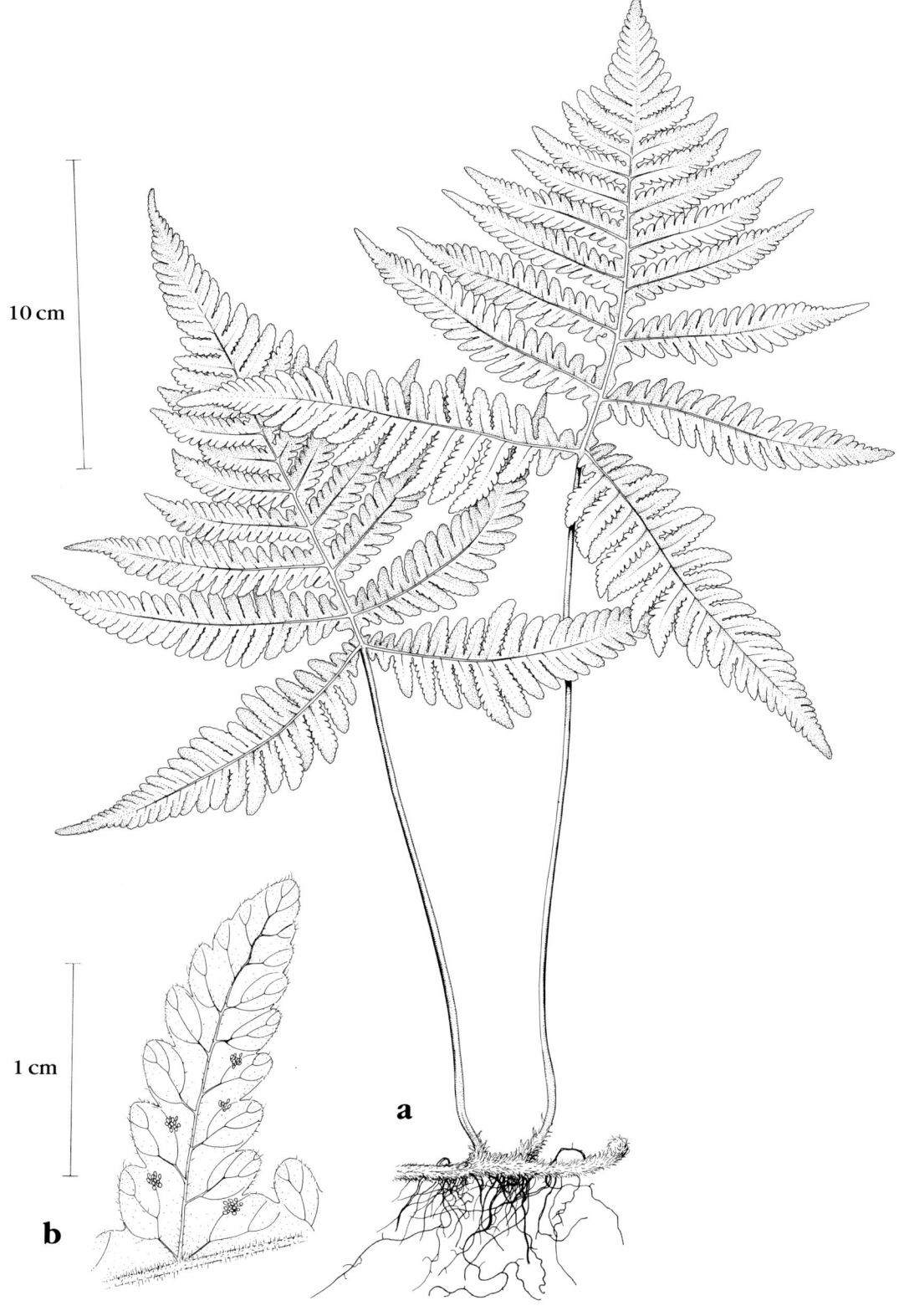

Phegopteris hexagonoptera
a. Habit; b. Lower surface of frond lobe with sori.

Pilularia L. Pillworts

A genus of six species found in temperate regions.

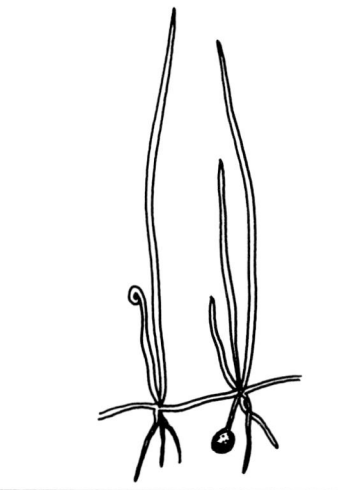

1. *Pilularia americana* A. Br.

COMMON NAME: American Pillwort

Anchored water plant. Rhizome creeping, slender, branching. Fronds erect, simple, filiform, devoid of pinnae, up to 10 cm tall. Sporocarps solitary near base of frond, borne on deflexed stalks arising at base of frond, globose, up to 3 mm in diam., covered with yellowish brown hairs, containing 2-4 sori, heterosporous; sori bearing megasporangia distally and microsporangia proximally; megaspores solitary in megasporangium, white, ovoid; microspores numerous in microsporangia, white, tetrahedral-globose.

HABITAT: Margins of lakes; Interior Highlands. Conway Co.: Cedar Lake; *D. Moore 470584* (APCR); Bailey Lake; *Taylor 2883* (SIU). Faulkner Co.: Beaverfork Lake; *J. Moore 6608* (UCA). Garland Co.: Lake Hamilton; *D. Moore 480532* (UARK). Logan Co.: Cove Lake; *D. Moore 490427* (UARK). Polk Co.: Lake Mena; *Massey 1329* (NCU). Sebastian Co.: near Ft. Smith; *Nuttall 180* (MO). Washington Co.: Lake Wedington; *D. Moore 480774* (MO).

RANGE: Georgia, Tennessee, Missouri, Arkansas, Kansas, Oklahoma, Texas, Nebraska, California, Oregon.

Pilularia was unknown in North America until specimens were collected by Thomas Nuttall near Fort Smith in 1819 (Dennis and Webb, 1981). Additional stations in Arkansas for this inconspicuous plant escaped discovery until 31 August 1942 when Dwight Moore collected it on Petit Jean Mountain around Bailey Lake, Conway County (Moore, 1947). Careful observation along the edges of lakes and ponds should yield additional records for *Pilularia americana* in the state.

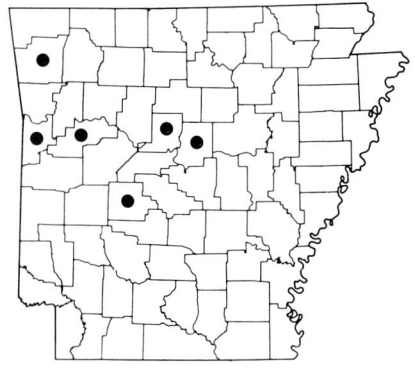

Pilularia americana

Conway Co.: *D. Moore 470584* (APCR). Faulkner Co.: *J. Moore 6608* (UCA). Garland Co.: *D. Moore 480532* (UARK). Logan Co.: *D. Moore 490427* (UARK). Polk Co.: *Massey 1329* (NCU). Sebastian Co.: *Nuttall 180* (MO). Washington Co.: *D. Moore 480774* (MO).

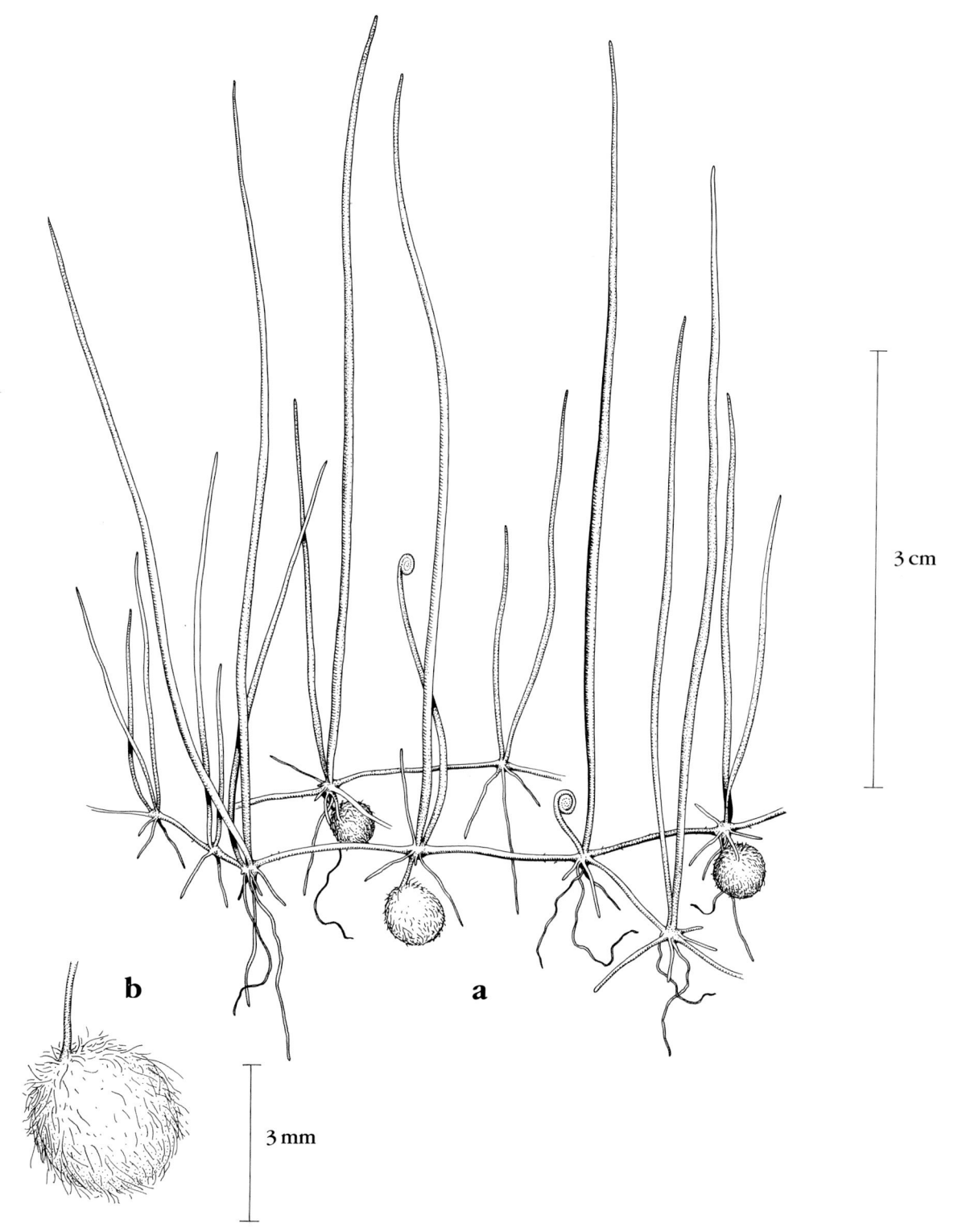

Pilularia americana
a. Habit; b. Sporocarp.

Polypodium L. Polypody Ferns

Rhizome long-creeping, scaly. Fronds evergreen, pinnatifid with alternate to subopposite divisions, glabrous, articulate near base; blades glabrous; veins forked, free. Sori submarginal to medial, round; indusium absent.

A genus of perhaps 1000 mostly epiphytic species, mainly of tropical regions.

Key to the species of *Polypodium* in Arkansas

1. Stipe and lower surfaces of blades scaly; blade divisions entire; veins obscure .... 1. *P. polypodioides* (p. 192)
1. Stipe and lower surfaces of blades scaleless; blade divisions remotely crenulate; veins obvious .... 2. *P. virginianum* (p. 194)

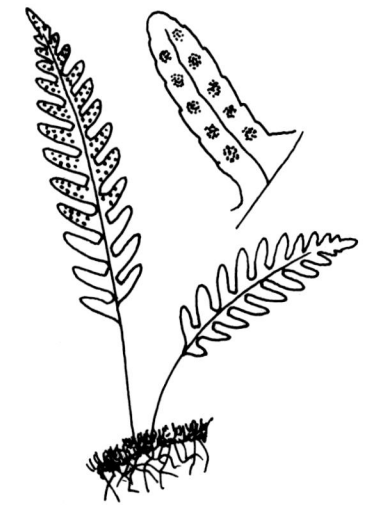

1. *Polypodium polypodioides* (L.) Watt var. *michauxianum* Weatherby

Acrostichum polypodioides L.
Polypodium incanum sensu auct., non Sw.
Polypodium ceteraccinum Michx.
Marginaria polypodioides (L.) Tidest.

COMMON NAME: Resurrection Fern

Rhizome slender, wiry; scales peltate, attenuate to apex. Fronds erect to pendent, pinnatifid, up to 20 cm long, scaly; scales orbiculate to ovate-lanceolate, erose, peltate, usually less than 1 mm long and with a blackish spot at point of attachment; stipe wiry, green to purplish black, scaly; blade deltoid to lanceolate, up to 12 cm long and 5 cm wide, scaleless above except along midrib, scaly below; blade divisions linear to oblong, entire, veins obscure. Sori submarginal; paraphyses absent.

HABITAT: On rocks or as an epiphyte on trees, especially oaks and elms.

RANGE: Southeastern United States.

Polypodium polypodioides var. *michauxianum* appears to be the most ubiquitous pteridophyte in Arkansas. Variety *michauxianum* differs from the West Indian variety *polypodioides* in that the upper surface of the blade is glabrous and the lower surface of the blade has erose rather than fimbriate scales.

Under moist conditions the fronds of *P. polypodioides* are fully expanded, but during dry periods, the fronds fold and curl upon themselves. These shriveled fronds quickly return to the expanded state when adequate moisture is again available.

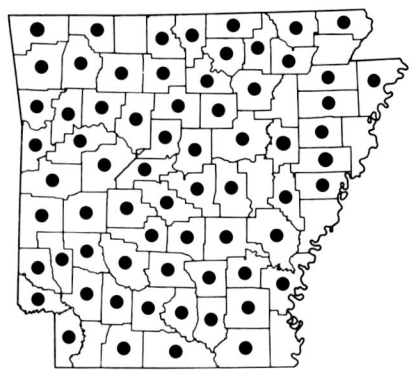

Polypodium polypodioides

Arkansas Co.: *Taylor 1867a* (SIU). Ashley Co.: *Taylor 1873b* (SIU). Benton Co.: *Peck 81-237* (ULAR). Baxter Co.: *Taylor 1848* (SIU). Bradley Co.: *Taylor 1145* (SIU). Calhoun Co.: *Johnson 284* (HXC). Carroll Co.: *Palmer 4528* (MO). Clark Co.: *Taylor 2179* (SIU). Clay Co.: *Hartsoe 376* (SMU). Cleburne Co.: *Taylor 1024* (SIU). Cleveland Co.: *Taylor s.n.* (SIU). Columbia Co.: *Taylor 1165* (SIU). Conway Co.: *Demaree 249162* (SMU). Craighead Co.: *Taylor 2882* (SIU). Crawford Co.: *Redfearn 24556* (SMS). Cross Co.: *Palmer 31658* (MO). Dallas Co.: *Taylor 2731* (SIU). Desha Co.: *Johnson s.n.* (UARK). Drew Co.: *Taylor 1149* (SIU). Faulkner Co.: *Taylor 2013* (SIU). Franklin Co.: *J. Moore s.n.* (APCR). Fulton Co.: *Demaree 5284* (UARK). Garland Co.: *Taylor 2196* (SIU). Grant Co.: *Taylor 2728* (SIU). Hempstead Co.: *Taylor 1179* (SIU). Hot Spring Co.: *Demaree 21194* (SMU). Howard Co.: *McSwain 43E66* (UARK). Independence Co.: *Demaree 17098* (SMU). Izard Co.: *Taylor 2138* (SIU). Jefferson Co.: *Locke 761* (UARK). Johnson Co.: *Johnson 54* (HXC). Lawrence Co.: *Taylor 1791* (SIU). Lee Co.: *Demaree 37378* (SMU). Lincoln Co.: *Demaree 13739* (SMU). Little River Co.: *Taylor 2149* (SIU). Logan Co.: *Palmer 24152* (MO). Lonoke Co.: *Buchholz s.n.* (UARK). Madison Co.: *Taylor 2001* (SIU). Marion Co.: *Taylor 1836* (SIU). Miller Co.: *Taylor 1911* (SIU). Mississippi Co.: *Medcalf 645* (US). Monroe Co.: *Taylor 2832* (SIU). Montgomery Co.: *Taylor 1076* (SIU). Nevada Co.: *Taylor 2747* (SIU). Newton Co.: *More & Demaree 6386* (UARK). Ouachita Co.: *Taylor 2628* (SIU). Perry Co.: *Demaree 27056* (SMU). Pike Co.: *Demaree 9507* (SMU). Poinsett Co.: *Demaree 28624* (SMU). Polk Co.: *Taylor 2549* (SIU). Pope Co.: *Redfearn 23888* (SMS). Pulaski Co.: *Demaree 8467* (SMU). Randolph Co.: *Taylor 2096* (SIU). St. Francis Co.: *Johnson 486* (HXC). Saline Co.: *Aingworth s.n.* (UARK). Scott Co.: *Taylor 2714* (SIU). Searcy Co.: *Emig 85* (MO). Sebastian Co.: *Taylor 2722* (SIU). Sevier Co.: *Culwell 3239* (UCA). Sharp Co.: *Demaree 26281* (SMU). Stone Co.: *Demaree 59388* (SMU). Union Co.: *Taylor 2633* (SIU). Van Buren Co.: *Palmer 25188* (MO). Washington Co.: *Demaree 2742* (SMU). White Co.: *D. Moore 451040* (UARK). Woodruff Co.: *Johnson 479* (HXC). Yell Co.: *Taylor 2622* (SIU).

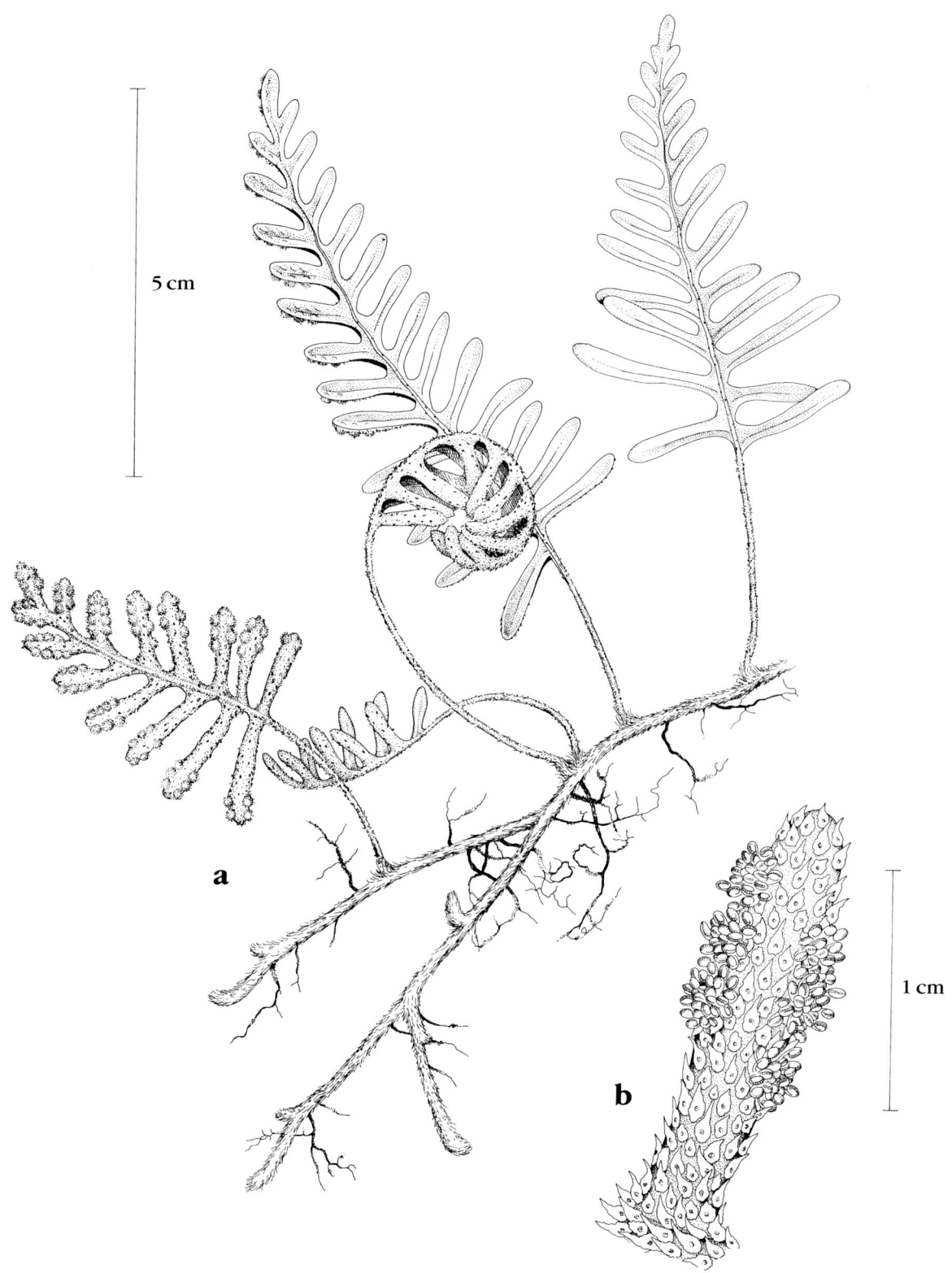

Polypodium polypodioides var. *michauxianum*
a. Habait; b. Lower surface of frond lobe with sori.

2. *Polypodium virginianum* L.

Polypodium vulgare var. *virginianum* (L.) Eat.
Polypodium vulgare var. *americanum* Hook.

COMMON NAME: Common Polypody

Rhizome thick, stiff; scales deltoid-ovate to linear-lancelate, obtuse to auriculate at base. Fronds erect to erect-spreading, pinnatifid, up to 35 cm long, scaleless; stipe green to stramineous; blade ovate-lanceolate to oblong, up to 25 cm long and 6 cm wide; blade divisions oblong, obtuse, remotely crenulate, veins apparent. Sori submarginal to medial; sporangia mixed with clavate, glandular paraphyses.

HABITAT: Usually shaded, sandstone outcrops; chiefly Ozark Mountains.

RANGE: Eastern and central North America.

Polypodium virginianum, as widely recognized, likely represents a species complex. Manton and Shivas (1953) detected diploid and tetraploid cytotypes in Canadian plants. Manton (1957) discovered a triploid cytotype which presumably resulted from hybridization of the diploid and tetraploid taxa. This triploid's chromosome pairing during meiosis (37 pairs and 37 univalents) indicates that the tetraploid is an allopolyploid. Evans (1971) provided additional chromosome counts, correlated morphological characters with the three cytotypes, and suggested *P. montense*, a western species, as a possible partner with diploid *P. virginianum* in the origin of the tetraploid.

As currently understood, the three cytotypes appear to be morphologically distinguishable on the basis of spore abortion in the triploid and differences in leaf blade outline between the diploid and tetraploid. Spores of triploid plants are mostly small, shriveled, and colorless. A few spores, however, are larger, globose, yellow, and at least appear to be viable. Diploid and tetraploid taxa produce abundant reniform, yellow, "normal" looking spores. Diploids, which bear ovate to nearly deltoid leaf blades, have their basal pair of leaf segments notched on the lower edge near the rachis. Tetraploids bear narrowly lanceolate leaf blades with their lower leaf segments unnotched but often reduced in size.

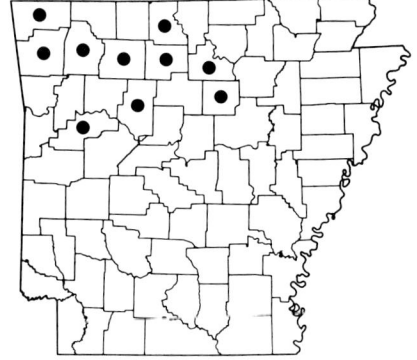

Polypodium virginianum L.

Benton Co.: *D. Moore 410014* (UARK). Cleburne Co.: *Babb 186* (ARKSU). Franklin Co.: *Johnson 526* (HXC). Logan Co.: *Taylor 1042* (SIU). Madison Co.: *Taylor 2002* (SIU). Marion Co.: *D. Moore 480728* (UARK). Newton Co.: *Palmer 27090* (UARK). Pope Co.: *Taylor 1214* (SIU). Searcy Co.: *Demaree 51919* (SMU). Stone Co.: *Taylor 2901* (SIU). Washington Co.: *Harvey 77* (MO).

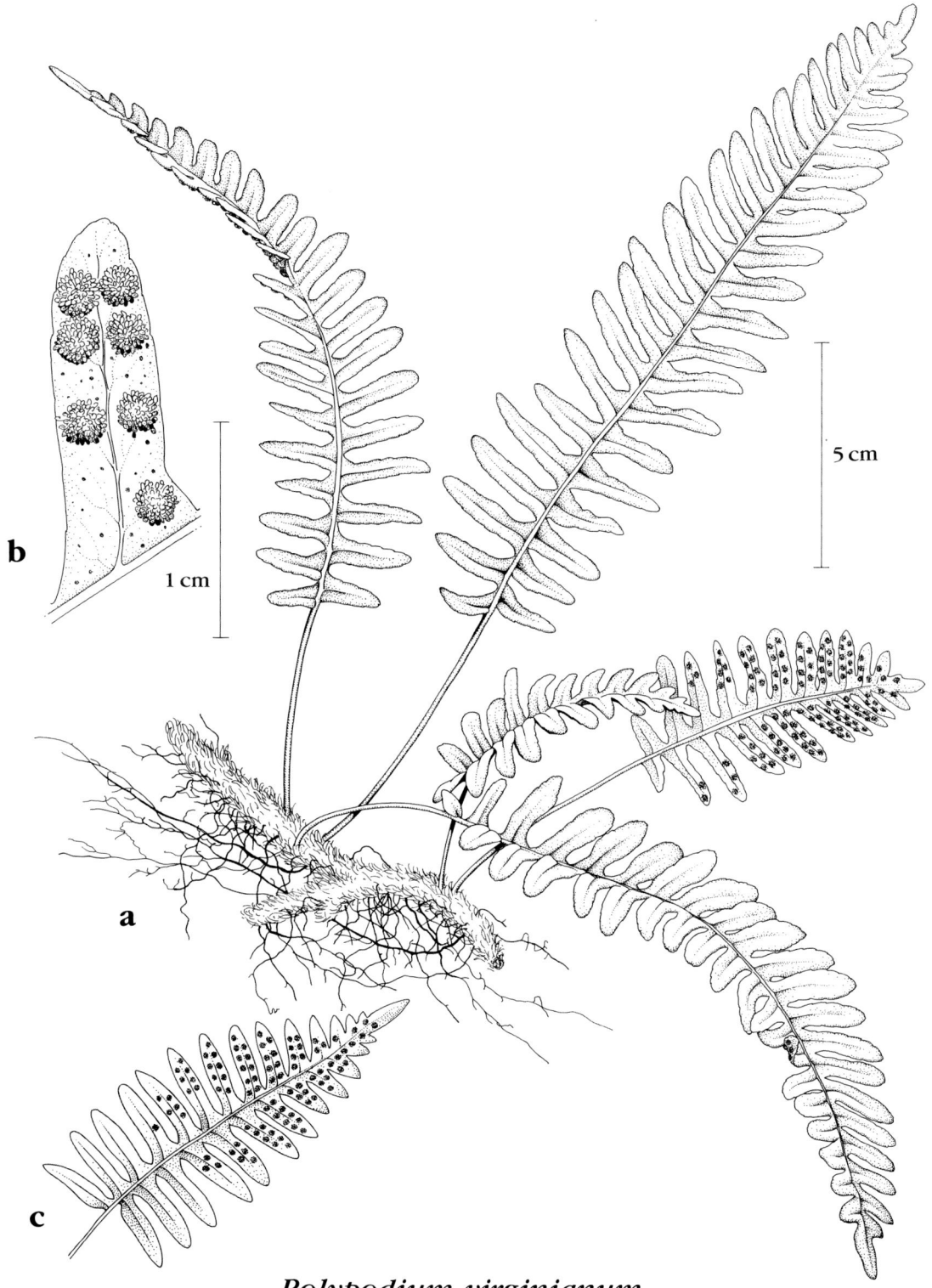

Polypodium virginianum
a. Habit; b. Lower surface of frond lobe with sori; c. diploid cytotype.

Polystichum Roth Holly Ferns

A genus of about 175 species, mostly of temperate regions.

1. *Polystichum acrostichoides* (Michx.) Schott

Nephrodium acrostichoides Michx.
Aspidium acrostichoides (Michx.) Sw.

COMMON NAME: Christmas Fern

Rhizome creeping, stout, covered by old stipe bases; scales ovate to linear-lanceolate. Fronds evergreen, erect to erect-spreading, pinnate, up to 75 cm long, stipe and rachis green to stramineous, scaly; blade lanceolate, up to 50 cm long and 15 cm wide; pinnae lanceolate to oblong, auriculate at base on upper margin; veins mostly once forked, free, dimorphic; fertile pinnae toward frond apex, abruptly smaller than sterile pinnae. Sori medial, round, borne on veins in two rows along pinna midvein; indusium peltate, soon shriveling.

HABITAT: Rich, rocky, wooded slopes and ravines, along stream banks, and in alluvial woods; throughout the state.

RANGE: Eastern North America.

Polystichum acrostichoides is one of the most common and widespread of the pteridophytes in Arkansas. Fronds of this plant which bear pinnae that are coarsely serrate to lobed and which sometimes have scattered sori extending to the tips of the lower pinnae have been recognized as f. *incisum* (Gray) Gilb. Specimens bearing these variously cut pinnae and scattered sori have been noted from a number of collections in the state.

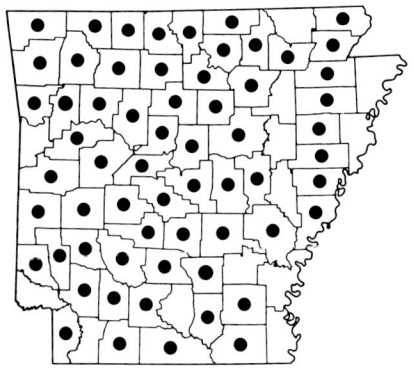

Polystichum acrostichoides

Arkansas Co.: *Wherry s.n.* (PH). Ashley Co.: *Taylor 1878* (SIU). Baxter Co.: *D. Moore 450747* (UARK). Benton Co.: *D. Moore 460154* (UARK). Boone Co.: *Demaree s.n.* (UARK). Bradley Co.: *Demaree 21015* (UARK). Carroll Co.: *Bush 15424* (UARK). Clark Co.: *Taylor 2174* (SIU). Clay Co.: *Demaree 27019* (SMU). Cleburne Co.: *Taylor 1021* (SIU). Cleveland Co.: *Locke 2268* (UARK). Columbia Co.: *Johnson 35* (HXC). Conway Co.: *Demaree 22791* (MO). Craighead Co.: *Demaree 3493* (SMU). Crawford Co.: *Taylor 1094* (SIU). Cross Co.: *Palmer 31660* (UARK). Dallas Co.: *Taylor 1134* (SIU). Drew Co.: *Palmer 44222* (SMU). Faulkner Co.: *Buchholz 929* (UARK). Franklin Co.: *Johnson 519* (HXC). Fulton Co.: *Wheeler 40* (F). Garland Co.: *Taylor 2194* (SIU). Grant Co.: *Taylor 2725* (SIU). Greene Co.: *Demaree 4009* (NY). Hempstead Co.: *Bush 1651* (NY). Hot Spring Co.: *Palmer 26575* (MO). Howard Co.: *McSwain 43 E65* (UARK). Independence Co.: *Demaree 17068* (MO). Izard Co.: *Taylor 2135* (SIU). Jefferson Co.: *Demaree 24084* (MO). Johnson Co.: *D. Moore 450264* (UARK). Lawrence Co.: *Taylor 1792* (SIU). Lee Co.: *Taylor 1184* (SIU). Logan Co.: *Taylor 1034* (SIU). Lonoke Co.: *Clark 680* (HXC). Madison Co.: *Taylor 1996* (SIU). Marion Co.: *Taylor 1236* (SIU). Miller Co.: *Taylor 1173* (SIU). Montgomery Co.: *Taylor 1074* (SIU). Nevada Co.: *D. Moore 420463* (UARK). Newton Co.: *Taylor 1222* (SIU). Ouachita Co.: *Demaree 16844* (MO). Perry Co.: *Taylor 2852* (SIU). Phillips Co.: *Taylor 1189b* (SIU). Pike Co.: *Demaree 9419* (SMU). Poinsett Co.: *D. Moore 31057* (APCR). Polk Co.: *Taylor 1068* (SIU). Pope Co.: *Taylor 1205* (SIU). Prairie Co.: *Taylor 1182* (SIU). Pulaski Co.: *Merrill 1425* (UARK). St. Francis Co.: *Demaree 22156* (MO). Saline Co.: *Palmer 8442* (MO). Scott Co.: *Taylor 1056* (SIU). Searcy Co.: *Taylor 1851* (SIU). Sevier Co.: *Brinkley 349* (F). Sharp Co.: *Schmitt 11* (ARKSU). Stone Co.: *Taylor 1252* (SIU). Union Co.: *Taylor 1154* (SIU). Van Buren Co.: *Taylor 2563* (SIU). Washington Co.: *Taylor 1104* (SIU). White Co.: *Johnson 455* (HXC). Yell Co.: *Taylor 1196* (SIU).

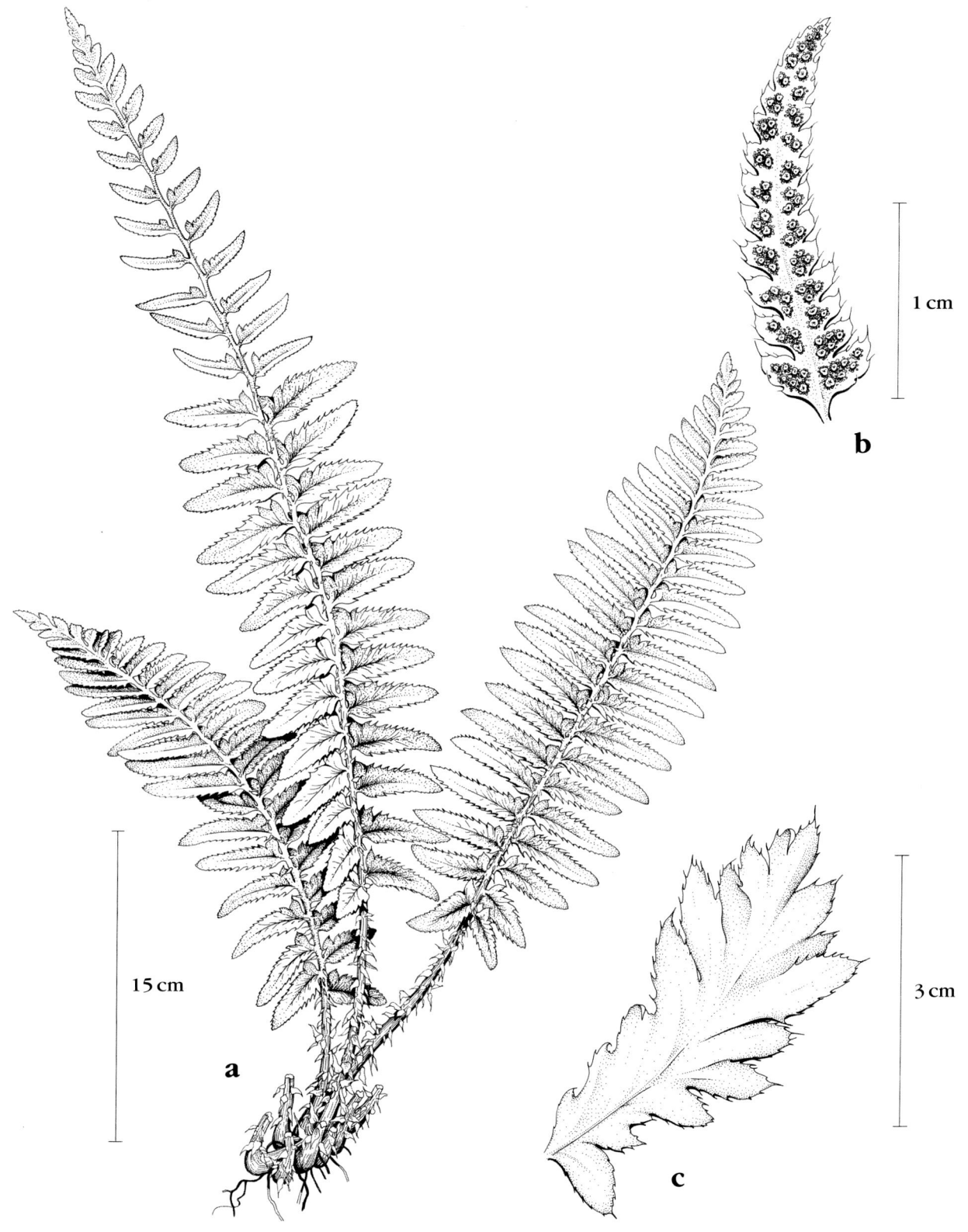

Polystichum acrostichoides
a. Habit; b. Lower surface of pinna with sori; c. f. *incisum*, pinna.

Pteridium Scop. Bracken

As revised by Tryon (1941), this genus is often treated as a single species, *Pteridium aquilinum,* composed of a number of regional varieties. It is one of the few truly cosmopolitan plants, being found on all continents except Antarctica.

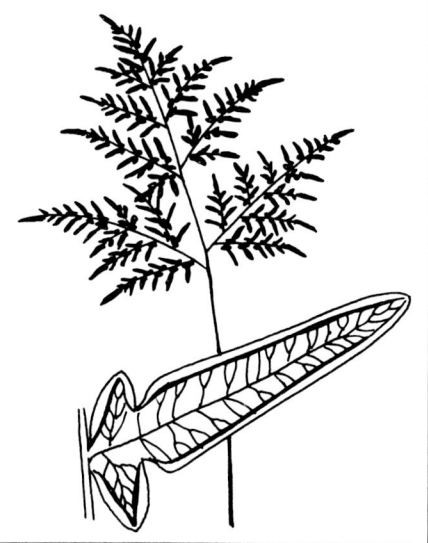

1. *Pteridium aquilinum* (L.) Kuhn

Pteris aquilina L.

COMMON NAME: Bracken

Rhizome subterranean, long-creeping, repeatedly branching, wide-spreading, often with a tuft of white to reddish brown hairs at apex. Fronds deciduous, erect-spreading, bipinnate-pinnatifid to tripinnate, up to 1.5 m tall, glabrous to puberulent; stipe rigid, reddish brown to stramineous; blade broadly deltoid to ovate, up to 60 cm long and 70 cm wide; pinnules or segments ovate to linear, entire to pinnatifid, margins revolute; veins forked, free. Sori marginal, with rudimentary inner indusium, partly covered by revolute margins of ultimate segments.

The two varieties of *Pteridium aquilinum* which occur in Arkansas, var. *latiusculum* and var. *pseudocaudatum,* intergrade to a considerable extent. Some populations have the broader ultimate segments characteristic of var. *latiusculum* but are nearly glabrous. Others possess the narrower segments of var. *pseudocaudatum* but have a sparsely puberulent margin and midvein. The presence of these intermediate populations precludes a clear distinction of the two taxa. Generally, var. *pseudocaudatum* is the more commonly encountered taxon in the West Gulf Coastal Plain, while more puberulent fronds, assignable to var. *latiusculum,* are found with greater frequency in the northern third of the state.

Key to the varieties of *Pteridium aquilinum* in Arkansas

1. Margins of pinnules or segments puberulent; longest, entire, ultimate divisions or lobes 3-7X longer than broad .... 1a. var. *latiusculum*

1. Margins of pinnules or segments glabrous or glabrate; longest, entire, ultimate divisions or lobes 6-15X longer than broad .... 1b. var. *pseudocaudatum*

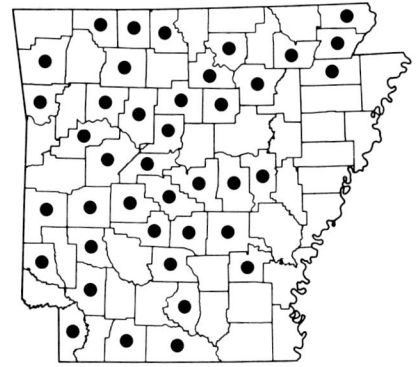

Pteridium aquilinum

Ashley Co.: *Taylor 1890* (SIU). Benton Co.: *D. Moore 450891* (UARK). Boone Co.: *Demaree s.n.* (UARK). Bradley Co.: *Demaree 23878* (SMU). Calhoun Co.: *Demaree 16616* (SMU). Carroll Co.: *D. Moore 410188* (UARK). Clark Co.: *Taylor 2181* (SIU). Clay Co.: *Richards 5353* (ARKSU). Cleburne Co.: *Smith 1488* (UARK). Cleveland Co.: *Taylor 1139* (SIU). Columbia Co.: *Taylor 1169* (SIU). Conway Co.: *Clark 45* (HXC). Craighead Co.: *Pyle 5819* (UARK). Crawford Co.: *D. Moore 50283* (UARK). Cross Co.: *Johnson 440* (HXC). Dallas Co.: *Demaree 19048* (SMU). Drew Co.: *Taylor 1148* (SIU). Faulkner Co.: *Buchholz 988* (UARK). Fulton Co.: *Taylor 2668* (SIU). Garland Co.: *Taylor 2860* (SIU). Grant Co.: *Demaree 16564* (SMU). Greene Co.: *Demaree 26697* (SMU). Hempstead Co.: *D. Moore 480477* (APCR). Hot Spring Co.: *Taylor 2859* (SIU). Howard Co.: *Demaree 9952* (SMU). Independence Co.: *Thomas 7778* (NLU). Izard Co.: *Taylor 2134* (SIU). Jefferson Co.: *Demaree 19457* (SMU). Johnson Co.: *Demaree 20213* (SMU). Lawrence Co.: *Demaree 31002* (SMU). Lee Co.: *Holmes 81* (SMU). Lincoln Co.: *Demaree 19185* (SMU). Little River Co.: *Taylor 2162* (SIU). Logan Co.: *Pyle 332* (UARK). Lonoke Co.: *Demaree 8406* (SMU). Marion Co.: *Demaree 29322* (SMU). Miller Co.: *Demaree 24486* (SMU). Montgomery Co.: *Taylor 2220* (SIU) Nevada Co.: *Taylor 2749* (SIU). Newton Co.: *Taylor 2701* (SIU). Perry Co.: *Wright P701* (UARK). Pike Co.: *Taylor 2171* (SIU). Polk Co.: *Demaree 15695* (SMU). Pope Co.: *Taylor 1206* (SIU). Prairie Co.: *Demaree 22307* (SMU). Pulaski Co.: *Taylor 2540* (SIU). Randolph Co.: *Taylor 2101* (SIU). Saline Co.: *Demaree 8545* (SMU). Sevier Co.: *D. Moore 401105* (UARK). Stone Co.: *Taylor 1256* (SIU). Union Co.: *Hoiberg 326* (SMU). Van Buren Co.: *Wherry s.n.* (PH). Washington Co.: *French s.n.* (APCR). White Co.: *Demaree 26892* (SMU). Yell Co.: *Demaree 20584* (SMU).

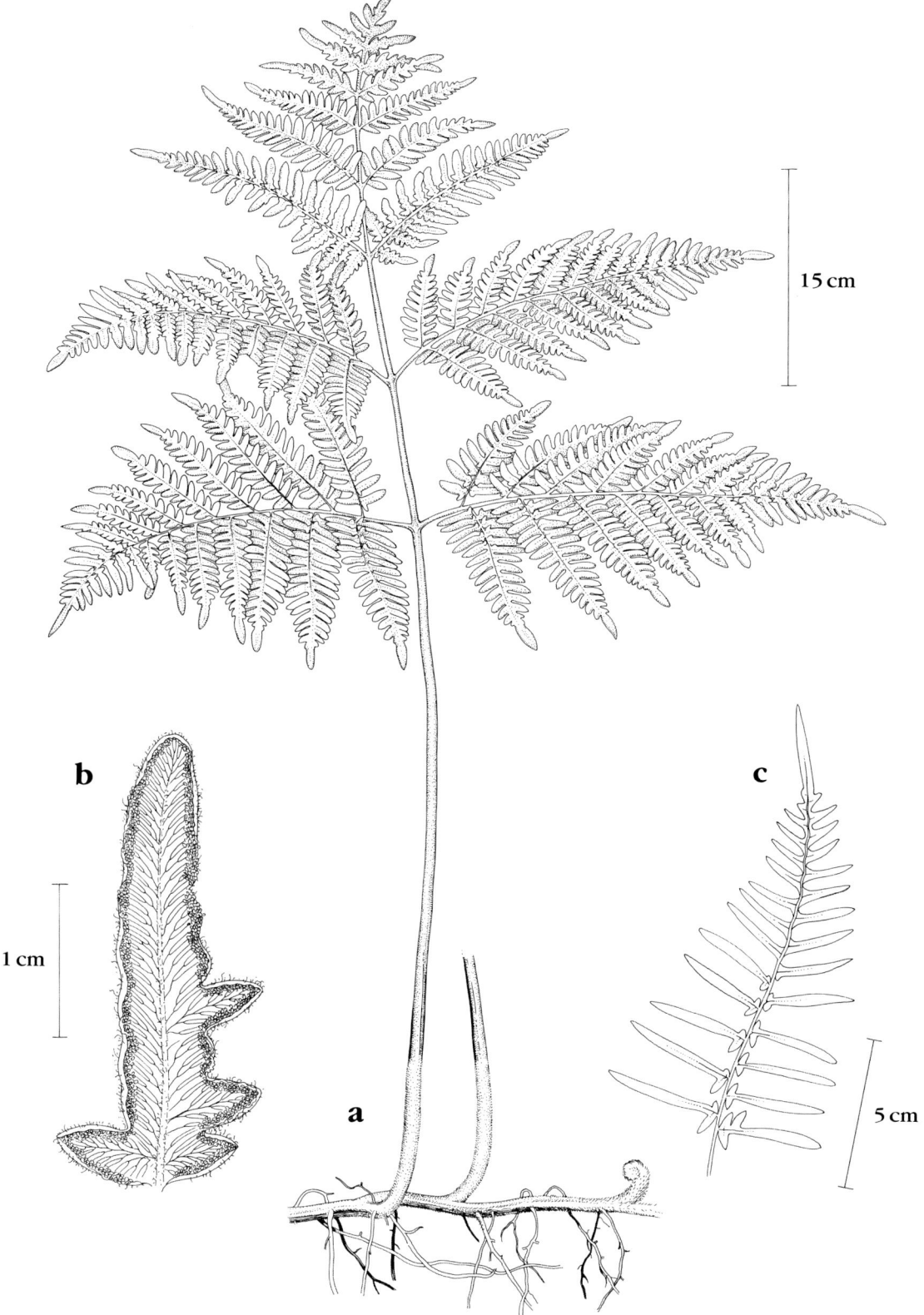

Pteridium aquilinum
a. Habit; b. var. *latiusculum*, lower surface of sporiferous pinnule; c. var. *pseudocaudatum*, portion of frond.

1a. *Pteridium aquilinum* var. *latiusculum* (Desv.) Heller

Pteris latiuscula Desv.
Pteridium latiusculum (Desv.) Fries

COMMON NAME: Eastern Bracken

Rhizome apex often with a tuft of whitish hairs. Stipe and rachis glabrous to puberulent; blade ciliate; entire ultimate divisions up to 1 cm wide, usually puberulent below along midrib; longest, entire, ultimate divisions or lobes 3-7X longer than broad.

HABITAT: Open woods, cut-over and burned-over areas, thickets, old fields, roadsides.

RANGE: Eastern North America, eastern Asia.

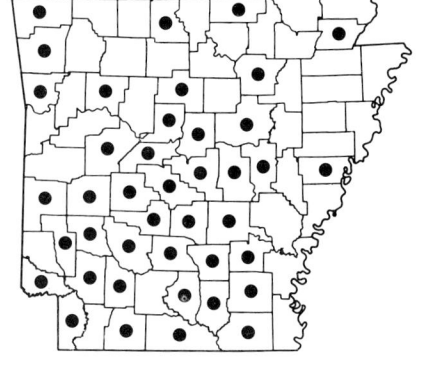

1b. *Pteridium aquilinum* var. *pseudocaudatum* (Clute) Heller

Pteris aquilina var. *pseudocaudata* Clute

COMMON NAME: Tailed Bracken

Rhizome apex often with a tuft of reddish brown hairs. Stipe and rachis glabrous or glabrate; blade glabrous or glabrate; entire ultimate divisions up to 7 mm wide, glabrous to sparsely puberulent below along midrib; longest, entire, ultimate divisions or lobes 6-15X longer than broad.

HABITAT: Open woods, cut-over and burned-over areas, thickets, old fields, roadsides.

RANGE: Southeastern United States.

Pteris L. Brakes

A genus of about 250 species of tropical and subtropical regions.

1. *Pteris multifida* Lam.

Pycnodoria multifida (Lam.) Small

COMMON NAME: Spider Brake

Rhizome short-creeping; scales lustrous, reddish brown to black, linear to linear-lanceolate. Fronds deciduous, ascending to pendulous, pinnatifid to bipinnatifid, up to 60 cm long, glabrate, dimorphic; stipe green to stramineous; blade ovate-deltoid, up to 40 cm long and 25 cm wide; rachis green, more or less winged; ultimate divisions linear to lancolate, serrate mostly toward apex, veins simple or once-forked, free; fertile divisions usually narrower than sterile divisions. Sori marginal, covered by scarious, revolute margins of ultimate divisions.

HABITAT: Garland Co.: tufa exposures at base of Hot Springs Mountain, Hot Springs National Park; *Taylor 2708* (SIU).

RANGE: Naturalized in southeastern United States, native of Asia, but readily excaping cultivation and now widely distributed in tropical and warm temperate regions.

Chandler (1941) first noted the above station of *Pteris multifida* in Arkansas. Although there has been considerable habitat modification in the area, plants continue to grow around the exposed tufa.

Pteris multifida

Garland Co.: *Taylor 2708* (SIU).

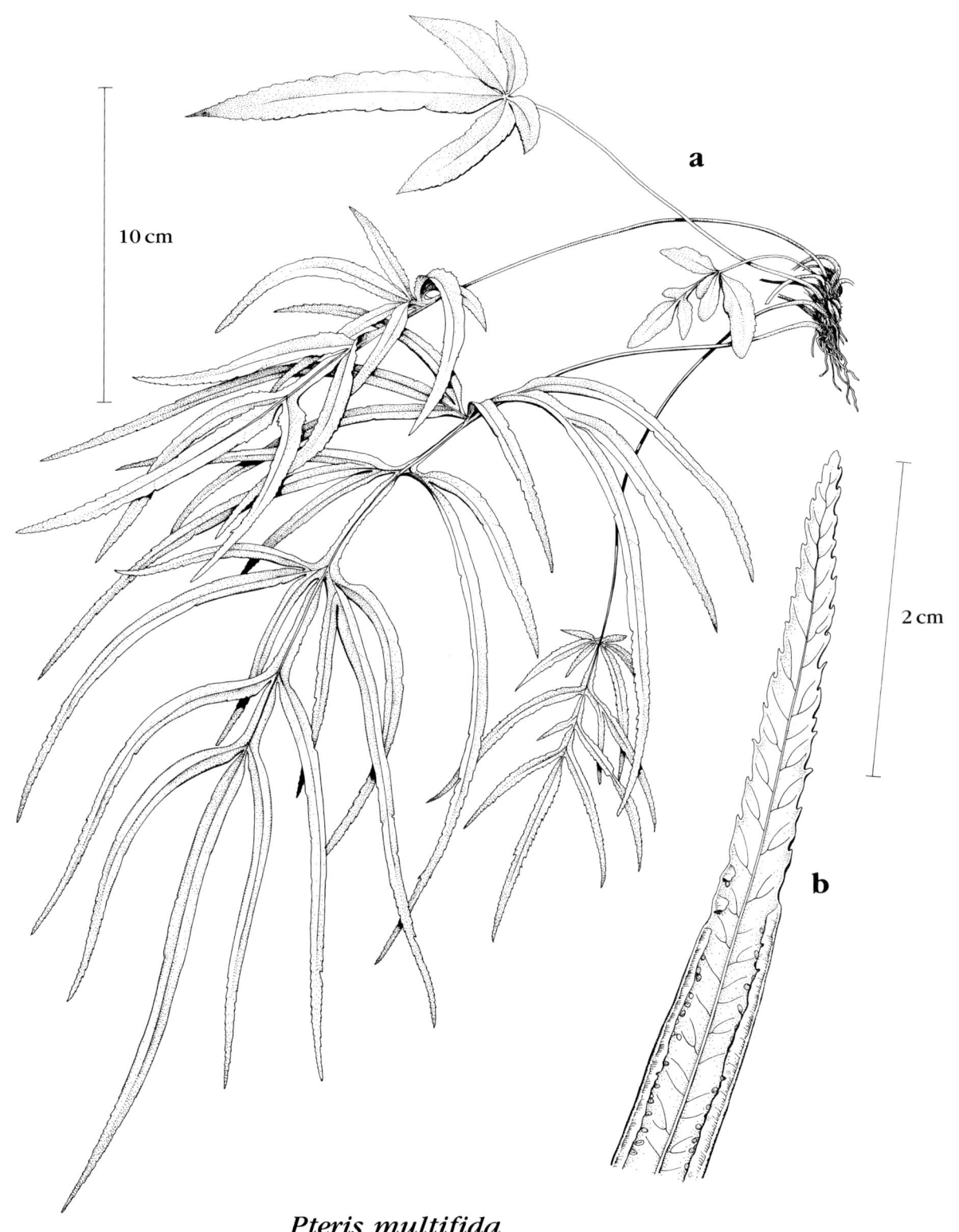

Pteris multifida
a. Habit; b. Lower surface of sporiferous frond division.

Selaginella Beauv. Spikemosses

Leafy stems and branches prostrate and creeping or decumbent to erect, anisophyllous and dorsiventral or isophyllous and radially symmetrical; roots adventitious. Leaves spirally arranged, spaced or crowded, ligulate, simple, ovate or linear-subulate. Sporophylls 4-ranked, appressed or ascending, imbricate, ovate-lanceolate, aggregatetd in a terminal tetragonal strobilus, with microsporophylls usually above megasporophylls; sporangia axillary, solitary, reniform to subglobose, splitting transversely, heterosporous; megaspores 1-4 per megasporangium, tetrahedral-globose, rugulate to reticulate or rarely smooth; microspores numerous in microsporangia, tetrahedral-globose.

A genus of about 700 species found mostly in the tropics. Alice Tryon (1949) has examined the spores of North American species of *Selaginella*. *Selaginella rupestris* and its allies have been studied by Rolla Tryon (1955).

Key to the species of *Selaginella* in Arkansas

1. Leaves spaced, ovate, membranous; plants herbaceous, delicate, with stems and branches prostrate and creeping
    2. Apices of dorsal leaves long attenuate with midrib extending into apex; mature megaspore surface shiny, laxly reticulate . 1. *S. eclipes* (p. 212)
    2. Apices of dorsal leaves acute or, if attenuate, with midrib not extending into apex; mature megaspore surface dull, tightly reticulate . . . .
    . . . . 2. *S. apoda* (p. 214)
1. Leaves crowded, ascending, linear subulate, stiff; plants evergreen, wiry, with stems and branches decumbent to erect
        3. Stems and branches ascending to erect, often tufted; roots copious; megaspores 230-430 **u**m in diam . . . . 3. *S. riddellii* (p. 216)
        3. Stems and branches decumbent, often matted, roots sparse; megaspores 400-590 m in diam . . . . 4. *S. rupestris* (p. 218)

1. *Selaginella eclipes* Buck

COMMON NAME: Buck's Meadow Spikemoss

Plants herbaceous, delicate. Stems and branches prostrate and creeping, often matted, up to 20 cm long, anisophyllous; roots sparse. Lateral leaves spaced, spreading oblong-ovate, up to 2.0 mm long and 1.3 mm wide, membranous, papillose, acute to acuminate, subentire to serrulate; dorsal leaves appressed, ovate to ovate-lanceolate, up to 1.8 mm long and 0.8 mm wide, midrib extending into apex, apex often hyaline and fragile, abruptly tapered, and long attenuate. Strobilus obscurely tetragonal, up to 3 cm long; mature megaspores usually 4 per sporangium, shiny white, 325-400 µm in diameter, laxly reticulate, muri broad with sloping sides, minutely pitted; microspores orange, 20-30 µm in diam.

HABITAT: Moist to wet, usually shaded, calcareous rock outcrops; Ozark Mountains.

RANGE: St. Lawrence River Valley and Great Lakes region southwest through Indiana, Illinois, Iowa, Missouri and Arkansas to Oklahoma.

Selaginella eclipes is rather subtly differentiated from *S. apoda*. According to Buck (1977) this taxon may eventually prove to be better treated at a subspecific level. On the basis of available collections, specimens referable to *S. eclipes* seem to be confined to the Ozark Highlands and Boston Mountains, while specimens of *S. apoda* with more tightly reticulate megaspore surfaces and less attenuate dorsal leaf apices are mostly absent from these regions.

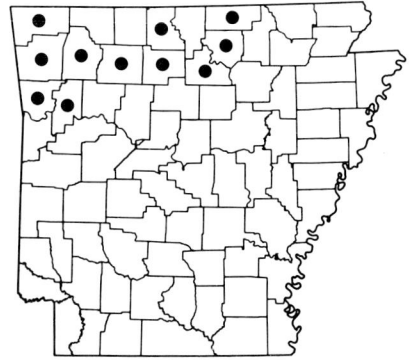

Selaginella eclipes

Benton Co.: *D. Moore 321202* (UARK). Crawford Co.: *Taylor 1096* (SIU). Franklin Co.: *Redfearn 23699* (SMS). Fulton Co.: *Redfearn 26438* (SMS). Izard Co.: *Taylor 1268* (SIU). Madison Co.: *Redfearn 18857* (SMS). Marion Co.: *D. Moore 350165* (UARK). Newton Co.: *Taylor 2690* (SIU). Searcy Co.: *Redfearn 14273* (SMS). Stone Co.: *D. Moore 450810* (UARK). Washington Co.: *Calicott s.n.* (UARK).

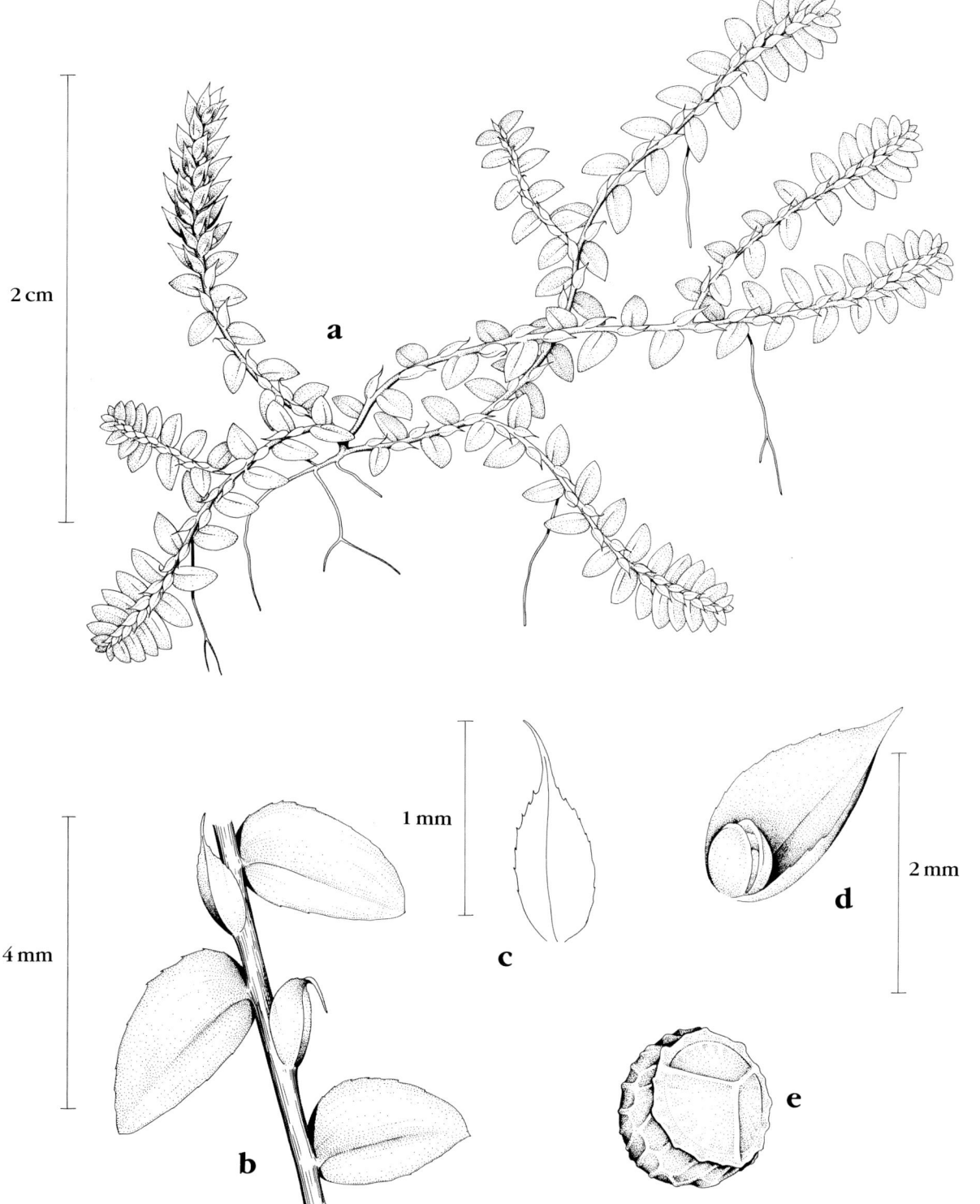

Selaginella eclipes
a. Habit; b. Upper portion of stem with dorsal and lateral stems; c. Dorsal leaf; d. Sporophyll with sporangium; e. Megaspore.

2. *Selaginella apoda* (L.) Mart.

Lycopodium apodum L.
Diplostachyum apodum (L.) Beauv.
Selaginella apus (L.) Mart.
Selaginella apoda (L.) Fern.

COMMON NAME: Meadow Spikemoss

Plants herbaceous, delicate. Stems and branches prostrate and creeping, often matted, up to 20 cm long, anisophyllous; roots sparse. Lateral leaves spaced, spreading ovate, up to 2.2 mm long and 1.5 mm wide, membranous papillose, acute to acuminate, subentire to serrulate; dorsal leaves appressed, ovate to ovate-lanceolate, up to 1.5 mm long and 0.8 mm wide, midrib not extending into apex, apex usually neither hyaline nor fragile, acute to attenuate and keeled. Strobilus obscurely tetragonal, up to 2 cm long; mature megaspores usually 4 per sporangium, dull white, 290-350 µm in diam., tightly reticulate, muri narrow with vertical sides, minutely alveolate and spinulose; microspores orange, 22-34 µm in diam.

HABITAT: Moist to wet, usually shaded, sandstone and shale outcrops, low meadows, seeps and sandy or clayey soils along stream banks.

RANGE: Eastern United States.

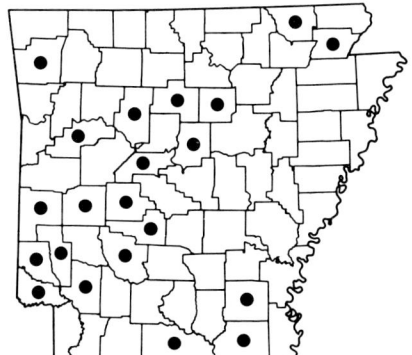

Selaginella apoda

Ashley Co.: *Taylor 1874* (SIU). Clark Co.: *Redfearn 24404* (SMS). Cleburne Co.: *Babb 1023* (ARKSU). Drew Co. *Demaree 17899* (MO). Faulkner Co.: *Taylor 2008* (SIU). Garland Co.: *Taylor 2557* (SIU). Greene Co.: *D. Moore 480681* (UARK). Hempstead Co.: *D. Moore 56128* (UARK). Hot Spring Co.: *Taylor 936* (SIU). Howard Co.: *Iltis 680* (UARK). Little River Co.: *D. Moore 50021* (UARK). Logan Co.: *Taylor 1044* (SIU). Montgomery Co.: *D. Moore 430154* (UARK). Perry Co.: *Issacs 3319* (UCA). Polk Co.: *J. Moore 3145* (UCA). Pope Co.: *D. Moore 520759* (UARK). Randolph Co.: *Taylor 2665* (SIU). Sevier Co.: *D. Moore 510094* (UARK). Union Co.: *Taylor 2631* (SIU). Van Buren Co.: *Johnson 292* (HXC). Washington Co.: *French 269* (UARK).

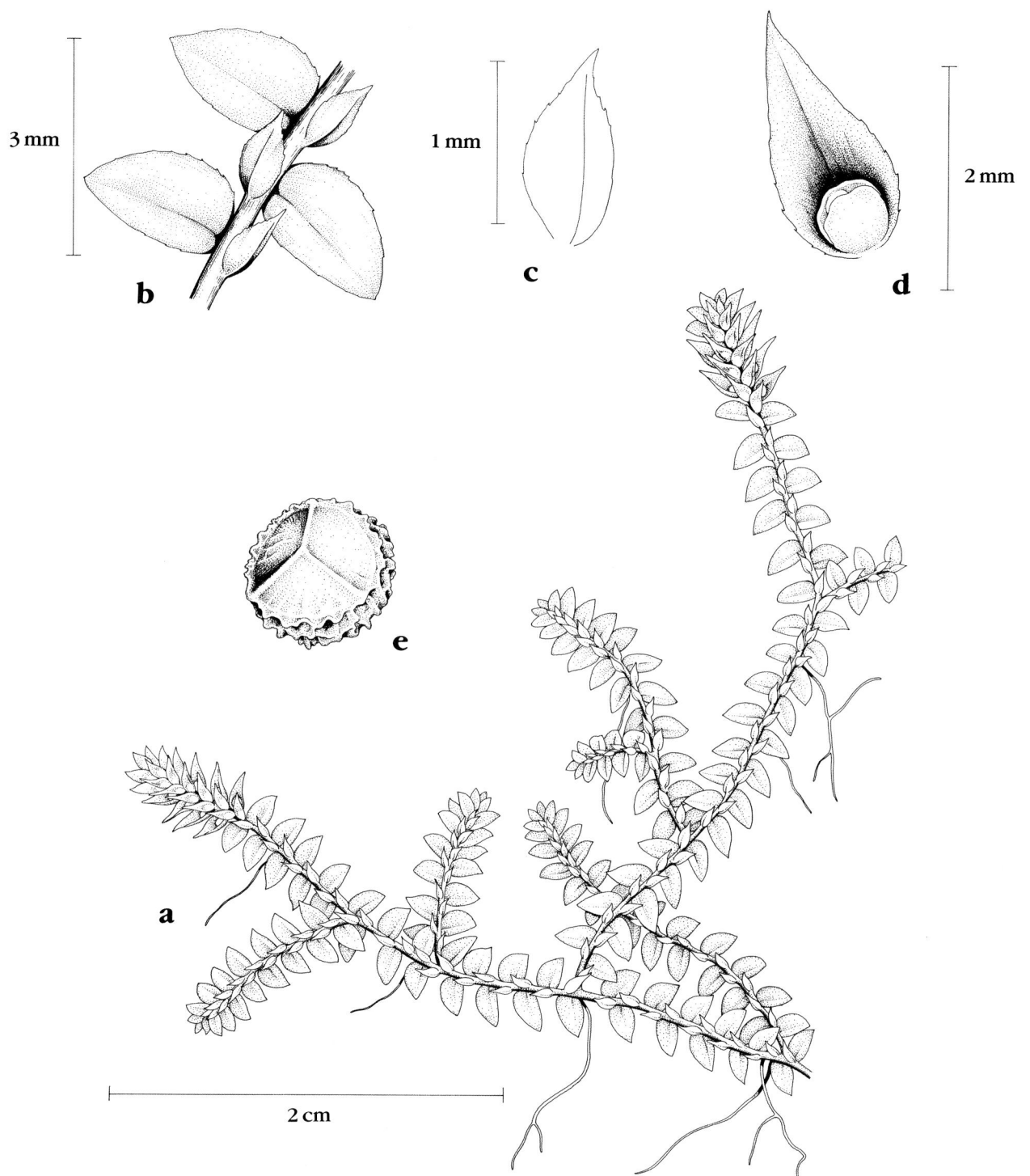

Selaginella apoda
a. Habit; b. Upper portion of stem with dorsal and lateral leaves; c. Dorsal leaf; d. Sporophyll with sporangium; e. Megaspore.

3. *Selaginella riddellii* Van Eselt.

Selaginella arenicola Underw. subsp. *riddellii* (Van Eselt.) Tryon

COMMON NAME: Riddell's Spikemoss

Plants evergreen, wiry. Stems and branches decumbent to erect, often tufted, up to 12 cm long, isophyllous; roots copious. Leaves crowded, ascending to appressed, imbricate, linear-subulate, up to 2.5 mm long and 0.4 mm wide, stiff, dorsally sulcate, bristle-pointed, with margins fimbrillate. Strobilus conspicuously tetragonal, up to 2.5 cm long; megaspores usually 4 per sporangium, white to light yellow, 230-430 µm in diam., rugulate to rugulate-reticulate, rarely smooth; microspores deep orange, 32-52 µm in diam.

HABITAT: Sandy, open soil. Nevada Co.: roadside along Hwy. 24; E of Bluff City; *Taylor 2747* (SIU). Ouachita Co.: hillside; N of Chidester Baptist Church, Chidester; *Taylor 2743* (SIU); dumping ground along Hwy. 368; *Taylor 978* (SIU). Pike Co.: outcrops along Little Missouri River; *Roberts & Bradford s.n.* (UARK). Pope Co.: sandstone bluffs above Arkansas River, Norristown Mountain, Russellville; *Tucker 6563* (SMU).

RANGE: Arkansas, Oklahoma, Texas, and Louisiana.

The first Arkansas collection of *Selaginella riddellii* was made in Pope County by Gary Tucker on 16 September 1967 (Tucker, 1971). Several years later additional stations for this taxon were discovered in the West Gulf Coastal Plain of Arkansas.

The extensive, fibrous root system of this species appears important in binding the loose, sandy soil in which it grows.

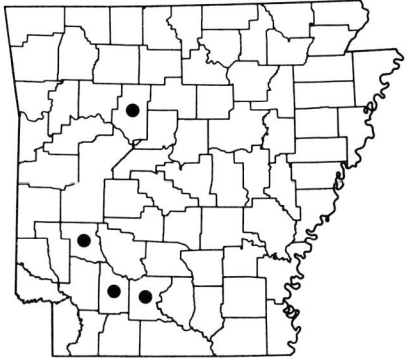

Selaginella riddellii

Nevada Co.: *Taylor 2747* (SIU). Ouachita Co.: *Taylor 2743* (SIU). Pike Co.: *Roberts & Bradford s.n.* (UARK). Pope Co.: *Tucker 6563* (SMU).

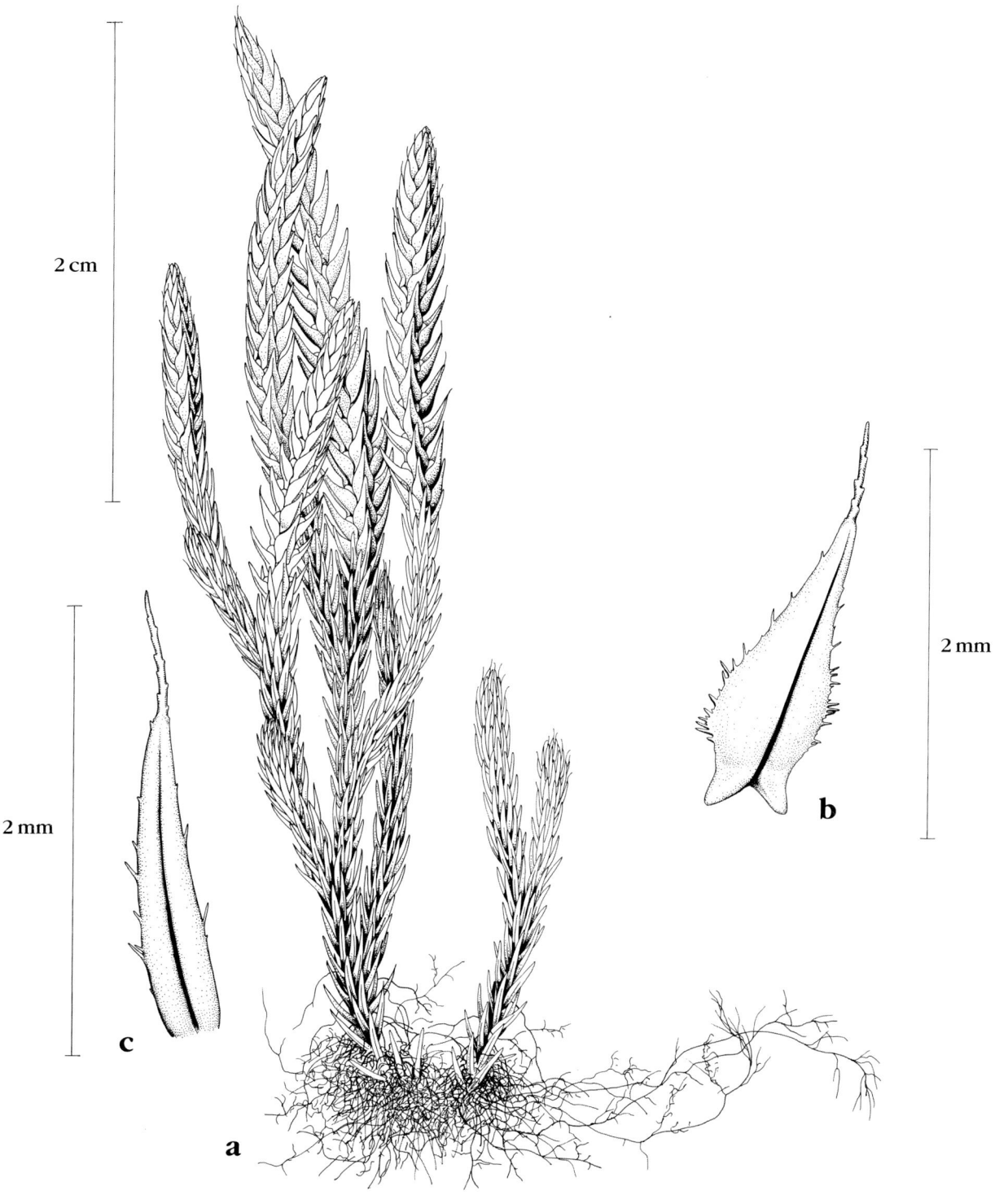

Selaginella riddellii
a. Habit; b. Ventral side of sporophyll with sporangium; c. Stem leaf.

4. *Selaginella rupestris* (L.) Spring

Lycopodium ruprestre L.

COMMON NAME: Rock Spikemoss

Plants evergreen, wiry. Stems and branches decumbent, often matted, up to 10 cm long, isophyllous; roots sparse. Leaves crowded, ascending to appressed, imbricate, linear-subulate, to 2.5 mm long and 0.4 mm wide, stiff, dorsally sulcate, bristle-pointed, with margins fimbriolate. Strobilus conspicuously tetragonal, up to 2 cm long; megaspores usually 2 per sporangium, yellowish orange, 400-590 µm in diam., rugulate to rugulate-reticulate; microspores deep orange, 35-65 µm in diam.

HABITAT: Exposed sandstone outcrops; chiefly Ozark Mountains.

RANGE: Northeastern North America, west to Montana and Oklahoma.

Lesquereux (1860) reported *Selaginella rupestris* in Arkansas from "sandstone, dry rocky places." However, no authentic Arkansas material was found to substantiate this report until 11 June 1927 when Delzie Demaree collected specimens at Calico Rock, Izard County. Since then Dwight Moore (1940a) and others have collected this species from a number of sandstone exposures, primarily in the northwestern and north-central portions of the state. Tryon (1955) states that *S. rupestris* is apogamous throughout much of its range. He has found that in the Appalachian mountain region north to southern Pennsylvania, *S. rupestris* usually appears to be a sexual species producing the normal tetrad of megaspores in each megasporangium. Outside this region he has observed that *S. rupestris* more often produces only one or two megaspores per sporangium. Arkansas material, which usually contains two megaspores per sporangium, supports Tryon's observations.

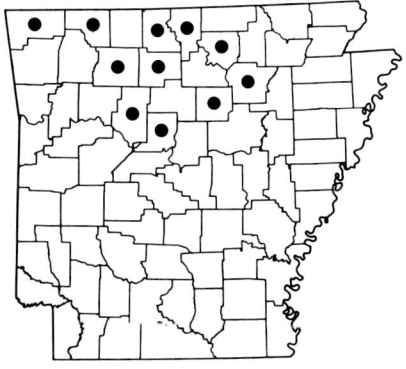

Selaginella rupestris

Baxter Co.: *Tucker 6809* (APCR). Benton Co.: *D. Moore 1350203* (MO). Carroll Co.: *Haus 1516* (UCA). Cleburne Co.: *Babb 1580* (ARKSU). Conway Co.: *J. Moore 1097* (UARK). Independence Co.: *Demaree 5979* (SMU). Izard Co.: *Demaree 32518* (MO). Marion Co.: *Redfearn 08163* (SMS). Newton Co.: *D. Moore 32490* (UARK). Pope Co.: *Redfearn 26772* (SMS). Searcy Co.: *D. Moore 350160* (MO).

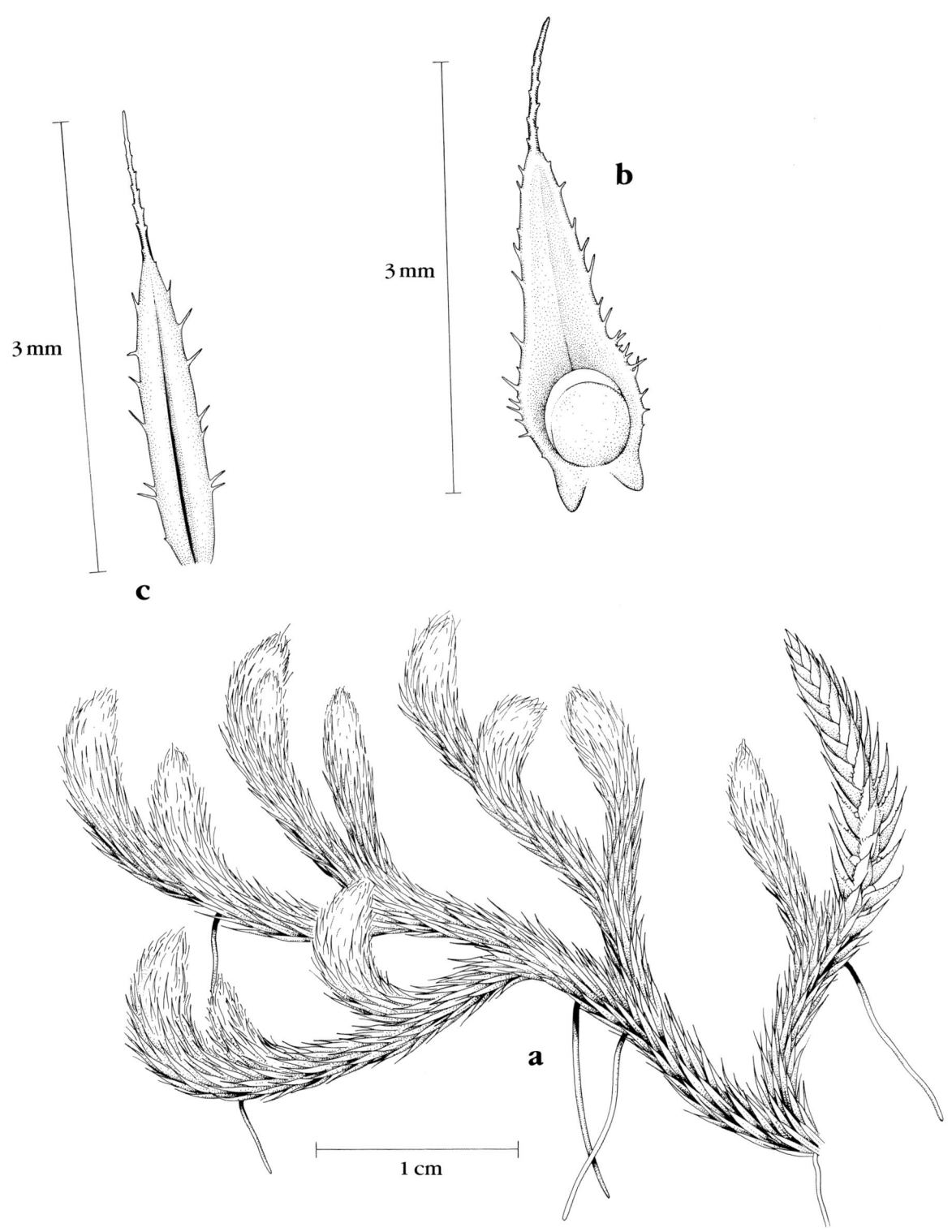

Selaginella rupestris
a. Habit; b. Ventral side of sporophyll with sporangium; c. Stem leaf.

Thelypteris Schmidel Marsh Ferns

Rhizome long-creeping, slender, scaly. Fronds deciduous, erect to erect-spreading, pinnate-pinnatifid to bipinnate-pinnatifid, puberulent, acuminate; stipe and rachis green to stramineous; blades deltoid to elliptic-lanceolate; rachis puberulent or pilosulous and glandular; ultimate segments ciliolate; veins simple or forked, reaching the margins. Sori submarginal to medial, round, borne on veins; indusium delicate, orbicular-reniform, attached at sinus.

A genus of approximately 1000 species from tropical to temperate regions. There are a number of morphologically definable subgroups in *Thelypteris* and Smith (1971) has monographed the neotropical species in section *Cyclosorus*.

Key to the species of *Thelypteris* in Arkansas

1. Fronds bipinnate-pinnatifid .... 1. *T. torresiana* (p. 222)
1. Fronds pinnate-pinnatifid
    2. Fronds elliptic-lanceolate; lower pinnae gradually reduced to small deltoid segments; sori submarginal; indusium glandular .... 2. *T. noveboracensis (p. 224)*
    2. Fronds deltoid or lanceolate; lower pinnae with little or no reduction in size; sori medial; indusium hairy or glabrous
        3. Fronds deltoid-lanceolate; upper surface of pinnae hirtellous along midveins; lower surface of pinnae and indusia hirtellous .... 3. *T. kunthii* (p. 226)
        3. Fronds oblong-lanceolate; upper surface of pinnae minutely tomentose along midveins; lower surface of pinnae minutely and sparsely pilose; indusia ciliolate .... 4. *T. palustris* (p. 228)

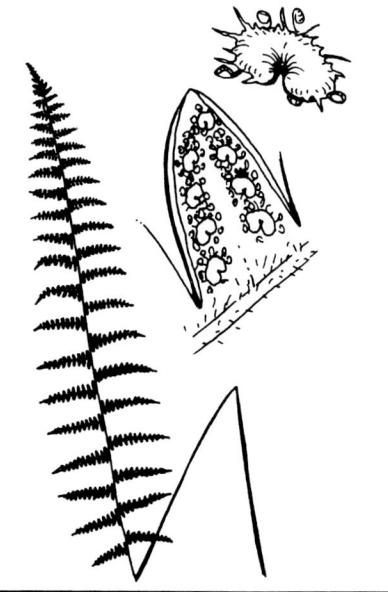

1. *Thelypteris torresiana* (Gaud.) Alston

COMMON NAME: Mariana Maiden Fern

Rhizome brown, pilosulous; scales lanceolate, ciliolate. Fronds bipinnate-pinnatifid, alike, up to 1 m long; stipe and rachis green to stramineous, glabrate; blade deltoid to deltoid-lanceolate, up to 70 cm long and 45 cm wide; pinnules pilose along midribs and veins. Sori medial; indusium delicate, pilose.

HABITAT: Ashley Co.: roadside at edge of field; timber access road, W of Crossett; *Taylor 3783* (SIU); roadside in lumbered pine forest; timber access road SE of Lake Georgia-Pacific; *Johnson 283* (HXC).

RANGE: Southeastern United States; native to continental Asia, but escaping from cultivation and now widely distributed in tropical and subtropical America.

Thelypteris torresiana was discovered in Florida in 1904 and has since been collected in a number of southeastern states (Leonard, 1972). The discovery of *T. torresiana* in Ashley County by David Johnson on 25 October 1975 extends its known range into southeastern Arkansas. Naturalized plants from the above localities are scattered in cut-over pine-hardwood forest and probably became established as a result of habitats created by lumbering operations in the area (Taylor and Johnson, 1979).

Thelypteris torresiana

Ashley Co.: *Taylor 3783* (SIU) and *Johnson 283* (HXC).

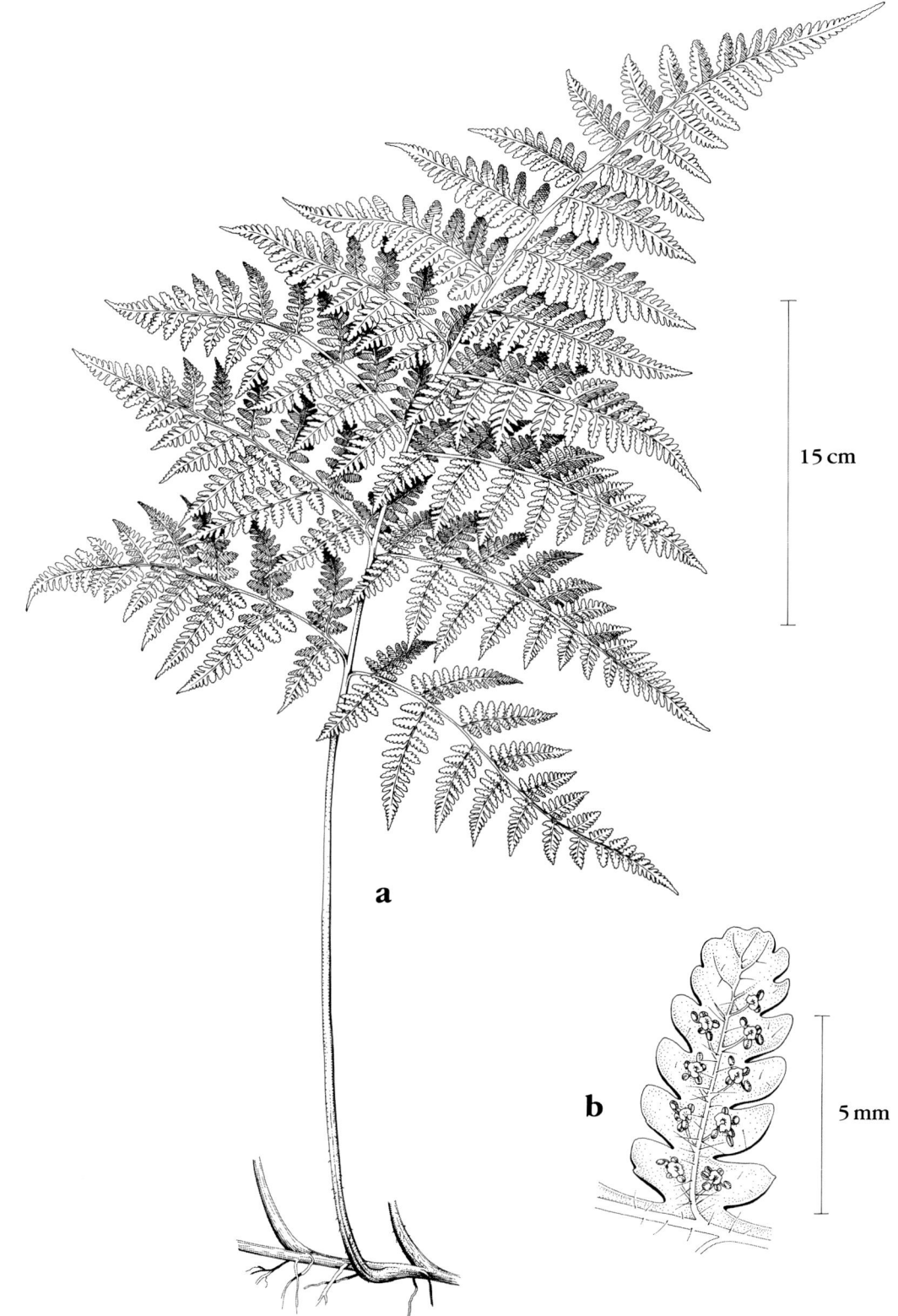

Thelypteris torresiana
a. Habit; b. Lower surface of pinnule division with sori.

2. *Thelypteris noveboracensis* (L.) Nieuwl.

Polypodium noveboracense L.
Aspidium noveboracense (L.) Sw.
Dryopteris noveboracensis (L.) Gray

COMMON NAME: New York Fern

Rhizome brown to black, glabrate; scales lanceolate. Fronds pinnate-pinnatifid, alike, up to 75 cm long; stipe and rachis green to stramineous, puberulent; blade elliptic-lanceolate, up to 60 cm long and 15 cm wide. Pinnae linear-lanceolate to deltoid, pilose; lower pinnae gradually reduced to small, deltoid fragments. Sori submarginal; discrete; indusium glandular.

HABITAT: Moist, rocky soils of woods and thickets along streams; chiefly Ouachita Mountains.

RANGE: Eastern North America.

Thelypteris noveboracensis reaches the southwestern extent of its range in the Ouachita Mountains of Arkansas. The Arkansas populations are well over 200 miles disjunct from the nearest reported stations in the Ozark Hills of southern Illinois and the Tennessee River Hills of northeast Mississippi.

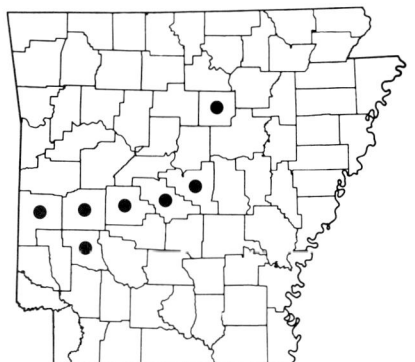

Thelypteris noveboracensis (L.) Nieuwl.

Cleburne Co.: *Johnson 393* (HXC). Garland Co.: *D. Moore 6278* (APCR). Montgomery Co.: *Taylor 1084* (SIU). Pike Co.: *Taylor 2903* (SIU). Polk Co.: *D. Moore 410261* (UARK). Pulaski Co.: *Johnson 112* (HXC). Saline Co.: *D. Moore 480154* (UARK).

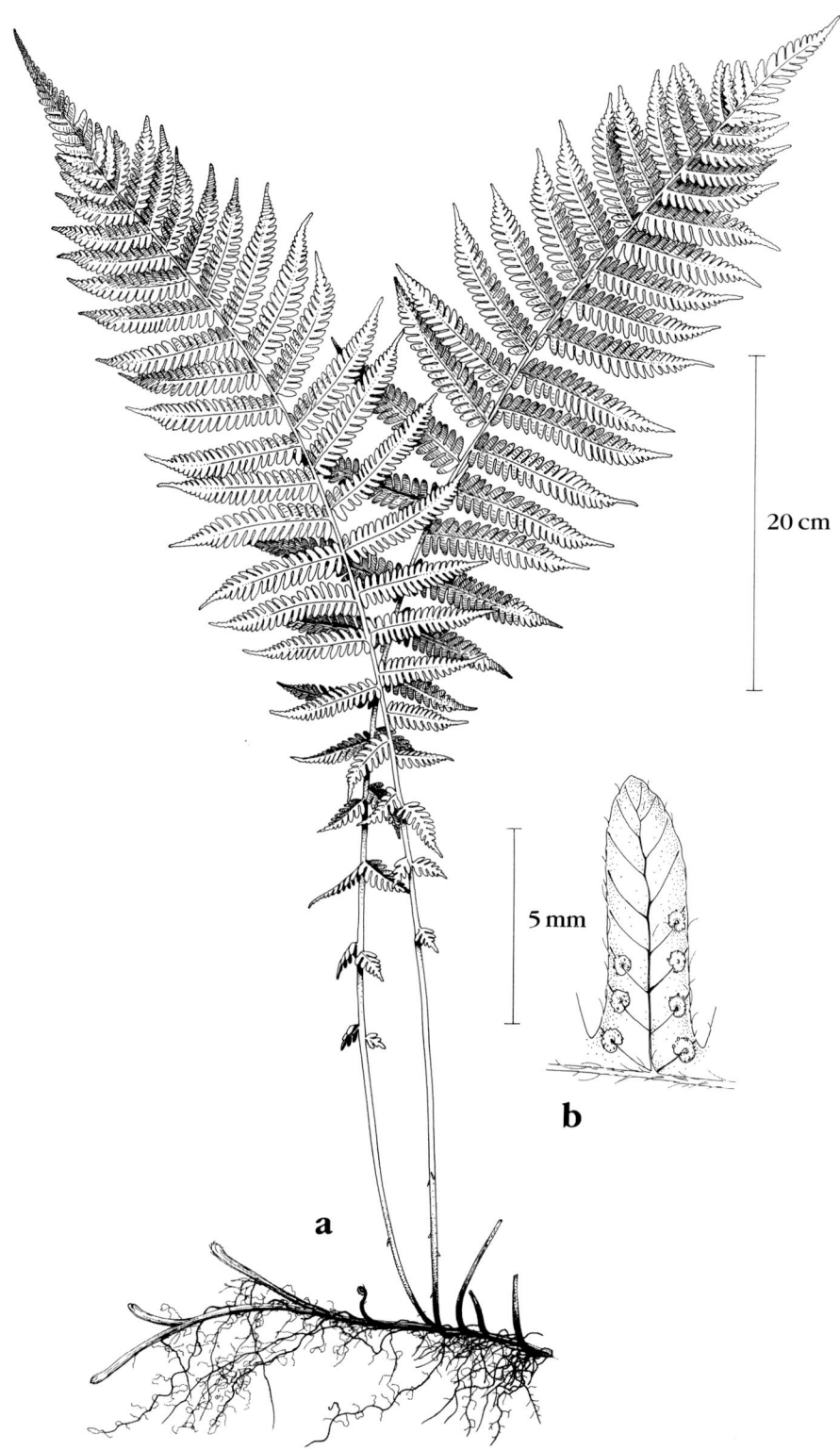

Thelypteris noveboracensis
a. Habit; b. Lower surface of pinna lobe with sori.

3. *Thelypteris kunthii* (Desv.) Morton

Thelypteris normalis (C. Chr.) Moxley
Dryopteris normalis C. Chr.

COMMON NAME: Southern Shield Fern

Rhizome brown, puberulent; scales lanceolate, ciliolate. Fronds pinnate-pinnatifid, alike, up to 1.2 m long; stipe and rachis green to stramineous, puberulent and minutely stipitate-glandular; blade deltoid-lanceolate, up to 70 cm long and 40 cm wide. Pinnae linear-attenuate, hirtellous and minutely stipitate-glandular below and along midvein above. Sori submarginal to medial; indusium hirtellous.

HABITAT: Ashley Co.: roadside at edge of lumbered pine forest; timber access road SE of Lake Georgia-Pacific; *Johnson 281* (HXC).

RANGE: Southeastern United States, West Indies, Middle America.

The Ashley County plants first discovered by David Johnson on 25 October 1975 are from what appears to be a naturalized population. Plants from the above locality are scattered in cut-over pine-hardwood forest and probably have become naturalized as a result of habitats created by lumbering operations in the area (Taylor and Johnson, 1979). *Thelypteris kunthii* has also been collected from Lee and Pulaski Counties. However, both of these collections were made from old garden plots and it does not appear that plants from these two sites have as yet adequately escaped cultivation to be considered naturalized.

Thelypteris kunthii (Desv.) Morton

Ashley Co.: *Johnson 281* (HXC).

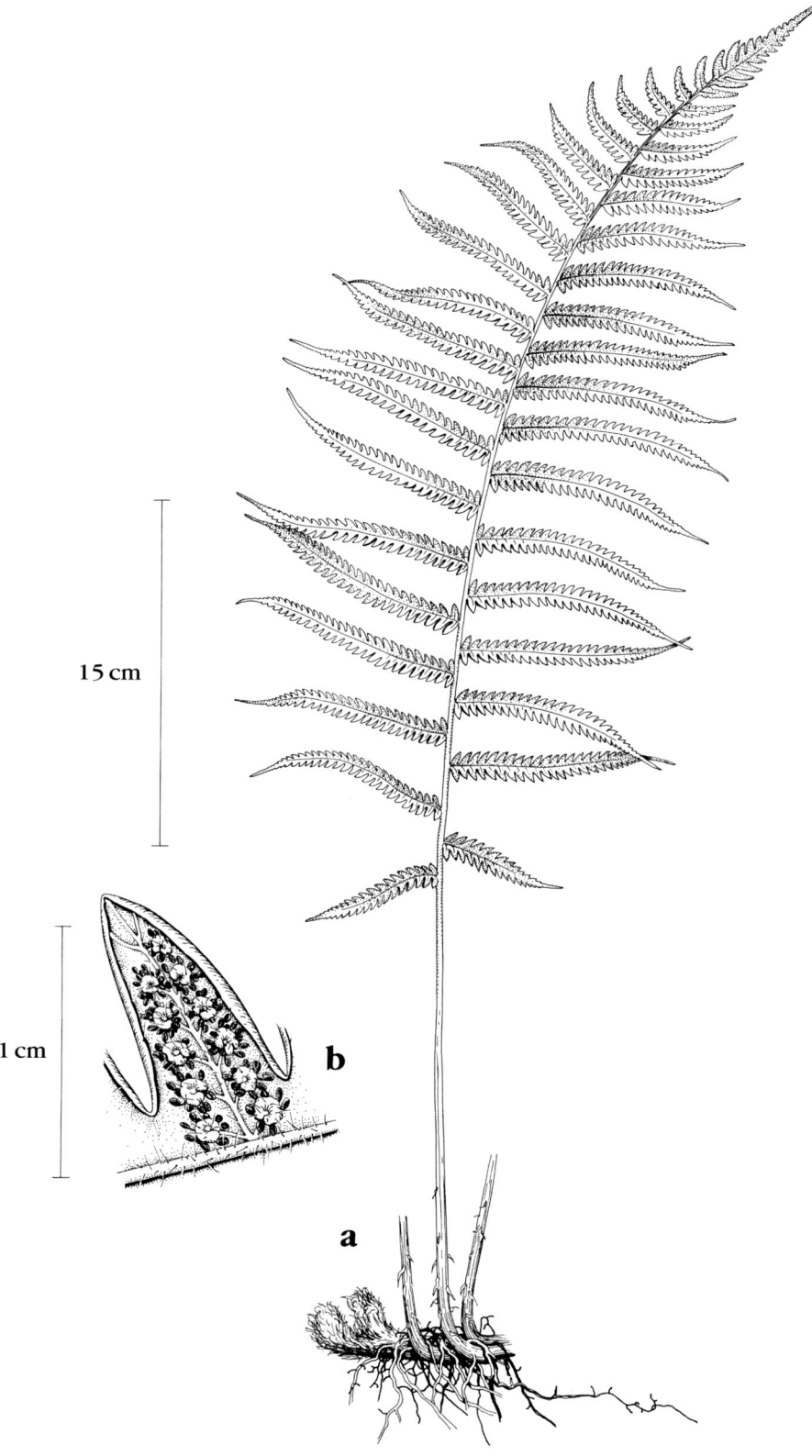

Thelypteris kunthii
a. Habit; b. Lower surface of pinna lobe with sori.

4. *Thelypteris palustris* Schott

Acrostichum thelypteris L.
Aspidium thelypteris (L.) Sw.
Dryopteris thelypteris (L.) Gray

COMMON NAME: Marsh Fern

Rhizome black, glabrate; scales deltoid-ovate. Fronds pinnate-pinnatifid to bipinnate, moderately dimorphic, up to 80 cm long; fertile fronds usually longer and slightly narrower than sterile fronds; stipe and rachis stramineous, glabrate; blade oblong-lanceolate, up to 60 cm long and 20 cm wide. Pinnae linear-lanceolate, minutely tomentose along midveins above, minutely and sparsely pilose below. Sori medial, often confluent; indusium ciliolate.

Two varieties of *Thelypteris palustris* have been recognized in Arkansas. Although most of the Arkansas material is clearly referable to var. *pubescens,* var. *haleana* has been collected from two populations in Drew and Bradley Counties (Demaree, 1943). These two populations also contain var. *pubescens* and forms transitional between the two varieties.

Key to the varieties of *Thelypteris palustris* in Arkansas

1. Fronds pinnate-pinnatifid; pinna midrib mostly without scales; lateral veins of fertile divisions mostly simple .... 4a. var. *pubescens*
1. Fronds bipinnate at least toward base of lower pinnae; pinna midrib bearing yellowish brown to dark brown ovate scales toward base; lateral veins of fertile divisions or pinnules mostly forked .... 4b. var. *haleana*

4a. *Thelypteris palustris* var. *pubescens* (Laws.) Fern.

Dryopteris thelypteris var. *pubescens* (Laws.) Weatherby

COMMON NAME: Hairy Marsh Fern

HABITAT: Low marshy areas around ponds and lakes and along streams.

RANGE: Eastern North America, Japan, northeastern Asia.

4b. *Thelypteris palustris* var. *haleana* Fern.

Dryopteris thelypteris var. *haleana* (Fern.) Weatherby

COMMON NAME: Hale's Marsh Fern

HABITAT: Bradley Co.: cypress swamp near Warren; *Demaree 19445* (SMU). Drew Co.: among grasses and sedges in swamp near Wilmar; *Demaree 24624* (SMU).

RANGE: Southeastern United States.

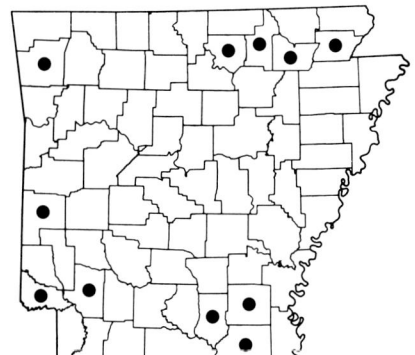

Thelypteris palustris

Ashley Co.: *Johnson 276* (HXC). Bradley Co.: *Demaree 19445* (MO). Drew Co.: *Demaree 24624* (SMU). Greene Co.: *D. Moore 480685* (UARK). Hempstead Co.: *D. Moore 480353* (UARK). Izard Co.: *Johnson 422* (HXC). Lawrence Co.: *Taylor 1794* (SIU). Little River Co.: *Palmer 8359* (MO). Polk Co.: *J. Moore & McWilliam s.n.* (UARK). Sharp Co.: *Wade 167* (UARK). Washington Co.: *Henbest 16* (UARK).

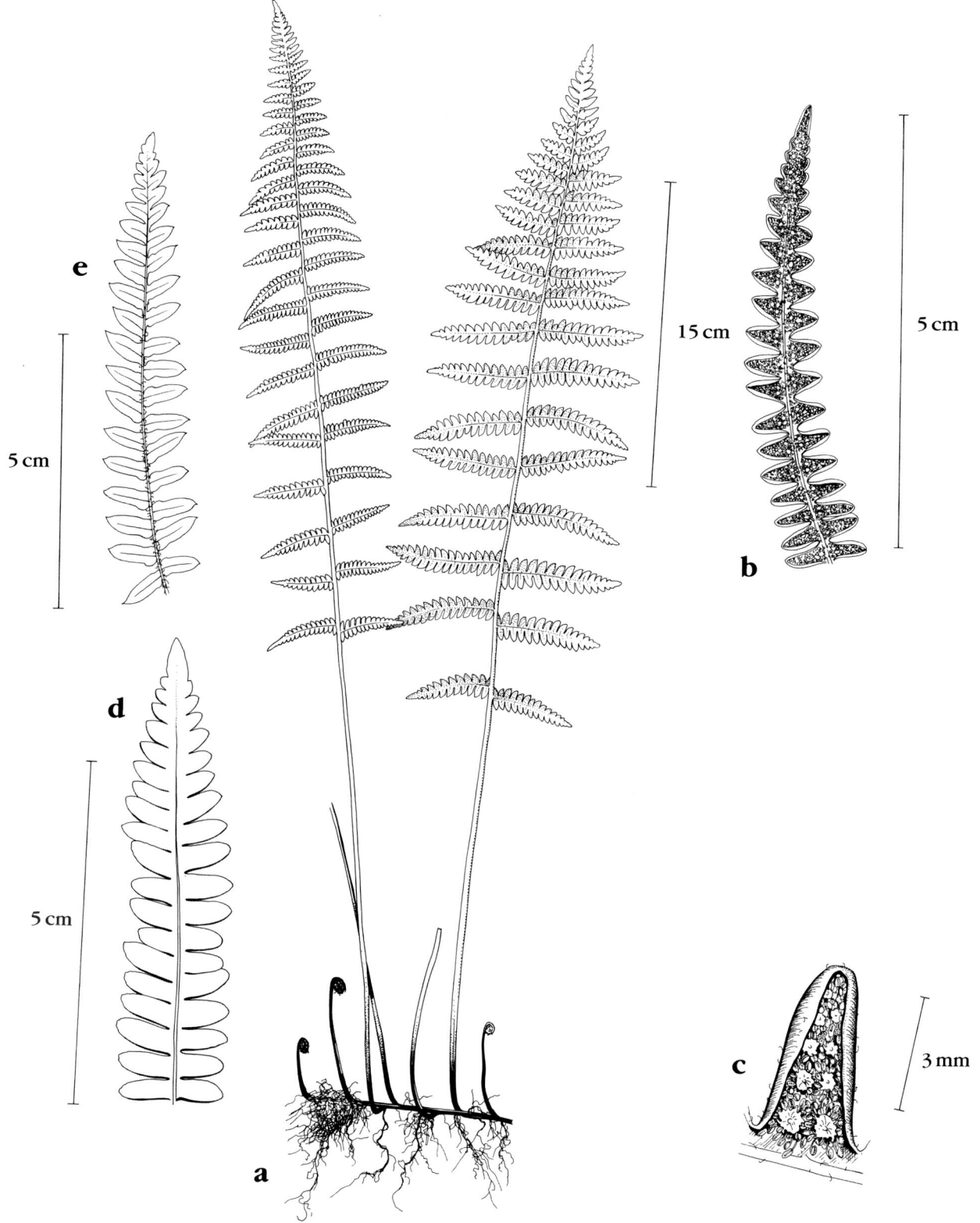

Thelypteris palustris
a. Habit; b. Lower surface of pinna with sori; c. Lower surface of pinna lobe with sori; d. var. *pubescens*, pinna; e. var. *haleana*, pinna.

Trichomanes L. Filmy Ferns

Rhizome long-creeping, wiry, black, tomentulose with septate hairs. Fronds delicate, membranous evergreen, usually pendant, glabrate to sparsely hairy; stipe green, winged above and often nearly to base; blade translucent, one cell thick; veins forked, free. Sori at edge of blade, terminating veins; sporangia clustered on an exerted, bristle-like meristem in a tubular or funnel-shaped indusium; spores tetrahedral-globose.

A genus of nearly 300 species essentially of humid tropical regions.

Key to the species of *Trichomanes* in Arkansas

1. Fronds bipinnatifid, usually more than 2 cm long; sori usually several to many per frond, terminal on lobes .... 1. *T. boschianum* (p. 232)
1. Fronds entire to undulate-crenate and lobed, less than 2 cm long; sori one to occasionally several per frond, terminating midvein .... 2. *T. petersii* (p. 234)

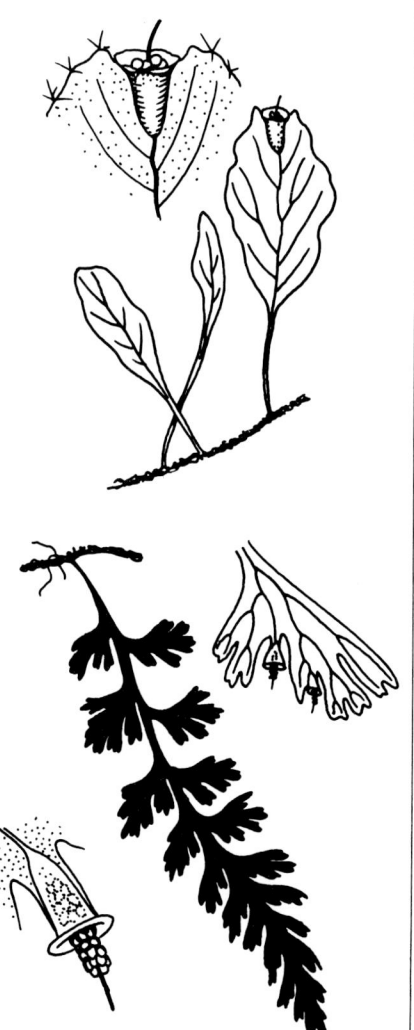

1. *Trichomanes boschianum*

COMMON NAME: Appalachian Filmy Fern

Fronds bipinnatifid, up to 20 cm long, bearing scattered, hyaline to brown, septate hairs; blade ovate to oblong-lanceolate, up to 15 cm long and 4 cm wide; blade segments ovate, lobed, cleft, or parted into elongate divisions normally containing a single vein. Sori usually several to many per frond, terminal on lobes; indusium tubular.

HABITAT: Under moist, overhanging sandstone outcrops. Cleburne Co.: NE of Greers Ferry Dam; *Taylor 1013* (SIU). Madison Co.: SE of Pettigrew; *Clark 1400* (MO).

RANGE: East central United States.

Delzie Demaree first collected *Trichomanes boschianum* in Arkansas on 20 August 1961 at the Cleburne County site (Wagner, 1962b). On 4 February 1962, another, more extensive population was collected by Maxine Clark in Madison County (Clark, 1962). A number of additional populations have been found near Clark's original station.

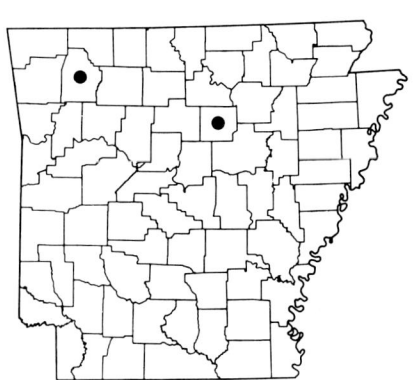

Trichomanes boschianum

Cleburne Co.: *Taylor 1013* (SIU). Madison Co.: *Clark 1400* (MO).

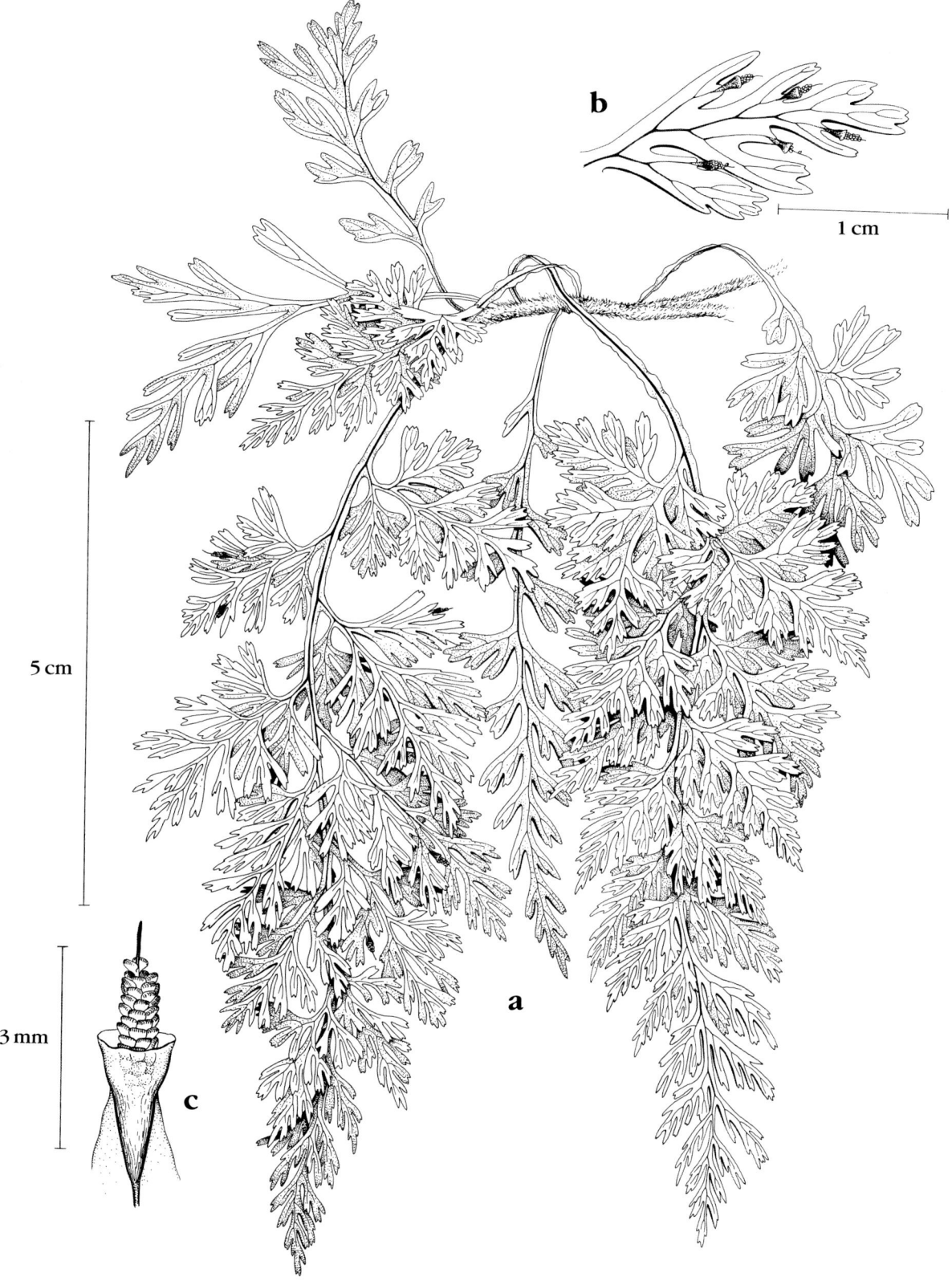

Trichomanes boschianum
a. Habit; b. Division of frond with sori; c. Sorus.

2. *Trichomanes petersii* Gray

COMMON NAME: Plateau Filmy Fern

Fronds entire to undulate-crenate and lobed, up to 1.5 cm long, bearing scattered, dark brown to black, stiffly branched hairs along margins; blade ovate to spatulate, up to 1.3 cm long and 8 mm wide. Sori usually one per frond, terminating midvein; indusium funnelform.

HABITAT: Conway Co.: sandstone ledge, Petit Jean State Park; *Peck 83-57* (LRU). Garland Co.: shale exposure around placer mine; *Peck 83-452* (LRU). Pope Co.: side of sandstone boulder in narrow drainage ravine SW of Pelsor; *Redfearn 21508* (SMS). Stone Co.: sandstone ledge along North Sylamore Creek; *Taylor 2897* (SIU).

RANGE: Southeastern United States, Middle America.

The Pope County station was located on 24 May 1967 by Donald Farrar and Paul Redfearn. Farrar and Redfearn (1968) noted that at this station the plants are somewhat atypical in that the blade bases approach a subcordate condition rather than the usual more acuminate base. Further, they found that the blade length to width ratio is smaller than in the typical form, and that the midrib shows a tendency to branch dichotomously so that the blade may bear two or more sori.

The diminutive size and cryptic habit of *Trichomanes petersii* make it easy to overlook.

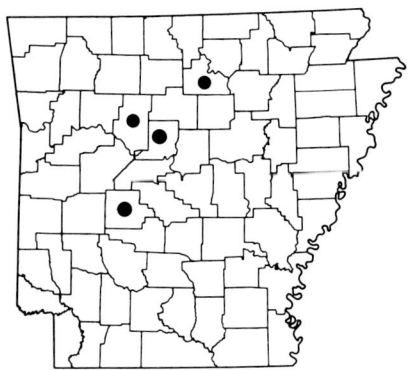

Trichomanes petersii

Conway Co.: *Peck 83-57* (LRU). Garland Co.: *Peck 83-452* (LRU). Pope Co.: *Redfearn 21508* (SMS). Stone Co.: *Taylor 2897* (SIU).

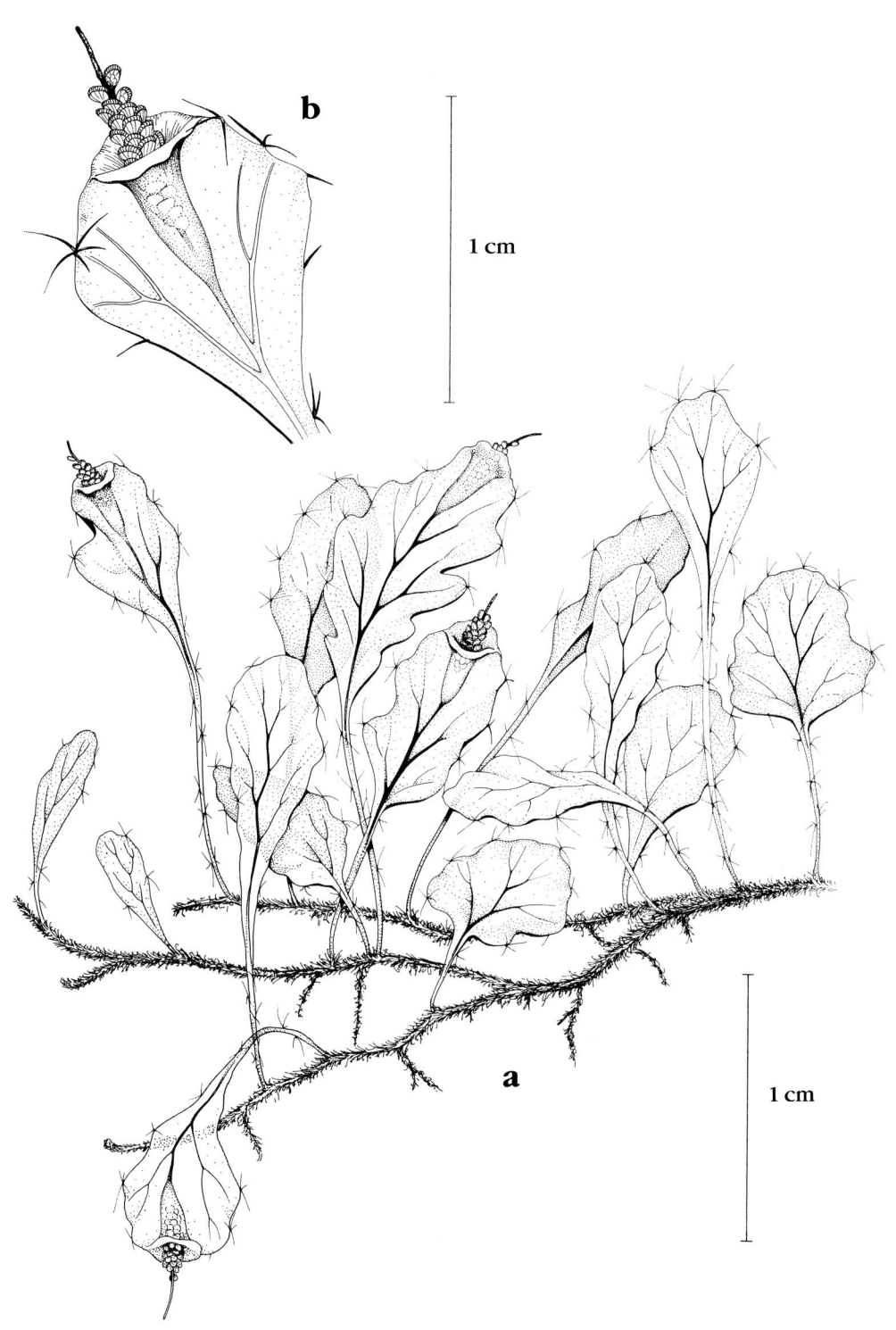

Trichomanes petersii
a. Habit; b. Portion of frond with sorus.

Woodsia R. Br. Woodsias

Rhizome short-creeping to erect; scales often with a dark medial stripe, linear-lanceolate. Fronds mostly deciduous, cespitose, erect to erect-spreading, bipinnate to bipinnate-pinnatifid, glandular; blade lanceolate; pinnules ovate to oblong; veins forked, free, not reaching the margins. Sori submarginal, round to slightly elongate, borne on veins; indusium cup-like, opening above and splitting into several segments, glandular.

A genus of nearly 40 species predominately found in north temperate regions. The most recent monographic treatment of *Woodsia* is by Brown (1964).

Key to the species of *Woodsia* in Arkansas

1. Rachis glabrate, bearing scattered light brown scales; stipe green to stramineous .... 1. *W. obtusa* (p. 238)
1. Rachis pilose with gland-tipped hairs, scaleless; stipe lustrous reddish brown .... 2. *W. scopulina* (p. 240)

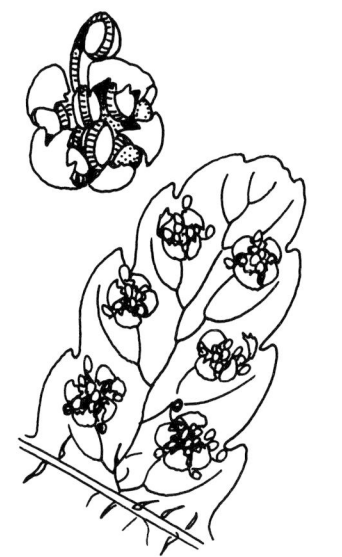

1. *Woodsia obtusa* (Spreng.) Torr.

Polypodium obtusum Spreng.

COMMON NAME: Blunt-lobed Woodsia

Rhizome scales reddish brown, often with a blackish medial stripe. Fronds bipinnate to bipinnate-pinnatifid, up to 45 cm long; stipe and rachis green to stramineous, glabrate, bearing scattered light brown scales; blade up to 35 cm long and 10 cm wide; pinnae deltoid-ovate to oblong-lanceolate, glabrate, glandular.

HABITAT: Well drained rocky or sandy soils of woodlands, rock outcrops, along roadsides and fence rows, occasionally on old rock walls.

RANGE: Eastern North America.

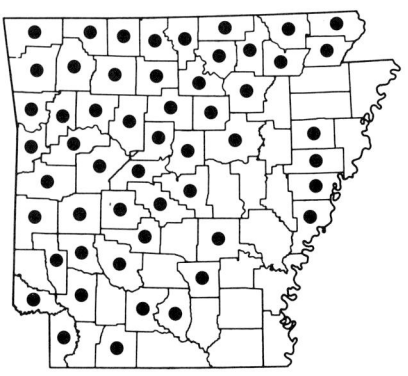

Woodsia obtusa (Spreng.)

Baxter Co.: *Taylor 1829* (SIU). Benton Co.: *Taylor 1121* (SIU). Boone Co.: *D. Moore 490380* (UARK). Calhoun Co.: *Demaree 22105* (SMU). Carroll Co.: *Palmer 4537* (MO). Clark Co.: *Taylor 2190* (SIU). Clay Co.: *Demaree 30417* (SMU). Cleburne Co.: *Taylor 1018* (SIU). Cleveland Co.: *Taylor 2737* (SIU). Columbia Co.: *Thomas 27931* (NLU). Conway Co.: *Demaree 23115* (SIU). Crawford Co.: *Taylor 1099* (SIU). Cross Co.: *Richards 3946* (ARKSU). Faulkner Co.: *Taylor 2011* (SIU). Franklin Co.: *Taylor 1129* (SIU). Fulton Co.: *Taylor 2666* (SIU). Garland Co.: *Taylor 2232* (SIU). Greene Co.: *Hess 1132* (SMU). Hempstead Co.: *Bush 5711* (MO). Hot Spring Co.: *Demaree 16539* (SMU). Howard Co.: *McSwain 43 E70* (UARK). Independence Co.: *Demaree 27150* (SMU). Izard Co.: *Taylor 2137* (SIU). Jefferson Co.: *Locke 1224* (UARK). Johnson Co.: *Taylor 1088* (SIU). Lawrence Co.: *Taylor 1786* (SIU). Lee Co.: *Demaree 37377* (SMU). Little River Co.: *Johnson 474* (HXC). Logan Co.: *Taylor 1033* (SIU). Madison Co.: *Taylor 1997* (SIU). Marion Co.: *Taylor 1229* (SIU). Miller Co.: *Taylor 1910* (SIU). Montgomery Co.: *Taylor 1081* (SIU). Newton Co.: *D. Moore 480228* (UARK). Ouachita Co.: *Demaree 63771* (SIU). Perry Co.: *Demaree 27051* (SMU). Pike Co.: *Taylor 2170* (SIU). Polk Co.: *Holberg 560* (SMU). Pope Co.: *Taylor 1200* (SIU). Pulaski Co.: *Demaree 17375* (MO). Randolph Co.: *Taylor 1081* (SIU). St. Francis Co.: *Demaree 22149* (SMU). Saline Co.: *Demaree 23042* (SMU). Scott Co.: *Taylor 2715* (SIU). Searcy Co.: *Taylor 1241* (SIU). Sebastian Co.: *Taylor 2712* (SIU). Sharp Co.: *Taylor 1817* (SIU). Stone Co.: *Taylor 1249* (SIU). Van Buren Co.: *Wherry s.n.* (PH). Washington Co.: *Taylor 1115* (SIU). White Co.: *Demaree 26902* (SMU). Yell Co.: *Taylor 1193* (SIU).

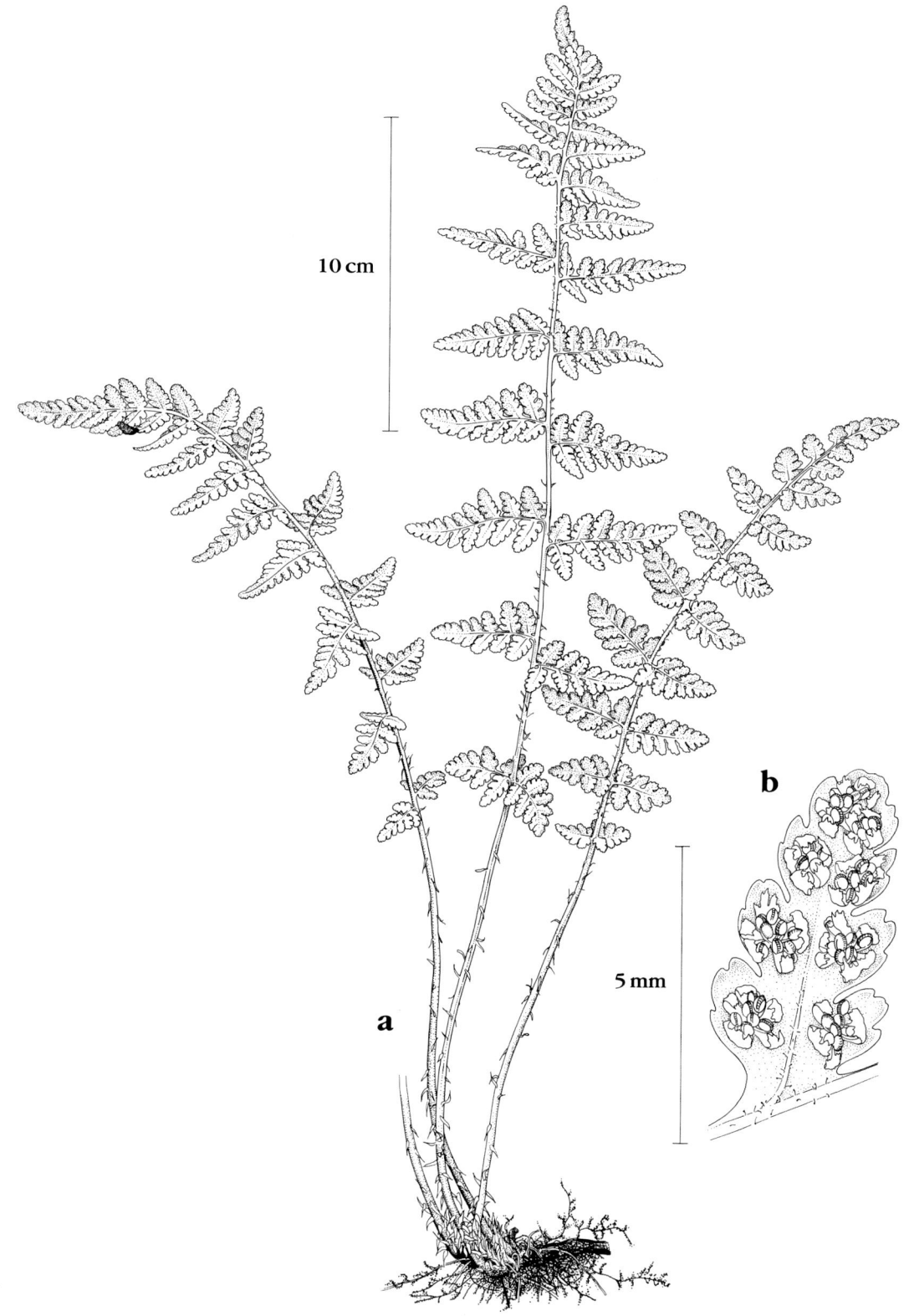

Woodsia obtusa
a. Habit; b. Lower surface of pinnule with sori.

2. *Woodsia scopulina* D. C. Eat. var. *appalachiana* (T. M. C. Taylor) Morton

Woodsia appalachiana T. M. C. Taylor

COMMON NAME: Appalachian Woodsia

Rhizome scales pellucid to light brown, often with an irregular, dark reddish brown medial stripe. Fronds bipinnate, up to 30 cm long; stipe and rachis lustrous reddish brown to stramineous, pilose, with gland tipped hairs, scaleless; blade up to 25 cm long and 8 cm wide; pinnae oblong-lanceolate, pilose with hyaline, jointed hairs mixed with minute, yellowish, stipitate glands.

HABITAT: Logan Co.: ledges of sandstone outcrops and talus on north side, near summit of Magazine Mountain; *Taylor 1045* (SIU).

RANGE: Arkansas and the Appalachian Mountains of Virginia, West Virginia, North Carolina, Kentucky, and Tennessee.

Palmer (1924) first collected *Woodsia scopulina* var. *appalachiana* in Arkansas from the above locality on 15 October 1923. This Arkansas station is interesting because it is over 500 miles distant from the nearest known populations of *Woodsia scopulina* in eastern Tennessee, western Oklahoma, and northern Iowa.

The Arkansas material of *Woodsia scopulina* is assignable to var. *appalachiana* on the basis of its indusia, which split into several relatively broad, erose segments. In this respect, the Arkansas material is similar to specimens found in the southern Appalachians. Variety *scopulina*, which is widespread in northern and western North America, has indusia that split into numerous, relatively narrow, linear-attenuate segments.

Woodsia scopulina

Logan Co.: *Taylor 1045* (SIU).

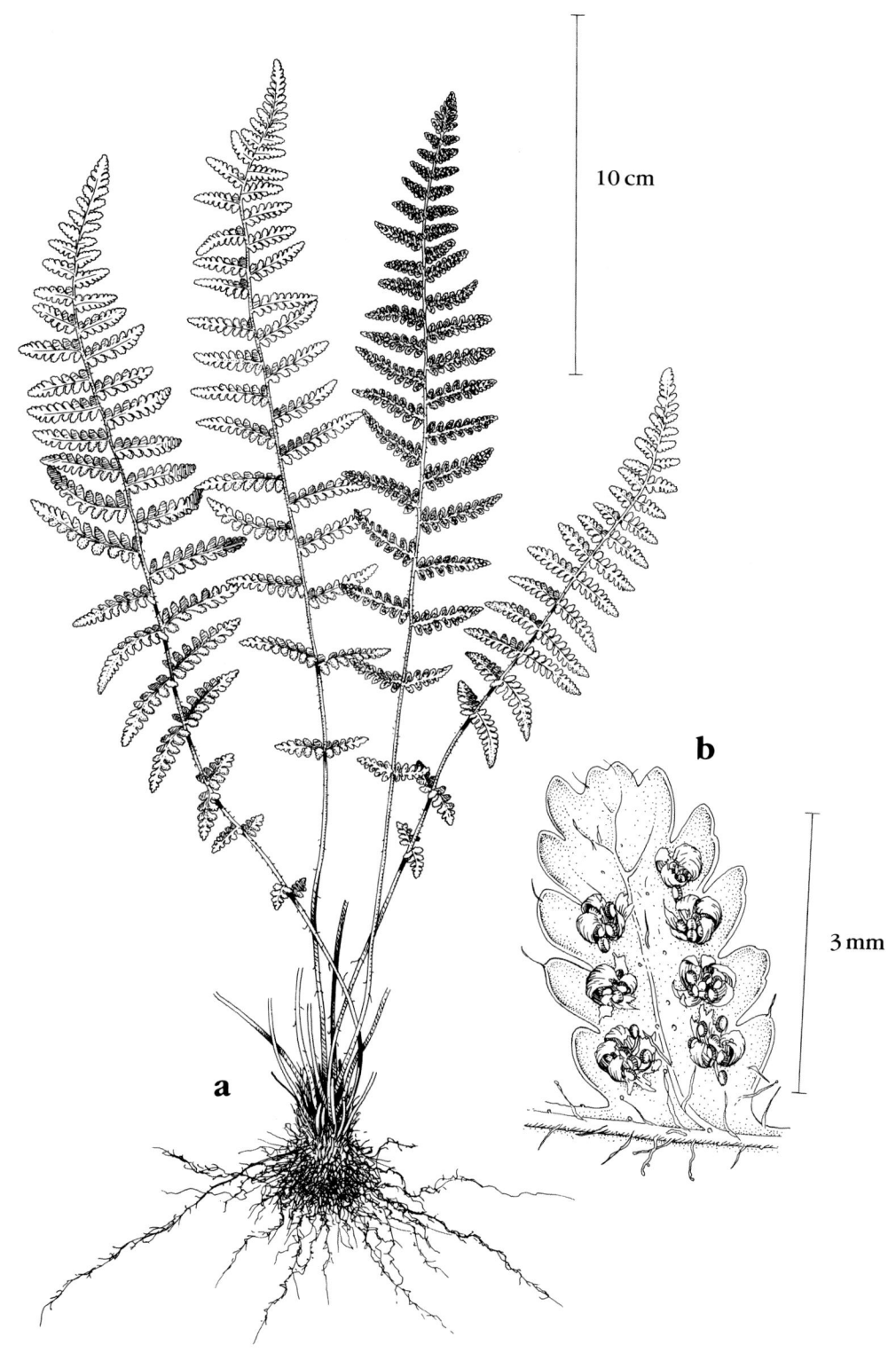

Woodsia scopulina var. *appalachiana*
a. Habit; b. Lower surface of pinnule with sori.

Woodwardia J. Smith Chain Ferns

A genus of about 11 species mainly of temperate regions.

1. *Woodwardia virginica* (L.) J. Smith

Blechnum virginicum L.
Anchistea virginica (L.) Presl

COMMON NAME: Virginia Chain Fern

Rhizome long-creeping; scales deltoid ovate to lanceolate. Fronds deciduous, erect-spreading, pinnate-pinnatifid, up to 80 cm long; stipe lustrous purplish red to stramineous; blade ovate to oblong-lanceolate, up to 50 cm long and 25 cm wide; rachis reddish brown to stramineous; pinnae linear-lanceolate to elliptic-lanceolate, veins partly reticulate forming a single series of linear to oblong areolae along midribs of pinnae and pinnae segments; pinna segments ovate to oblong, serrulate. Sori linear to elongate, borne on veins bordering outer edge of areolae; indusium glandular, attached by its outer margin, opening toward midrib.

HABITAT: Low, wet, sandy soil of woodlands; chiefly West Gulf Coastal Plain.

RANGE: Eastern North America, Bermuda.

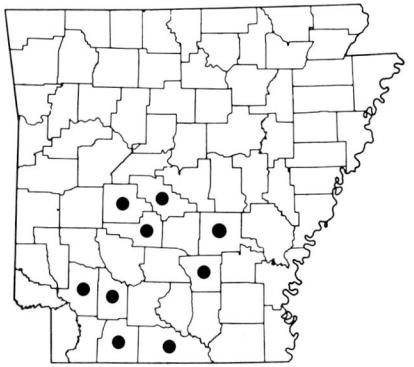

Woodwardia virginica

Cleveland Co.: *Taylor 1141* (SIU). Columbia Co.: *Taylor 1166* (SIU). Garland Co.: *D. Moore 410418* (UARK). Hempstead Co.: *D. Moore 56179* (UARK). Hot Spring Co.: *D. Moore 440081* (UARK). Jefferson Co.: Locke 1309 (UARK). Nevada Co.: *D. Moore 490643* (UARK). Saline Co.: *D. Moore 410434* (UARK). Union Co.: *D. Moore 410335* (UARK).

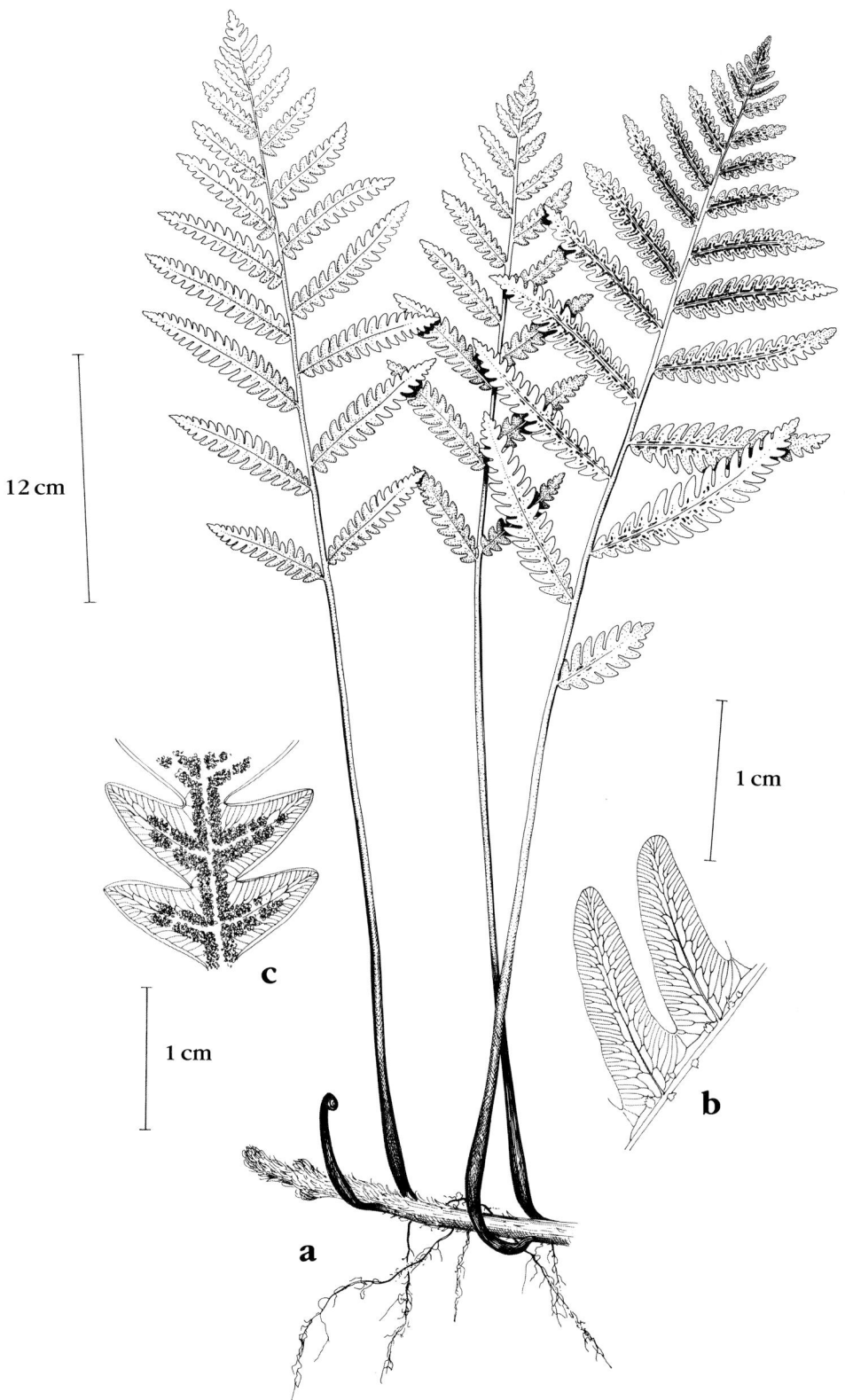

Woodwardia virginica
a. Habit; b. Portion of pinna; c. Lower surface of pinna with sori.

Herbaria from which specimens are cited

ACRONYM	INSTITUTION
APCR	Arkansas Polytechnic College, Russellville, Arkansas
ARKSU	Arkansas State University, Jonesboro, Arkansas
F	Field Museum of Natural History, Chicago, Illinois
HXC	Hendrix College, Conway, Arkansas
LRU	University of Arkansas at Little Rock, Little Rock, Arkansas
MO	Missouri Botanical Garden, St. Louis, Missouri
MEM	Memphis State University, Memphis, Tennessee
NCU	University of North Carolina, Chapel Hill, North Carolina
NLU	Northeast Louisiana University, Monroe, Louisiana
NY	New York Botanical Garden, Bronx, New York
PH	Academy of Natural Sciences, Philadelphia, Pennsylvania
SIU	Southern Illinois University, Carbondale, Illinois
SMS	Southwest Missouri State University, Springfield, Missouri
SMU	Southern Methodist University, Dallas, Texas
TENN	University of Tennessee, Knoxville, Tennessee
UARK	University of Arkansas, Fayetteville, Arkansas
UCA	University of Central Arkansas, Conway, Arkansas
US	Smithsonian Institution, Washington, D. C.

*Abbreviations mostly after Holmgren and Keuken (1981).

Glossary

Acuminate. Tapering to an apex with the sides concave (Fig. 6).
Acute. Tapering to an apex with the sides straight (Fig. 6).
Adaxial. Side toward the axis or stem.
Adventitious (roots). Arising from a part of the plant other than the base of the stem or rhizome.
Allopolyploid. Organism having more than two sets of chromosomes derived from two or more species by hybridization.
Alternate. Borne singly at different points along an axis.
Alveolate. Pitted. Full of small cavities.
Anisophyllous. Having more than one leaf shape.
Annulus. A series of thick-walled, elastic cells which function in opening and closing the sporangium.
Antheridium. Sex organ on prothallus which produces sperm (Fig. 3).
Apex. Top.
Apiculate. Ending in a short, sharp point.
Apogamy. Production of a sporophyte directly from the prothallus without fertilization.
Appressed. Pressed closely against.
Arachnoid. Cobwebby.
Archegonium. Sex organ on the prothallus which contains an egg (Fig. 3).
Areole. Area inclosed by a network of veins (Fig. 6).
Articulate. Jointed.
Ascending. Rising or curving upward.
Attenuate. Having a long, gradual taper.
Auricle. Ear-shaped appendage as a lobe at the base of some pinnae (Fig. 6).
Auriculate. With an auricle or basal lobe (Fig. 6).
Axillary. Borne in the angle formed by a leaf and stem or pinna and rachis.

Bipinnate. Twice divided. Blade cut into pinnae and pinnules (Fig. 4).
Bipinnatifid. Twice divided. Fronds divided with divisions deeply lobed (Fig. 4).
Bivalvate. Opening into two halves.
Blade. Flattened, expanded portion of a frond.
Bulbiferous. Bearing bulblets.
Bulblet. Small bulb produced on a frond, usually axillary.

Calcareous. Containing calcium. Limestone is a calcareous rock.
Carinal canal. Cavity in stem of *Equisetum* below the ridges.
Caudate. With a slender, tail-like appendage.
Cauline. Of or attached to the stem.
Chromosomes. Bodies located in the cell nucleus which carry genes. They are usually constant in number for any given species.
Ciliolate. Marginally fringed with minute hairs.
Clathrate. Latticed. Refers to scales composed of translucent cells with thick, darkened sidewalls that together give a lattice-like appearance, typical of *Asplenium*.
Clavate. Club-shaped.
Cleft. Cut about one-half way to midvein.
Concolorous. Uniformly colored.

Connate. Joining of similar structures.
Cordate. Heart-shaped (Fig. 6).
Corm. Bulb-like, solid, fleshy stem of *Isoetes*.
Cortical sclerenchyma. Thick-walled support tissue near the outer edge of the stem of *Equisetum*.
Costa (pl. costae). Midrib or midvein.
Creeping. Running along at or near ground level and rooting at the nodes.
Crenate. With rounded teeth.
Crenulate. With small, rounded teeth (Fig. 6).
Crisped. Curled.
Cuneate. Wedge-shaped (Fig. 6).
Cupulate. Cup-like.
Cytotype. The chromosome constitution of an organism.

Deciduous. Fronds not persisting throughout the year, not evergreen.
Decumbent. Reclining on the ground, with upper end ascending.
Decurrent. Extension of the blade or blade division down the stem or rachis.
Deflexed. Bent downward.
Deltoid. Shaped like a triangle.
Dentate. Toothed, with teeth pointing out at right angles to the midvein (Fig. 6).
Denticulate. Finely dentate (Fig. 6).
Dichotomous. Dividing into equal branches.
Dimorphic. Occurring in two forms, fronds or their parts not all alike.
Dioecious. Unisexual, bearing male and female reproductive bodies on different plants.
Diploid. Having two sets of chromosomes.
Dissected. Cut into parts, segments, or lobes.
Distal. Opposite point of attachment.
Distichous. Two-ranked. In two opposing rows in the same plane.
Divided. Separated nearly to the base.
Division. One of the parts into which a frond may be divided.
Dolomite. Common rock forming mineral of calcium-magnesium carbonate.
Dorsal. The lower surface of a frond; the back or outer surface of an organ.
Dorsiventral. Flattened so as to have distinct dorsal and ventral surfaces.
Doubly serrate. Margins with teeth of two different sizes.

Echinate. Covered with thin, tapering projections; spiny.
Eglandular. Without glands.
Elaters. Spatulate, hygroscopic appendages on the spores of *Equisetum*.
Eligulate. Without a ligule.
Elliptic. Form of flattened circle tapering uniformly to both ends.
Elongate. Lengthened; drawn or stretched out.
Emarginate. Having a shallow notch at the apex (Fig. 6).
Entire. Smooth margin, without teeth or lobes.
Ephemeral. Persisting only a short time.
Epiphyte. Plant which grows upon another plant but is not parasitic on it.
Erose. An irregular edge, as if gnawed.

Evergreen. Remaining green throughout the year.
Excrescence. An outgrowth or appendage.
Exserted. Projecting beyond surrounding tissue.
Exsiccated. Dried up.

Fastigiate. Erect and close together.
Fertile. Bearing sporangia and producing spores.
Fiddlehead. Coiled tip of a young frond.
Filiform. Thread-like.
Fimbriolate. Minutely fringed with hairs.
Flabellate. Fan-shaped.
Fleshy. Thick, juicy; succulent.
Flexuous. Zig-zagged; bent alternately in opposite directions.
Fluted. Having longitudinal grooves.
Forma (f.). Taxonomic category used to indicate a minor, often sporadic variant of a species.
Foveolate. Pitted.
Free. Separate, distinct; not united with other structures.
Frond. Fern leaf including stipe and blade.

Gamete. Reproductive cell; egg or sperm.
Gametophyte. Plant producing gametes; prothallus which bears archegonia and antheridia.
Gemma (pl. gemmae). Bud which detaches from parent plant and is capable of developing into a new plant.
Gemmiparous. Producing gemmae.
Glabrate. Becoming glabrous.
Glabrous. Without hairs.
Glandular. Bearing glands.
Globose. Spherical.
Glochidium. Barbed appendage on a microsporic massula in *Azolla*.

Haploid. Having one set of chromosomes.
Hastate. Spear-shaped with two divergent lobes at base.
Herbarium. Collection of dried, labeled, and systematically arranged plant specimens.
Heterosporous. Producing two kinds of spores; microspores and megaspores.
Hirtellous. Minutely covered with hairs.
Hispidulous. Minutely covered with rather stiff hairs.
Homosporous. Producing only one kind of spore.
Hyaline. Translucent.
Hybrid. Product of a cross between two species.
Hygroscopic. Readily absorbing moisture and changing in form or position because of this absorption.

Isophyllous. Having one leaf form.
Indusium. Thin sheet of tissue covering a sorus.
Incised. Cut sharply, deeply, and irregularly.
Imbricate. Overlapping.

Jointed. Having nodes or points of apparent articulation.

Keeled. Sharply creased or ridged below.

Lacerate. Irregularly cut as if torn.
Lanceolate. Lance-shaped; longer than broad; broadest above the base and tapering toward the apex.
Lanuginose. Woolly or cottony.
Lax. Loose, not crowded.
Logilate. Bearing a ligule.
Ligule. Small appendage above the sporangium on the leaves of *Isoetes* and *Selaginella*.
Linear. Long and narrow; more than ten times longer than broad.
Lineolate. Marked with fine lines.
Lobe. Shallow division rounded at its apex.
Lobulate. Having small lobes.
Lunate. Crescent-shaped.
Lustrous. Having a gloss or sheen.

Marginal. Placed on or along the edge.
Massula. Mass of microspores bearing glochidia in *Azolla*.
Medial. Midway between the margin and midvein.
Megasporangium. Sporangium in which megaspores are produced.
Megaspore. Large spore which produces a female gametophyte bearing archegonia.
Megasporocarp. Structure containing a megasporangium in *Azolla*.
Meiosis. Process by which a diploid organism produces haploid gametes.
Membranous. Very thin and translucent.
Meristem. Tissue in which dividing cells are capable of developing into various tissues or organs.
Micrometer (um). 1/1000 milimeter.
Microsporangium. Sporangium in which microspores are produced.
Microspore. Small spore which produces a male gametophyte bearing antheridia.
Microsporocarp. Structure containing microsporangia in *Azolla*.
Midrib. Central rib of a frond or one of its divisions. Essentially the same as midvein.
Midvein. Central vein of a frond or one of its divisions. Essentially the same as midrib.
Monoecious. Bisexual, having male and female reproductive structures on the same plant.

Novaculite. Hard, fine-grained siliceous rock used for whetstones.

Oblanceolate. Lance-shaped; broadest above the middle; reverse point of attachment for lanceolate.
Oblong. Longer than broad, with sides nearly parallel.
Obovate. Egg-shaped; broadest above the middle; reverse point of attachment for ovate.

Obpyriform. Pear-shaped with the broadest portion toward the apex.
Obtuse. Blunt, rounded apex or base.
Opposite. Borne directly opposed along sides of an axis.
Orbicular. Circular in outline.
Ovate. Egg-shaped; broadest below the middle.

Papillate (papillose). Bearing small, nipple-shaped protuberences.
Paraphyses. Sterile, club-shaped, structures found in the sorus of some ferns.
Pellucid. Clear, nearly transparent.
Peltate. Umbrella-shaped, with point of attachment toward the center.
Pendulous. Hanging downward.
Perennial. Of more than two year's duration.
Perine. Loose outer wall of a spore.
Petiolule. Stalk to a pinna, pinnule, or segment.
Pilose. With long, soft hairs.
Pilosulous. Minutely pilose.
Pinna (pl. pinnae). Primary division of a blade.
Pinnate. Once divided. Blade cut into pinnae along opposite sides of rachis.
Pinnate-pinnatifid. Pinnate with pinnatifid pinnae.
Pinnatifid. Pinnately lobed to divided.
Pinnatisect. Pinnately cut to the midrib.
Pinnule. Division of a pinna; secondary division of a bipinnate frond.
Pith cavity. Central cavity in the stem of *Equisetum*.
Proliferous. Producing buds, bulblets, or plantlets on the fronds.
Prostrate. Lying flat on the ground.
Prothallus. Small, membranous, generally heart-shaped gametophyte bearing archegonia and antheridia.
Proximal. Toward point of attachment.
Pteridologist. One who studies ferns and fern allies.
Pteridophyte. Any fern or fern ally.
Puberulent. Minutely hairy.
Pubescent. Bearing hairs.
Punctate. Dotted with minute depressions or pits.

Rachis. Midrib of a compound frond extending from apex to lowest pinna.
Radially symmetrical. Parts of a whorl all alike; whorl capable of being bisected into identical halves along more than one axis, forming mirror images.
Recurved. Bent or curved downward or backward.
Reflexed. Abruptly bent downward or backward.
Relict. Plant existing in isolation as a remnant from an earlier geological period.
Reniform. Kidney-shaped.
Reticulate. Forming a network.
Retrorse. Directed backward or downward.
Rhizoid. Filamentous, root-like structure lacking vascular tissue; found on prothallus.
Rhizome. More or less horizontally elongated stem producing fronds and roots.

Rhombic. Diamond-shaped; outline of an equilateral oblique-angled figure.
Rugulate. Wrinkled.

Saxicolous. Growing on or among rocks.
Scabrid. Roughened.
Scale. Thin, scarious outgrowth more than one cell wide on the surfaces of rhizomes and fronds.
Scarious. Dry, thin, membranous, not green.
Secund. Borne along one side of an axis.
Segment. Division of a pinnule; ultimate division of a tripinnate frond.
Senescent. Aging.
Septate. Being divided or partitioned by cross walls.
Serrate. Toothed, with teeth pointing forward toward the apex.
Serrulate. Finely serrate.
Sessile. Without a stalk.
Simple. Not divided into pinnae; not compound.
Sinus. Indentation or space between two lobes or divisions.
s.n. Sine numero. Without a number.
Solitary. Borne singly or alone.
Sorus. A cluster of sporangia, most often on the lower surface of fronds.
Spatulate. Spoon-shaped.
Species (pl. species). Variously defined but may be considered here as a group of plants that is recognized as being of one kind because it is more or less reproductively isolated from other groups of plants.
Specific epithet. The second name of a binomial or species name.
Spinulose. Having small spines.
Sporangiophore. Peltate appendage that bears sporangia in the strobilus of *Equisetum*.
Sporangium. Spore case.
Spore. One-celled reproductive body which germinates to form a gametophyte.
Sporiferous. Spore-bearing.
Sporocarp. Structure containing sporangia in *Marsilea, Pilularia,* and *Azolla.*
Sporophyll. Spore-bearing leaf.
Sporophyte. Spore producing plant; rhizome or stem bearing roots and fertile fronds or leaves.
Sterile. Lacking functional reproductive structures.
Stipe. Stalk of frond extending from lowest pinna to point of attachment on the rhizome.
Stipitate. Having a stalk.
Stramineous. Straw-colored.
Strigillose. Minutely strigose.
Strigose. Bearing stiff, sharp appressed hairs.
Strobilus. Cone; an aggregation of sporophylls or sporangiophores.
Suberous. Corky.
Sub-. A prefix indicating an approach to a condition, e.g., subentire meaning nearly entire, subopposite meaning almost opposite, etc.
Subspecies (subsp.). Taxonomic category below the rank of species.

Subulate. Awl-shaped, tapering from base to apex.
Sulcate. Grooved or furrowed longitudinally.
Sympatric. Occupying the same geographic region.
Synonym. Name rejected in favor of another name because of misapplication or difference in taxonomic judgement.

Taxon (pl. taxa). Any taxonomic unit into which an organism is classified, i.e., variety, subspecies, species, etc.
Tetrahedral. Pyramidal form with four triangular faces.
Tetraploid. Having four sets of chromosomes.
Tomentose. Densely covered with matted, woolly hairs.
Tomentulose. Finely tomentose.
Transection. Cross section. Section cut at right angles to the long axis of an organ.
Tripinnate. Three times divided. Blade cut into pinnae, pinnules, and segments.
Triploid. Having three sets of chromosomes.
Truncate. Ending abruptly as if cut or squared off.
Tuberculate. Bearing small rounded, pimple-like projections or tubercules.
Tufa. A porous limestone formed by precipitation from mineralized springs.
Tuft. Clustered; growing close together.

Undulate. With a wavy, up and down, margin or surface.
Unilateral. One-sided, e.g. unilateral indusia are attached only along one edge.

Vallecular canal. Cavity in the stem of *Equisetum* between the ridges.
Variety (var.). Taxonomic categeory used to indicate a variation within a species not sufficiently distinctive to be recognized at the species level.
Vascular. Containing conducting cells, i.e., xylem and phloem, for moving water and nutrients throughout the plant.
Vein. Strand of vascular or conducting tissue in the blade or any other part of the plant.
Veinlet. Small vein.
Venation. Vein pattern.
Velum. A flap of tissue partly covering the sporangium in *Isoetes*.
Ventral. The upper or inner surface of a frond, leaf, or other organ.
Verticil. A whorl; a whorled arrangement of similar parts.
Verticillate. Borne in verticils.
Villous. Provided with long, soft, fine hairs.

Winged. Bearing an expanded, flat, sometimes blade-like portion on either side of an axis.
Wiry. Flexible but springy.

Zygote. Cell formed by the fusion of sperm and egg.

Literature Cited

Bates, V. M., Jr. and E. T. Browne, Jr. 1981. *Azolla filiculoides* new to the southeastern United States. Am. Fern J. 71: 33-34.

Beitel, J. 1979. Clubmosses *(Lycopodium)* in North America. Fiddlehead Forum 6: 1-7.

Beitel, J., W. H. Wagner, Jr., and K. S. Walter. 1981. Unusual frond development in sensitive fern *Onoclea sensibilis* L. Am. Midland Nat. 105: 396-400.

Blasdell, R. F. 1963. A monographic study of the fern genus *Cystopteris*. Mem. Torrey Bot. Club 21: 1-102.

Boom, Brian M. 1979. Systematic studies of the genus *Isoetes* in the southeastern United States. M.S. Thesis, University of Tennessee, Knoxville.

_____. 1982. Synopsis of *Isoetes* in the southeastern United States. Castanea 47: 38-59.

Bowers, F. and P. L. Redfearn, Jr. 1967. *Lycopodium lucidulum* in the Boston Mountains of Arkansas. Am. Fern J. 57: 91-92.

Branner, J. C. and F. V. Coville. 1891. A list of the plants of Arkansas. Pages 155-242 *in* J.C. Branner, Annual Report of the Geological Survey of Arkansas for 1888. Vol. IV. Press Printing Co., Little Rock.

Britton, D. M. 1961. The problem of variation in North American *Dryopteris*. Am. Fern J. 51: 23-30.

Britton, D. M. and C. J. Widen. 1974. Chemotaxonomic studies on *Dryopteris* from Quebec and eastern North America. Can. J. Bot. 52: 627-638.

Brown, D. F. M. 1964. A monographic study of the fern genus *Woodsia*. Nova Hedwigia 16: 1-154.

Buchholz, J. T. 1924. Notes on Arkansas pteridophyta. Am. Fern J. 14: 33-38.

Buchholz, J. T. and E. J. Palmer. 1926. Supplement to the catalogue of Arkansas plants. Trans. Acad. St. Louis 25: 91-155.

Buck, W. R. 1977. A new species of *Selaginella* in the *S. apoda* complex. Can. J. Bot. 55: 366-371.

Chandler, A. 1941. *Pteris multifida* in Arkansas. Am. Fern J. 31: 112.

Clark, M. B. 1962. *Trichomanes boschianum* in Madison County, Arkansas. Am. Fern J. 52: 85-86.

Clausen, R. T. 1938. A monograph of the Ophioglossaceae. Mem. Torrey Bot. Club 19: 1-177.

Correll, D. S. and H. B. Correll. 1972. Aquatic and Wetland Plants of the Southwestern United States. Environmental Protection Agency, Washington, D. C.

Demaree, D. 1943a. Arkansas fern notes. Am. Fern J. 33: 75.

_____. 1943b. A catalogue of the vascular plants of Arkansas. Taxodium 1: 1-88.

Dennis, W. M. and D. H. Webb. 1981. The distribution of *Pilularia americana* A. Br. (Marsileaceae) in North America north of Mexico. Sida 9: 19-24.

Engelmann, G. 1882. The genus *Isoetes* in North America. Trans. Acad. St. Louis 4: 358-389.

Evans, A. M. 1971. A review of systematic studies of the pteridophytes of the southern Appalachians. *In* P. C. Holt (editor), "The Distributional History of the Biota of the Southern Appalachians. Part II: Flora." Virginia Polytech. Inst. Res. Div. Monogr. 2: 117-146.

Farrar, D. R. and P. L. Redfearn. 1968. *Trichomanes petersii* in the Boston Mountains of Arkansas. Am. Fern J. 58: 32-33.

Foti, T. L. 1974. Natural divisions of Arkansas. Pg. 11-34 *in* Arkansas Natural Area Plan, Department of Planning. Little Rock.

Gleason, H. A. 1952. The new Britton and Brown illustrated flora of the northeastern United States and adjacent Canada. I. Hafner Publishing Co., New York.

Godfrey, R. K., G. W. Reinert, and R. D. Houk. 1961. Observations on microsporocarpic material of *Azolla caroliniana*. Am. Fern J. 51:89-92.

Gupta, K. M. 1957. Some American species of *Marsilea* with special reference to their epidermal soral characters. Madrono 14: 113-127.

———. 1962. *Marsilea*, Botanical Monograph No. 2. Council of Scientific and Industrial Research, New Delhi 1-113.

Harvey, F. L. 1881. Classified list of the ferns of Arkansas with notes on the geographical range and habitat of the species. Bot. Gaz. 6: 188-190, 213-215.

Hauke, R. L. 1963. A taxonomic monograph of the genus *Equisetum* Subgenus *Hippochaete*. Beih. Nova Hedwigia 8: 1-123.

———. 1979. A taxonomic monograph of *Equisetum* subgenus *Equisetum*. Nova Hedwigia 30: 385-455.

Holmgren, P. K., W. Keuken, and E. K. Schofield. 1981. Index Herbariorum Part I, The Herbaria of the World. 7th ed. Bohn, Scheltema, and Deventer, Utrecht, Netherlands.

Holttum, R. E. 1969. Studies in the family Thelypteridaceae. The genera *Phegopteris, Pseudophegopteris* and *Macrothelypteris*. Blumea 17: 5-32.

Key, J. S. 1975. Pteridophytes of the Interior Highlands of North America. M.S. Thesis. Southwest Missouri State University, Springfield.

———. 1976. Forked fronds in *Asplenium rhizophyllum*. Am. Fern J. 66: 26-27.

Leonard, S. W. 1972. The distribution of *Thelypteris torresiana* in the southeastern United States. Am. Fern J. 62: 97-99.

Lesquereux, L. 1860. A catalogue of the plants of Arkansas. Pages 346-399 *in* D. D. Owen, Second Report of a Geological Reconnaissance of the Middle and Southern Counties of Arkansas Made During the Years 1859 and 1860. C. Sherman & Son, Printers. Philadelphia.

Liew, L. F. 1972. Numerical taxonomic studies on North American lady ferns and their allies. Taiwania 17: 190-216.

Manton, I. 1957. The problem of *Polypodium virginianum*. Am. Fern J. 47: 129-134.

Manton, I. and M. G. Shivas. 1953. Two cytological forms of *Polypodium virginianum* in eastern North America. Nature 172: 410.

Manton, I. and S. Walker. 1953. Cytology of the *Dryopteris spinulosa* complex in eastern North America. Nature 171: 1116-1118.

Moore, D. M. 1940a. *Selaginella rupestris* (L.) Spring in Arkansas. Am. Fern J. 30: 50-52.

_____. 1940b. Arkansas pteridophyta. Am. Fern J. 30: 105-119.

_____. 1941. Some noteworthy fern communities of Arkansas. Am. Fern J. 31: 63-71.

_____. 1947. Further notes on Arkansas pteridophytes. Proc. Arkansas Acad. 2: 69-70.

_____. 1950. A new fern record for Arkansas. Proc. Arkansas Acad. 3: 33-34.

_____. 1951. Some new records for the Arkansas flora. Proc. Arkansas Acad. 4: 61-63.

_____. 1957. New records for the Arkansas flora III. Proc. Arkansas Acad. 11: 6-10.

_____. 1958. New records for the Arkansas flora IV. Proc. Arkansas Acad. 12: 9-16.

Moore, J. E. and I. Hartsoe. 1955. A new location for *Ophioglossum crotalophoroides* in Arkansas. Proc. Arkansas Acad. 7: 63.

Moran, R. C. 1982. The *Asplenium trichomanes* complex in the United States and adjacent Canada. Am. Fern J. 72: 5-11.

Nuttall, T. 1821. Journal of Travels into the Arkansas Territory During the Year 1819 with Occasional Observations on the Manners of the Aborigines. Thomas H. Palmer, Philadelphia.

_____. 1835. Collections towards a flora of the territory of Arkansas. Trans. Am. Phil. Soc. 5: 139-160.

Palmer, E. J. 1924. Two interesting ferns from Arkansas. Am. Fern J. 14: 39-41.

_____. 1932. Notes on *Ophioglossum engelmannii*. Am. Fern J. 22: 43-47.

Pfeiffer, N. E. 1922. Monograph of the Isoetaceae. Ann. Missouri Bot. Gard. 9: 79-233.

Reed, C. F. 1965. *Isoetes* in southeastern United States. Phytologia 12: 369-400.

Scora, R. W. and W. H. Wagner, Jr. 1964. A preliminary chromatographic study of eastern American *Dryopteris*. Am. Fern J. 54: 105-113.

Scully, F. J. 1937. Ferns of Hot Springs National Park and vicinity. Am. Fern J. 27: 59-62.

_____. 1939. Ferns of Hot Springs National Park and vicinity. Natural History Journal No. 5. Hot Springs National Park.

Slosson, M. 1902. The origin of *Asplenium ebenoides*. Bull. Torrey Bot. Club 29: 487-495.

Smith, A. R. 1971. Systematics of the neotropical species of *Thelypteris* section *Cyclosorus*. Univ. Calif. Publ. Bot. 59: 1-143.

Smith, D. M. and D. A. Levin. 1963. A chromatographic study of reticulate evolution in the Appalachian *Asplenium* complex. Am. J. Bot. 50: 952-958.

Smith, D. M., T. R. Bryant, and D. E. Tate. 1961. New evidence on the hybrid nature of *Asplenium kentuckiense*. Brittonia 13: 289-292.

Smith, E. B. 1978. An atlas and annotated list of the vascular plants of Arkansas. University of Arkansas, Fayetteville.

Steyermark, J. A. 1963. Flora of Missouri. Iowa State University Press, Ames.

Svenson, H. K. 1944. The new world species of *Azolla*. Am. Fern J. 34: 69-84.

Taylor, W. C. 1976. Arkansas pteridophyta: description and distribution. Ph.D. Dissertation, Southern Illinois University, Carbondale.

Taylor, W. C. and D. Demaree. 1979. Annotated list of the ferns and fern allies of Arkansas. Rhodora 81: 503-548.

Taylor, W. C. and D. M. Johnson. 1979. *Thelypteris* in Arkansas. Am. Fern J. 69: 26-28.

Taylor, W. C., R. H. Mohlenbrock, and J. A. Murphy. 1975. The spores and taxonomy of *Isoetes butleri* and *I. melanopoda*. Am. Fern J. 65: 33-38.

Taylor, W. C., R. H. Mohlenbrock, and F. J. Burton. 1976. Variation in North American *Asplenium platyneuron*. Am. Fern J. 66: 63-68.

Thomas, R. Dale. 1978. Three additions to the Ophioglossaceae of Arkansas. Bull. Torrey Bot. Club 105: 234-235.

Thomas, R. D., P. S. Marx, and D. Lawson. 1974. Two Adder's-tongues new to Missouri. Am. Fern J. 64: 119-120.

Thomas, R. D., W. H. Wagner, Jr., and M. R. Mesler. 1973. Log fern *(Dryopteris celsa)* and related species in Louisiana. Castanea 38: 269-274.

Thompson, R. L. 1975. The vascular flora of Lost Valley, Newton County, Arkansas. M.S. Thesis. Southwest Missouri State University, Springfield.

Tryon, A. F. 1949. Spores of the genus *Selaginella* in North America, north of Mexico. Ann. Missouri Bot. Gard. 36: 413-431.

―――――. 1957. A revision of the fern genus *Pellaea* section *Pellaea*. Ann. Missouri Bot. Gard. 44: 125-193.

Tryon, A. F. and D. M. Britton. 1958. Cytotaxonomic studies on the fern genus *Pellaea*. Evolution 12: 135-145.

Tryon, R. M. 1941. A revision of the genus *Pteridium*. Rhodora 43: 1-31, 37-67.

―――――. 1955. *Selaginella rupestris* and its Allies. Ann. Missouri Bot. Gard. 42: 1-99.

―――――. 1960. A revision of the genus *Dennstaedtia* in America. Contrib. Gray Herb. 187: 23-52.

Tryon, R. M. and D. M. Britton. 1966. A study of variation in the cytotypes of *Dryopteris spinulosa*. Rhodora 68: 59-92.

Tucker, G. E. 1971. *Selaginella arenicola* ssp. *riddellii* in Arkansas. Sida 4: 275.

Wagner, W. H., Jr. 1954. Reticulate evolution in the Appalachian *Aspleniums*. Evolution 8: 103-118.

_____. 1961. Nomenclature and typification of two *Botrychiums* of the southeastern United States. Taxon 10: 165-169.

_____. 1962a. Irregular morphological development in hybrids. Phytomorphology 12: 87-100.

_____. 1962b. *Trichomanes boschianum* in Arkansas. Am. Fern J. 52: 84-85.

_____. 1966. Two new species of ferns from the United States. Am. Fern J. 56: 3-17.

_____. 1971a. The southeastern Adder's-tongue, *Ophioglossum vulgatum* var. *pycnostichum*, found for the first time in Michigan. Michigan Bot. 10: 67-74.

_____. 1971b. Evolution of *Dryopteris* in relation to the Appalachians. *In* P. C. Holt (editor), "The Distributional History of the Biota of the Southern Appalachians. Part II: Flora." Virginia Polytech. Inst. Res. Div. Monogr. 2: 147-192.

Wagner, W. H., Jr. and T. Darling. 1957. Synthetic and wild *Asplenium* X *gravesii*. Brittonia 9: 57-63.

Wagner, W. H., Jr., D. R. Farrar, and K. L. Chen. 1965. A new sexual form of *Pellaea glabella* var. *glabella* from Missouri. Am. Fern J. 55: 171-178.

Wagner, W. H. and D. Johnson. 1981. Natural History of Ebony Spleenwort, *Asplenium platyneuron* (Aspleniaceae), in the Great Lakes area. Canadian Field-Naturalist 95: 156-166.

Wagner, W. H., Jr. and W. C. Taylor. 1976. *Dryopteris* X *leedsii* and its westernmost station. Sida 6: 224-234.

Wagner, W. H., Jr. and F. S. Wagner. 1965. Rochester area Log ferns (*Dryopteris celsa*) and their hybrids. Proc. Rochester Acad. Sci. 11: 57-71.

Wagner, W. H., Jr. and F. S. Wagner. 1966. Pteridophytes of the Mountain Lake area, Giles Co., Virginia: Biosystematic studies, 1964-1965. Castanea 31: 121-140.

Wagner, W. H., Jr. and F. S. Wagner. 1969. A new natural hybrid in the Appalachian *Asplenium* complex and its taxonomic significance. Brittonia 21: 178-186.

Wagner, W. H., Jr. and F. S. Wagner. 1976. The role of foliar dimorphy in the systematics of ferns. (Abstr.) Page 44 *in* Botanical Society of America Abstracts of Papers. Allen Press, Inc., Lawrence, Kansas.

Wagner, W. H., Jr., F. S. Wagner, and D. J. Hagenah. 1969. The Log fern (*Dryopteris celsa*) and its hybrids in Michigan. Michigan Bot. 8: 137-145.

Walker, S. 1955. Cytogenetic studies in the *Dryopteris spinulosa* complex. I. Watsonia 3: 193-209.

———. 1959. Cytotaxonomic studies of some American species of *Dryopteris*. Am. Fern J. 49: 104-112.

———. 1960. Evolution within the genus *Dryopteris*. Proc. Linn. Soc. London 171: 130-132.

———. 1961. Cytogenetic studies in the *Dryopteris spinulosa* complex. II. Am. J. Bot. 48: 607-614.

———. 1962a. Further studies in the genus *Dryopteris:* The origin of *D. clintoniana, D. celsa,* and related taxa. Am. J. Bot. 49: 497-503.

———. 1962b. The problem of *Dryopteris leedsii.* Am. J. Bot. 49: 971-974.

———. 1969. Identification of a diploid ancestral genome in the *Dryopteris spinulosa* complex. Brit. Fern Gaz. 10: 97-99.

Waters, C. E. 1903. Ferns. Henry Holt and Co., New York.

Werth, C. R. and W. C. Taylor. 1980. *Asplenium* X *gravesii* discovered in Arkansas. Am. Fern J. 70: 28.

Widen, C.-J. and D. M. Britton. 1971. Chemotaxonomic investigations on the *Dryopteris cristata* complex in North America. Can. J. Bot. 49: 1141-1154.

Widen, C.-J., D. M. Britton, W. H. Wagner, Jr., and F. S. Wagner. 1975. Chemotaxonomic studies on hybrids of *Dryopteris* in eastern North America. Can. J. Bot. 53: 1554-1567.

Checklist of Arkansas Pteridophytes

___ *Adiantum capillus-veneris*
___ *A. pedatum*
___ *Asplenium bradleyi*
___ *A. X ebenoides*
___ *A. X gravesii*
___ *A. X kentuckiense*
___ *A. pinnatifidum*
___ *A. platyneuron*
___ *A. resiliens*
___ *A. rhizophyllum*
___ *A. ruta-muraria*
___ *A. trichomanes*
___ *Athyrium filix-femina*
___ *A. pycnocarpon*
___ *A. thelypterioides*
___ *Azolla mexicana*
___ *Botrychium biternatum*
___ *B. dissectum*
___ *B. lunarioides*
___ *B. virginianum*
___ *Cheilanthes alabamensis*
___ *C. eatonii*
___ *C. feei*
___ *C. lanosa*
___ *C. tomentosa*
___ *Cystopteris bulbifera*
___ *C. protrusa*
___ *C. tennesseensis*
___ *Dennstaedtia punctilobula*
___ *Dryopteris carthusiana*
___ *D. celsa*
___ *D. X leedsii*
___ *D. marginalis*
___ *Equisetum arvense*
___ *E. X ferrissii*
___ *E. hyemale*
___ *E. laevigatum*
___ *Isoetes butleri*
___ *I. melanopoda*
___ *Lorinseria areolata*
___ *Lycopodium appressum*
___ *L. lucidulum*
___ *Lygodium japonicum*
___ *Marsilea uncinata*
___ *M. vestita*
___ *Notholaena dealbata*
___ *Onoclea sensibilis*
___ *Ophioglossum crotalophoroides*
___ *O. engelmannii*
___ *O. nudicaule*
___ *O. petiolatum*
___ *O. vulgatum*
___ *Osmunda cinnamomea*
___ *O. claytoniana*
___ *O. regalis*
___ *Pellaea atropurpurea*
___ *P. glabella*
___ *Phegopteris hexagonoptera*
___ *Pilularia americana*
___ *Polypodium polypodioides*
___ *P. virginianum*
___ *Polystichum acrostichoides*
___ *Pteridium aquilinum*
___ *Pteris multifida*
___ *Selaginella apoda*
___ *S. eclipes*
___ *S. riddellii*
___ *S. rupestris*
___ *Thelypteris kunthii*
___ *T. noveboracensis*
___ *T. palustris*
___ *T. torresiana*
___ *Trichomanes boschianum*
___ *T. petersii*
___ *Woodsia obtusa*
___ *W. scopulina*
___ *Woodwardia virginica*

Index to Common and Scientific Names

Adder's-tongue Ferns 157-167
Adiantum 25-29
Adiantum capillus-veneris 28, 29
Adiantum pedatum 26, 27
Alabama Lip Fern 84, 85
American Pillwort 188, 189
Appalachian Filmy Fern 232, 233
Appalachian Woodsia 240, 241
Asplenium 31-53
Asplenium bradleyi 46, 47
Asplenium X *ebenoides* 48, 49
Asplenium X *gravesii* 52, 53
Asplenium X *kentuckiense* 50, 51
Asplenium pinnatifidum 34, 35
Asplenium platyneuron 38-41
Asplenium platyneuron var.
   bacculum-rubrum 38, 40, 41
Asplenium platyneuron var.
   incisum 39, 41
Asplenium platyneuron var.
   platyneuron 38, 39, 41
Asplenium resiliens 42, 43
Asplenium rhizophyllum 32, 33
Asplenium ruta-muraria 36, 37
Asplenium trichomanes 44, 45
Athyrium 55-61
Athyrium filix-femina subsp.
   asplenioides 56, 57
Athyrium pycnocarpon 58, 59
Athyrium thelypterioides 60, 61
Azolla 63-65
Azolla mexicana 63-65

Beech Ferns 183-185
Black-based Quillwort 124, 125
Black-stemmed Spleenwort 42, 43
Bladder Ferns 91, 94-97
Blunt-lobed Woodsia 238, 239
Botrychium 67-77
Botrychium biternatum 72, 73
Botrychium dissectum 74-77
Botrychium dissectum var. *dissectum* . 74, 75
Botrychium dissectum var.
   obliquum 74, 76, 77
Botrychium lunarioides 70, 71
Botrychium virginianum 68, 69
Bracken 201-205
Bradley's Spleenwort 46, 47
Brakes 207-209
Broad Beech Fern 184, 185
Buck's Meadow Spikemoss 212, 213
Bulblet Bladder Fern 94, 95
Bulbous Adder's-tongue Fern 158, 159
Butler's Quillwort 126, 127

Chain Ferns 243-245
Cheilanthes 79-89
Cheilanthes alabamensis 84, 85
Cheilanthes eatonii 82, 83
Cheilanthes feei 88, 89
Cheilanthes lanosa 86, 87
Cheilanthes tomentosa 80, 81
Christmas Fern 198, 199
Cinnamon Fern 172, 173
Cliff Brakes 177-181
Climbing Ferns 139-141
Cloak Ferns 148-151
Clubmosses 133-137
Coarse-lobed Grape Fern 74, 76, 77
Common Polypody 194, 195
Cut-leaved Grape Fern 74, 75
Cystopteris 91-97

Cystopteris bulbifera 94, 95
Cystopteris protrusa 92, 93
Cystopteris tennesseensis 96, 97

Dennstaedtia 99-101
Dennstaedtia punctilobula 100-101
Dryopteris 103-111
Dryopteris carthusiana 106, 107
Dryopteris celsa 108, 109
Dryopteris X *leedsii* 110, 111
Dryopteris marginalis 104, 105

Eastern Bracken 203, 204
Eaton's Lip Fern 82, 83
Ebony Spleenwort 38-41
Equisetum 113-121
Equisetum arvense 114, 115
Equisetum X *ferrissii* 120, 121
Equisetum hyemale var. *affine* ... 116, 117
Equisetum laevigatum 118, 119

Ferriss' Scouring Rush 120, 121
Field Horsetail 114, 115
Filmy Ferns 231-235
Fragile Ferns 91-93

Glade Ferns 55, 58-61
Grape Fern 74-77
Grape Ferns 67-77
Graves' Spleenwort 52, 53

Hairy Marsh Fern 228, 229
Hairy Lip Fern 86, 87
Hairy Water Clover 144, 145
Hale's Marsh Fern 228, 229
Hay Scented Ferns 99-101
Holly Ferns 197-199
Hook-spined Water Clover 146, 147
Horsetails 113-115

Interrupted Fern 174, 175
Isoetes 123-127
Isoetes butleri 126, 127
Isoetes melanopoda 124, 125

Jagged Ebony Spleenwort 40, 41
Japanese Climbing Fern 140, 141

Kentucky Spleenwort 50, 51

Lady Ferns 55-57
Least Adder's-tongue Fern 162, 163
Leed's Wood Fern 110, 111
Limestone Adder's-tongue Fern ... 160, 161
Lip Ferns 79-89
Lobed Spleenwort 34, 35
Log Fern 108, 109
Lorinseria 129-131
Lorinseria areolata 129-131
Lycopodium 133-137
Lycopodium appressum 134, 135
Lycopodium lucidulum 136, 137
Lygodium 139-141
Lygodium japonicum 140, 141

Maidenhair Ferns 25-29
Maidenhair Spleenwort 44, 45
Marginal Wood Fern 104, 105
Mariana Maiden Fern 222, 223
Marsh Fern 228, 229

Marsh Ferns 221-229
Marsilea 143-147
Marsilea uncinata 146, 147
Marsilea vestita var. *mucronata* .. 144, 145
Meadow Spikemoss 214, 215
Mosquito Fern 63-65

Narrow-leaved Glade Fern 58, 59
Net-veined Chain Fern 129-131
New York Fern 224, 225
Northern Maidenhair Fern 26, 27
Notholaena 149-151
Notholaena dealbata 150, 151
Northern Maidenhair Fern 26, 27
Notholaena 149-151
Notholaena dealbata 150, 151

Onoclea 153-155
Onoclea sensibilis 153-155
Ophioglossum 157-167
Ophioglossum crotalophoroides .. 158, 159
Ophioglossum engelmannii 160, 161
Ophioglossum nudicaule var.
   tenerum 162, 163
Ophioglossum petiolatum 166, 167
Ophioglossum vulgatum var.
   pycnostichum 164, 165
Osmunda 169-175
Osmunda cinnamomea 172, 173
Osmunda claytoniana 174, 175
Osmunda regalis var. *spectabilis* . 170, 171

Pellaea 171-181
Pellaea atropurpurea 178, 179
Pellaea glabella 180, 181
Phegopteris 183-185
Phegopteris hexagonoptera 184, 185
Pillworts 187-189
Pilularia 187-189
Pilularia americana 188, 189
Plateau Filmy Fern 234, 235
Polypodium 191-195
Polypodium polypodioides var.
   michauxianum 192, 193
Polypodium virginianum 194, 195
Polypody Ferns 191-195
Polystichum 197-199
Polystichum acrostichoides 198, 199
Powdery Cloak Fern 150, 151
Pteridium 201-204
Pteridium aquilinum 202-204
Pteridium aquilinum var.
   latiusculum 203, 204
Pteridium aquilinum var.
   pseudocaudatum 203, 204
Pteris 207-209
Pteris multifida 208, 209
Purple-stemmed Cliff Brake 178, 179

Quillworts 123-127

Rattlesnake Fern 68, 69
Resurrection Fern 192, 193
Riddell's Spikemoss 216, 217
Rock Spikemoss 218, 219
Royal Fern 170, 171
Royal Ferns 169-175

Scott's Spleenwort 48, 49
Scouring Rush 116, 117
Scouring Rushes 113, 116-121

Selaginella 211-219
Selaginella apoda 214, 215
Selaginella eclipes 212, 213
Selaginella riddellii 216, 217
Selaginella rupestris 218, 219
Sensitive Fern 153-155
Serrate Ebony Spleenwort 39, 41
Shining Clubmoss 136, 137
Silvery Glade Fern 60, 61
Slender Lip Fern 88, 89
Smooth Cliff Brake 180, 181
Smooth Scouring Rush 118, 119
Southern Adder's-tongue Fern 164, 165
Southern Clubmoss 134, 135
Southern Fragile Fern 92, 93
Southern Lady Fern 56, 57
Southern Maidenhair Fern 28, 29
Southern Shield Fern 226, 227
Sparse-lobed Grape Fern 72, 73
Spider Brake 208, 209
Spikemosses 211-219
Spinulose Wood Fern 106, 107
Spleenworts 31-53
Stalked Adder's-tongue Fern 166, 167

Tailed Bracken 203, 205
Tennessee Bladder Fern 96, 97
Thelypteris 221-229
Thelypteris kunthii 226, 227
Thelypteris noveboracensis 224, 225
Thelypteris palustris 228, 229
Thelypteris palustris var.
   haleana 228, 229
Thelypteris palustris var.
   pubescens 228, 229
Thelypteris torresiana 222, 223
Trichomanes 231-235
Trichomanes boschianum 232, 233
Trichomanes petersii 234, 235

Virginia Chain Fern 244, 245

Walking Fern 32, 33
Wall Rue Spleenwort 36, 37
Water Clovers 143-147
Winter Grape Fern 70, 71
Wood Ferns 110-111
Woodsia 237-241
Woodsia obtusa 238, 239
Woodsia scopulina var.
   appalachiana 240, 241
Woodsias 237-241
Woodwardia 243-245
Woodwardia virginica 244, 245
Wooly Lip Fern 80, 81

762-3
5-33
CC

DATE DUE			
SEP 19 1997			
RETURNED SEP 27 1996			
RETURNED DEC 2-1997			
DEC 14 1997			

DEMCO 38-297